A
MYTHIC
LIFE

A MYThIC LIFE

LEARNING TO LIVE OUR GREATER STORY

JEAN HOUSTON

Foreword by Mary Catherine Bateson

HarperSanFrancisco
An Imprint of HarperCollins*Publishers*

HarperCollins Web Site: http://www.harpercollins.com

HarperCollins®, ■®, and HarperSanFrancisco™ are trademarks of HarperCollins Publishers Inc.

Book design by George Brown

FIRST EDITION

Library of Congress Cataloging-in-Publication Data
Houston, Jean.
A mythic life : learning to live our greater story / Jean Houston ; foreword by Mary Catherine Bateson. — 1st ed.
Includes bibliographical references and index.
ISBN 0–06–250281–6 (cloth)
ISBN 0–06–250282–4 (pbk.)
ISBN 0–06–2511403–2 (intl. pbk.)
1. Myth.   2. spiritual life.   3. Houston, Jean.   I. Title.
BL304.H68   1996
291.1'3—dc20   95–21245

96 97 98 99 00 ❖ RRD-H 10 9 8 7 6 5 4 3 2 1

To the memory of Margaret Mead

Contents

✦

◆

FOREWORD

by Mary Catherine Bateson

What does it mean to live life in constant dialogue with myth? This is the question that Jean Houston explores in her autobiography, and the example that she offers to her readers. Such a dialogue (or struggle) within a single tradition is not new. It was the ordinary reality of human beings throughout millennia, continuing for indigenous peoples for whom ghosts and spirits are simply there. It has also been the goal of religious practice worldwide, where complexity involved a constant effort to focus attention and to hold doubt at bay, to pierce the cloud of unknowing and practice the presence of God, to recognize the Christ in every passing face, or to see all beings as Buddha, hear all sounds as mantra, and know all places as nirvana.

The dialogue with myth, or with history interwoven with myth, has been a focus of the life-history narratives of many writers living at the meeting place of different cultures, and striving for identity: Audre Lorde called her autobiography a "biomythography." Maxine Hong Kingston, in *The Woman Warrior*, weaves both myth and history into her effort to understand the present. Alex Haley's epic,

Roots, has been criticized for the interweaving of different ways of knowing the history of one family and of the African-American identity, yet it is precisely this kind of interweaving that gives the epic its power. But Jean Houston would have us live our lives in multilogue not with a single mythic tradition but with all the world's wealth of imagination and aspiration.

This makes for a very rich brew. Jean quotes my mother, Margaret Mead, as saying, when she first visited the home of Jean and her husband Bob Masters, "Such a strange place . . . nothing goes with anything, and yet somehow it all works. Like your mind, eh, Jean?" My father, Gregory Bateson, was an intellectual minimalist, deeply concerned about internal consistency, and yet he continued to value Jean's vision in spite of the fact that her weave of metaphor was the opposite extreme from his own fastidiousness. In recent years I have come to believe that, surrounded as we are with contradictory beliefs and perceptions, too careful a filtering may leave us with a lowest common denominator, a well-swept emptiness that makes us prone to demons. We must cultivate the skills of inclusiveness, delighting in diversity. Jean calls this "polyphrenia," the orchestration of many parts of ourselves, and "leaky margins," the accepting of other modes of experience. She is not introducing the archetypes and the elementals into a scheme of *explanation* but into a scheme of *understanding,* and she brackets with quotation marks her references to the "gods." Ontology, the study of what is, is not necessarily synonymous with epistemology, the study of what and how we can know. "The emphasis may shift to affirming things that are true but not accurate, rather than just those that are accurate but not true. Process itself will be celebrated along with the seeking of end goals."

This autobiography is what I have come to call a learning narrative, organized not around linear chronology but around a series of themes and the events that opened up understanding of those themes and have come to symbolize them. Learning is not linear, for it involves the combination and recombination of insights in reckless disregard of sequence, so that the past is reconfigured by growth—and perhaps only lies flat on the page when growth has ceased.

I find it helpful to read this book as the braided narrative of three aspects of Jean's character; this gives me a way through the polyphrenia of performer, teacher, and "midwife of souls." When my mind boggles at some extravagance of language or metaphor, when the "archetypes zoom in and zoom out," I remind myself that Jean is a jester in motley, taking after her father, who possessed "a comedic mind in search of an honest outlet." Willingly suspending disbelief, I thank heaven for the laughter. Hard on the heels of Athena, a crocodile crosses the stage—or has it learned also to zoom?

At the same time, Jean is a teacher in the sense of the word that we all need to explore for the future. As a teacher, she is a nurturer and appreciator, trying to make the most abstruse subjects user friendly, above all by engaging the student in active participation. She is learned in a number of complex fields, from theology

to neurology to fractal mathematics, but is at the same time a constant and om-
nivorous learner. The games and dances and lectures she offers her students form
a barrage (her word) of stimuli, from which each student necessarily draws something different. There is no set list of facts that must be retained, no standard conclusions to be regurgitated, but instead a deepened sense of possibility.

Lastly, however, Jean is one who performs hieratic acts that reunite heaven and
earth, past and present, and that make the necessary metamorphoses of life possible. "Transition is my middle name," she says, even as she speaks of the whole-
system transition that characterizes the globe today. How does the sinner recover
innocence, the boy become a man, the bigot become a lover of humankind? How
do sick people discover their own powers of self-healing, woundings become resources, and men and women become husbands and wives? By what process of
transignification can we learn to value and respect human diversity and the diversity of the living world? We have always known that for human beings, living in
and on systems of meaning, these transitions need to be marked by words. Jean
invokes theophanies and brings forth new states of possibility, habitually offering
the spiritual path of enrichment rather than austerity.

Memoirs and works of autobiography are playing an increasingly important
role today, offering alternative ways of being, none of which can be replicated but
each of which offers materials to be incorporated in a personal synthesis. We live
in a perplexing time, in which many people seek out narrow and exclusive formu-
lae to live by. The millennium, with all its attendant pathologies, lies ahead, but
there is no single way to meet it, to grow in imagination to live in the emerging
world. For myself, I prefer reading the stories of lives of search and learning and
improvisation—like this one—over new dogmatic assertions or self-help formu-
lae for contentment. We all compose our lives and worlds differently. With someone like Jean, with whom I have shared many experiences over the years, I can
relish the fact that even sitting in the same room with another person we see and
hear different things from what he or she does.

The braiding of personae in Jean Houston is a sign of one of the changes happening today. Modern society has been expert in dividing things up into different
categories and putting them into labeled boxes: home, church, hospital, school,
cinema, office. These boundaries are breaking down as we realize how little learning occurs in schools, how much of healing occurs in laughter, the lifelong spirituality of work and play and learning. Jean moves us beyond these divisions in a way
that is emblematic of our times. Yet this is inappropriately analytical language for
speaking about a book as zestful and exuberant as this one. We hear in Jean's narrative of her life about rejection and bereavement and the deep lessons these
teach, but woven through them all is the conviction that humankind, our kind,
evolves out of pleasure rather than out of pain.

Fractal Waves on God's Back Lot

When I was just under five years old, my father, Jack Houston, a comedy writer, brought me to the MGM studios in Hollywood, where he was working on a picture. As we were making our way to the middle of the studio, a little round man with a huge cigar and bright yellow pants came by and ordered my father to follow him to his office to discuss a scene. He was the producer of the picture my father was working on. My father grabbed me by the hand and started after him, only to be stopped by a magisterial wave of the producer's cigar.

"Leave the kid behind, Jack," the great man wheezed. "I can't stand kids."

My father gave me a worried glance, but I assured him, "I'll be okay, Daddy," since I had just seen Roy Rogers ride by on Trigger. Dad sat me on some steps, gave me a lollipop, and, shouting over his shoulder as he followed the little round producer, told me that he'd be back in no time.

No time turned out to be two hours, but it was also no time as we know time. For there on the street on the studio lot passed the storied humanity of every time and place. I scooted over as Marie Antoinette and part of the French court swished down the stairs in their elaborate gowns and white powdered wigs. I noticed that Marie was wearing tennis shoes. An Indian chief in full feathered headdress with interesting markings on his face came out of the commissary eating a hot dog and talking to Julius Caesar. They had to step out of the way as the French Foreign Legion (or was it the cast of *Kismet?*) riding on camels passed a Hindu actor riding an elephant. The camels spat, the elephant dumped, and the Hindu actor shouted words in English I had never heard before. It was quite impressive. Just then a talking airplane came walking down the street. "Gangway," it said, "for *Thirty Seconds over Tokyo.*" As it passed, I saw legs sticking out from under what must have been a cardboard mock-up. A bunch of cannibals with bones in their noses headed over to the rest room, only to be told by Madame Curie that it was out of order.

I looked up and down the street for my father, but he was nowhere in sight. I decided to follow a midget pushing a baby carriage. She turned a corner, and we were in ancient Israel, where Salome was playing poker with some of the twelve disciples on the table of the Last Supper. Judas was evidently winning, judging by the stuff he was raking in—too green and papery to be thirty pieces of silver. I sauntered through the open door of a Roman temple, past the statues of Jupiter and Venus, only to find myself in a cardboard English village of Shakespeare's time. Turning a corner, I found a knight in armor taking a snooze between the paws of the sphinx, while across the way Jesse James was ambling through a mock-up of a Maya temple. Was that woman in high heels and grass skirt who had just stopped to talk to him Dorothy Lamour?

Then it really got interesting. A fight broke out in the Dodge City Saloon, and I moved closer to watch. It was a funny kind of a fight; one cowboy kept hitting another cowboy over the head with a chair. Then he'd stop and take a rest, hold up another chair that was handed to him, and hit the same cowboy over the head again. The other cowboys sat back, chewed their gum, and read *Variety.* I tugged at the long red skirt of a woman dressed like Belle Starr, who was reading a movie magazine, and asked her in a loud whisper why that man kept hitting the other man with a chair over and over again.

"Quiet, honey, this is a shoot," she whispered. Then she added, "Is your ma one of the dancing girls?"

"I don't think so," I replied and wandered off quite literally into the sunset—in this case, a painted set of vibrant colors left over from *The Wizard of Oz.* A man in a monkey suit finally found me and took me over to the place where my father had left me. There I was retrieved by Mrs. Martha Washington, who told me in serious tones worthy of the mother of the country, "Your father is quite concerned about you. I am taking you to his office."

When we arrived, my father swooped me up, swung me around, and said, "Hey, kid, I was worried about you! Did Jack the Ripper find you?"

"No, Daddy, Mrs. Washington did."

"Oh, that's better," said my father.

"Daddy," I asked, looking at the letters on his door, "what does that say?"

"Well now, kid," he replied, "your mother has been teaching you to read. You figure it out."

"Well," I said, peering up at the door, "the first letter is a D and the second is an R. That's DR. Then there's an E and an A. That's a DREA."

"Go on," said my father.

"Then there's an M. DREA . . . Dream!" I shouted excitedly. "But there's more. There's an L and an A. DREAMLA . . . " Suddenly I got the whole thing, and it all made sense. "Dreamland, Daddy. Dreamland. Why do you call your office Dreamland, Daddy?"

" 'Cause that's where we are, kid, that's where we are."

That was Hollywood in the 1940s—a back lot of the collective history and unconscious of the human race. MGM itself was an archetypal dream factory and, with its associate studios, it made some 366 pictures a year. Most of the major themes and stories outlining the human condition got produced in the course of a year. This was the golden age of movie making, for having just emerged from the Great Depression and still in the throes of world war, we relied on the movies for our psychic health and much of our culture. Movies were the oozing of our dreams onto celluloid—soul stuff in high projection. Movie stars were just that—stars in our firmament—and as they traveled across the sky of our wonder, we followed them like mad astronomers. Many people were ritually bound by the cult of movie going, seeing some two hundred pictures a year. Gone was the hearth where the grandparents told the old tales. We thought we had found something better; we thought we could fall through the screen into mythic lives.

In the trance domain of the darkened theater, we became liminal, incarnating as a shy cowboy single-handedly taking on a gang of cattle rustlers. Losing our boundaries, we became Mr. Smith, an ardent but ordinary Joe, and cleaned up political corruption in Washington. When we plunged into despair, a wingless angel fell out of the sky and helped us revalue our wonderful life. The movies of the forties were the backdrop against which the events of my childhood unfolded. Born into a showbiz family, with a comedy writer father and a mother who had studied acting with Stanislavsky's leading lady and opened a drama school for children whenever money ran short, I seemed to come naturally by a life that has seemed at times as fantastic and mythic as the movies.

Looking back, I have come to realize that the Hollywood sets that I walked through as a child prefigured in fact and fantasy what was soon to become reality, my mythic life. I have been privileged and blessed to experience the wondrous varieties of human experience and culture firsthand. Over the last decade or so, I have often felt as if I were walking and living in God's own back lot. I have swum in the Ganges, trying to avoid a surge of wave-driven ashes that carried what I thought was a burned cow leg but that turned out to be the remains of a human cremation. I have followed a former president and his wife into their home in Plains, Georgia, where they told me how they had carved their own bedroom furniture. I have walked through a jungle in South America near the Orinoco and seen a nearly naked Indian man come out into a clearing with a transistor radio clapped to his ear, listening to a soccer game from Mexico City. I have planted rice with farmers in a remote part of China, and I have danced with lepers in the African Congo—dances so old that even time has forgotten them. At my partners' insistence, I reciprocated by teaching them disco dancing.

I have been allowed to accompany Aboriginal women in the center of Australia as they showed me how to find food in an utterly barren landscape, and I have discussed the quality of the new international cuisine with Julia Child at a hot dog contest on Wall Street. I've dived within the science-fiction landscapes of the Great Coral Reef and walked around the navel of the world that is Ayer's Rock, Australia. I've climbed into tombs in Egypt that no tourist ever sees, viewing walls still vibrant with color after nearly five thousand years, and I've witnessed the launching of the space shuttle Discovery in the dark of night as the horizon blazed orange and violet. I have seen trance dancers in Jogjakarta become horses, chew flowers and grass and nails and glass, and fall upon their swords with no apparent harm, and I have seen traders in the Japanese stock market scream themselves into a frenzy that recalled their samurai ancestors. I have been chased by tanks lobbing tear gas in countries torn by revolution, and I have addressed the United Nations. I have watched people die and people be born, both literally and spiritually, on every continent of the globe, and I have seen the dreams of millennia become real and the realities of the last hundred years fade away into dreams.

The mythic quality of my life, however, is by no means unique. It is only my individual version of the pattern taking place among us all: the local stories of our lives are bound up with the larger story happening the world over, and what our ancestors thought of as mythic is becoming mundane. We are becoming vulnerable to our own psychic depths as well as to the realities of other people. Thus the story of recent history is the story of convergence; everybody and everything is being woven together into a new world myth. The many worlds and realities that I saw as a child on the MGM lot are now part of everyone's reality.

The information revolution is an important aspect of this interpenetration, causing a disintegration of all traditional cultures, languages, sciences, religions, nations, races. We are participating in the creation of the global mind field. The planet is becoming self-conscious in all its parts through ourselves. Electronic circuitry has so wired the planet that within twenty years—a few hundred months—just about everything that the human race is doing or has ever thought about will be available at its fingertips. The human spirit is now coming in waves at us through computer, TV, CD player, and joystick. The electronic revolution is returning us to a tribal world of instantaneous information and dialogue.

My earliest memory is a prefigural anticipation of all this. I was about two and a half years old, and my father and I were walking along a curb in Hollywood. Suddenly I began to kick the cars along the side of the road. "Stop that, Jeanie," he admonished. "Why are you doing that, anyway?"

"Because where I come from, we do it much better."

"Do what?"

"Cars."

"Oh, you mean that you move people around better? No wheels, no gas, no piles of junk like these babies?"

"Yes."

"Well, how do you do it? If you can answer that one, kid, we'll make a million bucks."

"With music."

"Ah, shoot!"

A fractal wave connects this memory with my present life. Most nights when I am home, I turn on my computer and modem and tune in to the world. Through the Internet and several other networks, I am wired through the music of frequency to the planetary mind. My late-night hobby gives me back something of the feeling of my infant memory of traveling across great distances in moments. I can move through identities as well. On one network, using an appropriate name, I am a fifteen-year-old boy, playing Dungeons and Dragons with other fifteen-year-old boys who think I am a fifteen year old with a weird vocabulary. On another service and using another name, I was known for a while as the "queen of comedy," since I inherited my father's joke file and uploaded its better offerings into the CompuServe comedy files. And, on the more serious of the international networks, I often use my own name and nightly discuss global issues, green politics, and methods of encouraging cultural survival with people all over the world. These simultaneous, electronically linked, planetwide talks give me enormous happiness, for they seem to me "a blast from the past," a high-tech communion of ideas and feelings with many people from many different cultures. Somehow, these planetary conversations seem closer to my recollection of how we moved about "where I came from," a knowing that I suspect almost every child shares. Soon music, too, will be added, and I will be able to play a rhythm-and-blues riff on my computer-linked keyboard, while across the Atlantic in Ireland, a network buddy will add a Celtic fret with her harp, followed next by a pal in Delhi, who will introduce a cascade of raga notes from his sitar, which will be deepened and given Earth tones by an Aboriginal friend in Darwin, Australia, who will blow his didgeridoo into our transworld concert. Then we will all play together, making the planet's own music—the soul of the world in microchips; rhythm and RAM.

Most of us were raised in print culture, wherein principles of continuity, uniformity, and repeatability were elevated over the more organic principles of discontinuity, simultaneity, and multiple associations. Now the mythic flavor of the more ancient, organic perspective returns, and chaos theory becomes lauded as the way things work. We look for flow patterns rather than for linear cause-effect explanations. Resonance has become far more important than relevance, and nothing is truly hidden anymore.

How are people experiencing the nature of this new reality—the rising of the depth currents of all times, all cultures, and all experiences? Its effects are felt in the fascination with myth, the seeking of spiritual experience, the revival of the knowings of indigenous people, the beginnings of a world music that incorporates and sustains the knowings of many regions, styles of clothing that mix and match continents on a single body. Even on the shadow side, we find rising for a last stand the old tribal gods in their varying fundamentalist postures, before they are swept, not away—nothing is ever swept away—but into a new amalgam in which they, too, become part of the larger story. Today, and for all of us, all parts of the planet are catching all parts of the planet.

In order to prepare for these world changes, the human psyche is manifesting many different versions of itself. Psyche is moving at remarkable speeds past the limits most of us have lived with for thousands of years into an utterly different state of being. The contents of the psyche are manifesting at faster and faster rates—a dreamlike reality in which it is difficult to tell anymore what is news and what is drama, what is matter and what is myth. We live in chaos that we may have created in order to hasten our own meeting with ourselves. All over the world, in virtually every culture I visit, I find that images that were relegated to the unconscious are becoming conscious. Happenings that belonged to extraordinary experiences of reality are becoming more common, and many of the maps of the psyche and its unfolding are undergoing awesome change. Buddhist cybernauts share realities with secretaries who hold black belts in kung fu. Women Episcopalian priests draw ancient mazes on the floors of their cathedrals and lead their parishioners through the sacred geometry of dromenons, labyrinths that lead body, mind, and heart into rhythms of awakening and sacred remembrance. Economic advisers at the U.N. practice deep meditation and find solutions to the tribulations of countries in resources met in inner space.

Against this mythic template, the events and stories of our individual lives can be seen as small but potent fractals of the great fractal, which is the infinite mirroring of the soul of the world. What are fractals? Fractals are repetitions of the same general patterns, even the same details, at both ascending and descending scales. They tell us that the universe and all that it contains is made up of folded realities within self-similar worlds. The term *fractal* itself was invented by Benoit Mandelbrot, an IBM researcher, to describe the new geometry of shapes that form in the wake of dynamic systems.

Fractal patterns are all around us, above us, within us. Trees are fractals, with their repeated pattern of large and small branches, with similar details found even in the smallest twigs. Even a single leaf shows fractal repetitions of the whole tree in both its shape and the branching in its veins. Examine a broccoli or a cauli-flower, and you find fractal geometry at its best, with florets arranged in self-similar scales; for a total fractal experience, peel the leaves from an artichoke. Photographs taken through electron microscopes and far-ranging telescopes reveal that images from vastly different scales evoke a feeling of similarity and recognition. A spiral nebula that measures hundreds of light-years across looks remarkably similar to something that measures a thousandth of a centimeter, say the eye of a firefly. One can be seen as the fractal resonance of the other, the resonance of the microcosm to the macrocosm. The patterns in the weather, the turbulence in the winds, the rhythm pounded out by an African drummer, the rituals performed by queens and shamans and celebrants of the New Year, the courtship habits of peacocks and prairie dogs, the landscapes of nature and the inscapes of dreams—all embody fractal phenomena.

These examples point to the universality of the fractal as a central organizing principle of our universe; wherever we look, the complex systems of nature and time in nature seem to preserve the look of details at finer and finer scales. Fractals show a holistic hidden order behind things, a harmony in which everything affects everything else, and, above all, an endless variety of interwoven patterns.

Let us speculate now that if we could look at the events in a human life in the same way that we have looked at a tree, we might discover another order of fractals present in themes that recur in the leafings and branchings of happenings, events, moods, tragedies, and comedies. Track these themes backward through ancestral lives, and many of them may recur as waves, albeit in different contexts in the family of origin. And if one could go forward into the future, one would probably see these same waves of similarity in character, personality, and existential events repeating in one's physical and spiritual descendants throughout time. Many of the peoples of the world believe in some version of reincarnation and accept the idea that themes tend to recur through life after life in ways that recall fractal patterns, our larger life including many lives made up of mythic themes that karmically branch and leaf like a great tree over and over again.

A myth itself is a fractal, a repetition of patterns of becoming. Our personal stories weave between our local lives and Life writ large, the mythic equation of each life doing its part to illumine the screen of the world. When we reflect on our lives, it is possible to discern repeating themes and patterns, which if acknowledged and unfolded would allow us to see the bigger picture. Thus the sets I walked through as a child and the life that I now live are fractal waves of the same stories rolling through my earlier and my later life. But their deeper currents, as in all lives, may be nothing other than the fractal wave forms of the Mind of the Maker, the Creator or Creative Spirit who started it all in the first place.

The leafings and branchings of my own life seem improbably complex. Genetically, I began in a medley of cultures—a riot of ethnic DNA, Cherokees chasing the genes of Scottish warriors who are also poets and of Sicilian nobles who are also vintners. My education followed suit, taking me to every kind of school that America of the forties and fifties had to offer—about twenty in all before I was twelve years old. My life in the theater gave me incarnations in the soulscapes of women's possibilities—Antigone, Alcestis, Saint Joan, the Madwoman of Chaillot, Hamlet's mother. I was one of the few people who had a legal supply of LSD in New York City when I was twenty-one, and the research I performed with it gave me access to the layers upon layers of the cultures of the psyche, as I took depth soundings of the minds of well over three hundred subjects. When that work finished, I became a hierophant of inner space, leading thousands of students and seminar participants through the mysteries of the mind without drugs, designing unique journeys into the multiple realities and capacities of their embodied selves. And then I became a traveler in outward spaces, journeying as much as a quarter of a million miles a year, visiting every bioregion of the planet as teacher and adviser in human and cultural development. I have become a small fractal of the larger wave that is the global genesis of the possible human who, in turn, may help create the possible society.

Time is a juicy god. To discern the patterns of a life, we must become time amphibians, swimming backward and forward through the temporal seas. Time is not, as we so often think, a linear progression of one darn thing after another. Rather, it is a fluid medium in which everything is interconnected and in which each apparently unique happening is also a metaphor for other happenings, past and future. Time itself may be elemental. It is not a no-thing, a convenience with which to measure our passage through space. Rather, it has form as well as function and may be made up of nested, fractally resonant fields of previous, present, and perhaps future times. Time mavens, mystics, and physicists hint that past, present, and future are our little local ways of boxing the universe to make it plausible to consciousness. They hint further that reality may be shot through with hyperdimensions and multiple realities. Can such thinking give us clues to the hidden meaning and purpose of our lives? If we crack open the habits of our local constructs of form, space, and time, might we glimpse vistas of a reality larger than our aspirations, richer and more complex than our dreams?

In what follows, I propose to surf on a few of the fractal waves of my mythic life. The stories that I tell from my childhood and adolescence seem to me now to be like pulses from the depths, each of which set in motion a flood of events that crashed on the shores of my adult life. In dipping back into the sea of my becoming and riding some of these waves, I return, as it were, to my Essence—what in fractal mathematics is called the *strange attractor*, a construct that provides order, meaning, and direction to apparent chaos—to celebrate its patterns and to discern its future possibilities. I do not believe that any of us is history innocent. We each bear family history, cultural history, even the history of humanity itself morphically coded into the folds of our brains and the fields of our lives. The present emerging ecology of minds and psyches, our availability to each other, and our ability to dream one another's dreams and experience one another's biographies are parts of the interpenetrating fractal wave of the current time, psyche, and memory. We are being rescaled to planetary proportions, as we become fractally resonant and intimate with our own depths.

This is the story of my experience in this astonishing new world. I have been unusually blessed with opportunities to observe and participate in this changing reality. In charting these fractals, these riffs of my life and times, I hope to encourage my readers to examine the currents of their own lives so as to discover that they, too, are living mythic lives.

1

✦

HyBRID
VIGOR

It is July 1993. I am sitting on the ground in an Aboriginal camp in Arnhem Land in the Northern Territories, Australia. Above me is the Southern Cross, the great curling sweep of the Milky Way, and a sky with stars so bright, so blazing, one can reach up and touch them. By their light I can make out the face of Audrey, an Aboriginal woman of high degree sitting near me. We are listening to the sounds coming from the main camp nearby; click sticks and the drone of the didgeridoo punctuate the songs and dances of the circumcision ceremony for the boy soon to be initiated into the secrets of Aboriginal life. He is only six years old, not twelve or thirteen, as most boys facing this rite always had been. The elders want to immerse him in Aboriginal life before the double threat of alcohol and Christian fundamentalism lays claim to him.

Members of the related clans have gathered from all over the Northern Territories to attend this corroboree. One of the relatives is a fundamentalist preacher, and he has brought with him a generator and sound system supplied by a church in Mississippi with which to preach against the ceremonies. Throughout the week, he has tried to drown out the ancient rituals, his amplified voice contesting with the sounds and traditions of fifty thousand years. Audrey grinds out her cigarette with disgust.

"What is he saying, Audrey?" I ask.

"He is saying that our ways, the ways of our ancestors, the ways of the Dreamtime, are rubbish and the only true way is through Jesus. You know, Jean, the whitefella came, killed our people, took away our land, and now the whitefella religion wants to kill our spirit. This land I hold is the place where the Pelican Dreaming meets the Brown Snake Dreaming. It is the most sacred land, for it holds another world within it. It holds the Dreaming. It holds my ancestors. It holds the future."

"How can we tap into this future, Audrey? How do we make the Dreaming come back?"

Audrey lights another cigarette, and it is some minutes before she responds. As she considers her answer, I reflect on the days that we have spent in the Aboriginal camp. We were led here by an American musician, who had made his way to the Walker River area the previous year searching for the source of the didgeridoo, the long horn instrument made of a hollowed-out tree branch that, in the hands of the right performer, is capable of the most hair-raising range of sounds. The musician had been welcomed into the clan and invited to return and bring a small group of strangers and foreigners to experience life in the camp. During our days here, we have walked barefoot through the woods and by the river, gone fishing with the Aboriginal women, learned to dig for yams and tubers, swum in the billabong (after the crocodiles had left), drunk endless cups of agonizingly potent tea made in tin billies over the open fire, absorbed the subtle and indirect teachings of the women leaders of the tribe, listened with inner ear to the duet sung by Pelican and King Brown Snake within the open plain landscape that was also the place where the Dreamtime lived, watched the children play, and applied white paint and feathers and danced and sung by firelight at the corroboree held for the young boy's ritual.

Throughout our time at the Aboriginal camp, many of us have felt as if we were nested in another world—the Dreamtime. Ngarungani, the Dreamtime, is the depth world flowing through this world. It is always and never, a time that never was and is always happening. It is the force that spiritually maintains the world and has to be constantly recreated through ritual, meditation, and prayer if the world, the clan, and the self are to be renewed. The Dreamtime includes a mythological distant past when the creative spirits moved over the land, shaping it, naming it, calling it into being, and generally getting it ready for the human populations that they soon would create. Wherever these creators went in their travels through the land, they left some evidence of their presence—a watercourse formed from their tracks, a rocky outcrop that came about through the weapons or other objects left, a deposit of red ocher from the blood they spilled, a depression left by the mark of their buttocks where they sat or by their body as they slept, water holes or soaks where they had passed water or dug using their sacred emblems, and so on. All over the continent of Australia are examples of these remembrances, each holding part of the sacred spiritual substance, the life force of the characters concerned.

After the world was created, some of these ancestors went into the other land in the sky to watch over their descendants, while others left images of themselves painted in caves—the Wandjina, star-headed figures dressed in what look like spacesuits, who many Aborigines insist were extraterrestrials. But before the great ancestors entered the Dreamtime, they taught their descendants, the Aboriginal people, all they needed to know to live in harmony with nature and with one another. They left instructions that formed the basis of ceremonies by which young people could become grown-up men and women, responsible leaders of the community well versed in the laws of nature. These sacred laws are contained in the legends, the stories, the myths that are passed on from generation to generation. Additionally, the ancestors left sacred sites and objects full of their power, the essence of life itself, to be preserved in the hands of the old men and women.

One enters the Dreamtime in order to contact the ancestral spirits of the Dreaming, the great creative powers who not only made the world but who continue to exist in present and future time and who will release their life-giving power to those who seek them. The totems of the Aborigines can serve as agents to establish this relationship, and each person is connected to totem objects—animal, creature, or plant—and considers the self and the clan the embodiment of the totem in human form. The camp we visited was the place where in the Dreamtime, the ancestral creative spirits known as Pelican and King Brown Snake are said to have met, and they continue to meet, rendering the site potent with sacred energy. Here the Dreaming is particularly strong, and we feel it, so much so that it seems that the mythic time beyond time is overwhelming our little local time.

We are shattered and brought back to the cruelties of local time and history when two of the elders of the tribe recall for us how as children in the early part of this century they had experienced attacks by white bounty hunters. They had seen many members of their families killed; they themselves had hidden from the hunters and barely survived. The elders claim that spirits of the murdered ones are still very much present, haunting the camp, asking, "Why did they kill us? What is it the white man wants?"

I have heard this question repeated the world over—among the Maori of New Zealand in their elaborately carved Maraes, in the councils of the Navajo at Window Rock, among the Inuit in northern Alaska, the Dogon in Mali, and black mothers in the inner cities of Detroit and Chicago. What is it the white man wants? They tell of unspeakable cruelties, acts of genocide, repression, the willful destruction of nature and property, and the subversion of native cultures through church, state, corporation, and alcohol.

"Why are the white people so greedy?" asked a Shoshone woman, tears streaming down her face, after a lumber company had come in and without warning chainsawed *many acres of her precious pine trees. "I think they are crazy," she added, looking over the hills now ravaged of their beautiful trees.*

A friend in publishing has just sent me chapters from a soon-to-be-released book that uses statistics to suggest the lesser intellectual capacities of certain races and the higher intelligence of others, especially the white one, which is deemed crazy by much of the world. I fear that if this book with its insular and outrageous view of "genetic intelligence" is taken seriously, masses of people, often the very ones who have the greatest sensitivity and intelligence concerning the Earth and her needs, could become officially marginalized.

Audrey has finished her cigarette and is ready to talk again. "We bring back the Dreamtime by sharing our different ways of knowing—blackfella, whitefella, allfella. But first we have to bring back that knowing. For my people to remember their know-ing, I have an idea. It is so big an idea that it must come from the Dreamtime. I want us to create an Aboriginal community here that the people will build themselves, with houses made of wood, not these ugly tin houses that the government sells us and that kill our spirit.

"We will start a school here. I'm a teacher, and I know how to do it—a school that will teach the children the old language that they have forgotten and the secrets of the bush—the healing flowers and plants, the knowledge of the ancestors. We will start our own businesses. We will help our people get off the dole, and with the help of the ancestors who are living among us, we will remember who we are and what we will yet become. And then we can help you whitefellas, brownfellas, yellowfellas become all that you can be, too. My grandmother stands behind me now in the Dreaming as I tell you these things."

In the background the whine of the fundamentalist minister singing a nineteenth-century Protestant hymn in an Aboriginal language suddenly ceases. Later I find out that all his listeners had left to join the corroboree; the ancient chanting drew them back one by one to the initiation ceremony. Eventually the minister, too, gave up and, feeling the deeper pull of his heritage, took his place among the men and beat the click sticks for the ceremony.

Audrey suddenly points to the star-bitten sky. "Look, a satellite is crossing the Southern Cross."

We watch its quick declension, a star in a hurry, heading east for New Zealand, Tahiti, the United States.

"My ancestors are here, all of them present with us now," says Audrey. "Where are yours?"

My ancestors, too, were there in the Dreamtime, oblivious to the passage of time and the barrier of space. There were my great-aunts—Rosa, Nena Maude, and Nanny—showing me, as they did when I was a child, the long parchment on which is painted the Houston family tree with its curling branches, strange fruit, exotic blossoms, and a lot of day-to-day apples having their own particular worms.

The brawny trunk line indicates the Houstons of Texas and Louisiana, a strange, hyperactive bunch noted for their height and chronic wit. An early account by a neighbor in Virginia in 1743 says, "The Houstons are tall beyond what is good and seemly. All the day they do sit around the porch telling jokes and laughing in a manner most strange. I fear they suffer from the brain fever."

One gnarled and weathered branch is occupied by Sam Houston, that great original who was at once statesman, alcoholic, wordsmith, depressive, military genius, visionary—a gallant monument of a man who would stalk the floors of Congress dressed in white-beaded buckskins to defend the rights of the Indians and who found his soul when living with the Cherokee. Another branch is related to Robert E. Lee, the elegant gentleman scholar who, contrary to all his natural inclinations, was required to lead the armies of the South in the Civil War. A branch also descends from the Adam and Eve of Virginia, William and Mary Randolph, with Thomas Jefferson thrown in as a distant cousin.   ·

Many among the clan have proved consistent in their luck, the pattern of which was established by one of the first Houstons to arrive in America. He escaped from Scotland with his wife and eight children in the last years of the seventeenth century. After great hardships and many swashbuckling adventures, including escaping with his family from the pirates who boarded their ship, he arrived in the promised land and promptly drowned in the Delaware Water Gap.

The size of the Houstons has long been a source of considerable pride to many of them. Often at family gatherings, virtue is calculated in feet and inches. A tape measure is always present, and children gain in honor and distinction as they shoot up way beyond the average height for their age.

"The taller you are, the nearer to heaven," a great-aunt once told me. It was a thing of shame for me that my shorter Sicilian genes stunted my growth, and I reached my full height at the age of eleven—a paltry five feet eleven inches. My shame was balanced somewhat at gatherings of the Todaros, my maternal Sicilian tribe, where it was not uncommon for a short relative to look up and up at me and exclaim, "Eh, Gina, what kind of manure do you put on your shoes to make you grow so high?" However, when with the Houstons, I was continually reminded of the Junoesque proportions of my great-grandmother, a six-foot-two-inch steer-wrestling matriarch renowned for the loudest voice in Hook County, Texas. She occupied a house at the top of a hill overlooking a valley town. People told time by her. Every morning for years, she would arise at precisely 5:30 A.M., stand outside on her porch, a mammoth vision in her long white nightgown, stretch out her immense arms, and moan in a voice said to be heard for miles around, "Ohhhhhhhhhhhhh, Mother of God!"

This announcement sped across years and nations to reappear in the mouth of my Sicilian grandmother, whose constant litany to mark all wondrous or dolorous occasions was "Ahhhhhhh, Mama de Jesu!" But then, for all us hybrids (and that is most of us), the fine wind that blows the new direction of time also sweeps together the remnants of cultures that, until now, were widely dispersed from each other. Big mamas speak of the Great Goddess, the feminine face of God, regardless of their own particular liturgy or locale. Archetypes zoom in and zoom out wearing different costumes to fit different cultural mind-sets, but ultimately they are members of the same psychic family. For us hybrids, the shock of this discovery spurs the search for common spiritual ground, the Dreamtime that embraces all apparent contraries; it means sinking the plumb line into the genetic soup and coming up with—everybody!

For we are divided from the possibility of knowing everybody by the famous six degrees of separation: east and west, north and south, above and below. Add a few degrees more, and we find that our ancestors have met and mated and melded us into the conglomerate stock that makes us so richly, so variously human. To celebrate this variety is to assimilate it, to open the psyche to the muchness we all contain. I do not hold with those who believe that generations just peak and shrivel, leaving little of their experience to their descendants. I suspect, rather, that the spiraling genes trail clouds of memories along with genomes for specific qualities. Blue eyes, black hair, a tendency to be tall or short, fat or fatuous are but the externals, the obvious givens. Stewing in the juice surrounding these givens are recollections of being chased across Spain by woolly mammoths, heaving on Irish seas in little coracle boats, burying babies on every land and continent. To recall our common origins is to remember floods and famines, meteors and mass migrations. It is to recall the myths of humankind and to know without having read the great tales of the heroes and heroines with a thousand faces who still occupy the inscapes of consciousness. Ultimately, it is to remember star stuff and the very act of creation, to recall ourselves as Godseeds, the spawn of the universe, pioneers on the frontier of Mind at Large.

We are all immigrants, strangers perpetually settling strange lands, and we carry the collective memory of experiences that make us wise beyond our local knowings, deeper than our life histories warrant. Of this I am certain, for I have taken many depth soundings of the psyches of many people the world over. Get beneath the surface crust of consciousness, and all the scripts are present—every soap opera, adventure story, myth, legend, and fairy tale, wisdom figures as well as daimons, angels, and gods. They are part of the great untapped resource that we all bear as part of our natural equipment, and in the course of this book of a life lived mythically, I hope to guide the reader to some of the ways to discover this larger life that we inhabit but rarely use.

I soon found that genealogy is a bag of mysterious blessings. You can spend your entire life at it, as did several of my elderly relatives, who occupied their days surrounded by family trees, charts, and tracings, looking for the bar sinister and hoping against hope for that happy day when they could prove their honorable credentials and be received into the bosom of the Grand Order of the Daughters of the Barons of Runnymead. Occasionally, the royal quest was rewarded by the discovery of a curious original among the fruiting ancestors, a unique and deviant strain who made up for all the tedium of forebears by the bright, exotic signals of his or her life. Such was the case with one ancestor, a Polish-Jewish trader who sold axes and firewater to a certain Cherokee tribe. The chief ran out of trading goods and instead offered his own daughter in marriage to the trader. The two were married—nice Jewish girls being hard to come by on the frontier—and their first child's name was the equivalent of "Scarecrow" Rosenblatt. Further testimony comes down to us that the Rosenblatt *père* remained a curious polymorph among the Indians. Dressed in Indian clothes, he always wore a yarmulke on the Jewish holy days. He tacked a mezuzah to the wigwam and insisted that his elk be slaughtered to strict kosher standards. Scarecrow had a bar mitzvah and also underwent the traditional Cherokee puberty rites. He was eventually thrown out of the wigwam of Rosenblatt and the Cherokee tribe when he married a white Christian woman from Tennessee. One of the daughters of this union married a Houston, and, skipping a hundred and fifty years or so, this brings us up to my father, Jack Houston.

The original jack-of-all-trades in the course of his growing-up years in Texas and Louisiana, my father managed to become an undertaker, short-order cook, stock market board marker, lumberjack, movie extra, violin player at weddings, janitor, cotton picker, wildcat oil rigger, chiropractor, reducer of fat women, press agent, perfume salesman, cowboy, hobo, phony waiter, professional love letter writer for other people, longshoreman, and Clara Tidwell (a lonely hearts columnist). This takes us up to about his twenty-fourth year. The number and diversity of these professions testifies to many sudden departures—owing, perhaps, to an excess of creativity. Always, my dad would think up a new and better way of performing his chores, and almost always there would be a catastrophe.

There was the time, for instance, when he took a job as an undertaker in order to romance the mortician's daughter. Both the romance and the job were going smoothly until my dad decided to invent a better way of embalming. His method consisted of folding the body into a rain barrel filled with a solution that hardened on the skin and gave a lovely shine. The problem was that when he tried his innovation out on a deceased gentleman, a Mr. Clyde Travis McIntire, the tallest man in Commerce, Texas, the body couldn't be unbent, and my dad had to place it in the coffin sitting up. At the funeral, folks thought it very sophisticated to have a corpse sitting up. They changed their minds, however, when the heat of the sun made the corpse begin to straighten out and raise its arms in a mystic hosanna, accompanied by a symphony of small firecracker pops as it became increasingly unglued.

On the basis of this experience, my father quite naturally decided to become a chiropractor. But that venture, too, ended in catastrophe when he took on the reducing of fat women as an addition to his chiropractic practice. When they refused to do the exercises my father prescribed, he invited them to wrestle with him. "Put my shoulders to the floor," he challenged them. That they did with vast enthusiasm. (Perhaps this was a prefigural event of the thousands of people I would coax to the mat all over the world to perform all manner of psychophysical exercises.) As some of these women weighed over 300 pounds, and my father at that time weighed no more than 165, there was no contest. Several broken ribs and a torn cartilage later, he decided to throw in the towel and look for greener and thinner pastures.

He answered an ad from Macy's department store in New York City announcing a position available as supervisor of a new reducing and exercise salon. Hopping a freight train, he arrived in New York, penniless, in a suit held together by safety pins. The manager of the elegant Macy's salon was aghast. "But you are supposed to be a woman!" the manager cried. "We hired a woman for this job. Aubrey Houston. Aubrey. That's a woman's name."

"Oh no, sir. Back home in east Texas, that's a man's name. But if you don't like it, you can call me Jack. They used to call me Crackerjack when I was a kid on account of how I was always the first to find the prize—but lately I've shortened it to Jack and—"

"But this changes things drastically. We couldn't possibly hire you. The ladies who frequent Macy's are extremely sensitive and high-class. In the delicate matter of weight reduction, they would be deeply offended if we brought in a man to attend to this most personal and intimate matter." And then with an evil glint in his eye, the manager suggested that Dad try Gimbels.

Two months later, in a typical reversal of fortune, my father found himself holding the bubble dancer Sally Rand by the ankles while dipping her into a vat of honey. He had become a press agent in order to support the vanity publishing house he had started, and Sally Rand, who thought he was cute, was helping him with his Busy Bee Honey account. From the metaphysical point of view, I would have to say that my father's life was ruled by the goddess Whimsy and her accomplice, some Puckish sprite. A letter he wrote to his Aunt Kate around 1935 tells it all: "New York is the grandest place—you can get away with anything! This morning I dropped about a thousand wriggling worms in the subway car at the height of the rush hour. Folks screamed and hopscotched over the little crawlers, but don't doubt that they'll ever forget Lillian's Live Bird Food anytime soon. Tomorrow I'm hiring a couple of guys to scrub down 52d Street and Fifth with French perfume. Their shirts will read Marlene's Perfume. Well, it's a living."

From the time that he learned to walk, my father was always turning the world inside out, upside down. Paradox and the absurd were the only realities he ever really believed in, comedy the pinnacle of the human expression. So there he was in the middle of the Depression, dropping Ping-Pong balls from the top of the Empire State Building, posing as a waiter at Mrs. Roosevelt's favorite restaurant so as to squirt her all over with soft ice cream for a newspaper picture. Clearly, his was a comedic mind in search of an honest outlet. (Years later, when he was writing jokes for President Roosevelt, the First Lady, much to his embarrassment, remembered him and in her gracious way forgave him.) Finally, destiny knocked. Cliff and Pat, a couple of radio comedians my dad was trying to plug, called him up and said that their writer was drunk. They asked if he could write them a five-minute comedy routine.

"Sure," said my dad. "How much does it pay?"

"Twenty-five bucks."

"Twenty-five bucks just for a bunch of jokes?"

"Yeah."

He was hooked, and the world today is a hundred thousand jokes richer for it. Soon he was writing for Ed Wynn and Eddie Cantor at the same time. This was followed by stints for Charlie Stupenagel, Walter O'Keefe, Joe Penner, Henny Youngman, Edgar Bergen and Charlie McCarthy, Jack Benny, George Burns, and just about every name in the comedy business. Between 1936 and 1986, he kept countless folks in stitches as they sat by the radio, in front of the television screen, at the movies, at variety acts, and at theaters of the legitimate stage (he was also a Broadway show doctor).

There was always laughter in the house. Jokes and quips, sight gags and prat-falls were the daily bread of our lives. I remember Dad once saying to me, "I suppose my big trouble is that I laugh too much. Most of the worries of the average person and the worries of the world aren't very serious to my way of thinking." Of course this included dwindling bank accounts, preparing for the future, finding a house to live in or a school to go to. Laughter was the great fixer, since my dad was certain that the Almighty had conjured up the Earth for his own vast amusement. He would have approved the old Apache tale that goes, "The creator made man able to do everything—talk, run, look and hear. He was not satisfied though, till man could do just one more thing—and that was laugh. And so man laughed and laughed and laughed. And the creator said, 'Now you are fit to live.'" Having grown up in a sea of laughter, having been marinated in humor from the womb, I, too, have come to believe that humor is the next best thing to God.

I've often wondered why massive laughter can be elicited by the slightest provocation of a joke or a mildly comical episode. Perhaps it is because we humans are stocked with so many subpersonalities, so many dimensions of consciousness in addition to our storehouse of personal history, that we are always sitting on a dangerous powder keg. What humor and laughter do is permit a release of this hothouse of stored emotions and feelings, letting the unconscious up for air, as it were, while it blows off steam. Laughter under social conditions also allows the soul to be congregationalized, and instead of meeting in mutual enmity and distrust, we allow our unconscious responses to become socialized, trusting, and openly infectious. Thus laughter lifts our spirits, surprises and sometimes shocks our expectations, allows us to cross boundaries, reorders our priorities, and gives us access to ideas and associations we rarely ever thought to have. Different worlds and ways of being conjoin and come up funny.

The one pattern that seems to underlie all varieties of humor is that of bisociation—seeing a situation or event in two mutually exclusive associative contexts. An example of this would be the story about the marquis at the court of Louis XV unexpectedly returning from a journey and, on entering his wife's boudoir, finding her in the arms of a bishop. After a moment's hesitation, the marquis calmly walks to the window, leans out, and begins going through the motions of blessing the people in the street. "What are you doing?" cries the anguished wife. "Monseigneur is performing my functions, so I am performing his." With jokes such as these, we jump the track of ordinary consciousness and reach a world governed by an unexpected set of rules. Our minds are purged of ordinary habits and probabilities, and we are renewed in laughter. This not only gives us a larger universe, it gives us different laws of form—the basis for all acts of creation. We tend to live in the late modern Euro-American standard-brand universe. But what about the weirder universe, or even the weirdest one just down the quantum block? Laughter carries us light-years in moments. Move one universe over, and you have the classic story of the interloper from one universe entering another and coming up against its different set of rules.

The story is told of the tractor salesman driving up to a farm and being startled to see the farmer lifting a large pig up to the branch of an apple tree. As the salesman watches in amazement, the pig bites a large apple off the branch, whereupon the farmer gently puts the animal down and picks up another pig, who gobbles up his own apple from the tree. This goes on for quite a few pigs, until the salesman can no longer restrain himself.

"Excuse me," he says to the farmer, "but wouldn't it be easier to pick all the apples yourself and let the pigs eat them off the ground?"

"Might be," allows the farmer as he reaches for yet another pig. "But what's the advantage?"

"For one thing," says the salesman, "it would save a lot of time."

"Could be," says the farmer. "But what's time to a pig?"

Atop a mountain in Ojai, California, a pink marble sphere has been placed over my dad's ashes. Carved into it are the words he wrote as his own epitaph: "He Made a Billion People Laugh." Recently, I had to arrange to move these ashes from one mountaintop to another when the property he was buried on changed hands. Since the pink sphere was not yet in place, we were not quite sure where Dad's dusty remains were buried. When I arrived at the property, I was met by Cleopatra, the owner's large black dog, who went slinking off into the bushes and wouldn't come, regardless of our calling and cajoling. Up on the mountaintop, I was handed a pair of dowsing rods, which my friend assured me would help me find my father. Skeptical but game for anything since I was sure that my father would have gotten a kick out of the procedure, I went dowsing for Dad. The rods were unmoving until I reached a particular spot, where they started spinning with abandon. Sitting on the spot, I attempted some kind of conversation with Dad. "Hey, Dad," I said, "if you're down there, give me some proof that I'll find acceptable." A few moments later, the shy dog suddenly had a change of heart and came galloping up the mountain, pausing only to roll in the mud before racing over to me and covering me with mud and kisses. A proof, a veritable proof! When we dug at the spot, with the dog's help, I might add, we found the metal box containing Dad's ashes.

A year or two after his career as a comedy writer began, my father met my mother at a YMCA dance.

"You look like a fairy princess," he said.

"You look like Gary Cooper," she said.

("Oy vey," said Jean-to-be, waiting in the wings. "I'm going to look like a cross between Gary Cooper and a fairy princess!")

The Dreamtime shifts, and a second trunk emerges from the family tree, this one rooted in volcanic ash.

My mother's ancestors were vintners on Mount Etna. For hundreds of years they were willing to risk all to get the perfect grape, which, they believed, could be grown only in the volcanic soil. I have visions of them snatching up vines as they ran down the mountain every quarter century or so when the volcano erupted, their heels licked by lava, only to return and plant again. Another branch of my Sicilian family belonged to the minor nobility. Their sons filled the ranks of army officers for generations, fighting the hordes of marauders who came to Sicily's shores in successive waves—Greeks, Arabs, Normans, Spaniards, Turks, Moors, the armies of the pope. Always they were defending themselves from invaders, always trying to recover what of theirs had been snatched or lost, always playing out the eternal return of the story of Demeter and Persephone. Sicily is the home of Demeter, the place where her daughter Persephone was said to have been playing among the flowers when the Earth opened up and Hades himself grabbed Persephone and took her down to the underworld to make her his bride and queen. The Sicilian landscape is littered with memories of the goddess and her search for Persephone; the ecstatic ritual of the Sicilian Easter is celebrated as a thinly disguised memory of the myth, as the Madonna goes wandering in search of her lost child after his crucifixion. Hades, of course, continues to exact his tribute in the underworld of the Mafia.

My mother was born in the ancient city of Syracusa and came to America at the age of six. Her father, Prospero Todaro, was the younger son of a Sicilian nobleman. Having few prospects in that land of stern primogeniture and rebelling against the cycles of war and politics, Prospero became an anarchist. Longing to live in a more innocent land, he brought his family to New York just before World War I and managed to prosper by dint of hard work and an import-export business (salami, olive oil, provolone). He was a legendary eater who thought nothing of putting away pizzas by the stack. His belly began at his chin; he knew of his feet only by rumor.

My mother had gone to Columbia and Fordham and was by day a statistician and analyzer of stocks and bonds for the Hanover Bank. Her brother had told her that the only thing you needed to know to be a statistician was how to count from one to ten. With this basic knowledge as background, a master's degree in economics, and a strong streak of mysticism, she created an almost infallible system for predicting which stocks were going to go up. Her method had something to do with hunches. By her early twenties, she had made the bank an enormous amount of money—in the middle of the Depression. Bank executives came from all over the United States to learn the mysteries of her system.

"It's all in believing," she would explain to them in her fey but pleasant manner. "Every morning when I come to the office, I look at the stock market quotations and say to the newspaper, 'I know, *I believe,* that hidden there in all that print is the name of the stock that's going to rise tomorrow.' And then I let my eyes glance up and down the page until, all of sudden, one stock leaps off the page and begins to tingle. And I tell the stock manager about the stock that tingled, and he buys it, and we make lots of money." The executives would leave, baffled and distraught.

Perhaps you think that my mother's system of market analysis is just too far out to be the truth. Friends I have described it to have protested that they wouldn't mind if a bit of Fordham economics was mixed with mystical intuition, but they complain that my account of it must be more entertaining than factual. On the contrary, I tell them, my mother has always been fey, an inhabitant of several worlds, a woman who sees angels, is prescient about the future, intuits deeply, and operates on many levels simultaneously. Even now in her mideighties, when she meets new people, she tells them in her very gracious manner all about themselves, often extolling wonderful qualities and possibilities that seem to rise up from the unread pages of their lives. Most leave saying that they feel they have been truly seen and known for the first time.

By night my mother had a secret life—one that in the eyes of her family would have been almost as exotic as her method of predicting the market. She studied method acting with Maria Ouspenskaya, the grand old Russian actress who had been Stanislavsky's leading lady. While her parents thought she was studying at the Columbia Library, like a good Sicilian girl should, she was in fact playing the title role of *Hedda Gabler* in an off-Broadway production. (Just to show how the past comes back to haunt one, years later when my mother thought I was studying in the Columbia Library, I was actually running LSD experiments in a Bronx hospital.)

Audrey is listening intently to my tale of two families. Something seems to bother her.
"How could they eat together, your mother's and your father's families?"
    "What do you mean, Audrey?"
    "When clans that live far away from each other go walkabout and meet, they do not always know each other's food. Or the food of one clan is forbidden to the other. One clan can eat kangaroo but not wombat. Another eats wallaby but not bandicoot. This is a serious thing. The wombat eaters have grown up under different skies and have different spirits than the kangaroo eaters. Now it is changing, and the clans try to eat each other's food, but it is very difficult."
    "You're talking about what we call multiculturalism, Audrey."
    "I'm talking about the mixing of the clans."
    "But that is inevitable."
    "But it isn't easy. They eat such different foods."

On the day that my father was to ask my mother's family for her hand in marriage, he arrived for the ritual Sunday Italian dinner. He didn't know it at the time, but he was to be put to a Herculean test by this meal. You must remember that he appeared to the Todaros to be the complete alien—very tall, blond, blue eyes, a Texas drawl, and a slaphappy, cowboy-jester manner. If he had come from another planet, he might have been more recognizable. As it was, he was of a different species, a Visigoth entering Rome, a member of one of the invading nations that had trashed Sicily. The only way they knew of making him prove his worth was by observing his ability to consume the many courses of a Sicilian Sunday meal.

Twenty-one people sat down to dinner at the long table with all the extension leaves in. My grandmother brought out the antipasto, and the gastronomic voyage was launched. The antipasto that day was a kind of cornucopic fantasy consisting of cold cuts (salami, mortadella, prosciutto, pepperoni); cheeses (provolone, gorgonzola, bel paese, caciocavallo); pickled vegetables (eggplants, peppers, mushrooms, pimentos, ceci peas, green, black, brown, and purple olives, stalks of fennel, celery, stuffed artichokes); and fish (broiled shrimp, tuna fish eggs, pickled squid, and baked clams). All this was served with many loaves of Italian bread and great decanters of lusty homemade wine. At the end of this first course, my father sighed deeply, loosened his belt, and said, "Well, that was just great. What's for dessert?"

The family murmured ominously. "Dessert," said one of them finally, "is at least six hours away."

"Lasagna!" my grandmother announced happily, and everybody looked hungry again. The lasagna was served with a side portion of meats stewed in tomato sauce, including meatballs, braciola, pork chops, and hot and sweet sausages. Spaced along the table every few feet were huge pyramids of freshly grated parmesan.

"This is some trough you put out here, ma'am!" my father said to my grandmother. "Boy, would my granddaddy's prize hog like to be snorting around here!" The family looked dubious.

"*Mangia! Mangia!*" the old lady encouraged my father. "Oh I'm a-mangaying, ma'am. You just keep bringing it out, and I'll mangay every last smidgen."

"*Zuppa!*" my grandmother sang out, and everybody was ladled out great steaming portions of chicken soup with tortellinis floating in the broth like a flotilla of doughy islands.

"Turca . . . Rozabeeffa . . . Hamma!" (My grandmother was trying to speak English for my father's benefit.)

The turkey was stuffed with chestnuts and sausages. The ten-pound roast beef was sitting in a forest of wild mushrooms my grandmother had brought back from Brooklyn's Prospect Park the day before, having given them the never-fail silver quarter test, and the ham was shimmering in a tomato aspic.

"*Pesce!*" A whole stuffed carp appeared.

With these were served the "vega-tables," a baker's dozen of leaf and legume extravaganzas; the *insalate,* a crunchy green jungle awash in olive oil and vinegar; and many glasses of wine and cream soda.

Whenever my father faltered in his labors, my grandmother would shake a plump finger at him and say, "You too skinna. *Mangia* some more."

"*Mangia, mangia,*" the family would thunder in chorus.

"Reminds me of the time I lost out to Fatso O'Rourke in the pie-eating contest at the Texas state fair," my father mused unhappily. Just then he had a bright idea on how to keep the family from observing his intake too closely. "Hey, would y'all like to hear some jokes?"

"*Mangia!*"

Dutifully, painfully, wearing a smile on his face that was no longer a smile but a muscular contraction of agony, my father continued to ingest and imbibe the unending processional that crossed his plate and filled his glass.

The laws of chemistry finally caught up with him. For a man whose stomach had been nurtured on a diet of grits, fried chicken, and black-eyed peas, the present culinary trip had driven him into what I would later learn to call an altered state of consciousness. He watched his plate in silent fascination as epic and fantasy emerged from the depths of the gravy. The romaine flapped its spiny green wings and soared over the great Byzantine mushroom temple with its inlaid floor of salami mosaic. Speeding over drought-ridden fields of fried eggplant, it paused over the sausage-crusted volcano and peered into its fiery crater of tomato sauce. But what really upset him was the plague of stinkbuds that sprouted all over the plate. My mother patiently explained that this was garlic, the essential ingredient of a Sicilian meal, but my father knew them only as stinkbuds, the things that the old healing women down South wore around their necks to frighten off the "Run-at-yous."

He was somewhat distracted from his vision when a booming operatic baritone shattered the air with an intense and passionate rendering of "Ritorno Sorrento." The family joined in on the second verse, dark thunder in their voices, the Italian words trembling with deep and terrible yearnings. My father had never heard a song invested with such fervor before. His experience of family singing was limited to merry little choruses of "Little Brown Jug" and "The Old Gray Mare." Sometimes, a poignant note would be introduced with "Home on the Range."

As the family moved into an apocalyptic version of "O sole mio," my father, as he later described this scene to me, noticed that their faces and bodies had changed. They were the Todaros no more but the nightmare inhabitants of the world of Hieronymous Bosch. Devils and grotesques surrounded him on every side. At either end of the table a troll and a banshee bared their fangs and began to shout maledicta at each other. This was the weekly "discussion" between Uncle George and Uncle Paul, whose political beliefs were a mere 180 degrees from each other. Having grown up in the genteel South, my father had never heard such raging fury in family discussions, except perhaps in moments of concerted agreement as to the behavior of the Union army. As both of my mother's brothers were lawyers, the acrimony quickly moved from brilliant briefs for the far left and right sides of the political spectrum to all-out epithets of outrage and name calling.

"Communist!"

"Fascist!"

"Marxist dupe!"

"Wall Street oppressor!"

"Proletarian pinko!"

"Bourgeois decadent!"

"Lousy red! "

"Fascist pig!"

"Second-Avenue Trotskyite!"

"Brooklyn capitalist!"

"Desserta—eight kindsa!" my grandmother announced, and with a flourish the curtain rose on the final act—cannelloni, zabaglioni, a rice and candied fruit pie, rum cream puffs, sweetened chestnut puree buried under mounds of whipped cream, cheesecake, pound cake, and a galaxy of cookies.

Much later and with a satisfied groan, my uncles pushed back from the table. "Now, Jack, did you want to talk to us about something?"

The table became deathly still. The circle of Sicilians—olive skinned, black haired, eyes like pools of darkness—watched as my blond and blue-eyed father got shakily to his feet and tried to speak.

"Yes. I would like to tell all of you swell folks . . . that I would like to merry Marry . . . uh, I mean, marry Morry . . . meery? Mary merry? Murray?"

He suddenly keeled over and passed out.

There was a long silence from the table. Then my grandfather's basso profundo was heard to ask in Sicilian, "Eh, Maria. Where did you get this donkey?"

One week later my parents eloped. A week after that, my mother bought a southern cookbook and attempted a not-too-successful rendition of chicken-fried steak. Perhaps it was the olive oil she used to fry the steak or possibly the additions of oregano and parmesan cheese. Today, when restaurants boast cuisines that marry continents and foodies drool over Aztec gravlax and Tibetan foie gras, the innocence of early departures from regional cooking may seem jejune. Back then, and for many, even now, it bespoke a dread before the coming of jump time, when cultures, in a frenzy of rapid and whole-system transition, would move beyond time-honored phobias and leap into early stages of a planetary civilization. The primal territory of tongue and stomach were to be the meeting grounds of this emerging ethos, taste buds tingling with signals of capture or rapture. But as the palate grows ever more planetary, the ancestral life in which it is housed demands equal time, with the result that in the late twentieth century we are witnessing the phenomenon of cultures reestablishing themselves. And the ancient myths that underscored each civilization are returning to be retold and resold. The tribal wars that beset the evening news are the shadow of this attempt, the tragic last stand of the separatist position that has ruled so many millennia.

All of us have moved, step by faltering step, into the ocean that beckons us to swim farther out and suffer a sea change into something rich and strange. We are becoming members of at least three cultures—our primary family and clan with its distinctive cultural features; the secondary one of mix and match, which includes profession, political party, skills, interests, and other cultures; and now a third one, the global culture, whose attributes of world music, the information highway, travel, media, and, above all, food take us into a new phase for which history has no precedent.

My parents' marriage was an early attempt to work out culture clash, and on the surface my mother and father seemed eminently suited for the venture. They were already hybrids themselves—a mystical statistician actress and a southern agnostic clown. I was to be the repository of this blend, a Cuisinart kid mixing science and spirit, comedy and culture and possessing a certain talent for cooking up complex dishes. Above all, the hybrid blend gave me a passion for the possible—anytime, anywhere.

My life began in a gagman's riff. How many among us can say that they were bought from the hospital for 350 jokes? While I was being born, almost two months prematurely, my father paced outside the delivery room, talking to himself and frantically jotting down jokes.

"What do you get when you cross a melon, a collie, and a baby? Right! A melancholy baby. No, even I know that stinks. Okay. Did you ever hear the one about the rabbi, the priest, and the baby. . . . Stop. Keep your mind on the joke. Okay. A baby walks into this bar, see . . . Ah, the hell with it."

Shortly thereafter I came into the world, a shriveled bundle of not-yet-ready-to-be-bornness. When he saw me, for the first and last time in his life my father was shocked into speechlessness. "That's no baby girl," he stammered, "that's a puppy—a red, wrinkled, horrible looking puppy. I'd be ashamed to take that thing to the pound."

"Oh, don't worry," said the nurse. "She'll get better looking. They all do. She'll have to stay in an incubator for a while, but then she'll be fine."

That was my first confrontation with my father, who now had a serious problem on his hands. He needed 175 dollars to pay the bill to keep me in the incubator until I was big enough to leave the hospital. No matter what I looked like, my father was in desperate need of some quick cash.

Henny Youngman, a radio comedian on the *Kate Smith Show,* was currently my father's only source of income. "Hello, Henny? This is Jack. Listen, that baby I was telling you about? Well, she just arrived. . . . No, by pony express. . . . Henny, let me get to the punch line, will you? I've got to have 175 bucks, so could you let me have an advance on the jokes I sell you, so's I can pay for the incubator? Whaaat?! That's like fifty cents a joke! I could do better over at Grand Ole Opry selling gags to the horse. . . . Okay. . . . All right. I'll deliver them in a couple of days."

Recently, in an ancient hatbox, I found the 350 jokes that sprung my mom and me from the hospital. They're not exactly dazzling, but then, neither was I.

As I recall, virtually everything in my early life was circumscribed by comedy. Take my naming, for instance. I had no name until the day of my baptism. My father kept dreaming up southern or southwestern names like Daisy Darlene and Maple Belle, which my mother, with understandable foresight and charity, rejected. They fought the hardest over the name Scarlett, my father having just read *Gone with the Wind* for the third time. It was finally decided on the day of the christening to leave everything to fate and to let my Sicilian grandmother name me. She was still undecided in the car as we rode to the church where the ceremony was to take place. She kept reciting names to herself, trying them out on her tongue. The problem was that her tongue was thoroughly Sicilian.

"Pasqualina," she trilled to herself musically. "Seraphina. Maristella. Agnese. Santuzza. *Ah sì. Che bella nama.* Santuzza!"

My father was adamant. I was an American baby who needed an American name. "Jill? Joan? Jane? Maud?" my father suggested hopefully.

"*Discrazia,*" said my grandmother with disgust.

She returned to intoning names more fitting for some Puccini heroine. "Perpetua. Fiorina. Graziella. Annunciata."

A few minutes later at the baptismal font, when the terrible decision could be put off no longer, she announced to the priest and all gathered, "I tinka we nama de bambina Gianuzza Houstini!"

"Jinootsa!" my father fairly shrieked. "That does it. I put my foot down. Father!" he said to the priest. "Excuse me. My mother-in-law here is a good, kind, religious Eye-talian lady, but she doesn't have any sense of American sounds. Now look, maybe you can do us all a favor. You name the kid. You think up an American name that's the nearest thing to Jinootsa."

The priest thought for a few moments and then shook his head. "Beats me. Can't think of a thing."

"Me neither," said my father. He then had a sudden inspiration.

"Father, who's your favorite actress?"

"Janet Gaynor," said the priest instantly.

"Named!" said my father. And they proceeded with the christening.

As they left the church my mother said, "I don't like it."

"What don't you like, Mary?"

"The name Janet. It just doesn't suit Jeanie. That's it—Jeanie. We'll call her Jeanie. Her legal name is Janet, but her real name is Jeanie."

And that's the last I ever heard of Janet. But not, I'm sorry to say, of Gianuzza. My grandmother spent the rest of her life convinced that was my only legitimate name.

Audrey seems to be looking beyond me to the place just fifty yards back that is the most sacred site of the camp, where it is said that the Dreamtime of the creative ancestors is strongly present.

"But who is your parent beyond your parents?" she asks.

"What do you mean?"

"Who is your ancestor in the Dreamtime? If you do not know who it is, you are only half alive. Your Earth parents are not your only family."

I begin to suspect what she means. Many traditions hold that we are double parented, and the creative ancestors and their totems of the Aborigines can be thought of as archetypal partners and sponsors who present us with both abilities and challenges. Whether they are numinous borderline persons or constructs of the creative unconscious, we cannot say. But whatever or wherever they be, they, like the spirits of the Dreamtime, have made an enormous impression on the human psyche.

This past year my mother, at eighty-seven, has been remembering many things of long ago with great acuity. One of the things she remembers may shed some light on my two-year-old memory of having come from someplace else. I asked her if she recalled anything special from the time when she was pregnant with me.

"Oh yes," she replied. "During that time I often had the same dream. A limousine would come and pick me up and take me to a palace."

"What kind of palace, Mother? A palace like the Renaissance palaces we saw in Venice?"

"No, it was more like a temple. The whole place was filled with music. And there was a beautiful lady there dressed in blue who always greeted me so warmly. I believe she was a goddess. We would sit and listen to the music and talk and she would tell me . . ." At this point my mother, no matter how many times I would question her, lapsed into Italian to recount the conversation. The conversation generally had to do with the baby inside her whom the beautiful lady would claim was her baby, too. My mother would strongly contest this claim, but the lady would only laugh and say, "You'll see," whereupon they would both become quiet and listen again to the music. When I asked my mother the name of the beautiful lady, whom she called Blue Dell, she faltered and then said, "Tell me the names of some goddesses."

"Well, there's Isis, Astarte, Aphrodite, Hecate, Tara, Demeter, Spider Woman, Corn Mother, Kwan Yin, Hera, Hathor, White Buffalo Woman, Persephone, Artemis, Sekhmet, Bridget, Cerridwen, Athena—"

"Stop, that's it. That's who it was. She told me her name was Athena."

Two fractal waves converge here, both of them essential to my later pursuits and both coded, it would seem, in the womb—my memory of music or frequency as the core nature of reality and my sense of an archetypal friendship and partnership with Athena, which has been with me most of my life.

Dr. David Cheek and other prenatal psychologists who study the mental and emotional development of the unborn child maintain that some form of hearing and understanding is available to the human fetus. Further, they say, the human fetus is a "feeling and interpreting organism from the moment its mother is told she is pregnant until the time of delivery." It acquires its information through hormonal channels, auditory ones, and, quite possibly, psychic ones as well, including telepathy and clairvoyance. Hypnotic age regression of adults remembering episodes in their fetal life suggests that the consciousness of the unborn is able to pick up and be influenced by the mother's experiences of delight as well as distress.

I know what my distress was. My father wanted me aborted, since he felt he was not yet able to support a baby. "You've got to be practical, Mary," he reminded her over and over. "We can't afford a baby, and I'm sick of living with your parents. I can't stand the smell of garlic anymore. You can have a kid later, after I get on the *Bob Hope Show,* and we move out of here."

My mother, Catholic and Sicilian, refused and perhaps found solace in a dream world of limousines, temples, and goddesses who wanted the child born. And, perhaps, the dream world was "real." Perhaps it was similar to or even the same as the Dreamtime of the Aborigines, the world behind the world, the domain of music and delight and numinous borderline persons who knew a logic higher than the merely practical. This is what I choose to accept, and why not? For without my mother's constant return to this dream reality, I might never have been born. As it was, her distress over my father's demands may have accounted for my premature birth, but the delight of her dreams may have influenced my entire future intent.

"And so, Audrey," I conclude, "that's the story of my family background. That's how I got here." She lights a cigarette, and we both watch the smoke coil into the night sky, snaking its way into the Dreamtime. "Your mother knew how to visit the Dreamtime and learn from your ancestor spirit, who you call Athena. That one, she made you get born. Your father had a name like my whitefella name," she says after a few deep drags on the cigarette. "Maybe we are all related. Maybe we are all just one letter different. You have many races in you. So do I. So do most blackfellas here. Nobody anymore is just one thing or the other. Or if they are, they soon won't be. My husband Phillip, he is quite light, and I am very dark. Is that so with your husband, too?"

I think for a moment and realize it is, my skin being olive toned, while Bob's English background makes him very fair. "But what's inside of you," she continues, "is light and dark, all mixed together. The same with me. How do we make it work? I have a good whitefella schooling. I teach those things I learned. Phillip knows how to apply for grants, build buildings, run machinery. But we also know how to catch sea turtles, make color dyes from roots, talk to our ancestors, travel in the Dreamtime. If all these worlds—blackfella, whitefella, yellowfella, redfella—don't be true to their own dreaming while they come together in a new way, we will have no world soon. I have the seeing, and I know that is so."

I am haunted by Audrey's knowing. The hound of heaven woofs at my feet each morning, urging me to do something about it. I have help. My hybrid body and soul fit me for the work that I do—helping people discover within themselves the many cultures and, therefore, many potentials of mind and body that all of us contain. I treat cultures themselves like persons, helping them to deepen and recover their genius and integral knowings while linking with other cultures and ways of being, including the emerging planetary civilization. My work has taught me that we are truly living in a time of harvest of the world's cultures and the planet's history. It is as if every kind of society that has ever existed, as well as the different human capacities that each elicits, is alive today—from the few remaining examples of Paleolithic people deeply attuned to the rhythms of nature and their own inner spirit, to high-tech societies that are collapsing into inwardness, searching for the green world within to redeem the gray world without.

With the entire spectrum of historical social development at hand and with the present fractal move toward planetization, I discover that the world is set for a whole-system transition. In this transition all cultures, regardless of where they are socially or economically, have something of supreme value to offer the whole. For example, many members of European-derived cultures reveling in technique and objective mastery are sadly lacking in the depth of spiritual awareness and psychological relationship found in Aboriginal cultures. Societies less technologically advanced have continued to develop spiritually over the millennia, until now they are immensely brilliant and luminous versions of themselves (or were, before the tragic intervention of colonialism). If the genius of so many cultures can be brought together, as I believe is now happening, the current crisis of social breakdown and moral disorder can be transformed into the creative symbiosis of the coming world civilization, allowing the findings of each culture to seed the others while preserving and enhancing its individual cultural style and differences.

Part of my work has been to study, collect, and apply human capacities as they have developed around the world under different environmental and social conditions. How Africans walk and think and celebrate spirit, how the Chinese teach and study and paint, how Eskimos experience vivid three-dimensional inner imagery, how the Balinese learn to perform artistic endeavors so rapidly and with such high craft, how a tribe along the Amazon raises happy and nonneurotic children, why certain children in India raised amid traditional music develop extraordinary skill in mathematics—these are capacities no longer limited to place and culture. In this new world of hybrid vigor, all these potentials once nurtured in separate societies are now available to the entire family of humankind.

The world mind has gone walkabout. The membrane that used to preserve the barriers between tribes, nations, and ways of being is shot through with holes. Everything has gone hybrid—music, language, religion, art, food. Yesterday for dinner I made Chinese wonton stuffed with Sicilian olives, sun-dried tomatoes, artichokes, basil, Szechwan pepper, and parmesan cheese. I did this while wearing Austrian shoes and an Indonesian print shirt and pants, listening to an album called *Earthbeat* in which American musicians weave jazz melodies through ninth-century songs sung by Russian peasants. My Japanese Akita dog slobbered hungrily at my side while I cooked, and at the nearby fax machine, my long-haired white German Shepherd pawed at the messages rolling out to me from Thailand, Norway, Greece, Bangladesh, and Brooklyn. My hybrid family background has spawned, like a Mandelbrot picture, an unending series of fractal offshoots.

And yet despite this joining and melding, cultures are becoming more what they are, not less. Maori people, Native Americans, Australian Aborigines, Chinese Hakka folk, and so many other indigenous peoples are attempting, as Audrey did, to recover the old ways of their culture while they are moving into complex relationships with other cultures. This applies to individuals as well. My friend Brendan, whose relatives are Irish, has taken to learning Gaelic with a vengeance, while my highly expressive business manager Fonda, whose grandparents came from Italy, lards her speech with Neapolitan patois, explaining all her theatrics with the catch-all, prideful "I'm Italian!" I sometimes think that all of this is a ruse of Mother Gaia herself, who, after all, loses one of her species every twenty-five minutes or so. Perhaps human cultures are the organs of the Earth's psyche, and recovering their distinctiveness is the psychic equivalent of recovering species that the Earth requires for her functioning.

In this time of much change and the compounding of complexity, we need to use capacities that we never knew we had—capacities rarely used or even lost, perhaps, since childhood or the childhood of the race. We might refer to these capacities as evolutionary accelerators. They propel us from beneath the surface crust of sleepy consciousness and our own human nature and biology. They help us, too, to move beyond the shutters of our local cultural windows so as to have the courage and capacity to nurture all forms of the possible human and the possible society. For undoubtedly we are patterned and coded with potentials, few of which we ever learn to use. It is as if we had in our bodies and minds a vast orchestral range of a million keys, and we have learned to play but a small fraction. The journey to discover what these missing keys are and how they can be used is what my life is all about.

Several months after my birth, the doctor who examined me commented on how well I was doing for a premature baby. "Hybrid vigor," he said. "That's what it must be. What did you say this baby's background was?"

"Scottish-Sicilian and some Cherokee Indian," my mother replied.

"Well, then, she's going to have quite a life," the doctor responded.

And so she has.

Our visit to the Aboriginal camp is coming to an end. As we prepare to depart, Audrey asks us to speak with the two elders who had seen the massacre by the white bounty hunters and the unhappy spirits who still inhabit the place. "They have something important to tell you," she says. The two old men arrive and announce that something has changed. The spirits had come again that day to say that they had seen this group of white people come to the camp. This time the whites had lived like the people themselves, had painted and danced and sung and talked and listened. That fact had released the Aboriginal spirits from their years of misery; they told the elders they were now ready to "go in" and could leave happy. And what is more, they said, the land itself was healing and the Dreamtime returning.

✦

2

New Adams and New Eves

It is March 1989. I am lecturing on paradise and its inhabitants in the Mystery School, an institution of curious learning that I created to teach the things I love best—history, philosophy, the new physics, psychology, anthropology, myth, and human potentials. This year we are studying the major myths of many cultures, and we inaugurate the series with a session on the themes that run through the mythic remembrance of Eden. This remembrance is the equivalent in many ways of the Australian Aborigine's memory and experience of the Dreamtime—an ever-present origin that contains the stories of creation and the ancestors and a continuing domain of creation that abides and evolves within our deeper nature. The myths and metaphors of paradise serve as symbolic codes for gaining access to the pattern of evolutionary existence. In mythic parlance, through them, we enter once and future times to discover who we are and what we yet may be.

I have been telling my students that many societies hold the memory of a golden age far in the past, when people were different than they are now. They moved beautifully, they were without stress, they sensed and experienced the world exquisitely, they conferred with archetypes and angels and knew one another's souls. They had natural wisdom, loved greatly, and lived long lives, continually celebrating and enjoying their optimal existence.

Rachel raises her hand. "What about in the Jewish tradition, Jean? Adam's a clump of mud, Eve's a rib, and no sooner do they get created but they really screw up and get kicked out of paradise!"

"Yes, but that's just the kosher version," I reply. "In Jewish folklore, you have quite another story. Adam and Eve are portrayed as so magnificent that their very skin is luminous. They know everything and can understand and communicate with animals and plants. The tradition says that God not only revealed the geography of the entire Earth to Adam and Eve but also gave them the ability to see into the future."

"They had access to the ultimate computer that runs the whole show," Rachel observes. "Maybe that's the real scoop on the tree of knowledge. It's a computer, and the Big Boss is saying, 'Don't mess around with my data base!' "

"Or maybe it's the memory of what we all have stored within us from the start. After all, a myth is something that never was but is always happening. And the fact that so many of these early myths and scriptures tell us much the same story about our potentials shows us not just where we may have been but also what is coded within us—a second nature that is so much greater than our usual one. Evolution may require that we go back to the future, exploring in ancient myths the future of our own possibilities. Adaba, the Babylonian first man, was said to have been 'equipped with vast intelligence. . . . His plane of wisdom was the plane of heaven.' What does that sound like to you?"

"CompuServe!"

"The Mayan scriptures of the Popol Vuh describe the people of the first age as having a kind of seeing in which their gaze embraced everything; nothing was concealed from their knowing. They were so far-seeing and had so much clarity and insight that they had the same understanding of the world as the gods."

"So what happened?"

"The gods got worried and gave us myopia, so that we could only understand what's close at hand."

"It figures."

Ben, a student of Eastern religions, takes the mike. "In China, Taoists saw the first times as ones in which we were all one with the Tao—nature's way—and therefore shared in her intelligence. Lao Tzu said that in primitive times intelligent people had an intuitively penetrating grasp of reality that could not be stated in words. It's as if in our original state, we are in tune with everything and pick up the waves of universal knowing. It's like the Zen concept of beginner's mind. But you have to tune your body and mind first in order to get into that state. That's no small feat."

"That reminds me of a story," I reply, and I proceed to tell one of my favorites: how my father reinvented the human being.

It is 1939, and the World's Fair has come to Flushing Meadow, New York. Futuristic towers with names like the Perisphere rise up like giant white organs of generation, and multicolored pennants fly from daunting pavilions. This is Camelot as the World of Tomorrow. One is borne through it on moving esplanades or traveling chairs that take you into the year 1960, with its perfect roads on which cars routinely speed their quiet way at a hundred miles an hour. The booming grandpa voice of H. B. Kaltenborn assures you of "a brave new world built by united hands and hearts. Here brain and brawn, faith and courage, are linked in high endeavor. . . ."

Should you pass the two hundred buildings that house the glorious near-future and find your way to the end of the exhibit area, you will discover a number of tents where some of the more questionable but interesting endeavors are housed. In front of one of the tents stands a young man with a Dagwood haircut. It is my father. He is wearing an old-fashioned nightgown with a magnet attached to its hem. He calls this garment "Ye Staye Down Nightie." A placard explains that its purpose is to prevent waking up frozen in the middle of the night with your nightgown up around your neck. The magnet makes the nightgown stick to the foot of the bed. Of course, it has to be an iron bed. Situated on the tables are a number of objects serving as testimony to the untrammeled imagination, among them:

A portable fireplug that holds your parking place until you return. You leave the fireplug in the spot where you wish to park. When you are parked, you store the fireplug in the trunk of the car.

A statue that shrugs its shoulders to frighten off pigeons.

A backward calendar for people who don't think they'll like tomorrow.

Over the entrance to the tent is a sign that reads:

JACK HOUSTON AND HIS CRAZY INVENTIONS

At this moment he is beginning to demonstrate to the small crowd a contraption that looks like a robotic junk pile. He calls this bungled assortment of parts the Redesigned Man or, more familiarly, Junior. He is explaining that his inspiration for this apparition was the Old Testament.

"The problem with God is that he really didn't sit down and think out the consequences of his inventions. Everything was hot off the drawing board with the good Lord. Take human anatomy, for instance. It's a string of boo-boos from top to, uh, bottom. Now I'm going to show you good folks this morning what God would have come up with had he spent a few more days tinkering with Adam."

He proceeds to demonstrate the many improvements.

"Now just look at my face. It's overcrowded! Who needs two eyes within a couple of inches of each other? Now you'll notice that with Junior here, I've put one eye in the middle of his forehead and another at the end of a finger. That's so when he loses his keys or money in a dark theater, he can reach his eye finger down to the floor and search for whatever he's lost, and because of his other eye, he doesn't even miss seeing the movie!"

When someone in the crowd observes that Junior has no mouth, my father counters that the problem is that God, in his absentmindedness, put the mouth in the wrong spot. And sweeping an old cowboy hat off the monster, he reveals a great grinning mouth in the top of the head.

"Now this fine gent has a decided advantage over all of us. He can put his lunch in his hat, and while he drives to work, he can eat his lunch without taking his hands off the wheel.

"And look, now, at the nose! My nose is all wrong, poking out there for no particular reason. If it has to stand out, let the nose stand waaaaay out and perform a service, like an elephant's trunk."

He reaches into the back of his creation and pulls a wire, which causes Junior's nose to unfurl and stretch out into the audience a good five or six feet.

"You will notice that at the end of the nose trunk are six fingers. These are good for all sorts of things."

The fingers reach out and pat a pretty girl who is standing nearby.

"Now, about feet. We have too much of us spread out all over the floor. Shoes are expensive, and toes are completely useless. But this magnificent specimen has the perfect answer to feet . . . wheels! If all of us were built like Junior with wheels for feet, we could eliminate the automobile and solve the traffic problem."

"How do you tell the boys from the girls?" a bobby-soxer asks with a snicker.

"I was afraid somebody was going to ask that. Actually, I've put in a little invention of mine that does away altogether with—"

"Hey," a young man interrupts. "Didn't I see you and your inventions in the *New York Post*? Weren't you the 'Screwball of the Week'?"

Just then a howl is heard coming from inside the tent.

"Ohmygod, the baby!" my dad exclaims. The object of his worry is me, for he had left me inside his latest invention, the Electronic Nursey. This contraption was supposed to keep a baby amused whenever it had to be left alone. If the baby cried and wriggled, a circuit would engage and the cradle would rock. If that didn't work, Kate Smith would come on singing "God Bless America." If the baby was still crying, a large pink mammalian structure filled with milk would descend slowly and gently into the baby's mouth.

At the moment, however, things are not going as planned. I am crying, all right, but the cradle is heaving violently from side to side and up and down to the sound of Kate Smith booming "God Bless America." Unfortunately, the needle is stuck on "AmericaAmericaAmericaAmericaAmerica." And instead of descending smoothly and gently into my mouth as designed, the large pink mammalian structure keeps bopping me in the mouth. Luckily, my mother has also responded to my wails and plucks me out of the malfunctioning Nursey. If she hadn't, I might have grown up looking like Walter Matthau.

"Sorry, Mary," my dad explains. "I was busy with Junior and . . . My problem is that everything I invent works—almost."

Early imprinting is a curious thing, a fractious fractal that never goes away, and the whole episode may well have knocked into my tender and trusting little head the wish to follow in my father's audacious footsteps and take on the task of inventing the possible human. I have plied my trade of reinventing people with both the physiological and the psychological equivalents of insulated wires and needle-nosed pliers. I have probed long and deep into the mystery of why people fail to use their full powers, why we have become botched and malfunctioning versions of what we could be. What went wrong? And where? And how? Was my dad right—were we too quickly pulled off the design board of evolution? Was paradise lost, and with it the memory of the possible human?

In my studies of the three-part structure of the human brain, I have pondered whether the neocortex, that part of the brain that makes us human, may have developed too fast and grown too large some thirty thousand years ago. There it sits, I speculate, nested on its throne of beasts and reptiles—the earlier brains that have moved back in the skull to accommodate the sumptuous if juvenile brain of their new monarch. These earlier brains conspire while they protect, plot fights and flights while they advise and pretend to consent. Sometimes, in my more whimsically troubled moments, I think we humans are the result of a Ph.D. project of some graduate student god-in-training, who subsequently flunked his finals. Like my father and his inventions, everything that this young god created worked—almost. The intention was good, but the subsequent product seems to be missing a number of essential parts. There is no question but that we are patterned and coded with possibilities few of which we ever learn to use. Why do we live at a fraction of our potential? What keeps us from full use, and what, if anything, can be done about it? And why are we haunted by the memory of "once upon a time," when we were all that we could be but can't remember where or when?

I signal Mickey Houlihan, my sound engineer, to play mystical background music. I tell my students to close their eyes while I invoke the Dreamtime of paradise. "As you go deeper into the Dreamtime, tell me what you remember about being in paradise. It can be something that actually happened, or it can be something that never happened, but still you remember. . . ." As the music and my voice carry them deeper, hands begin to go up.

"I remember when everything was possible and the first smells of autumn would glow through me."

"I remember when each moment felt spacious."

"I remember love, loving, and being loved."

"I remember riding bareback and taking the horse in for a swim."

"I remember the lush cool greenness of a rain forest pressing in around me and how safe and healthy I felt."

"I remember being very small and the world being very big and the night being very dark and the stars being very bright and the breeze being very balmy. And someone downstairs that made everything very safe."

"I remember the moment when I was willing to die because I was a part of everything."

After many have spoken, I recite the opening words of Wordsworth's poem of remembrance of paradise in early childhood:

There was a time when meadow, grove and stream
The earth, and every common sight,
To me did seem
Apparelled in celestial light,
The glory and freshness of a dream. . . .

My longtime student and friend Judith Morley rises in confirmation, speaking lines from the same poem:

Our birth is but a sleep and a forgetting:
The Soul that rises with us, our Life's Star,
Hath had elsewhere its setting,
And cometh from afar:
Not in entire forgetfulness,
And not in utter nakedness,
But trailing clouds of glory do we come
From God, who is our home. . . .

The memories of childhood, the myths of paradise all tell us that we are born of deeper stuff, which we have forgotten. But in those moments of rapture, high creativity, love, communion, or sheer grace, we sometimes remember. The embers banked deep within us never really go out. Through the grace of the unexpected or the power of conscious work on the self, they can be kindled into fire in the belly, passion in the mind.

My lyrical side trip into Wordsworth annoys Rachel. "Embers?" she fumes. "It's steel and silicon we're heading for. A hundred years from now my grandchildren are going to be part robot."

It's true. We are already well into the morning of human-machine interface. We may come in trailing clouds of glory, but we are soon met by the spume of nuclear smoke. Technology already does or soon will partner the major experiences of human life—from conceiving babies to dying. Human capacities will soon be en-hanced by biomachine interfaces—fetuses spawned in tubes and raised like gup-pies in hospital incubation tanks, organs replaced routinely by clever machines, grandmothers past menopause giving birth to their own grandchildren, genes spliced and looped. The human body is being redesigned, microelectrodes im-planted in the brain to expand one's senses and extend one's memory, reality me-diated through computer-synthesized virtual forms, and even death delayed or defeated. Human-machine hybrids are the likely arbiters of this brave new world. The resurrection of Junior in a form light-years beyond my dad's zany conception is almost assured.

But what of it? For all the apparent ascendancy of androids and artificial intel-ligence, nothing can take the place of human development from inside out. The ironies of science fiction address this dilemma by portraying a future in which fantastical technologies abound but people and their social structures remain about the same. In fact, more often than not they have regressed—galactic empires run by medieval lords; societies replete with transporter beams, warp speeds, intergalactic starships, and phaser weapons, but differing not a whit from the ideologies and prejudices that made a holocaust of the twentieth century. Su-permen and superwomen engineered to replicate their own organs and access in-formation through modules implanted in their brain are caught in the same old emotional pain and trauma. The Faustian claims of those who speak for new gen-esis forget the wisdom of ancient stories, which tell us that the power of gods in the hands of those who have not done their human homework leads inevitably to disaster.

However, the prospect is not entirely grim. Any new high-tech advance seems to call forth a corresponding development in high touch: advanced medical tech-nology has as its corollary the rise of preventive and holistic medicine; television viewing is balanced by personal growth seminars; computers are offset by a prolif-eration of crafts or do-it-yourself skills and hobbies. Though high technology can lead to human betterment, technological benefits can never preempt innate human capacities or supplant the exhilaration we feel in their expression. We hu-mans are a vast system of systems and subsystems; to make conscious use of the complex wisdom of the body is to achieve a sublime orchestral experience of the self and its many ecologies, which technological enhancement can never give. Nothing can replace the paradise of natural use.

My seminars and workshops proceed from the premise that an inner Eden ex-ists in each of us in the form of latent human capacities, which can be awakened and called into play. At the Foundation for Mind Research, my husband Robert Masters and I have sought clues to this latency in many fields—history, literature, anthropology, psychophysiology—and performed research into the nature of the brain and consciousness. Using various techniques, ancient and modern, and ap-plying the "spare parts" of human potentials garnered from my research and travels all over the world, I have guided thousands of research subjects and well over a million seminar participants to redesign themselves as more possible humans. Our studies show us that the fall from paradise is no mere metaphor, that we humans endure the loss of many exquisite abilities, and many balanced and beautiful ways of functioning have become distorted, inhibited, or blocked. Since we humans are infinitely variable, so, too, the losses differ from person to person and from culture to culture. But few of us have escaped serious crippling. Almost everybody is much less than he or she has the capacity to be.

Consider my fantasy of the possible human, a once and future person, who may be both what we were and what we may yet become:

The first thing that you notice about her is that she enjoys being in her body. A fullness of being inhabits that body, with its flexible joints and muscles, its movements fluid and full of grace. One senses an ebullience in the bones, an appetite for delight. She is given to long pleasures and short pains, in contrast to most of us, who experience long pains and short pleasures. And if her natural zippiness and boundless curiosity entice her into situations where she gets physically hurt, she is able to control any bleeding and accelerate her own healing.

Like the yogi adepts in the Himalayas, she can voluntarily control involuntary physical processes and stay warm in cold weather and cool in hot. (This is true in emotional climates as well as physical ones.) She can also self-regulate skin temperature, blood flow, heart and pulse rate, gastric secretion, and brain waves. Indeed, she can consciously enter into alpha and theta brain wave states for meditation and creative reverie, drop into delta whenever she wants to go to sleep, and call upon beta waves when she needs to be alert and active. Scanning her body, she self-corrects any function that needs improving.

This new Eve celebrates acute senses, which are not limited to five, for she enjoys synesthesia or cross-sensing, the capacity to hear color and touch the textures of music, capture with her nose the smell of words, and taste the subtlest of feelings. Since her sensory palette is so colorful and wide ranging, she engages and is engaged by the world as artist and mystic, seeing infinity in a grain of sand and heaven in a wildflower. The splendor of her sensory life graces her with an accompanying gift, an excellent memory, for she is so present to the perceptual richness of everyday life that little is lost or disregarded and all is stored in her memory banks for later review and delectation. She can time travel into these memories, walk around in them as if they were happening now—talking to this friend, reliving that moment of joy, even holding the hand of a long-ago loved one. Thus she need never feel lonely, for the past is as present as the present.

And wherever in the past wounding occurred, she can visit that time in her mind as the wiser version of her former self and bring understanding, compassion, and wisdom to the occasion. This practice can free capacities that may have been frozen in the painful past and yield fruitful consequences for her present and future development. She is thus a time player, able to speed up subjective time when she needs it to go faster or slow it down so as to savor lovely moments or have more time to rehearse skills or review projects.

Meredith's hand is waving wildly. "Hold it, Jean. Back up a little. Exactly how would this possible human go about healing her own past?"

"Come here, Meredith, and I'll demonstrate. Are you up for it?"

A nervous laugh. "I think so. . . . Sure, why not?"

"Then I ask you to recall some incident in your past when you felt wounded, alone, in need of a friend."

"The night my husband had his heart attack and died. I was so shocked and frightened and unbelieving that I still feel like a part of me died then."

"I invite you to choose some part of that long night to begin the process of healing for yourself."

Meredith shifts uncomfortably. "Maybe the worst moment, as I see it now, was when they wheeled him into the elevator to take him to the cardiac care unit. He lifted his hand and waved at me. I was standing by the admission desk waiting to give them the necessary information and worried about money. I wasn't really afraid for his life at that time. After all, I had gotten him to the hospital, and in my innocence I thought that meant he would be all right. Part of me knew that I should run over and give him a kiss or touch his hand, but I was too busy and too cluttered with mundane worries. He died in the elevator. They brought him back for a while, but he never re-gained consciousness."

I realize there are several ways of working with Meredith. I could invite the person Meredith is now, with her expanded capacities for compassion and love, to move into the scene directly, make herself known to the Meredith who was present originally, and then move over to her husband, gather him in her arms, and give him blessing and gratitude and love from the wealth of experience and life that is Meredith's today. Or the Meredith of today could enter the scene, make herself known to the Meredith of the wounding, and urge that Meredith to move to her husband and touch him one more time. I discard both of these options because of the shame Meredith carries from not having performed this action in the past. I don't want to imply to her that reliving the scene in her imagination changes what actually happened.

In the end, I ask Meredith if she would be willing simply to be with the Meredith of the wounding in that moment of feeling pulled and yet pulling back. That seems to get at the major issue, Meredith's difficulty in listening to and obeying her instincts to move toward people in pain or need. She often says that she is too shy or doesn't want to intrude or feels herself stuck.

Meredith agrees. I ask her to stand in loving communion with that stricken Meredith at the hospital admissions desk, to feel again—but with compassion—the push-pull in her, to acknowledge that she learned in childhood "not to make a spectacle of herself," which included any show of emotion in front of strangers. Did she feel, I asked, any resentment toward her husband for being sick, for making her worry about how to pay for his illness? "Of course I did," Meredith agrees. Could Meredith hold that sense of shame with equanimity, understanding, and even self-forgiveness?

"That's much harder," she replies. Nevertheless, she agrees to hold the hurting Meredith imaginatively in her arms—the Meredith who did not yet consciously know that the future would bring her husband's death, the one who did not have the long view—and to talk to her kindly and gently.

I ask her to stay with that Meredith throughout the long night that followed, to sing to her, to remind her of happy days with her husband, to show her images of the future, to listen to the birds singing as the dawn came and the doctor arrived to tell her that it was over. I ask her to walk with that Meredith back to her home and to comfort her by being a guide through the days and weeks of pain that followed.

All this takes place within a few minutes of actual time. When the process ends, I ask Meredith to look once again at that moment of being by the desk. She reports, "It has shifted; it's much more flexible. There's a sense of communion with my husband that is very strong. There is light coming from him and from me now, and I can easily add the presence of eternity and angels—they're just there. The images are moving now. My husband gets up from the stretcher and I move toward him and we begin to dance—he loved to dance. I hear music playing."

Since that time Meredith tells me it is much easier for her to hear her inner music and to touch or assist someone when her inner wisdom is alerted.

This session with Meredith reminds us that each possible human is, not a member of some collective *Übermensch,* but a profoundly individual and precious demonstration of life in its infinite variety. This is certainly true on the physical plane and unimaginably more so when it comes to experiencing the internal realms. Indeed, the possible human can think in inward images and experience subjective realities as strikingly as she can know objective ones. She listens to inward music as complex as any symphony, in fact often richer, for instruments and sounds are added that are unknown or too expensive for any formal orchestra. She views new movies on her inner screen whenever she wishes, for she knows that it is the nature of the brain to provide stories, well-wrought novels for the Inward Television Station (ITS). She uses these images to entertain herself as well as to provide the materials of creativity and invention. She is already an adventurer into a vast reservoir of virtual realities and needs no machine to assist her. She knows that self-creating works of art are always budding out of the fields of her mind, and she can capture and rework them as she wishes.

Consciousness for her is a vast landscape, a continuous landscape, and she travels its length and breadth at will. She enters a state of meditation here, a region of deep trance there, finding shortcuts into the realms of fantasy and imagination, spelunking her way into the caves of creativity. She continues to discover the many cultures of her psyche and has matriculated in the Innerversity, studying all manner of knowledge and wisdom that these cultures within provide.

She has many friends and allies in the inward and imaginal worlds, the most important of whom may be the beloved of the soul, the spiritual friend who is her archetypal partner and the companion of her depth reality. And, whenever she feels ready, she journeys to the source places of her soul, where she partakes of the everlasting waters of life and spirit. She lives daily life as spiritual exercise, and her radiance affects all who meet her, for she is deeply empathic, knowing herself part of a seamless kinship with all living things. Being more, and using more of herself, she feels and cares more deeply about the decay and degradation in the social and moral order. In spite of evidence to the contrary, she recognizes others as God-in-hiding, and in whatever way she can, she calls them back to their own possible humanity. She is one about whom we might say, "The human heart can go to the lengths of God."

This possible human is not mere fantasy. Processes to develop these capacities have been developed in our three-year-long human capacities training programs as well as in Mystery School. I have described my work as a kind of psychenaut program "to put the first human on Earth."

I have found that most people, given opportunity and training, can learn to think, feel, and know in new ways, to become more creative and more imaginative, and to aspire within realistic limits to a much larger awareness, one that is superbly equipped to deal with the complex challenges of modern life. True, we have never achieved the fully functioning person described above, but we are getting closer.

Enhanced human capacities begin with what we generally think of as our most concrete reality—our own bodies. The human body, however, is anything but concrete. It is amazingly malleable and contains various evolutionary time zones. We inherit in our bodies and nervous systems the remnants of the earliest vertebrates as well as the fruits of mammalian evolution. And we also contain as latency the substance of what we will yet become. The brush of angel wings stirs our souls as some long-forgotten paradisiacal memory of the future. Thus the question is moot whether we are the more who have derived from the less, as Darwin supposed, or the less who have derived from the more, as certain theologians and esoteric thinkers hold. I take a more poetic view, believing with T. S. Eliot that "time past and time future are gathered in time present." Thus any practice that seeks to enhance human awareness and functioning must be based in these inherited potentials, which carry within themselves the seeds of evolutionary unfolding.

Michael Murphy writes in *The Future of the Body* (Los Angeles: Tarcher, 1992) about how earlier aspects of evolutionary development move toward extraordinary complexity and application in later stages:

We can cultivate somatic awareness and control . . . because nerve cells that evolved from analogous structures in the earliest vertebrates are deployed throughout our bodies. Relaxation exercises are effective because we possess a parasympathetic system that developed during the long course of mammalian evolution. We can become creatively absorbed in work, perhaps, because we have inherited capacities for catalepsy, analgesia, and selective amnesia that facilitate escape and hunting. In short, self-regulation skills, regenerative relaxation, and performance trance, like other kinds of creative functioning, are based on capacities that developed among our animal forbears. And while transformative practices draw upon our animal inheritance, they also employ uniquely human activities. The imagination we use to enjoy books can be cultivated to induce metanormal cognitions or to facilitate extraordinary physical skills. The self-reflection we sometimes practice when confronted by difficulty can be deepened by means of sustained meditation. . . . (340)

In 1972, at an Association of Humanistic Psychology meeting in Montreal, my husband, Bob, and I met a fascinating man who embodied some of the characteristics of this once and future human. His name was Moshe Feldenkrais, an Israeli and a respected physicist, and he was a living paradox. Gentle and angelic one moment, he could be bellicose and primeval the next. He entered psychophysical work in order to repair his knees, which had been much damaged by vigorous competitive jujitsu. After strengthening his own body, he began to offer his knowledge of the body to others who were injured or in pain, and his practice had grown as news of his astonishing results spread. Short and massive, Feldenkrais seemed larger than life; to me he was a living testimony that such people tend to have larger-than-life virtues as well as faults. Feldenkrais had the greatest practical understanding of the human brain and nervous system of anyone that either Bob or I had ever met. In Montreal, we watched him straighten a cruelly bent back in less than twenty minutes, a feat that seemed like a biblical miracle. But, no, Feldenkrais insisted, it was science.

Clearly Feldenkrais had discovered a path to the possible body. He prescribed exercises that involved repeated movements of a group of muscles and joints and were aimed at bringing the entire surface of the body into consciousness. If you want to improve, say, the functioning of the elbow, you move it many times in all the ways that the elbow is capable of moving, including ways that you haven't moved it since childhood. This action serves to alter the brain cells that are responsible for movement of the elbow. As a result of this focused attention, even if the elbow has been stiff and unmoving for years, it will start to bend with a child's flexibility. Bob and I have developed this work along our own lines and applied it to the many people participating in our research and seminars. We have seen changes in functioning and awareness that most physiologists would deem impossible. Early on, we encouraged a roomful of retired nuns in their seventies and eighties to sit down on the floor and perform a series of gentle, repeated movements on the right sides of their bodies. After about thirty minutes, most of them were able to pick up their right foot and place it near to or even on top of their heads! Then, by repeating the same movements on the left side *in the imagination only,* they were able to place their left foot near to or on top of their head in only five minutes. (This is a demonstration of the "generalization" technique. If you learn something slowly and completely on one side of the body, you can achieve the same results on the other side simply by rehearsing the action in the muscular imagination or kinesthetic body.)

The Mystery School is convulsed. Mark speaks for all. "Hey, Jean, what earthly good is that demonstration, and whatever would the old nuns do with their right or left foot once it was on top of their heads?"

That was the same question the mother superior had asked. "The point, Mark," I reply, "is that in accomplishing this feat, the nuns had radically reorganized their brains and motor functions and showed that they were potentially far more flexible and free in their bodies than their lifestyle warranted. To be perfectly truthful, the mother superior found this realization to be a mixed blessing, as the aged sisters who continued to do this kind of psychophysical exercise became very sprightly and demanded to be sent out into mission work once more—or at least to teach in an inner city school."

Feldenkrais often stayed with us, and he and Bob formed a mutual admiration society. Bob thought him the most intelligent and refined person he had ever met, while Moshe told Bob that he had more natural aptitude for psychophysical work than anyone he had ever taught. For four years, Bob worked up to eight hours a day doing the Feldenkrais exercises. Within the first year of practice, he thought he had achieved more in physical flexibility and awareness than he had in twenty-five years of yoga, with the result that even today, in his late sixties and weighing 2 . . . much, he can in many ways move more freely than the finely conditioned dancers that he often trains.

On one of Moshe's longer visits, he and I sat down and wrote together the world's worst book. The shouting back and forth between us tended to obscure all attempts at literary merit, although the ideas were quite interesting. In the book we argued that developing and integrating the older and newer parts of the brain might depend on a child's being able to recapitulate within the first three years of life the critical movements of phylogenetic development. We speculated that if the young child fails to engage in the rocking, creeping, crawling, and swinging motions of the fish, amphibian, reptilian, and various mammalian stages, connections between one evolutionary level of the brain and another would be inhibited. This could result in aberrations and pathology, lack of coordination, and possibly antisocial or even autistic behavior.

We each subsequently published our own versions of these ideas, mine in *The Possible Human.* I also developed a series of exercises to allow individuals and groups to experience the evolutionary sequence of movement and behavior. I conjectured that it would be possible to effect healing and integration by enacting physically these various stages and their relevant movements regardless of one's age. Generally speaking, performing this recapitulation of many millions of years in a few hours awakens a deep sense of evolutionary process in the body, begins the resolution of trauma experienced in infancy or early childhood, and aligns the various parts of the brain into conscious service for the whole person.

More specifically, with each stage we "remember" a variety of paradises. Rolling from side to side as both fish and newborn baby, we sense the great ocean womb of union and of living in an absolutely supportive environment. Enacting the stage of the amphibian, when baby and ancient creature with heads raised pull themselves along the ground on their forearms, we remember the urging of the sun to rise out of the ocean to live at least part of the time in the air. This trains us in the capacity to live comfortably and productively in two worlds. The dynamic push of the reptile, when the baby learns to crawl but is still on her belly, reminds us of our deep contact with the Earth and its vast energy source. The early mammal's movements, when the baby begins to crawl along on all fours, cause us to remember the childhood of mammalian life, the beginning of our active socialization. The monkey stage brings movement up and down and all around. Its great gifts are curiosity and wonder, experimentation and imitation.

The next stage embodies the movement patterns of the great apes, the vital stage of individuation and self-possession. No wonder we call this stage in humans "the terrible twos." The movements of early humans bring our creative imagination into play. People at this stage spontaneously begin to speak, make rhythm and music, and discover fire, tools, rituals, and worship. Beyond the stage of present humanity, we explore the possible next stage of evolution. I have observed many groups enacting this part of the process. They seem to engage in an alternating pattern of ritual communion and radical separateness. People weave and dance together in angelic groups, then go off by themselves to meditate. Always the movement of the body is beautiful, as is the way people gaze on each other in wonder and astonishment.

To the uninitiated, the sight of hundreds of people slithering like reptiles and leaping like monkeys is astonishing, to say the least. I will never forget a day in the mid-1980s in Miami Beach, when two elderly Jewish women stopped to observe several hundred of my students leaving the fish stage behind as they emerged from the waves and flopped on the beach to drag themselves along toward sun and sand like early amphibians.

"What's that, Sadie?" one asked the other.

"Oh, Sarah, don't pay any attention. It's just one of those *meshugenah* cults."

Then there were the elegant businessmen at the finest and fanciest hotel in Houston, Texas, who came through the wrong door, only to observe some five hundred of my students thumping their chests, grunting, and otherwise enjoying the stage of the great apes. Gazing solemnly, one turned to the other and drawled, "You know what this is, don't you, Brad? It's an Amway convention."

Actually I call it *prolepsis,* going forward by recapitulating the past.

"No, no, not prolepsis!" my students complain. "I'm not dressed for it."

However, within moments, mats cover the floor, watches, earrings, and belt buckles are removed, and for the next three hours evolutionary history comes alive. When we finish, I call them all together in a great huddle. Looking around, I see faces and bodies that resemble new Adams and new Eves. Even Rachel looks angelic.

"How do you feel, having completed the stages of evolution?" I ask.

"Integrated . . . unblocked . . . free . . ." they exclaim.

"I liked being a reptile the best," Rachel reports. "Especially getting to crawl all over everybody."

"Now scan your bodies," I suggest. "You may notice that each stage has its own transcendent function, a kind of metalevel of performance and awareness when applied to the human stage. For example, what is the genius or metalevel of the fish when acquired on the human level?"

"It's the ability to live in a more fluid fashion. It's freedom to be."

"And what's the metalevel of the amphibian stage?"

"As my amphibian self, I can operate in different contexts without fear. I can move out of old habits and enjoy different ways of being."

"What is the genius of being reptile?"

"Stick-to-it-ness! I feel a momentum in me now to really finish what I start out to do."

"And the early mammal?"

"I feel more gregarious. . . . . I'd like to nurture everybody here!"

"How about the genius of the early monkey?"

"I find myself curious about everything—like why you are wearing that plaid shirt with those batik trousers."

"Because I feel like it. Okay, what happens to you on the metalevel of being a higher monkey?"

"A sense of power. My own strength. I am who I am!"

"What about the early human?"

"Well, it's definitely not the Flintstones. It's a passion for discovering meaning and a sense of having all the capacities I need to create new things. After all, I survived an Ice Age."

"And then there is the modern human. What is the metalevel of being who you are right now?"

"Speculation. Partnering evolution and helping to cocreate the world. Reinventing ourselves and saving our environment. Exploring the dimensions of inner and outer space. Doing what we are doing now."

"And finally, what can we say of the next stage of evolution, the extended human?"

For answer, there is only silence and a smile.

As my psychophysical work continued to develop, I integrated imagery and creativity studies into exercises aimed at improving and developing body movement and awareness. Thus some psychophysical work involves imaging optimal body states while in trance and with accelerated mental processes. I found that within several minutes of actual physical time, experienced subjectively as an hour, one could achieve results equivalent to what might be obtained by several hours of actual physical work. I found that our bodies house many mansions—what other cultures call the subtle bodies, the most practical of which is the kinesthetic body, or body of muscular imagination. By going back and forth between movements felt inwardly in the kinesthetic body and the same movements performed outwardly in the physical bodies, people can make far more progress in enhancing a skill or physical function than they would ordinarily.

Also, it soon became clear that students and research subjects who were engaged in psychophysical work learned more completely and with greater ease to apply the potentials gained in inner space, such as the improvement of memory, the capacity to think on many tracks at the same time, and the ability to tap into the great mythic and symbolic realms of the deep self. Not surprisingly, I observed what the ancients of the Eastern and Aboriginal worlds have always known: access to the transpersonal domain lies within the gates of the attuned body. Our brains are stargates, our bodies celled of mysteries that invite us to enter into a larger body, a richer field of mind, and a spirit that comprehends them all.

As for myself, when it came to the spectrum of human capacities, I soon discovered that my own talent lay in the realm of playing with time. Nature has offered us the great gift of stretching time to counteract the shortness of our lives. Since adolescence, these days, seems to last until about age thirty-one, and since we seem to know little before the age of fifty, it behooves us to use our capacity to self-orchestrate time so that we may live hundreds of years within our given allotment of four score and ten or so. Indeed, working with time may be one of the greatest of all human capacities and one that is essential to the development of the possible human.

I myself have been no stranger to temporal oddities. Once, at nineteen, while I was engaged in the sport of jumping out of airplanes, my parachute refused to open, and it was only after experiencing my entire life go by at what seemed its original speed that the chute finally opened. Then there was the night in June 1972 when I woke up with the firm conviction that I would not live out the year. There was no apparent objective reason for this awareness; I was in good physical and mental health and was looking forward to the next year's work. Still, my death would not go away, and daily I felt the presence of the final boundary of my life. I made wills, settled affairs, and lapsed into a mild melancholy over my sweet but soon-to-be-short life. In October of that year, I was visiting my father, his second wife, Polly, and my young half-brother, Steve, when I suddenly knew that my death was imminent—within a matter of hours. On this particular evening, I was scheduled to hold a public conversation with the science fiction writer Ray Bradbury. As my father led us to his car to drive to the event, I suddenly turned around, hoping to let this cup pass from me. "Where do you think you're going?" my father demanded. "We're already late."

"I don't think I want to go tonight, Dad."

"You have to go. You're debating Ray Bradbury."

"Actually, I prefer Isaac Asimov."

But the dreaded destiny prevailed, and soon we were speeding along the Ventura freeway at seventy miles an hour. In the spirit of life in the California fast lane, no car was more than a few feet away from the tail of another. As I sat in the backseat behind my father, I knew I was only seconds away from my end, and indeed, it came. A yellow Cadillac two lanes over spun out of control and swerved at a ninety-degree angle into the path of the blue car directly in front of us. Instantly, I entered an alternate realm of time. Everything happened in slow motion, and I strangely enjoyed the sight of the two cars rising to meet each other in the air over the freeway like two dancers in an elegant pas de deux. I remember that I had all the time in the world to think about who they resembled. Was the yellow car Nureyev or was it Nijinsky? And the smaller blue car, which rose and turned with such elegance, wasn't it certainly Margot Fonteyn? Somewhere in the back of my mind, where instincts for survival still lurked, the reptile hissed a warning, and I realized that we were in grave danger. But with the slowing of time, I could see perfectly the series of actions that we needed to take to avoid the crash. I pondered the plan for what seemed a long time before I spoke. "Now, Dad, swerve to the right, now to the left, and accelerate." I looked back and watched as the cars so gently floated down and met the waiting pavement—and some twenty-four other oncoming cars as well. Each buckled beautifully, an accordion of collapsing steel. Somehow, miraculously now in front of all the chaos, we pulled over to the side—in a slightly more normal time sense—and did what we could to help in the rescue.

I believe that what happened is that I entered an alternate time line and thereby avoided the death that would have been certain in the normal course of events. The change in consciousness changed my destiny, and later that evening I could feel, like distant echoes, the wounds in my body that I would have received had probability taken its tragic course. I had become liminal, moving beyond the structures of ordinary time and entering into zones of reality in which the script can be rewritten, the future restructured, and the path uncovered to reveal yet another forking.

What a gift to consciousness is the recognition of our multiple streams of time! Most of us have had some experience of breaking out of the monochronic monotony of one-damn-thing-after-another. Time flies; time crawls or stands still. We regularly experience the spectrum of party time, hanging-out time, condensed time, wasting time, scheduled time, falling-in-love time, anxiety time, creative time, borning time, dying time, meditation time, timeless time. Ecstasy and terror have their own temporal cadences, and in high creative moments as well in mystical experience, the categories of time are strained by the tensions of eternity. I think, for example, of the time trauma that once enveloped my associate, Peggy Rubin, when she was suddenly called in at the last moment to learn and perform the difficult role of Linda Loman in Arthur Miller's *Death of a Salesman*—a near-impossible task in "normal" time. The utter necessity of it led her to enter into subjective time and to find there all the time she needed to learn the part and to play it beautifully. As she described her experience to me later, "In that twenty-four hours, I found I was dancing with time. I had tons of time, and yet none at all."

I have been called by some a walking time bomb, because in my research and seminars I often blow to smithereens people's normal experience of clock time. I do this by deconditioning people from their usual frame of mind with regard to time and, after guiding them into trance, introducing them to the more fluid categories of space and time that operate in the depths of the psyche. I call the experience alternate temporal process (ATP). After inducing a trance or altered state, I might begin by telling my subject or student, "Now I'm going to give you considerably more time than you need to do the following. You will have one minute of objective or clock-measured time, but with special time alteration, that one minute will be just as long as you need to live out a very interesting adventure. This adventure may seem to take a minute, a day, a week, a month, or even years, but you will have all the time you need, although only a minute of clock time will have passed. Now begin."

Most people report that their internal experiences seem a great deal longer than one minute, and for some time itself becomes meaningless. The most commonly reported experience is taking a trip around the world. I have been astonished at the lavish and lengthy descriptions offered by these one-minute world travelers. Once one is introduced to the worlds of alternate time and time expansion, such feats, which are evidently natural to the possible human but not, generally, to the ordinary one, become part of normal experience.

Lift the barriers of time, and you also lift the blocks to creativity, learning, and memory. For example, my friend Gay Luce, at one time chief science writer for the National Institutes of Mental Health, had been stuck for months on the last third of a book she was writing for the NIMH on biological rhythms in medicine and psychiatry. I taught her the ATP technique. I then guided her into a fairly deep trance state and took her to a place in her subjective world where the book was already finished and in its final form. I gave her ten minutes of clock time, equal subjectively to all the time she needed, to read the last third of the book, which appeared open to her there. At the end of the ten minutes, she reported that she had finished reading her book and was, in fact, quite pleased with it. I then turned on a tape recorder and asked her to read the last third of the book aloud. She did so, and then returning to ordinary reality, she took the tape and spent the next several days typing out the remainder of the book as she had read it in her inner world. When the book was published, it won a number of awards for science writing. I continue to wonder why the usual blocks and recalcitrance generally do not apply during ATP. Could it be that we simply do not have enough time to mobilize our stuckness? Or is it that we simply reach domains of our self that operate out of a higher innocence wherein neither the constraints nor the limitations of our habitual life are relevant?

As evocateur and voyeur of the multiple realms of time, I have witnessed my students rehearse and improve skills that would normally take them months. Using ATP, my students have written novels, poems, and plays, completed doctoral dissertations, composed symphonies, improved their skills in yoga, golf, dancing, tennis, and weaving, retrieved long-lost memories, and investigated in full detail possible futures and courses of action and selected ones they wish to carry out. In one case, which I describe more fully in *The Possible Human*, Ewert Cousins, a professor of medieval theology with poor conversational abilities in French and Italian, improved in his use of these languages after thirty minutes of ATP in which I guided him to embody the word that signified for him the essence of each language (*tendresse* for French, and *mangia bene* for Italian) and to travel through France and Italy talking to everyone he met. When he took the same trips in real time and space in the following weeks, he found himself visiting many of the same places he had visited in his subjective journey and was able to run a major academic conference on Saint Bonaventure in French and Italian.

My Airedale, Saji Jinootsa, who has attended virtually every Mystery School session to date and is an essential participant in the process, comes over, tail wagging questions.
   "Soon. We'll go out soon," I say.
   No that's not it. She paws my knee and wuffles throatily, trying to say something.
   "What is it, Saji? What is it that you really want?"
   "She's just like us," says Ben. "She doesn't really know what she wants. She's just in a state of yearning."

I have experimented with the realization that communication on profound and remarkable levels is not limited to humans but can reach out across species boundaries to encompass chimpanzees, dolphins, and, in my life especially, dogs. From all this I conclude that most beings—satisfied slugs and contented armadillos notwithstanding—are in a state of evolutionary yearning to be more than they are. Yearning comes with the territory of living.

Many of us have known a transitional dog or cat, a four-legged friend in search of a more evolved doghood or catdom. My own experience of this was with my great friend Oliver, another Airedale who from his earliest months was trying to tell me that he was more than he appeared to be. It wasn't that he was just an unusually brilliant dog who invented games, was an artist at Frisbee, and followed all human conversations with unusual interest. His private passions indicated a complex emotional life as well. When he was about eighteen months old, a lovely young woman from Kansas came to be our housekeeper for the summer. Oliver developed a tremendous crush on her. He followed her everywhere and gave her long and soulful looks. Janice remarked, "It's like having a boyfriend." She once asked him, "Oliver, do you want to marry me?" Oliver leaped up, placing his paws on her shoulders, and kissed her tenderly on the lips. On another occasion, when Oliver came upon Janice and her human boyfriend embracing, he fell into a howling rage. When Janice returned to college that fall, Oliver sat in her room by her chair for three months and mourned, pulling out his hair and howling like some ancient lamenter. The following year, Janice returned as our housekeeper for the summer and was again followed all over by the love-besotted Oliver. When she went back to school, Oliver again fell into months of deep mourning.

Oliver and I were famous for our duets. He would accompany me in his high tenor as I sang opera. One day he came up to me, his tail wagging madly, vocalizing in an operatic manner and looking at me meaningfully.

I sensed that he was trying to impart some critical message. "Oliver, what is it you want? Do you want to sing? We always sing. What are you trying to tell me?"

Oliver stopped wagging his tail and looked thoughtful, clearly trying to figure out how to communicate what he had in mind. At last he began to sing, but with a brilliant clarity, holding a perfect note without wavering. At that moment, my mind meshed with his, and I knew what he wanted. "You want to sing on key, don't you?"

His tail signaled the affirmative.

I launched into an aria from *Rigoletto*. Oliver waited for his chance, and when I hit a high C, he attempted an exact emulation. "Ahhoooooo," he sang, with much feeling and technical brilliance. We continued singing together for a while—a mysterious interface between human and dog, carried by the music of Verdi into interspecies consonance.

When we ended, I was so excited I ran to get my husband. When I launched again into the aria with Bob looking on, Oliver backed away grumbling, clearly unwilling to share our secret.

The following day, Oliver came up to me again, his tail flagging yet another brave notion. "What do you want to do today, Oliver? Send me the thought."

Oliver opened his mouth and cut loose with a weird barrage of growls, hoots, and whines that seemed an attempt at speech.

"You want to speak, that's it?" Oliver's tail signified the affirmative. "Okay. Try my name: Jean. Jeeeeaan."

In response, Oliver worked his jaws laboriously but produced only a disappointing squeak. Suddenly, he lay on his back as if he knew that only in that position could he make truer sounds.

"Jeeeean," I encouraged him,

"Eeeeeee," Oliver responded.

"That's just great. Now try your name, O-l-i-ver."

"Raaaah-grrrrrr," Oliver replied. "Raaaaah-grrrrrr!"

I was wild with excitement. A new boundary had been crossed. Oliver and I had transcended the great linguistic divide between human and beast. By this point in my professional life, I had held long sign-language conversations with Washoe the chimpanzee and had spent time swimming with and being taught elaborate games by dolphins, but never before had I reached such an unexpected and emotionally charged breakthrough.

Again I ran to get my husband. As before, all that Oliver would do with Bob present was cast baleful glances at me and move away complaining.

Transition is my middle name. It is what my life and work are all about, playing midwife to the transition that is trying to occur in humans, animals, relationships, and even cultures. All of us everywhere are in that state that Oliver typified with his attempts to move beyond the barriers within his body and mind and answer a higher call.

How often in my life do I feel the equivalent of his plaintive "Raaaaah-grrrrrr!" and struggle with mind and mouth to express that for which I have no talent and less training! Shakespeare, as usual, says it best: "Man, proud man, drest in a little brief authority, most ignorant of what he's most assured, his glassy essence, like an angry ape, plays such fantastick tricks before high heaven as make the angels weep."

In the course of our research at the Foundation of Mind Research over the last thirty years, my husband and I have explored many ways to respond to this yearning that besets us all. We have tried to unshackle natural powers in adults and to prevent their initial inhibition in children. In this time of change and complexity, humans need to use capacities that we never knew we had, or that we have rarely used, even perhaps lost since childhood. We might refer to these capacities as *evolutionary accelerators*. They propel us from beneath the surface crust of sleepy consciousness and our own human nature and biology.

Such statements may sound utopian, the fancies of a lobbyist for Atlantis, but nothing is more urgent today than the need to overcome the archaic constraints of tribalism, nationalism, and ecological mayhem. Time is warping, space is shrinking, and we have entered a period of global interdependence that the human species may not survive if we retain our lethal habits of consumption, aggrandizement, paranoia, and manipulation. Human life may end in a blaze of blinding light if we continue to restrict the mind, thwart its potential, and refuse its willingness to prepare for life in a universe larger than its aspiration, more complex than all its dreams. It is time to educate ourselves to the web of kinship and fellow feeling necessary on this endangered planet, awakening the potentials that lay dormant while humanity played the role of conqueror of nature and other people. We are challenged, as never before, to achieve a new humanity and a new way of nurturing the species to achieve its genius in harmony with nature and each other. As the poet Rainer Maria Rilke said, "We must assume our existence as broadly as we in any way can; everything, even the unheard-of, must be possible in it. This is at bottom the only courage that is demanded of us: to have courage for the most strange, the most inexplicable."

My students and I have moved outside for a break. The trees and bushes are ripe with the coming of spring. Crocuses peep purple and white through the softening ground. The air promises a renewal of life. The pine forest is bursting green and aromatic.

Saji Jinootsa is rolling in ecstasy. I notice a group of students doing something in a muddy corner of the field. I walk over to observe. They are scooping up mud and forming it into the likeness of a human being.

"What are you doing?" I ask.

"Playing God," one of them responds. "Isn't that what comes next?"

3

✦

THE MANY
FACES OF GOD

It is September 1993 at the Parliament of World's Religions in Chicago. This is only the second time in a century that there has been such a gathering, the first being the 1893 parliament, also in Chicago, when West met East. That historic meeting of faiths brought Hinduism and Buddhism to North America and began a global ecumenism of spiritual culture from which there was no turning back.

Before me I see a wide representation of Hindu, Buddhist, Muslim, Christian, and Jewish faiths and all their branches, and now the shamanic world as well: Native Americans, African shamans, Inuit spirit folk, Maori spiritual leaders, and holders of the sacred traditions of the Australian Aborigines. The Goddess is also very much in attendance, as witnessed by the large numbers of feminist spiritual leaders, theologians, and followers of the Wiccan way. It is the world spirit taking a walk with itself. Only fundamentalists are lacking, and they are outside picketing, although occasionally one or more will venture in, filled with the wrath of the true faith.

I have given a speech on the future of spirituality to an audience of several thousand. Later in the week, I sit in on a meeting between Catholic and Buddhist monks and nuns who give papers and discuss their understanding of kenosis, *emptying the mind for union with the fullness of God for Christian contemplatives, and* sunyata, *the void that is the ground of being for Buddhists.*

The Dalai Lama attends this historic meeting, and we all feel the singular and merry presence and blessing of this awakened being. His Holiness has played a role both broad and deep throughout the parliament. Officially the revered leader of Tibetan Buddhism, he seems more a representative of the planet herself as he travels from group to group, calling for a deepening of their spirits, a sharing of their knowings, and a reconciling and honoring of their differences.

I am profoundly moved by this occasion as I am also by the depth and subtlety of the panelists whose lives and focus have for the most part been so different from mine. Whereas these monks and nuns have pursued the spiritual path of the via negativa, *the simplification of life, joined to meditative practices that empty consciousness, my path has been the* via positiva, *a life of mythic complexity and a pursuit of ultimate reality through bringing more and more content into consciousness—an attempt to develop sufficient hooks and eyes to catch the pluriverse.* Plerosis *(filling) rather than* kenosis *(emptying) has been my spiritual practice.*

What then, I wonder, can I offer to this discussion? Then it occurs to me that the missing term in this colloquy is nature and the natural world within ourselves and, by extension, the biology and physics of consciousness. I raise my hand and say that the critical factor in both kenosis *and* sunyata *is the tree. In the Western world, I explain, the man-god Christ finds his most complete emptying, which is followed by his resurrection, while hanging on a tree, whereas in the East, the god-man Buddha realizes* sunyata *and achieves his enlightenment while sitting under the tree. The tree is the vehicle of transcendence for both.*

Likewise, the tree is our human scaffold—our body and brain—and holds the key to our transformation. It is this biological tree that is nature's garden within us and that we are given as the vehicle with which to explore spiritual dimensions, the consummate reality. Thus, I conclude, there is a potent opportunity for Eastern and Western practitioners of contemplative methods to map together the gardens of these inner states as well their emotional and physiological correlates. What glory could emerge—the undiscovered country of the world soul—in the meeting of previously divided and distinguished worlds!

A rabbi once bemoaned to me the fact that so many people born Jewish were not attending synagogue except on High Holy Days. He feared they were losing their spiritual life. As I thought about this, I saw before my inner eye people I had met with names like Shakuntala Schwartz, Sri Devi Epstein, and Thunder Cloud Tanzman. Then I understood. "Why, Rabbi," I said, "I think the Jews are probably the most religious people on Earth."

"How can you possibly say that?" he asked in astonishment.

"Easily," I replied. "It's self-evident. In America, Jews make up the greatest number of Sufis, Hare Krishnas, Tibetan and Zen Buddhists, and most certainly Native American–style shamans."

"You're right," he said after some moments of palpable shock. "But what does this mean, Jean?"

What indeed? The changing of reality seems to require the spiritual equivalent of other voices, other shores. The spirit blows where it will, and lately it wills to blow everywhere, carrying us into a spiritual multiculturalism that seems to have its own agenda. Thus Episcopalians become Sufis, Methodists become Bahai's, Catholics jump into New Thought, a goodly number of feminists become Celtic witches, and Jews cover the religious map.

These trends aside, most Westerners seem to prefer staying in the temperate zones while they are questing for greener spiritual pastures. Few ever go south. Why? Because those who do must leave behind the comfort of the great divide between body and mind, nature and spirit, this reality and that—the divide that keeps us safe from the holy terror of Goddedness. As Michael Ventura has so wonderfully observed, in African metaphysics there is no great divide; nothing is totally other. The human world and the spirit world intersect and feed each other, and in the meeting, the world is "hotted" up. By the same token, African spirituality also makes the world "cool," art and consciousness impassioned by the flowing vitality of spirit. Through music and rhythm carried by slaves, and then by all those musicians and music influenced by slaves, Africa has loosed its spirit upon the world. There is virtually no place that is not touched by its pulsing metaphysics incarnated in jazz, blues, soul music, gospel singing, rock 'n' roll—music that takes us south in our psyches. Hot music loosens the religious corsets in which, until recently, most of the Western world has been so firmly encased. By changing the ways in which we move, dance, and sing, Mother Africa has given us access to spirit we never thought to have.

In this unbound state, more of us are able to seek spiritual renewal in other traditions, perform the spiritual practices and rituals born of radically different cultures and times, and even deepen our own traditional faith with a judicious borrowing of the spiritual techniques of other paths. As spiritual technologies have always been the major ways in which humankind has discovered the outer reaches of human nature, the present mix and match of spiritual cultures could result in extraordinary change in mind, body, and behavior. As the millennium draws to a close, creativity is running wild through the ways of spirit. Spiritual reality will never be the same, but perhaps that's just as it should be according to the ticking clock of evolution.

When I was a small child, my major adventure with the nature of reality came about through a rich and rampant early exposure to the varieties of Catholic experience.

My father was an ambulatory Protestant. He had been raised in the Southern Baptist church, but after falling in love with a variety of young women of various

Protestant denominations and joining their churches in order to romance them, he finally had to become a Roman Catholic in order to marry my mother formally after their elopement. (No Sicilian in Brooklyn recognized the legitimacy of a civil ceremony.) Duly, he took religious instruction from a young priest at Saint Patrick's Cathedral. I gather that they talked little theology but traded a great many jokes. Finally, with the wedding approaching, the young priest said, "Jack, you're just a natural-born pagan, and your religion is comedy. Here, I'll give you a kind of learner's permit so you can get married in the church. But any kids you and your wife have, you've got to promise to send them to Catholic school. We don't want them ending up like you!"

"Sure, Father. Anything you say. Did I ever tell you the one about . . . ?"

The year I was five, my father, who up to then had been a writer on Bob Hope's show, was temporarily suspended due, it was said, to "an excess of high spirits." I think he must have played some cornball practical joke on Hope, who did not suffer humiliation lightly. We found ourselves broke and moving from California to live with my mother's parents in the Sicilian section of Brooklyn, or "Brookalina," as my grandmother called it.

My Sicilian grandmother, Vita Todaro, led a double life. During the week she was a sweet, plumpish woman who cooked enormous Italian meals, crocheted endless bedspreads and slipcovers, and sang the American songs of the 1920s in a high, birdlike voice. "It treee o'clock in da morneee, I dansa whola night trouuu. . . ." But on Sunday she turned into *la signora splendida e spirituale.* She had her own church in the basement for the older Sicilian women of the community. They would meet in the morning before the 11 A.M. mass and listen to her preach to them in Italian on spiritual subjects often having to do with the feminine aspect of God. The wonders of the Madonna were a frequent subject of her discourses.

Since I understood a good deal of Italian in the Sicilian dialect, I took to attending these meetings but was often puzzled as to why there was so little mention of Jesus Christ. When I asked one old woman why this was, she responded with words similar to those I heard years later from another old woman in a church in northern Italy. When asked why all the women in the church were worshiping the Madonna and nobody was near the statue of Jesus, she replied, "Eh, that's because everybody knows that it's the mama who does all of the work!"

My grandmother, whom I called Nana, seemed to put a good deal of emphasis on prayer, contemplation, and ways of dealing with Mary, the saints, and the Holy Spirit. She insisted that the blessed ones were near companions. They were there to commune with, to carry on long discussions with, and even, on occasion, to berate. I recall that soon after coming to Brooklyn from California, my grandmother took me into the church and said, "Eh, Gianuzza, I showa yousa how to speaka to da Santa. Yousa watcha."

She went up to a statue of Saint Anthony and lit a small candle. "Santa Antonio," she began in her most reverent manner, "*Mio figlio Salvatore è molto malata.* (My son Salvatore is very sick.) He's gotta busta appendix. Now yousa fixa okay, and I makea yousa a bigga candle." Nana then lifted her hand to the top of her head to show how very large the candle would be. She then turned to me, "Yousa watcha, Gianuzza. Dissa will worka."

Next day, my uncle Sal was worse. My Nana trotted me back to the church and said somewhat huffily, "Dissa time it a really will worka. Yousa watcha how I talka to da santa." She marched up to Saint Anthony. "Eh! Tonio! *Mio figlio* isa worsa. Yousa betta fixa or elsa!" The next day Sal was no better. Grimly, Nana pulled me along back to church without a word. This time she stood in front of Saint Anthony, shook her head in disgust, and with a mighty whoof, blew out the candle she had lit. Then turning to another saint, she addressed it with extraordinary sweetness, "*Santa Catarina, mio figlio Salvatore . . .*"

However she went about it, my grandmother taught that you must experience and interact with the divine life, not just worship or talk about it. It was clear that the women found my grandmother's sermons and spiritual counseling much more involving than those of the priest of the local Catholic church we would all attend after my grandmother's services.

I remember being profoundly shocked the first time I went to the local church. Since my baptism, I had not been in a Catholic church. The priest's sermon was a Dantean catalog of the afflictions we would meet in hell and especially of the gruesome punishments that Jesus himself would mete out to all sinners, which, the priest made perfectly clear, was everybody present today. "Nana," I whispered to my grandmother, who was shaking her head with the same disgust that she would later give to the statue of Saint Anthony, "is that our Jesus he's talking about?"

"No, *figlia mia,*" she whispered back. "Datsa justa Jesu of da priests, not Jesu of yousa and me. Yousa and me, we know da real Jesu." And with that she turned around to face the women of "her" congregation who were sitting behind us and, in an ancient Sicilian gesture of disbelief, pulled down her lower eyelid. The women laughed, while the priest, wholly unawares, proceeded to vent ghoulishly on the barbecuing of women in hell.

When the service ended, I made my way up to the statue of Jesus. It was an especially contorted figure of the crucified Christ brought over from Sicily, replete with many slashes, bloody streamings, and green glowing skin. What with the statue, the heavy smell of incense, and the priest's sermon, I felt both sick and rebellious. "No," I found myself saying. "No, no, no, no, no." It wasn't just that at that moment I knew that the Jesus given to us by the church was not necessarily the true Jesus; it was my child's perception that something had gone terribly wrong here and the world was the worse for it. That sent me on a journey of asking many questions and exploring many ways of spiritual understanding. As far as Christianity was concerned, I set about looking for the historical Jesus as well as the perennial Christ; for the perfected one as well as for the one who is deeply human; for the God-in-man who is utterly other and for the man-in-God who is the beloved of the soul. Feeling dread and even nausea before the horrendous acts done in the name of Christ, I have also bowed in reverence before a simple act of Christian charity. I have struggled with the prism of theologies reflecting the many different ways of seeing Jesus and have known deep anguish at the polarizing effects these have had, dividing nation from nation and family from family and setting up ambivalence in the human soul.

On my travels all over the world, I have seen too many instances of Christian missionary work gone sour. Too often, I have encountered native peoples who once had a rich and fertile spiritual and mythic tradition thousands of years old that has been demythologized, ridiculed, and virtually destroyed by well-meaning clerics. In recent years I myself have received late-night phone threats from fundamentalists for my views. At one national Catholic educators' conference where I was a main speaker, police officers had to surround the convention center to protect me from a fundamentalist group who walked around the area with signs proclaiming me a GNOSTIC. (Actually, being hit over the head with such a sign would not be a bad way to die!) And yet, I have also seen many acts of unconditional loving-kindness and human service by people whose views of the Bible permit only the most literal interpretation.

To someone studying the infinite varieties of Christian theology, it sometimes seems that there are as many Christs as there are Christians. However, whoever Jesus may be, he continues to speak to the broadest and the deepest issues of the human condition. Not long ago, as a fractal culmination of these concerns, I wrote *Godseed: The Journey of Christ* as an attempt to provide readers with an experiential involvement in the life and message of Jesus. Using dance, movement, ceremony, and an array of psychological and spiritual exercises, the processes in the book guide one into the mysteries of identity, love, miracles, resurrection, and the ancient sacred journey.

My personal sacred journey began in the Catholic schools of Brookalina. There I was, five years old and theologically precocious, when my father remembered his promise to the priest who had given him his religious instruction. "Time to go to Catholic school, Jeanie," he announced. Seeing my crestfallen face, he added, "Don't worry, we'll make it fun. We'll gag up your catechism!" And that he did, giving me the most interesting questions to ask the nun who was my first grade teacher.

"Sister Theresa, when Ezekiel saw the wheel, was he drunk?"

"Sister Theresa, I counted my ribs and I counted Joey Mangiabella's ribs, and we have the same number of ribs, and so do all the other boys and girls. See?" (At that moment, on cue, all the children in the class lift up their undershirts to prove the point.) "So if God took a rib out of Adam to make Eve, like you said, how come . . . ?"

Then there were the Jesus questions.

"Sister Theresa, how do you know that Jesus wasn't walking on rocks below the surface when he seemed to be walking on the water?"

"Sister Theresa, when Jesus rose, was that because God filled him full of helium?"

Perhaps you are imagining a shy child posing these queries in a trembling voice to the beatific nun in the darkened quiet of the classroom after all the other children have left. Not at all. They were presented with all the delicacy of a circus calliope in the middle of a class and generally when the mother superior was visiting. Poor dear little Sister Theresa. Convent life had not prepared her for the theological sallies of my father's comic agnosticism. He had by that time written for Amos and Andy, Fibber McGee and Molly, Fred Allen, Bob Hope, and Abbott and Costello. In fact, for the latter, he had introduced his version of the trinity by helping to create for them (he claimed) the notorious routine "Who's on First, What's on Second, Nobody's on Third." With these eminent credentials, he was ready to raise the comic consciousness of the Catholic Church.

Sister Theresa reached her limit one day when I asked my very own question, one I had given a great deal of thought to and one that many a Catholic child has pondered. Before asking the nun, however, I checked out the question with my good friends and fellow theologians from the first grade, Joey Mangiabella and Cookie Colozzi. They assured me of the importance of the question for their lives and urged me to go ahead. As it happened, the mother superior and principal of Saint Ephraim's Catholic School was visiting our class that day. I figured that if Sister Theresa didn't know the answer, the mother superior certainly would.

I put up my hand. "Sister Theresa, I have a question!"

"Yesh," she lisped, with a worried glance at the mother superior.

I looked around at the other children. "Go on. Ask her," they encouraged.

"Did Jesus Christ ever have to go to the bathroom?"

All the little children leaned forward to hear the answer. The mother superior got up hurriedly and left the room.

"Well, did he?"

A storm was brewing under Sister Theresa's habit. Finally it exploded. "Blashphemy, blashphemy, blashphemy!" she lisped and raged. "Sacrilish and blashphemy!" She looked around, her eyes wild. Finally she spotted the supply cabinet and stormed over, pulling out oak tag and india ink. Like a female Savanarola, she jumped on a stool, tacked up the oak tag, and in large india ink letters wrote:

JEAN HOUSTON'S YEARS IN PURGATORY

From that day on, any time I asked a theological question of an original bent, especially about Jesus, Sister Theresa pulled out the bottle of india ink, climbed up on the stool, and X-ed up more years in purgatory, telling me all the while that this is what Jesus wanted. Each *X* stood for a hundred thousand years! At the end of the first grade, when I had turned six, I had three hundred million years in purgatory to my credit. (Actually, I got off lucky. If she'd been a priest and had more clout, it might have been hell that I'd have been assigned to.)

On the day of the great totaling up of all the *X*s, I returned home, emotionally and spiritually devastated by the vision of spending eternity being roasted on a spit with time off to be on the swallowing end of a million miles of Italian spaghetti. (Sister Theresa's theology led her to equate endless torment with eating. Perhaps that's why she weighed only ninety-five pounds.) Doubtless, I would have persisted in my torment and been scarred for life but for what happened next.

In the throes of the dark night of the soul, junior edition, I stumbled into the house and refused to look at my father. He caught my aura of gloom as he looked at me from over his typewriter. "What's the matter, kiddo? Oh, don't tell me. I know. You think you caught the chestnut blight, your hands are turning green, and your toes are taking root."

"Daddy," I blurted out, "I have to go to purgatory for three hundred million years, and it's all your fault!"

"Greeeeat, Jeanie-pot-pie! You topped my lines. Keep that up and I'll put you on the air opposite Henny Youngman!"

"But it's true, Daddy! Sister Theresa added up all the years and says that because of the questions I ask in school I've got to go to purgatory for . . . Why are you laughing? Stop laughing, Daddy! It's not funny!"

My father stopped howling long enough to swoop me up on his shoulders and start moving his feet to the sound of a train clickety-clacking down a track.

"Watch out!" he hooted. "Here comes the Purgatory Special! Purgatorypurgatorypurgatorypurgatorypurgatory. Toot, toot!"

And, gathering steam, he raced with me on his shoulders out the door and into the street, running down the sidewalk, keeping up his "Purgatorypurgatorypurgatorypurgatorypurgatory" all the way.

From high on his shoulders, I watched the amazed faces of the Sicilian neighbors. As we raced by, Mrs. Pasqualini leaned out of her window and screamed, "Eh, dere goesa Crazy Jack. Eh, Pazza, Crazy Jack, you betta watcha outa or yousa gonna fall ana breaka da head of da bambina!"

As my father raced across the main avenue, barely avoiding speeding cars but never losing his beat, I shouted, "Where are we going, Daddy?"

"To the movies, honey-pot! To see how the real saints had it. You think you got troubles? Wait'll you see how they hogtied poor old Bernadette!"

Within a few minutes we were seated inside the Brooklyn Fortway Theater watching *The Song of Bernadette*, a 1940s classic starring Jennifer Jones as the French peasant girl who sees a vision of Mary while praying at the grotto in Lourdes. Surrounding us in the dark were good Italian Catholics who were clearly deeply moved by this inspiring religious film. When Miss Jones first appeared on the screen, the old lady sitting next to me murmured, "*Che bella questa santa*" (what a beautiful saint) and crossed herself, rattling the many religious medals she wore pinned to her black dress.

Right from the start, I identified with Jennifer Jones. What she was, I knew, was what I was—a misunderstood saint! Of course my parents were nicer than hers, but I had Sister Theresa, so we were even. Then came the holiest and best part of the picture when the spectral white vision of the Virgin Mary appears to Bernadette in the grotto. I was beside myself with devotion, but I knew I shouldn't fall to my knees, because if I were kneeling I wouldn't be able to see the picture from behind the seats. Instead, I limited myself to a verbal outpouring of rapture, "Oh boy! Oh boy! Oh boy!"

The people in the audience were as entranced as I. The old lady beside me was muttering, "*Ah Santa Vergine! Santa, Santa Vergine,*" over and over again. Suddenly, out of nowhere, blasphemy! A long, whinnying, mulelike laugh began to fill the theater. It wouldn't stop, and it was coming from one person. My father. He was striving mightily and unsuccessfully to control himself.

"Daddy! Shhh! This is the holy part!"

"Yeah. I know," my father brayed, "but that's old Linda up there on the screen playing Mary. You remember Linda the starlet, honey, Linda Darnell? We met her at that party in Beverly Hills and she tried to get me to . . . Good old Linda. I told her she'd go far."

And with that he sputtered and choked like an old Model T, only to dissolve helplessly into an unrelenting roar. People in the audience were turning around, and they weren't happy.

"Daddy," I ordered, desperate now, "go to the bathroom!"

Thankfully, he obeyed, stepping over the knees of the old woman who stabbed the air in an evil gesture after him and hissed, "*Diablo . . . Diablo!*" Other members of the audience took up the chant and gesture, which followed my chuckling father up the aisle.

He returned sometime later, semichastened, with only an occasional snort to remind us of his true feelings.

At the end of the movie, I leaped out of my seat and began running home, heady with purpose. I knew what I had to do. My father called after me, "Hey Jeanie-pot, wait for me. What's the matter? Are you mad at me?"

"Yes."

"Well, take my hand. At least to cross the street. Where are you going anyway?"

"I don't want to tell you, Daddy. You'll laugh at me."

"No I won't. I promise. I won't laugh at you."

"Yes you will, Daddy. You can't help yourself."

"No, I promise. I won't laugh."

"Well, okay. I'm going to see the Virgin Mary."

"You are? What a good idea. Let's go together."

With that, he grabbed my hand and began skipping and singing down the street, trying to lure me into a Dorothy and the Tin Man routine: "We're off to see the Virgin, the Wonderful Virgin of Lourdes. We'll join the hordes and hordes and hordes and hooooooordes . . . The hordes to see the Virgin of Lourdes. Wonderful Virgin of Lourdes. We're off . . ."

"Quit that, Daddy! I've got something to do. Let me go."

With a fierce tug, I broke free and raced down the block, only to call back, "And don't follow me! This is serious!"

Back home, I ran upstairs to one of the guest bedrooms that contained a deep closet with a wall safe set into the back. The hangers were empty, since my dog Chickie had chosen this spot in which to have and nurse her eight puppies; they were now only about a week old.

As I considered the closet, it seemed to me the closest thing I could find in Brooklyn to a grotto.

Picking up as many puppies as I could, I dragged the protesting Chickie out of her nursery. The grotto cleared, I fell on my knees and clapped my hands together in prayer, and staring devotedly at the wall safe I prayed, "Please Virgin Mary, please pop up in the closet the way you did for Bernadette. I'd really like to see you." I then remembered my grandmother bribing the saint. "If you come, I'll give up candy for a week . . . two weeks. Okay?"

No Virgin Mary.

"Uh, Virgin Mary? Listen. I'm going to shut my eyes and count to ten and you be there in the closet when I finish counting. Okay? 1-2-3-4-5-6-7-8-9-10."

No Virgin Mary—only Chickie carrying a pup back by the scruff of its neck to the site of my hoped-for visitation. I pulled the dogs out again and kneeled down for some serious spiritual bargaining.

"Look, Virgin Mary? This time I'm going to count to . . . twenty-three, and when I open my eyes, you try to come down from heaven and get into the closet. And I'll give up candy and cake and ice cream and chicken with garlic and lemon sauce. And, Virgin Mary, I'll even give up stuffed artichokes if you'll come down and see me. Okay?"

I counted slowly with my eyes closed, trying to imagine at the same time the Virgin Mary winging her way down from the skies like some great white bird and hovering over the Brooklyn Bridge looking for my house. I was sure she'd make it. At the count of twenty-three, my eyes popped open.

No Virgin Mary. Just three more pups in the closet. I dragged the dogs away.

"Virgin Mary? Maybe you don't know where I live. It's 1404 Avenue O. It's the brick house with the stoop out in front. Etta Canzaneri is jumping rope there. You go to the second floor and turn left. Okay. Now I'll count to forty-one and you should have plenty of time to find it."

Well, she must have gotten lost, for she never did show up, at least not in the closet. I kept on trying for a while, counting to even higher numbers—59 . . . 87 . . .

103 . . . 167—but all I opened my eyes to was an ever-growing pile of puppies. By this time I had given up all sugars, all starches, and virtually all calories. The only thing I kept was broccoli, which I detested. Finally, I resigned myself to the fact that my efforts to lure heaven had failed. I gave up the ghost to the dogs, as it were.

Empty and exhausted, I wandered over to the bay window and sat there, drawing up my legs and looking out at the fig tree blooming in the back yard (only Sicilians can make fig trees bloom in Brooklyn, with an ingenious use of smudge pots). Sitting there, drowsy and unfocused, I must in my innocence have unwittingly tapped into the appropriate spiritual doorway, for suddenly the key turned and the door to the universe opened. Nothing changed in my outward perceptions. There were no visions, no sprays of golden light, certainly no appearances by the Virgin Mary. The world remained as it had been. Yet everything around me, including myself, moved into meaning. Everything became part of a single Unity, a glorious symphonic resonance in which every part of the universe was a part of and illuminated every other part, and I knew that in some way it all worked together and was very good.

My mind dropped its shutters. I was no longer just a little local "I," Jean Houston, age six, sitting on a windowsill in Brooklyn in the 1940s. I had awakened to a consciousness that spanned centuries and was on intimate terms with the universe. Everything mattered. Nothing was alien or irrelevant or distant. The farthest star was right next door, and the deepest mystery was mystically seen. It seemed as if I knew everything, as if I was everything. Everything—the fig tree, the plane in the sky, the pups in the closet, the planets, Joey Mangiabella's ribs, Linda Darnell, the Atcheson, Topeka, and the Santa Fe Railroad, Uncle Henry (the black porter who took care of me on the train across the country), the little boy fishing in the lake who waved to me on the train when I was crossing Kansas, the chipped paint on the ceiling, the mind of God, the Virgin Mary, my Nana's special stuffed artichokes, my Mary Jane shoes, galaxies, pencil stubs, my father's typewriter, the silky ears of corn in a Texas cornfield, my Dick and Jane reader, and all the music that ever was—was in a state of resonance and of the most immense and ecstatic kinship. I was in a universe of friendship and fellow feeling, a companionable universe filled with interwoven presence and the dance of life. This went on forever, but it was actually only about two seconds, for the plane had moved only slightly across the sky.

Somewhere downstairs a door slammed, and my father entered the house laughing. Instantly, the whole universe joined in. Great roars of hilarity sounded from sun to sun. Field mice tittered, and so did angels and rainbows. Laughter leavened every atom and every star until I saw a universe inspirited and spiraled by joy, not unlike the one I read of years later when Dante describes his great vision in paradise, "*D'el riso d'el universo*" (the joy that spins the universe). This was a knowledge of the way everything worked. It worked through love and joy and the utter interpenetration and union of everything with the All That Is.

In this direct knowledge, I later learned, lay the mystical experience. This experience is not something to be kept sacrosanct in esoteric cupboards. It is coded into our bodies, brimming in our minds, and knocking on the doors of our souls. It is our natural birthright, and naturally it is most available when we are still children. As a child it charged me and changed me and probably gave me the impetus to do the things I later did. It showed me the many faces of God, and for weeks afterward I went around seeing this face in every creature, plant, and person—even in Sister Theresa, who was somewhat bothered by my beaming approval of her inner self.

I am in a crowded foyer of the Palmer House, where much of the Parliament of World's Religions is being held. Suddenly the milling crowd parts like the Red Sea as a formidable force of nature and spirit moves through. It is Ma Jaya, and she is something else again. A street-smart woman of Jewish background and culture, she was living the life of a thirtysomething Brooklyn matron, complete with children and Italian husband, when she had an enlightenment experience while doing yoga exercises in the bathtub. This took her to India and a new life as a Hindu adept and most original spiritual teacher. Her heart is huge, and she has founded a center in Florida where she and her associates take care of babies infected with AIDS.

Here she comes, radiant with spirit, a vision in a billowing wine and gold sari and Asian jewelry, her Mount Rushmore face abrim with good humor, a yenta *who is also a* yidam *(a spiritual power).*

Suddenly someone breaks through her entourage, a pasty-faced man in a wrinkled seersucker suit. "Do you know Jesus?" he demands accusingly.

Ma Jaya gives the man a ravishing smile. "Know him!" she exclaims, and then adds in her pungent Brooklyn accent, "Why, dahling, I'm his mother!"

It has been said unkindly of mysticism that it begins in mist and ends in schism. This is both unfair and untrue, for after childhood ended, I remained in a state of yearning. This yearning took the form of spiritual exercises and inner work in order to touch "home," as it were. I soon found that theophany takes many different forms and is available in every kind of religious practice. In my eighteenth year, however, I discovered to my shock that some of the most honored of religious thinkers did not share this belief.

I was playing the cigar-smoking grand duchess of the Austrian-Hungarian empire in our college production of Ferenc Molnár's comedy, *The Swan*. As the budget of Barnard College's dramatic society was lean, I was providing myself with my own eighty-five-cent cigar for each performance. I generally carried it in the paper sack that bore my lunch. One day, several of us undergraduates were invited to listen in at a luncheon gathering for the great Jewish philosopher and theologian, Martin Buber. Buber spoke with a thick accent, his long beard wagging as he addressed essential issues of the I-Thou relationship with the divine. We had been studying Buber's work in class, and I was especially anxious to fathom the subtleties of his thought. I leaned closer, my eyes glued on his hirsute mouth while I unwrapped a carrot from my lunch and began to munch on it. Suddenly, Buber looked at me, dropped his jaw in shock, and exclaimed, "*Gott in Himmel!*" All eyes turned to me, and my face blazed scarlet with embarrassment when I discovered the cause of Buber's upset. In my extreme focus on the old philosopher, I had unwrapped my cigar instead of my carrot and was nibbling on that!

After this fiasco, my professor, Jacob Taubes, felt sorry for me and promised to sneak me into a select audience of professors of religion to hear Buber once again. He advised me to try to make myself invisible so as not to distract the great man. I did as I was told, and since the room was crowded and there were no more seats, I sat on the floor next to a remarkably handsome man who seemed vaguely familiar.

Professor Buber began to talk about the *deus absconditus* and about how God had hidden his face from his people. He spoke movingly about the sense of the absent God during the Holocaust as well as about the duty of Jews to hold the faith in spite of the horrors of recent history. As he spoke, I could not help but notice that the handsome man next to me was becoming agitated. Finally, he could stand it no more and raised his hand. "Yes, Mr. Campbell?" said Buber, recognizing him. Suddenly I saw that the handsome man next to me looked like the jacket picture on a book that had in my childhood, as I will tell in the next chapter, sent me questing into myth. I had met many movie stars in my time and had taken them for granted because of my father's business, but here I was sitting next to a real star. My heart thumped so loudly I was afraid he'd hear it.

"Professor Buber," Joseph Campbell began, "you are using a word in a way that I don't understand. The word is *God.*"

Buber was astonished. "You don't know what I mean by *God?*"

Campbell continued, "No, because you are speaking of God as absent. Now I've just recently returned from spending seven months in India, where people find God everywhere. They play with God; they sing and dance with God. There is no absence of God among the Hindus."

Buber drew himself up to his full five feet, raised his arms almost in an exorcism, and boomed out the words, "How can you dare to compare . . . ?"

Instantly, Jacob Taubes, the moderator, jumped in, trying to save the occasion, "I think that what Mr. Campbell means is, what do *you* mean by *God,* Professor Buber?" But it was too late. We had all heard what had almost been said. And I was, if anything, more shocked by Martin Buber than he had been with me.

I left the hall troubled and disheartened. I had just witnessed the polarity that existed between two of my intellectual heroes. I could understand Buber's concern with the apparent absence of the sense of God, given recent history. But why would he, who spoke so luminously about our relation to God, seemingly deny the authenticity of the experience and spiritual traditions of Eastern religions?

Campbell's question and Buber's soul-searing response made such a strong impression on me that I was driven to compare, and I began an intensive study of the philosophies that informed the world's religions. Campbell's great book had introduced me to *The Hero with a Thousand Faces.* Now, seven years later, his encounter with Buber propelled me to pursue the thousand faces of God. As I explored the ways in which humanity had perceived and sought the divine, I recalled my six-year-old experience of the great interwoven symphony of reality wherein the pups in the closet, the fig tree in the yard, and my idea of the Virgin Mary were all parts of the same joyous resonance in which everything was holy. It seemed to me that the multiple faces of God that are celebrated by many of the world's religions express the sense that in the One, there are the many, while through the many is to be found the One.

I am reminded of a recent experience in southern India when I was visiting Hindu village temples. The management of the large corporation I was training seemed amused by my interests in rural spirituality. A Brahmin corporate executive said, "You don't want to go to those places. The people in the villages are very primitive, very superstitious." The following day found me in a temple, examining the many rudely carved, brightly painted statues of the Hindu gods. A white-haired old farmer came over to me, his hands gnarled from so many years of plowing with his water buffalo. "You see that goddess there, sister? That is Lakshmi. She brings us abundance and the fruits of the field. And over there with the elephant head, that is Ganesh, who brings us protection and many good things. Here in front of us is Shiva. He lets things die so that new birth can happen. And around us you see Parvati, Vishnu, Durga, Saraswati, Rama, and Sita. But really, sister, they are all *nama rupa,* that is, different names and forms for the one God who contains them all." *Nama rupa* is, in Hindu philosophy, the ultimate statement of the varieties of religious expression. I thought of the Brahmin executive and wondered if he could possibly say anything deeper or more luminous than had this old farmer.

My concerns led me to pursue doctoral studies at Columbia University and Union Theological Seminary in philosophy of religion. While there, two events became critical to my developing thought. The first, the invitation to participate in research into the effects of LSD on human personality, is described in a later chapter. The second was one of those comical misunderstandings upon which an entire worldview can arise. Or so it happened to me.

The first year I was at seminary, German theologian Paul Tillich delivered the lectures that would become the third volume in his systematic theology. He spoke with a pronounced accent and frequently used a term that seemed essential to his argument. He pronounced this term with great enthusiasm, passion even, and we knew it was key to his most critical reflections. The term was *wokwoom.* "Und ve find zat ze *Heilsgeschichte* zat comes forth from ze *Wokwoom* . . ." We students would be electrified every time Professor Tillich referred to the *wokwoom,* but we would then cast hasty guilty glances at each other, since not one of us knew what it meant. We had all looked up the term in lexicons, both German and English, sacred and profane, but to no avail. Thus we determined to discover the meaning for ourselves. After class, groups of students would gather to explore the meaning and implications of the term. Our intense and prolonged speculation led us to consider an epistemology of *wokwoom,* a hermeneutics of *wokwoom,* and, of course, the *Heilsgeschichte* of *wokwoom.* (We did know that *Heilsgeschichte* meant salvation history.) The Marxes, both Karl and Groucho, supplied further ideological tinder to the now incendiary term, for *wokwoom* was fast becoming the ontological foundation of all being. By the end of the semester, we had compiled a sizable manuscript of formidable philosophic theology around this term. Yet my fellow students longed for some revelation and urged me to raise my hand and address the great man, who, truth be told, was very fond of women.

I prepared a question with the words *ontological, phenomenological,* and *epistemological* in it and raised my hand.

"Yes, Miss Houston?" Tillich recognized me. I stood up and opened my mouth to speak, but then, looking around at the hundreds of older and wiser male graduate students, I promptly forgot my question.

"Yes, Miss Houston, vat is it?"

My mind a hopeless blank, I blurted out a question of blithering naïveté, "Professor Tillich, how do you spell *wokwoom?*"

"Yes, *wokwoom,*" Tillich replied, and turning to the chalkboard he spelled out, v-a-c-u-u-m.

What a revelation! We slapped our foreheads in recognition. Of course! The *wokwoom!* That's what it was all about. Get rid of all the empty space in an atom and get down to its essential hard substances, and you haven't got much left. Take the remaining material substrata of the atomic structure of all living human beings, put them together, and what have you got? Matter the size and weight of a very heavy grain of rice. The rest of our extension in space and time is—the *wokwoom!*

But the question arises, "What's in the *wokwoom?*" Physics teaches us that nature abhors a vacuum, so something must be in it. Is it consciousness, mind, God, archetypes in the form of numinous borderline persons, hyperdimensions, transcendental objects, the patterns of creation yearning at the threshold of reality to enter into space and time? Perhaps the classic call in the hero's journey, or the call that quickens us into newer being, comes from the vacuum—the great no-thingness, nirvana, the realm of utter darkness, emptiness, *kenosis,* and *sunyata,* and yet the place of utter potentiality, the emergent zone, the Mind of the Maker. Physicist David Finkelstein once said that a general theory of the vacuum would have to be a theory of everything.

What rises from the vacuum? Is it the field of all fields, the sea of potential containing no particles and yet the place wherein all particles come about as the excitement or fluctuation of energy? Certainly, many of the great creation stories are coded archetypal tellings of this possibility—remarkably similar to speculations in modern physics, with the blowing on the waters of chaos by the energy wave or breath of spirit, which itself comes out of the vacuum. Consider the account of the cosmic egg spun out of the void found in the Hindu Vedas. Modern physics joined to theology would suggest that creation occurs because within the vacuum is the hyperdimensional consciousness, which many call God, who spins out energy fluctuations (the Big Bang, among other things) resulting in photons and electrons or the fields of potential pattern and of potential matter and form. Over billions of years, these fields interact to create living things, which further complexify until, in our part of the universe at least, the human experiment occurs. Human beings differ from other species in that we have become conscious that we are spun out of consciousness. Also unlike other species, human beings stay in a state creatively unstable enough to be available to the rhythms of the evolutionary pulse coming from the depths of being and consciousness.

We might then see high creativity or the experience of mystical insight as one of moving from the foreground of particles and matter to the background of consciousness. Thus arise the mystic's experiences of an unfathomable oceanic depth beyond depth and of falling into the vacuum. This speculation leads me to suggest that we need halfway houses for *wokwoom* swimmers. Too often, we pathologize by edict and diagnosis people who simply have moved from the foreground to the background for a while. When I live and study with indigenous people, I find that they do not make a great distinction between interior and exterior reality. The Great Nature without is reflected in even greater nature within. Thus these peoples tend to have a sense of a deep ecology between inward and outward worlds. They have not "closed their accounts with reality," as philosopher William James warned that the West is doing, and thus they are often far more cherishing and nourishing of those who have adventured for a time into inward worlds. They know the value of these worlds and take care of the traveler until he or she returns. Because the inward journey has been honored and given status, the journeyer often returns bearing gifts—new songs, dances, suggestions for planting, a gift of healing, a new story, even, of how the world works.

It is after midnight in the lobby of the hotel. A man from Ghana, in flowing robes and beaded cap, sits down on the floor with his drum. He is a member of the Yoruba tribe. As he begins to beat out a complex rhythm, conference members of all countries and all faiths begin to gather and to sway, clap, move. I watch with astonishment as Sikhs and Sufis, Wiccans and Buddhists, and even several collared Methodist ministers are compelled by the rhythm to join the dance. This is a very complex metaphysics of soul, this drumming, equal to the metaphysics in stone of the cathedral builders and the metaphysics in text of the writers of scripture. To the Western mind, interpreting the deeper message of the drum is well nigh impossible, unless, perhaps, by way of higher physics and wave frequency theorems.

As I dance, I try at the same time to observe the changing faces, the many faces of God. The drumming and the dancing seem to bring forth the very energies that create or call forth the God within us. In Africa these gods are thought to be themselves dancers, frequency waves and rhythms that are closer to the great rhythms and patterns than our local selves. To dance, then, is to pray, to meditate, to enter into communion with the larger dance, which is the universe. And because the universe dances, as the man from Ghana explains to me later, "he who does not dance does not know what happens."

We exist on a flimsy spur of local consciousness overlooking the great expanse of being. Whenever we get shaken up or shaken loose, whether it be by going mildly mad or by exploding with paroxysms of God-awesome knowing, the surface crust of consciousness breaks like cracking ice and we fall into the depths from which we came. The habits of a lifetime, even one's most esteemed accomplishments, can dissolve in the waters of these depths. Consider what happened to Thomas Aquinas. There he was at the summit of his career, having produced works that addressed every possible moral, theological, and philosophical question. This man of huge body and intellect, weighing, it is said, almost four hundred pounds, would sit on his poor donkey, with two secretaries riding at either side of him, dictating the *Summa Theologiae* to one and the *Summa Contra Gentiles* to the other while eating an endless baloney sandwich. Who could be more substantive and certain than Thomas? Then, while celebrating mass in a Neapolitan church, he fell into the *wokwoom* and had such a profound experience of unitive depth that he was unable to write, talk, or even tell about his experience—or much of anything else, for that matter.

I see him sitting there, his once-brilliant eyes now rendered childlike, his large mouth gaping like some mystical idiot. His good friend comes and begs him to tell him what has happened. Thomas finally replies, "Reginald, I cannot. For what I have seen makes all of my work seem mere straw."

Many have had this experience, some by virtue of grace, others by years of search and inner discipline, others by taking one or another journey of transformation, and still others through some kind of trauma that lowered the corporeal resistance that keeps us firmly entrenched in the foreground. By delving into the background, one is able to bring the great intentions and cosmic purposes and patterns into the foreground of our own space and time. What is true of the experience of individuals is also true of cultures and, by extension, of the planet. Unprecedented trauma and unequaled challenge have created an opening in the foreground of existence; through it, perhaps, may rise the background of consciousness and psyche, of high pattern and deep purpose. As one who regularly takes depth soundings of the psyches of people in many cultures, I have to conclude that something is rising out of the vacuum of divine no-thing-ness, and it contains the seeds and codings of all that can ever be.

I began to observe these things while in graduate school, when I commenced guiding LSD experiences. Then, about the same time, Professor Horace Kallen, the great social philosopher who helped found the New School for Social Research in New York, made me an offer that I could not refuse. Kallen, then in his eighties, had been as a young man the Harvard graduate assistant of the American philosopher and psychologist William James. I had met Kallen at a party and told him about how important James's work was to me and how his masterly study, *The Varieties of Religious Experience,* had become so critical to my own thinking and research. Several days later, Kallen called me to his office and told me that just before he died in 1910, James had made him executor of some of his scholarly and course work. "I think it's time for me to pass on the torch that James passed on to me," he said. "And so, what I would like you to do is to offer a course that will deal with *The Varieties of Religious Experience* in the light of modern research into states of consciousness. I believe that William James would have wanted that."

Since the policies of the New School were among the most liberal of any university, Kallen suggested that, along with my lectures, I try to offer experiential demonstrations of some of the varieties of religious experience. I was overwhelmed by the honor of being asked to carry on the tradition of James, and I marveled at the opportunity to explore nonchemical ways of evoking these kinds of experiences. And so, with Kallen's blessing, I began offering field trips in subjective realities. Using hypnosis and trance, guided meditation, and later even a vertical metal swing called an Altered States of Consciousness Induction Device, I took students in my New School course (and several years later, students at Marymount College) through inner realms of imagery and subjective realities.

After an initial experience of abstract images followed by images or feelings with more psychological content, my students would often experience a kind of visionary anthropology made up of fairy tale narratives, myths, archetypal figures, visits to "other worlds" and "other dimensions," and similar science fiction–like schema ("I am traveling at enormous speeds to the other end of the galaxy. I arrive at a planet where everything is made up of iridescent cubes of intelligence . . ."). It was fascinating to notice how many elements of the traditional hero's journey came up during these visits to inner worlds. This suggested that, despite cultural variations, the pattern of the hero's journey might be coded universally in the human mind and psyche.

After some time in these inner worlds had elapsed, I would tell my students, "You are about to experience something that can be very powerful, a symbolic death and rebirth." Next, I would tell them that a symbol would now arise in their consciousness that stood for their essential self. Once they sensed this, I would ask them to observe this symbol as it grew smaller and smaller, until at last it disappeared. "Then," I would add, "you may experience a kind of dying, and when this has been known fully, there will be a rebirth. Please know that you do not have to have this experience but that it is now available to you if you do want to have it."

One student in this course described his experience by saying that after seeing his symbol—a circle vanishing in a point of light—he felt himself go totally silent in waiting. He wrote,

> Then there was a tremendous slow-motion explosion and upsurge and outgo of energy all around and from the point where the light disappeared. It was incredible. Then the circle grew and grew to infinite proportions within me, and all the sound was white. It was a silent Beethoven symphony throbbing all over the place. All the colors in the world were transformed in the whiteness and alive glow of this fire. . . . I grew huge and transparent, filled and permeated with the light and fire. And I thought: My God is a God of love and he lives within me. When I opened my eyes, the whole room was living brown; when I shifted my vision from the wood to the books and the ceiling, I was part of all there was, yet wholly myself. Beautiful, is all I can say.

I wondered then, as I wonder now, what are we to make of such religious and mystical experiences? Why, when the suggestion is given, are they so natural and ordinary and so readily evoked? My fractal as an evocateur of spirited experience looks back to one day in the Kid Preacher church, as my father called it, when as an eight year old I ignited a Dionysian frenzy of salvation. The story has become part of the mythic repertoire in my family's telling of the "life of Jean," but it actually happened. In fact, it warned me how close to the surface is religious ecstasy and how easily it can be called forth and misused.

My sojourn in the Catholic Church had ended shortly after my experience in the closet. It was not just that I had no future in it, judging from my long-term assignment in the hereafter, but also that we were on the road so much I never did settle down to getting any kosher religious instruction. Instead, I joined my father in one of his favorite pastimes while traveling, visiting unusual church services and prayer meetings. My father was especially drawn to the shouting, stomping, rolling-in-the-aisles variety. He seemed to be of the opinion that the noisier and more boisterous the service, the better, and the better for you, the religion. He would leap into the proceedings with vast enthusiasm, hollering "amen" at all appropriate and inappropriate places and singing the hymns with extraordinary gusto. Next to him, Elmer Gantry was a little old lady in a rest home. These antics endeared him immediately to the souped-up congregations, with the result that we had to wade through endless quantities of black-eyed peas, southern fried chicken, and hand-cranked ice cream offered by way of thanks.

While my dad was strenuously engaged in whooping it up every Sunday, I was busy getting saved. When, at the end of the service, the preacher would call for "all you miserable sinners to rise and come forward and be washed anew in the blood of the Lamb," I would be the first out of my seat and down the aisle. Soon I'd be standing in the midst of a crew of guilty-eyed farmers, pimply faced youths, and ripely endowed women in their thirties. I'd grin up at the preacher, ready for anything salvation entailed. It never entailed much. A few songs, a few words, and many handshakes were all.

I kept getting saved over and over again, hoping that one time salvation would really live up to the vivid pictures the preachers always painted, but it never did. I think that what I hoped for was some communal experience that would get me back to the ecstasy and understanding I had known in Brooklyn. So I kept trying. The year I was seven I got saved eighteen times.

My parents were embarrassed. I remember once my mother tried to restrain me forcefully as I responded like a jack-in-the-box to the preacher's regulation call.

"Cut that out, Jeanie," she admonished while jerking me back down in my seat. "You're no more a sinner than Chickie the dog is!"

"I know, Mother, but maybe this time they'll have a *real* lamb bloodbath!"

My behavior utterly appalled my father. "Mention sinner anyplace, and this kid zeroes in like a homing pigeon," he'd complain.

"No more sinners' churches!" my father announced one Sunday when we were on the road. "From here on out—happy religion!"

"Where are we going this morning, Daddy?" I asked brightly, already looking forward to my next saving.

"We're going to a Kid Preacher church, honey-pot. It's just made for you. You can jump up there in the pulpit and kibbitz to your heart's content, and there's nobody around to save you!"

The full name of the Kid Preacher church was something like the Southern Primitive House of God Reformed—Snake River Division. It had a regular adult minister but also took seriously the injunction "and a little child shall lead them." We got wind of what this meant the moment we entered the church. Up there in the pulpit (actually, it was up there *on* the pulpit) was the four-year-old Reverend Little Petie. He wore large glasses and a Halloween cape for a cassock. I hated him. The members of the congregation who were for the most part ten times his age were straining their necks forward, hanging onto his every lisp. When we sat down, he was evidently in the middle of a scriptural commentary. It had something to do with fish.

"And Dethuth thaid to all the fithies, 'Fithies! You better be good and mind, you hear? Or elth I'm gonna thpank you.' And the fifthies thay, 'Yeth thir, Mr. Dethuth. We mind. When you go up to the monten top and preach to all the po-folk and come thupper time they gets hongry, we's gonna leap right out of the water and land in their lapth tho'th y'all will haf the miracle of the loathe and the fithies.'"

"Amen, Little Petie!"

"Praise the Lord!"

"What do you think of him, Daddy?" I whispered to my father nervously. I thought he was pretty good and was getting anxious.

"Out of the mouths of babes and sucklings cometh forth thit," he muttered sotto voce, in the only thing approaching an obscenity I'd ever heard out of him. He quickly shifted gears and beamed and nodded at the people around our pew. "Wonderful, wonderful! So talented!" He dropped his voice and whispered to me, "You can do better than that, honey-pot. First chance you get, you run on up there and show them what *real* preaching is all about."

"Oh, Daddy, do I have to? I'm scared!"

"*You,* the descendent of Sam Houston and Scarecrow Rosenblatt, scared of a bunch of Louisiana hog callers like our friends and neighbors here? You, the scion of a long line of Sicilian bandits, scared?"

"But, Daddy, I . . ."

"Shaddup and preach!"

With that, he pushed me out of my seat and in the direction of the adult preacher who was now calling for any children who felt they had the spirit on them this morning to come forward and share a message with the congregation. Around me I could see several other little kids wearing hangdog expressions as their mothers pinched and prodded them toward the pulpit. The minister, a simpering fat fellow with a too-jolly air, spotted me almost immediately.

"Ah, a little girl has come forward to give us the Word of God," he giggled. "And what's your sweet little name, honey?"

"Jean Houston," I answered reluctantly.

"And how old are you, Miss Jeanie?"

"Eight."

"Oh, an older child." He seemed disappointed but then decided to make the best of it. "Well, Miss Jeanie, do you feel the wings of the Lord beating on your little soul this morning?"

"No."

"Oh. Well, what are you going to talk to us about?"

"I don't know . . . yet."

"Well . . . ah . . . the Lord works in mysterious ways . . . his wonders to perform. So, you just climb up here on this chair behind the pulpit and call on the Lord for inspiration. Brothers and sisters, we shall now hear from the pure innocent heart of another one of the Lord's sweet cherubs!"

I stood up on the chair and looked out over a sea of smirks, sneers, and assorted bad thoughts.

"Brothers and sisters!" I began, my mind as empty as a clam's wallet. "Brothers and sisters . . . praise God!"

"Praise God," they all echoed dutifully.

"Praise Sam!" my father responded, one beat behind them.

"Sam," I wondered. "Sam who? Sam Houston? Sam Goldwyn?" In my family they occupied equal status. Maybe my father was trying to tell me to begin my sermon by roaring like the MGM lion. No, it couldn't be that. Maybe I'd just better open my mouth and see what happened.

"Brothers and sisters!" I began again. "My great-great-great-granddaddy, General Sam Houston, was a very big man . . . and a very big drunk."

I began to warm to my subject. "That's what the Indians called him, Big Drunk. Why, come Saturday night, he'd get so smashed, he'd think he was a big old blackbird—a raven—and he'd go running down the streets flapping his arms and waving his pants in the air."

"Amen!" roared the congregation.

"Yeah, amen . . . Well, anyway, on one of those nights when he thought he was a raven, he dreamed he flew plumb up to heaven . . . right up to the shoulder of God."

"Amen!"

"There he perched and sat a spell, and it occurred to him to ask God a question."

Now I was inventing freely. " 'God,' he said, 'what do you folks in heaven do for fun? You don't drink, do you?' 'No,' said God. 'You don't gamble?' 'No,' said God. 'You don't fistfight or arm wrestle?' 'No,' said God. 'Well, what do you do, anyway? You all seem so happy. You must do something.' 'We have bonfires,' said God. 'What do you mean, bonfires?' asked Sam. 'Well, you see, Sam,' said God, 'it's this way. Anytime any one of you people down there on earth confesses his sins and gets saved, we up here get to keep the dried up old husks of these here sins, and when we have enough of them, we fire them up into a bonfire. Then we have a big barbecue picnic and roast weenies and marshmallows, and the big angels have a harp contest, and the little angels play leapfrog over the bonfire, and everybody tells jokes and laughs and laughs. That's what we do for fun.' "

"Amen!"

"Amen, Jeanie!" shouted my father, and then broke into one of his *long* cackles, the one with the whoops and the hollers in the middle of it.

I was beginning to feel as high as Sam on a Saturday night. At that moment what would be a lifelong love affair with audiences kicked in. With all this appreciation, anything was possible. Anything. Why, I might just . . . At that point the minister came fidgeting toward me, his hamster cheeks parted to reveal about forty-seven very nervous teeth.

"Thank you, Miss Jeanie. That was most . . . interesting. Now you can sit down and—"

"Oh, no, Reverend. I'm not finished. I haven't told the brothers and sisters how to get saved yet!"

And with a wave of my hand I motioned him back to his seat and resumed my sermon.

"Would you like to get saved now?" I bellowed.

"Yes!" they thundered back.

"Would you like to help build a bonfire in heaven?"

"Yes!" came the resounding reply.

"Would you like to get washed in the blood of the Lamb?"

"Yes!"

"Oh, no," I could hear my father groan, the shock of recognition rising fast within him.

"Have you got any lambs around?"

This threw them for a moment. They looked at one another and shook their heads. This was obviously a dead end. Well, no matter. I'd go for second best. "Have you got any . . . any . . . catsup?"

A lady arose and proclaimed with some excitement, "There's a whole case in the church kitchen downstairs. I'll get it."

"Hot dog!" I chortled to the congregation, slapping my knee. "Are we ever going to have ourselves a saving!"

Here the minister bustled his way up to the pulpit again, his face a study in pure, undiluted heebie-jeebies.

"Miss Jeanie," he quaked, "I really do believe we have come to the end of—"

"Reverend," I cut in, "you asked me a while back if I felt the wings of the Lord beating on my soul."

"Why, yes, I did but—"

"Reverend, I feel a whole squadron of angels flapping inside of me. I feel a heavenly hurricane stirring up my soul, and I have been picked! I *know* I have been picked to save these good people and bring them back to the Lord!"

"Amen, Miss Jeanie!"

"Amen . . . amen . . . amen . . . amen."

"Here's the catsup, Miss Jeanie!"

"Thank you, ma'am. Now, folks, are you ready to light the all-time heavenly bonfire?"

"Yes!"

"Are you ready to come on up here and confess your sins so's I can save you?"

"Yes!"

"Then come on up, everybody, and the saving will begin!"

About thirty people piled on up to the front. I struggled to open the bottle of catsup. Finally, I gave it a mighty whack and managed to loosen the top.

"Okay, brothers and sisters! First we need some kindling wood. We need some little sins to get the bonfire going. Who around here has got some little sins to confess?"

"I do," volunteered an Adam's-appled fellow.

"Spill the beans!" I ordered.

"Uh . . . well . . . I . . . uh . . . oh, I cain't. There's too many people around. . . ."

"You don't get saved unless you fess up. Fess up! C'mon, you can tell us." I began to clap my hands rhythmically. "Fess up. Fess up. Fess up. Fess up."

The rest of the congregation immediately took up the chant and kept it up throughout the entire gothic proceedings.

"Fess up! Fess up! Fess up! Fess up! Fess up! Fess up!"

"Well, I uh . . ."

"Speak louder!" I commanded. "It's only a little sin."

"I caught my girlfriend, Melba Dowd, with Virgil Carp and so set fire to the haystack!" he boomed.

"Hooray!" I cheered. "Now you get to be saved. Now you just stand there and let me pour the blood of the Lamb on your head."

With that, I tilted the bottle of catsup and let loose all over the poor fellow. Perched as I was in the pulpit five or six feet over the crowd, my aim wasn't too good.

"Now that we've got some kindling, we need a log. Who has a big sin to confess? I want to hear from somebody with a very big sin."

"I have," said a sweet little old lady. "I have a terrible big sin to confess."

"Fess up!" said I, readying my bottle of catsup.

She came forward, a brittle-boned, blue-veined great-grandma, her frail, small voice lost in the chanting cacophony around us.

"Well . . . I . . ."

"Speak up!" I demanded mercilessly. "Anybody with a log sin has got to reach the ears of heaven."

Heaven must have helped, because when she opened her mouth a second time, there issued forth a phenomenon that was more thunderclap than voice. "*I promised the Almighty that I'd never dip snuff again, but last week I had a backsliding.*"

I wasn't too sure what snuff was, but it sounded sinister enough for me.

"*Saved!*" I roared and, shaking my bottle quickly, made her look like she'd had a run-in with a Mack truck.

"Oh, we're really lighting that fire upstairs today. I can smell it burning. Okay, who's next?"

They came tearing over now, all frenzied up to leap into that bonfire.

"I sent my husband, Gurney, to the undertaker before I was right sure he was dead!"

"Saved by the blood of the Lamb! Gimme another bottle of catsup."

"I played doctor with Wanda Mae Luckadoo." This from the Reverend Little Petie.

"Saved!" said I, adding an extra splash of catsup. "And don't do it again."

As the confessions and the savings proliferated, below me in mad ecstasy surged what looked to be a very jubilant bunch of war victims. This would have gone on for some time had my father not come running down the aisle.

"Hold it," he shouted. "Hold it, everybody. I want complete quiet here because I got the biggest sin of all to confess. I got the number one sin."

The quiet rolled in like a wave.

"What's your sin, Daddy?" I asked, delighted to have won so familial a convert.

"You're my daughter. That's my sin!" And, with that, he reached up, pulled me down from the pulpit, and, with a resounding whack on the you-know-where, my career in the ministry ended.

What did not end was the evangelical cast of my oratory. Even today, I can speak on the most abstruse intellectual subjects and make them sound like a hopped-up tent meeting sermon, which led one pundit to remark recently that if you could roll up Rollo May, Vanessa Redgrave, and Billy Graham into one person, you'd have Jean Houston.

I continued, over the years, to create a great variety of procedures to help students and research subjects have spiritual experiences. Some procedures are every bit as noisy and messy as my early foray into the pulpit. I also developed a model that corresponded to the dimensions of reality that I saw in so many people. The model suggests that body, mind, soul, and spirit are on a continuum with each other but operate on different frequencies, with their own vibrational languages. Because of this, we face the difficulty of bringing the metalanguages of the soul and spirit into the body. That is why we fumble and look for healing fictions.

My healing fiction consists of a model or map for the three major realms of experience. My names for these realms are the "I Am," the "We Are," and the "This Is Me." My model assumes that we humans are nested in several realities, each one greater and more encompassing than the other, so that once we descend into the *wokwoom* or get beneath the surface crust of consciousness, we discover that we are citizens in a much larger universe. In secular psychology we take it for granted that our existential life is the larger part of our existence, while psyche is some anomalous misty stuff that we relegate to the basement. In sacred psychology, however, we discover that it is not psyche that exists in us, but we who exist in psyche, just as the larger life of psyche exists within the realm of God. The distinctions that I draw, then, are between the realms of the historic and factual (This Is Me), the mythic and symbolic (We Are), and the unitive, source level of being (I Am). Each realm seems to have its own reality. While each is reflected within us, each exists independently of us as well. Our local selves are not the only center of reality, nor do they singularly create all we behold and experience, as some New Age psychologies suggest. Neither, however, can we escape from any part of experience, existence, or reality, for all are woven together and all invite—indeed, require—our participation. Whenever we neglect one or the other realm, we feel as if we are losing life, as if some vital part of us is leaking away. Many people live half-lives, turning the rheostat down to a very dim version of who and what they really are. Through my work I try to offer the challenge for us each to become fully aware, fully conscious cocreators in all three realms.

The first and certainly most familiar realm, the This Is Me reality, refers to everyday, ordinary existence—our biographies. It is bounded and limited by geographical space and calendrical time. When we operate in this realm, we are guided by habit, personal conditioning, and cultural patterns. Our local realities are structured by definitions of gender, physical characteristics, name, profession, family, and other relationships and affiliations, all of which cease to exist when we die. This Is Me is the mask we wear, the persona of our everyday existence, the categories of our curricula vitae.

And yet, many of us perpetually yearn for the self from someplace else. The ambivalence many people feel toward their own bodies grows out of this more fundamental ambivalence of being locked in by the This Is Me. That you and I exist by reason of being embodied, caught in the claustrophobia of circling seasons, that we are incarcerated in flesh and see through its veiled portals—oh, so dimly—is the source of much of our frustration, most of our confusion, and a good deal of our resentment. We often feel that our souls could soar and visit many realities if they were not pinned like butterflies to the flesh of our mortal form and the time of its containment. From this ambivalence has grown those mystical philosophies that affirm the soul's superiority to the body and offer practices to facilitate its escape. Unfortunately, these have too often prevented the integration of body, mind, and psyche. These practices find their opposite extreme in Western materialist philosophy, where resentment takes the form of denying the soul altogether, regarding it as a chimera, a ghost without gas, a hapless gargoyle overlooking the flying buttress of a medieval cathedral. This Is Me then becomes the be-all and end-all of existence. Were that actually so, life would be no more than a cul-de-sac, a dead-end world sans poetry, sans music, sans inspiration, sans everything.

But I, for one, cannot believe that this is so. Many people have allowed me to tap into the streams of realities that exist within them, and what I see in these streams are other realms. I must conclude that our local existence is nested in the domain that I call the "We Are." This is the abode of symbols, guiding archetypes, and myths. Enduring in an eternal world outside time and space, and thoroughly transhistorical, the We Are realm functions as the contact point for sacred time and space, the container for that which never was but is always happening. Since its source is complex, its coding is intense.

By this I mean that the archetypal image bears within itself multiple meanings, moods, potentials, dimensions. Thus the human psyche is inherently polytheistic, which is why sacred psychology has to honor the gods and goddesses in everyone. To me, what we call "gods" are actually encodings of particular energy patterns from the We Are realm seen with certain qualities and moods to help us relate to them more personally. That is to say, this realm is the place where the self joins its larger possibilities—often perceived as gods and goddesses. In Sanskrit, these beings are called *yidams,* personified rivers to the ocean of being. The gods— Yahweh, Athena, Asclepios, Sophia, Shiva, Quetzalcoatl, and thousands of others— are forces that have crystallized in the consciousness of human cultures and are revered as personalized emanations of a greater and unnameable power coming from both within and beyond the psyche. Sometimes they assume a humanized, semihistorical form, as with Jesus, Krishna, Buddha, Kwan Yin, and Zoroaster. We may feel a particularly loving resonance with such beings who have been elevated to godhood, identifying with both their numinous power and their storied humanity.

Virtually every culture has tapped into this archetypal realm to acquire the energies of the stories that illumine rites of renewal and social transformation. For example, since the We Are realm is the residence of creation myths and the energies of origins, many cultures have their priestesses, priests, shamans, and rulers enact a central creation myth at the time of the new year. They play the parts of the gods who conquer the principles of chaos, restoring order and recreating the world. In this way, they bring the Great Time of creation and the deeper reaches of the psyche back into the local world of the This Is Me. In so doing, nature is restored, and the psyches of both community and individual are granted the healing energies of new life.

Today, what we call the gods come down to us as the imaginative products of earlier historical ages—Greek, Roman, Egyptian, Germanic, Native American, Middle Eastern. They are, in fact, numinous borderline personalities. Embedded in earlier myths and ways of being, they serve as vehicles through which we may come to understand our strengths as well as our shadows. They grant us perspective into the ways in which certain behavioral patterns dominate our lives. Part of the emergence of an archetypal spirituality and mythology is the ongoing story of our allowing the gods their growth as we in turn deepen our humanity. Only then can we see the divine beings as partners in creation. The divine-human partnership has thus become the leading archetypal image for our time. This partnership is one that mystics and poets have long known to be true, for myths and archetypes communicate from the poetic level of mind and thought, allowing nature to speak to the imagining soul rather than just presenting us with scientific laws and probabilities. This poetic mind is of a higher order of coherence, because it has color, aesthetic form, rhythmic relation; it belongs to a finer frequency of the mind-brain continuum. Indeed, evidence exists that in certain states of consciousness, the mind-brain system appears to move into a larger wave resonance, a frequency that may itself be nested in a continuum of mind beyond the field of the experiencing body. In this state, mystics and highly creative people come back enriched and enlivened to do or think remarkable things. When we meet myths and archetypes in this state, we can speak directly to the inner imaginal realm in which mind, nature, and spirit converge, and our highest potentials become available to us.

I once studied fifty-five of the most creative thinkers, scientists, and artists alive in America. These people had sustained a high level of creativity over many years. I talked to them at length, ran tests, and observed them when they were both "on" and "off" their creative bent. What I found is that most had trained themselves to delve consciously into depth levels of reality in which the forms and creations of their imaginative life and works were conceived. They drew their insights not only from their own capacious minds but also from the great creative archetypal realm wherein are "stored" the principles that source new ideas and forms.

During these studies, I also discovered that a majority of them felt that they were partnered by an archetype. It was as if they felt they were two beings and that their local self was the exotype of a more primary archetype. Thus, in Emerson's words, they were never less alone, than when alone, or less at leisure, than when at leisure. I have found that with many people, a sense of relationship with an archetype, especially one that is experienced as a spiritual partner, a beloved of the soul, amplifies the deeper aspects of the self. This relationship disengages us for a while from the demands and demeanings of our local, ego-focused personalities and allows us to view our personal concerns from a universal perspective.

I myself have always had the sense of the nearness of an archetypal ally. Indeed, I doubt that I could have accomplished a fraction of what I have done without this sense of partnership. As my mother's prenatal dream of Blue Dell hints, my ally was there before I was born. She is an Athenalike being who grants me impetus when I am tired, who fills me with the passion for the possible, even when I am aware of little passion within myself, and who, above all, presents me with a suitcase full of unique and wonderful knowings, which will require more than one lifetime to unpack.

Beyond and within the other two realms lies the realm I call the "I Am." This is the realm of Being itself, pure potency, love, the very stuff of reality. This is the realm many know as God. This does not mean "the gods," for they live in the We Are; rather, it means God as the ground and unified Essence of being. About this realm nothing and everything can be said. The I Am is the supreme fractal wave from which everything branches, out of which everything comes forth. We bear its signature in the wave forms of our cells, the curvings of our histories. The poet tells us that "the human heart can go to the lengths of God." But I would add from my own experience that the lengths of God are also always going toward the human heart. We are signaled all the time by the pulsings of original grace, whether through the loving eyes of another or the sheer all-encompassing glory of a fig tree seen by a six-year-old girl in Brooklyn.

Perhaps the purpose of evolution is to create cocreators, who can help transform the potentials existing in matter and ideas into new forms, richer meanings, and higher art. In such an all-encompassing task, we participate in the totality and vigor, the creativity and generosity of divine life. The seed within, which held and nurtured the divine spark, is now fully grown, and we find ourselves transplanted into the vast gardens of universal life. This shift from the personal-particular to the personal-universal may well be a deep and essential requirement for an emerging planetary society. Otherwise, locked into our own experiences and cultures, we will have neither the passion nor the moral energy to cocreate with others a belief in a world that works. We are now in the process of learning to see with our souls—combining our life's experience with our deepest archetypal knowings.

I foresee a time when daily life will be lived by many as spiritual exercise.

Later that week in Chicago, many prayers and benedictions are offered by spiritual leaders to celebrate the closing of the Parliament of World's Religions, crowned by a speech by the Dalai Lama. At the conclusion of the ceremony, dancers from many religious traditions come onstage to perform a world dance. Suddenly almost everyone in the audience is up and dancing a circling dance in the aisles. I leap up and grab hands to join in, an African man in flowing robes on my right and, on my left, a Muslim woman, her face partially covered with a veil. As hundreds of people spiral and curl past each other, faces are ecstatic, for this is the living spiral of the world's religions meeting each other in joyful recognition. I lose my shoes, but no matter, for there is only the dance.

The crowds are leaving Grant Park. The mood of joy and high spirits continues. Outside, on the sidewalk, several representatives of a Christian fundamentalist church are passing out comic books showing Jesus damning all nonbelievers to perdition. They confront the people coming out of the park, warning them that they are doomed to hell and that the only way to salvation is through accepting Jesus and reading the Bible literally.

I notice an African man; his skin is ebony black and his robes snowy white. The fundamentalists also notice him. One of them, a burly chap in a checkered shirt, goes up to him and asks, "Do you accept Jesus Christ as your Lord and Savior?" The African man answers, "No, my brother, but the God in me sees and honors the God in you."

"Blasphemy," says the fundamentalist and turns away.

4

✦

The Mything
Link

It is October 1987. I have spoken this evening at the Museum of Natural History in New York at a celebration honoring the life and work of Joseph Campbell, who has recently died. Returning home, I feel pulled into sleep, as if something is requiring that I enter a dream world, and I do so quickly. Almost as soon as I lay my head on the pillow, I begin to dream. Although it is a simple dream, it disturbs me greatly, and all night I fight the bed so that in the morning my muscles are strained and aching.

In my dream Joseph Campbell suddenly shows up, his face gray and wan, and says to me, "Jean, come to Riverside Drive and help me with the correspondence."

I reply, "Joe, I've got all this work to do. I'm due here, and I'm supposed to be there. In the next month I've got to be in six different countries. I can't possibly come and help you with your correspondence. I'll send you somebody else to help you."

"No, Jean, you've got to come," Campbell insists.

But I send somebody else. And he sends that person back and shows up again and says, "Jean, please come and help me with the correspondence." I continue to make very legitimate excuses and to send Joe people with secretarial skills to help him. This goes on most of the night. But Joe always comes back and asks that I myself come and help with the correspondence. Finally, at dawn, I agree.

When I arrive, Campbell's face gets back its ruddy color, and he says, "Ah, now we can really get to work!"

I wake up, sore and with strained muscles, but no longer needing to dream.

In the days that follow I continue to be haunted by the dream. I know I haven't gotten it. Why should Joe ask me to help with his correspondence? He never did so in his lifetime. And why Riverside Drive? Of course, I went to school in the area around there for years, first at Barnard College and then graduate school at Columbia University and Union Theological Seminary. I also lectured in philosophy and religion at Columbia. But Joe hadn't taught there; for many years, he was a professor at Sarah Lawrence. Or did the phrase mean "at the river's side," the emblematic mythic place, where life and history flow by, the eternal streaming of the Tao?

Some weeks later I tell the dream to a friend, Marvin Sussman, whose wisdom and experience I value. "Why, Jean, it's so simple," Marvin says. "He meant the correspondences. You're supposed to help find the correspondences between myth and everything else—history and science and psychology and what's trying to happen in the world—the pathways from the past and the pathways to the future."

My response is the classic shock of recognition. "Oh! Of course. That's it!"

And indeed, why not? For Joseph Campbell and I have shared a long history. As I reflect back, I remember that we have indeed explored together many of the correspondences by which myth sheds its radiant light on the multiplicity of human learnings as well as the mysteries of the human heart. But there is more left to be done. Perhaps by remembering those times together I will know where along life's riverside I have yet to go to find the correspondences, the mything links.

When I was ten years old, a book came into my life that opened me to the world of myth and deepened forever my understanding of the ways of spirit. It was Campbell's *The Hero with a Thousand Faces,* and it primed my deepest knowings and wildest imaginings. It was also the fractal seed of my eventual meeting with the man who later became my friend, my research subject, my colleague, and the inspiration for my lifelong search for correspondences. In this book, Campbell draws upon the vast archive of the world's stories that tell of the journey of the hero and his transformation. A pattern of details and incidents emerges from these stories, a potent similarity in theme and sequence among the sacred stories of many times and cultures, and they show the world's peoples to be at the core more alike than different.

As I read, my child self identified with every stage of the journey. Each story that Campbell told began with the call to adventure, a grand summons beckoning the hero to leave an outmoded condition and journey forth into new ways of being. "Hot dog!" I thought. "That's me! I feel the call every minute."

Indeed, my family was always being called. The phone would ring in New York, and when my father hung up, he was likely to say, "Okay, everybody, off to Hollywood." Or Chicago. Or New Orleans. And the packing would begin. My hero's journey was a very literal one that took me to forty-three states and twenty schools before I was twelve. It was the golden age of radio, and comedy writers were the migrant workers of showbiz, following the laughs from city to city: New York, Chicago, St. Louis, Los Angeles, Dallas, New Orleans, Miami, Washington, New York. We were always on the train—traveling to shows, from shows, with shows. Whenever I dream about my childhood, I hear the accompanying score of a train moving along the tracks.

In those days, before every house had a television, America had not yet melted; the pot was still brimming with many distinct cultures and ways of speaking, eating, worshiping, relating. Unique adventures lay just across the county line. A mom-and-pop roadhouse (so different from today's characterless franchise highway inns) invariably provided savory and unsavory characters and wild and woolly tales worthy of a chapter in the great American novel of the forties. Cross state lines, and the world shifted. When one changes realities as much as we did, reality itself appears fluid astonishing, bizarre. Quite simply, reality becomes mythic. Each phone call that sent us on the road was for me an open door to a mythic life.

The next stage in Campbell's cycle of the hero's journey is the refusal of the call, putting the summons off or delaying it because it comes at an inconvenient time or because one doesn't feel worthy. I felt worthy enough, but I had to keep putting off the call, because I was just ten going on eleven, and my parents wouldn't let me run off yet to find my destiny. This being a child was a tremendous nuisance.

For example, I had recently joined an international pen pal club and was writing to Sikhs, Hindus, and Buddhists in Asian countries, all of whom were invariably men. I valiantly studied the scriptures of these religions and would spend days at the local Theosophical Society library, boning up on Eastern faiths. I would write long and, I thought, very adult-sounding essays to my correspondents on the differences between Eastern and Western religions. In return, I would receive charming missives with little religious content but full of questions about job opportunities in America. Then, generally around the third round of letters, I would open the envelope to find a proposal of marriage and a picture of my bearded, turbaned intended. "I have bristling black mustachios," one Sikh correspondent wrote me as part of the enticement to accept his proposal. I responded indignantly, telling him that I was only ten years old, to which he responded that ten was a perfect age for marriage.

However, Campbell made it clear that the journey of the hero was also an allegory of the soul's journey toward enlightenment. I looked up *allegory* in the dictionary and figured I'd be able to do that part without packing a suitcase and taking off without my parents.

The hero then tries to cross the threshold of adventure to enter a realm of amplified power. In the traditional journeys, this stage involves leaving the world of ordinary reality and entering the inner, visionary realms. "Now you're talking!" I said. "I've been trying to get back to that state since my experience of trying to see the Virgin Mary in the closet when I was six. What's keeping me from it?"

What can keep one from it, Campbell's book informed me, was the guardian of the threshold. Often a monster, typically unfriendly, the guardian is given to schedules, fixed habits, and attitudes cast in concrete. A worthy adversary, in our everyday life, the guardian can show up in supervisors, relatives, and friends who are given to primitive reptilian behavior, usually being overprotective of the status quo. At worst, this guardian devours us or turns us into a wimpy version of itself. At best, it hones our pluck and cunning and requires that we fool it with witty ways to get past its snatching arms. At ten, I'd been to so many schools and had contended with so many local dragons that I felt I knew all about this one. What had worked for me was to tell the guardian jokes, surprise its expectations, trot out my father to meet it, and then, if none of this worked, decide that it didn't matter anyway because soon we'd be moving and I'd find a more complacent monster in another state who'd let me by.

No, the real threshold guardian was in myself, I decided, the part of me who would not release my hold on consciousness enough to let me dissolve my boundaries and ooze into that deeper realm. Already, the *via positiva* had me in its grip. I had changed realities so often that I had not one but a number of personalities within me and could bring them out as occasion and local culture warranted. A New York street-smart persona, I had discovered, would never do in a public school in Biloxi, Mississippi. For the sake of survival, I had become not split, as in schizophrenic, but multiplied, as in polyphrenic, aware of a large inner cast of characters and personalities. To dissolve all of them to enable me to cross the threshold into an inner world presented an enormous task for my consciousness. Suddenly, in the midst of these reflections, I saw how to get past the guardian! All I had to do was bring my entire inner crew to the threshold along with me and take them all across at the same time. That would keep the guardian too busy to be more than a nuisance.

Once across, the hero is swallowed by the unknown, be it a whale, a wolf, a sarcophagus, or a cave. This stage, known as the belly of the whale, permits us to dissolve our identity in order to be rewoven into a stronger and brighter form. In the process, we die to our modernity and are reborn to our eternity. The belly of the whale comes in many guises. It can take the form of a depression or ingression or even of a strong need to get away from it all. To attempt this stage, I'd lie down behind the clothes in a closet and imagine myself losing all my physical parts, then my mental parts, and then my feelings. I had read up on Hindu and Buddhist yogic practices in the library, so I had some idea of the procedure. The only problem was that after losing all my parts, I'd generally lose my consciousness, too, by falling asleep. Life in the void didn't seem to be my form. However, I'd generally awake refreshed, in good spirits, and happy to get out of the closet and back to Mr. Campbell to find out what was next on the hero's agenda.

It was the road of trials. In the hero's journey, this is a time of incredible tests and extraordinary adventures. Campbell tells us that this is where "the hero moves in a dream landscape of curiously fluid, ambiguous forms, where he must survive a succession of trials." Generally, this sequence is the favorite of storytellers, epic poets, and novelists, for they can give full vent to the dread we all feel before the unknown and the unbound, be it in desert, wilderness, sea, or in the corresponding labyrinth of our own unconscious life. One is hurled into adventures and challenges for which one has had little preparation, and yet somehow one finds the resources to survive.

As far as I could see, I was constantly on the road of trials. It wasn't just my family's traveling and facing constantly changing landscapes, teachers, schools, and kids. No, my road of trials mainly took the form of my father's notions of survival training. His pushing me into the pulpit of the Kid Preacher church was a typical example, but other challenges had also raised people's eyebrows.

"Teach me to swim, Daddy," I had asked one day at the beach when I was about three.

"Sure, kid, climb onto my shoulders, and we'll wade out to sea." Once we were at about my dad's neck level, he flung me off and told me to dog-paddle. Somehow I managed to swim back over to him. Later I became quite a good swimmer. That same year, my father noticed that I was afraid of a particular friend of his—the big black dog who lived next door. He helped me face this particular trial by putting me outside with the dog and closing the door to my screaming. The dog chased me around the house until I fell; then it proceeded to cover me with kisses. I've since become kin to dogs. Then there was the time around age five when I asked my father to teach me to ride a two-wheeler. He took me to the top of the inclined driveway, perched me on the bike, and pushed me downhill, telling me to stay on as long as I could. I still have the scars on my knees from that episode, but I became quite a good biker. Each time he hurled me into the jaws of death, he did so with the words "Never be afraid of anything!" This has gotten me into many pickles and peculiar places: wars, plagues, the back alleys of inner cities, and the offices of heads of state.

But when I thought beyond the obvious, I realized that my essential road of trials stemmed from the fact that my mind was growing in directions and depths that seemed quite other from my parents, especially my dad. I felt myself to be theologically precocious and philosophically deft and knew that somehow I had to protect my budding mind from the onslaughts of his chronic laughter. What I rightly feared was that any serious thought I offered could and generally would be turned into a comedy skit and, what was worse, that I'd go along with it.

"Dad, I've been thinking about the meaning of the resurrection. . . ."

"Oh, yeah, the old J. C. routine. Now you see him; now you don't."

I capitulated. I had wanted to talk about what was eternal in the human soul, but instead I said, "Yeah, the old upsy-daisy."

"Great, kid, you topped my line."

Back to Campbell to find a solution. He wrote of magical helpers and supernatural allies. Fine and dandy, I thought, but where to find them? I looked up at the ceiling and intoned, "Okay, gods and goddesses, angels, supernatural allies, whoever and whatever you are, come and get me!" Just then the dog came over, leash in mouth to be taken out. We walked down Madison Avenue, and I stopped, as I always did on these jaunts, in front of a shop that displayed a fourth-century B.C.E. marble frieze of Demeter and Persephone. It cost two hundred dollars, so of course I couldn't buy it, but I thought it one of the most beautiful things I had ever seen and was happy just to gaze at it daily. Somehow, it seemed deeply familiar, a remembrance of things past and yet to come.

This day, however, it was no longer in the window. I went into the store, and the owner, a Viennese Jewish gentleman in his late seventies, told me it had been sold. Observing my crestfallen state, he said to me, "I see you every day looking through the window. Come, maybe it is time you should be learning about antiquities. If you like, I will teach you." His name was Dr. Biedermeier, and he had been one of Sigmund Freud's antiquities dealers in Vienna. He took me into the back, and there, in marble and bronze, were statues and busts and friezes of the gods and goddesses and legendary figures of Greece, Italy, and Egypt. I felt as if I had died and gone to classical heaven. The supernatural allies had showed up, and in their most literal forms. I handled them, felt their faces and forms burn into my mind, and came to know them as intimate and daily friends. The deity I would hold in my hands during the day would occasionally show up in the dreams that night, vivid and fully realized, taking me on a journey through time and space. For the next several years I visited the store regularly and learned not only how to appreciate, mend, care for, and date antiquities but also, and more important to me, how to understand the meaning these mythical figures had for the minds that made them.

"You must always try and feel these works of art in terms of the time and the people who made them," Dr. Biedermeier told me. "My big argument with Dr. Freud was that he was always presenting the stories of these figures in terms of modern psychoses. You must never do that, Jean."

"I'll try not to, Dr. Biedermeier," young Jean promised, having traveled to ancient Greece with Hermes before waking up that morning. Through the grace of fractal principles, it followed that when I grew up to become an avocational archaeologist and collector of antiquities, I came to own many of the figures of the gods of the ancient world, and my home eventually resembled the jumbled displays of mythical figures I first saw in the shop of my mentor.

The next stage of the journey brought the hero to the deepest point of the cycle, there to be recognized by the Father/Creator, to achieve sacred marriage with the Goddess or the inner beloved of the soul, and to enter upon his apotheosis or transformation. The first part was easy. I just went up to my father and announced, "Dad, I want you to recognize me as a true heroine."

"Sure, but what's the gimmick?" asked my dad, who was already dangerously close to laughter.

"No gimmick, Dad, you just have to recognize me. It's what happens to every hero who finally gets to. . . . Just a minute, I've got to check something." I ran back to consult Campbell. "Who gets to the 'nadir of the mythological realm,'" I said triumphantly.

"And that's where you are, huh?"

"Yes. So you have to play your part. C'mon, Dad, play your part. I need it for my apotheosis."

"Oh, well now, that's different. I'll do anything for an apotheewhatsis. I haven't had one of those in a coon's age. Okay, I'll tell you what we're going to do. . . ."

Dad went to a theatrical costume house and got me rigged up as Joan of Arc carrying a sword and wearing a long cape. He dressed up as Joan's fool (or fool of a father) and held the hem of my cape as we walked down Broadway. Every so often he would stop and answer the natural queries of people with, "This here is my daughter Saint Jean. She's a heroine, and I recognize her. How 'bout that?" I took it for about four blocks before I said, "Okay, Dad, that's enough. I feel recognized."

I didn't know what to do about sacred marriage but figured that my consort would come along in due time. I just hoped my beloved wouldn't have bristling black mustachios. But what was I going to do about it now? I had read somewhere that the Navajo say that if you take one step toward the god, the god takes ten steps toward you. I was beginning to feel something or someone moving toward me, and when I did, the sweep of emotion would be immense, a sweetness that dissolved for an instant all barriers, a remembrance of what or whom I was part of. And then it would diminish, as if to say, "Not yet, not yet," and I would be left only with my yearning and a promise.

My apotheosis, I decided, would also have to wait awhile. Campbell, however, had offered an alternate way of meeting this stage; it had to do with stealing the boon for which one was questing—an elixir of life, the fire of immortality, the key to knowledge, some big-time reward. "Intrinsically," Campbell wrote, "it is an expansion of consciousness and therewith of being."

"Expansion of consciousness!" What terrific words! I went around our apartment saying them over and over, singing them out in different keys and melodies. I didn't know it then, but I had indeed received my boon in those words, my life's gift, my own particular elixir—the commitment to bringing expansion of consciousness to whomever I could and wherever I was able.

That left only the magic flight back across the threshold with the boon intact so that, with it, one can restore the world. At this moment, one becomes the master of two worlds, able to bring the greening power of the depth world into the graying world of ordinary space and time. But how should one act after having been on the hero's journey? I had no magic potions for changing the world. What was worse, I had no opportunities for doing so. There was school, of course, but wait a minute! What about the Mertz sisters, Helene and Gertrude? They were red-haired twins with bad eyes who came from an abusive, poverty-stricken family. They wore the same clothes day after day and so were mocked by the generally well-to-do children of P.S. 6. They cringed when any of these children looked at them, for they had been victims for so long, they expected only mean treatment, and that is often what they got. As they had been kept back, they were a year or so older than the other girls and therefore more physically developed. The boys found great sport in grabbing their brassiere straps from the back and snapping them. Although they were not unintelligent, their general demeanor had led the teachers to think they were backward, and with these kinds of expectations, they couldn't answer questions when they were called on and frequently failed their exams. I went to school determined to befriend Helene and Gertrude Mertz.

At first they were suspicious, as all previous overtures from other girls had always ended in a setup for ridicule. I persisted and invited them home for dinner. My mother was very welcoming, and my father soon had them laughing. I always took great delight in the fact that my parents were kindly, generous people who treated all people as special, regardless of their circumstances. As I was class president, I put the sisters under my "protection," and that seemed to work. When some kids persisted in their cruelty, I tried embarrassing them by reciting the Golden Rule. When that didn't do the trick, I announced, "Boy, are you in trouble with the law of karma." Noting their confusion, I would say, "See, you don't even know what that is. It means for every bad thing you do to another person you're going to get bad things back to you ten times more. You just wait and see." And if that didn't work, I moved down a moral slot or two and invited them to put on boxing gloves and meet me after school. That always worked, as both my dad and my uncle Paul had given me lessons since age six. As a result, Gertrude and Helene were accepted more and more those years. I never found out what later happened to the sisters, although when I was in graduate school, I saw one of them through the bus window smiling and pushing a baby carriage.

My mother, who had been following my reading and enactment of the hero's journey, took me aside when I had finished the book and my version of the journey. I had been complaining that I had not attained to mastery of two worlds. She said, "Yes, you have, Jeanie. There is only one mastery, and that is compassion."

I also learned from my heroic journey that once you answer the call to a larger life, there is no turning back. Indeed, each of us might usefully consider where we find ourselves right now on the cycle of our own particular journeys. Have you heard a call to the larger life? Have you refused it, and if so, why? Have you accepted the call but then met with monsters of recalcitrance who refused to let you pass across the threshold to your own deeper capacities and possible life? Did you finally outwit these monsters and get across? Are you caught in the belly of the whale through despair, depression, or just plain sloth? Have unusual allies or helpers shown up? A telephone call at the right time? A book falling open at an important passage? Do you find yourself in the midst of the road of trials, and if so, do you experience it as full of adventures or as just one damn crisis after another? Is there awaiting you a sacred marriage or a transformational friendship? Do you feel the yearning for the inner beloved of the soul? Are you seeking atonement or attunement with your father or mother for what that person may or may not have done to you? Do you require recognition from a parental or authority figure? Are you finding a boon, an insight, a project that may bring some healthy solution to your own and the world's problems? Have you crossed the magic threshold and come back into ordinary life with a sense of accomplishment? Are you planning to rest for a while, or are you raring to start the journey all over again? Or perhaps you find yourself, like the rest of us, in several different stages of the journey at the same time.

Perhaps it was because I began to "think mythically" at such an early age that I pursued a mythic life. Or perhaps mythic life pursued me. My memories are blessed with happenings that seem the stuff of legend: swimming with dolphins, talking in sign language with chimpanzees, working as a teenager on projects with Eleanor Roosevelt, eating fried worms at a banquet in China, discussing the nature of God with Dag Hammarskjöld, living with lepers in southern India, wrestling all night in July of 1969 with a depressed friend to stop her from committing suicide while on television men were landing on the moon, and, of course, the many events that provided the vital ingredients for this bouillabaisse of a book. But then there are the mythic things I have not done—giving birth, raising a family, farming land. The fact that these actions seem so ordinary makes them in no way less extraordinary. They are the holy things that tell us that we are part of the God-life incarnate, cocreators and stewards of creation.

People tell me that I am uniquely blessed with opportunities. And yet, when I examine others' lives, I find that too often they are walking blind and deaf through a garden of possibilities—some of which are whistling, "Yoo hoo, over here! Hey, dummy, listen! Here's a new friend for you! There's a new road for you to take, a fresh role for you to master. C'mon, pay attention!" And through it all, they sleepwalk, mumbling, "Nothing ever happens. Nothing ever happens." Only when the opportunity for a larger life throws itself directly across their paths do they stumble into possibility. I have lived mythically because I have caught the fleeting glimpse of opportunity from the corner of my eye, said yes to risk, and sought out adventure.

Of course, this pattern was primed by my accepting life as inherently mythic and therefore as an "exploration into God," as the poet Christopher Fry puts it.

I have thus come to believe that life is allied with myth in order that we may advance along an evolutionary path carrying us nearer to the spiritual source that lures us into greater becoming. For this purpose, myth remains closer than breathing, nearer than our hands and feet. I think it is built into our very being. Myth is not a no thing, an insubstantial conceptual will-o'-the-wisp. It is coded into our cells and waters the seas of the unconscious. It dwells in our little finger and plays along the spine as well as the spirit. It grants us access to the DNA of the human psyche, the source patterns originating in the ground of our being. It gives us the key to our personal and historical existence. Without mythic keys we would have neither culture nor religion, no art, architecture, drama, ritual, epic, social customs, or mental disorders. We would have only a gray world, with little if anything calling us forward to that strange and beautiful country that recedes even as we try to civilize it.

It is January 1970. Joe Campbell has agreed to be my research subject to allow us to explore together the nature of mythic imagery. He relaxes easily, and I take him down to a place where most people begin to see the images of the inner world. Finally, when I think he is ready, I ask, "What do you see there, Joe?"

"Nothing," he replies.

"Well, then, I will have to take you deeper," I respond.

"It's no use, Jean. I've never seen an inner image."

"What?!"

"That's right. I'm one of those people who are entirely without imagery."

I am stunned, amazed, almost furious. "Then how can you write about symbols and myths and their images?"

"Because I feel them in my muscles, know them in my bones. Having been athletic most of my life, I am what you would call a high kinesthetic type. In the nothingness behind my eyes I feel a kind of screen, and behind that I sense the adventures of inner space as vividly as if I were having them myself. It must be like what Helen Keller felt when she traveled to the heaven of Swedenborg in her imagination. You must remember that these mythic worlds are held in the workings and the systems of the body as well as in the mind. They're all there, Jean, whether you see them in pictures like your husband Bob does, or hear them as music or words the way you tell me you do, or sense them in your muscles as I do. So, yes, I can tell you what's going on—a great deal."

As Joe recounts his kinesthetic adventures, I witness rising out of his body great epics worthy of a master bard. When he finishes, I don't know whether to laugh or cry, so astonished am I. Finally I say, "Good Lord, Joe, I've just seen your muscles ripple with the Arabian Nights. *And where did that Odyssean voyage come from, your liver or the marrow of your bones?"*

Inspired by this experience, I decided to test Joe's hypothesis that myths are corporeal or at least contained innately in the memories of sinews and the caches of
the brain. It would be easy to dismiss Joe's ready access to the great stories of humankind. After all, he had studied and taught them for years. But what about
those who had little or no such access? True, I had already heard hundreds of research subjects in altered states of consciousness describe adventures of the soul
so grand, so mythic, and yet so redolent of universal themes that I could readily
testify to the existence of a collective pool of myth and archetype residing in each
human being as part of his or her natural equipment. But I was dealing here with
adults who had by this time heard and incorporated vast amounts of overt and
veiled story and symbolism. If I were going to explore the phenomenon of myths
as givens of our existence, I would have to look for them in their purest form in
the minds of children—and not just any children, but ones who had not been exposed to radio, television, or movies, from which they could have picked up
mythic stories. Nor was I looking for the ordinary adventure tale of the kind that
naturally teems out of the child mind; I was after something else, at once more
imaginative and more mysterious. I was looking for the causal zone of myth. After
a search, I was able to locate a number of children whose parents refused to have
any media in the house. As I talked with them, I sometimes felt that I was listening
to embryonic Joseph Campbells.

For example, there was Jimmy, a very verbal child around three years old. I said
to him, "Jimmy, tell me a story."

"I don't know any stories," he replied and proceeded to chew his hand.

"Yes, you do," I insisted. "Please, Jimmy, tell me a story."

He took his hand out of his mouth and examined the scab on his knee. "What
kind of story?"

"A new story. Tell me a new story."

He thought a while, rubbed his eyes, and said, "Okay. Once upon a time there
was a little boy."

"Ah, that's nice," I said encouragingly.

"And he had a mommy."

"Mmmmm."

"And he loved his mommy."

"Oh yes," I beamed, thinking that I was getting no nearer to myth.

"So he married his mommy."

I became suddenly alert.

"And they had many babies."

I was so shocked, I could not speak.

"And that's the end of the story." Jimmy wandered off. I called after him,
"Come back. Tell me the rest of the story. What happens next?"

"I don't remember."

"Yes, you do. You do remember!"

Jimmy went over and patted the cat, his mind working, trying to remember. Finally he said, "Everybody got mad at them and . . . and . . . I'm going now. I don't like this story." With that, he toddled off to the porch. My nearly six-foot frame stumbled hastily after his three-foot-one. For here, maybe, was the alchemical key, the gold of Troy, the vindication of Carl Gustav Jung. I couldn't help thinking of the punch line of the old Jewish joke, "Oedipus Schmedipus, as long as he loves his mother!"

"Come on, tell me, Jimmy. What happens next?"

"I don't remember."

"Yes you do. Try to remember."

Jimmy stared out into the distance for about a minute. I thought I'd lost him, but no, he was genuinely trying to recall something.

"He goes away."

"With whom does he go away, Jimmy?"

"With . . . with his sister."

"That's right. And then?"

"And then . . . and then . . . everybody likes him again!" Jimmy ran off after the dog, his story truly completed. For Jimmy had told the full story, not stopping at the complex resulting from the marriage with the mother, as Freud had. Out of the marrow of his still-unmarked mind, Jimmy had intimated the more ancient tale that Sophocles, in his nineties, had told in his great and final play, *Oedipus at Colonus.*

Sophocles' tale tells "what happened next," as Oedipus, blind, outcast, and wandering, is led by his sister-daughter Antigone through the byways of Greece, searching as well the labyrinths of his own mind. People at first are terrified of him, the man who killed his father and married his mother, plowing the field in which he himself had been sown. But soon they decide that since Oedipus has already transgressed the major taboos of this world, it is safe to tell him their troubles. And so all through the land they seek him out: "Oedipus, have I got a story for you!" Eventually Oedipus and Antigone end up at Colonus, on the outskirts of Athens. There Oedipus is met by the young king Theseus, who himself has just returned from the labyrinth of Crete and who knows a man made wise through suffering when he sees him.

"Welcome, great man," says Theseus to Oedipus. "Abide here with us, you who have seen and known so much. Be for us a sage, a counselor of our peoples."

Oedipus agrees, and Athens becomes one of the first cities in Europe in which the human soul touches the sky. But the gods become worried, for with the help of Oedipus, human beings are becoming wiser than they. "We, too, need a counselor," they say. "We need Oedipus." So the gods arrange for a great earthquake. The ground opens, the sky is rent, and Oedipus is taken up to Mount Olympus to become a god. As Jimmy said, "Everybody liked him again"—everybody, people with their griefs, gods with their games, and psychologists with their clients. And I for one learned that out of the mouths of babes comes the remembrance of things deep and wise and woven into the regions of the unconscious or into the body (or does it matter?). We humans are the storied, mythic links between the great patterns of existence and the local experiences that assure their continuity in the world of time and history. The boy is father to the man (and the girl the mother to the woman), but the child is also the key to the eternal. The child remembers, and so great is this remembrance that it can be told only in codings that, like the storied spirals of DNA, contain immensities. Ergo, myth.

The hero's journey I first took when so very young has never left me. In my current work I often use variations of this pattern as the loom on which to weave journeys of transformation drawn from the world's great myths and stories. I find that regardless of the culture, people will go further and faster in developing human capacities if their training is tied to a story, especially a myth. For myth transcends and thus transforms our usual blocks and conditionings, carrying us into a realm in which these need not constrain us. And if the myth is a familiar one, present in the fabric of the culture, it works even better.

I think of a seminar I gave at Lanavala, India, using the ancient epic the *Ramayana* as the basis for work in psychological and social transformation. The seminar was attended by leaders in government, health, education, social welfare, and organizational management. As we followed the journey of Rama and Sita from palace to forest, from Sita's abduction by the demon Ravana to her deliverance by Rama and his allies, and as we enacted the roles of the myriad characters and events that are the essence of the soul of India, people were fired to make innovations in their own lives. In the course of the ten-day experience, seminar participants wrote poetry in the style of Valmiki, reputed author of the *Ramayana;* gave *darshan,* or deep seeing, to their fellow participants; renewed the art of meditation in the forest silence of their minds; and made a leap of faith toward their own possibilities as Hanuman, the noble monkey and ally of Rama, had leaped across the sea to Sri Lanka. Allied with the armies of Rama, participants fought and conquered their own demons of self-diminishment and despair, until finally, as an act of bhakti yoga, the yoga of spiritual love, they met the inner beloved of the soul, just as Rama found his Sita again. At the end of the epic, Rama and Sita discover themselves to be the god and goddess Vishnu and Lakshmi, called into human form to drive out evil forces and initiate an enlightened social order. So, too, in a final process, participants acknowledged their own divine nature and made plans to act accordingly.

In the five years since that seminar, I have heard from a number of the people who attended about its effect on their lives and work. A Brahmin woman wrote to me of the work she has done organizing the illiterate and impoverished women of the *shudra* (untouchable) caste so that they have their own banking system, job training program, and meeting places where they learn new skills and empower one another. A man who had arrived at the seminar depleted and depressed wrote that as he became the divine monkey Hanuman and explored his own capacity for creative play, he finally admitted to himself that he hated his job of many years. He left it and is now working in partnership with his wife in human resources management, creating new paradigms for business in Asia. A Parsi psychologist sent me word of a center he had created to help free people of phobias and obsessive behaviors by incorporating creative rituals that draw upon ancient as well as spontaneous procedures. He was inspired, he said, by seeing the way I worked with ancient texts, extending them to make them fresh and relevant. In working with his patients, he observed firsthand how ancient myths and rituals are embedded in the human psyche for good or ill. My work demonstrated, he said, that when mythic material remains latent, unused and unexplored, it can lead to pathological behavior. Release the latency, carry the story forward, and a miracle of liberation occurs in the psyche. One can get on with it!

Wherever I am in the world, I find that working with a mythical figure (or a historical person who has through time and legend been rendered mythic) allows people to see their own lives reflected in and ennobled by the story of a great life. Such work leads students into the discovery of their own larger story, for when actively pursued, myth leads us from the personal-particular concerns and frustrations of our everyday lives to the broader perspective of the personal-universal. Working with myth, we assume the passion and the pathos of Isis as she seeks to recover the remains of her husband Osiris; with Parsifal, we take on the quest for the Grail; we labor with Hercules and travel with Odysseus into the archetypal islands of inner and outer worlds. We explore new ways of peacemaking with Gandhi, learn the art of inventing society with Thomas Jefferson, and discover the basis for democracy with the peacemaker Deganawidah, creator of the Iroquois League. With the Persian mystic and teacher Rumi, we search for the beloved of the soul; we join in sacred marriage and descend to the underworld with the great Sumerian goddess Inanna. Gradually we discover that these stories are our own stories, that they bear the amplified rhythms of our own lives. After becoming Isis and Odysseus and White Buffalo Woman and Emily Dickinson, we return to our own lives deepened and enhanced, filled with a sense of the fractal resonance of the mythic life within our own. Having assumed the ancient stories and their persona, having walked in the shoes of folk who lived at their edges, we inherit a cache of experience that illumines and fortifies our own.

This joining of local life to great life is a central experience of what I call sacred psychology. It differs from ordinary psychology in that it provides ways of moving from outmoded existence to an amplified life that is at once more cherished and more cherishing. It requires that we undertake the extraordinary task of dying to our current, local selves and of being reborn to our eternal selves. When we descend into the forgotten knowings of earlier or deeper phases of our existence, we often find hidden potentials, the unfulfilled and unfinished seedings of what we still contain, which myth often disguises as secret helpers or mighty talismans. When the story I am working with involves finding talismans, I lead students into enactments aimed at rediscovering skills they had once known, lost perhaps in childhood—a capacity for art or music, for example, or even a sense of empathy. When special helpers like Merlin or the Good Witch are part of the story, I take students down into a private interior place where they meet the master teacher of the quality or capacity that they wish to acquire in their conscious lives. I view these forgotten or neglected potentials for living the larger life as deep codings of the source—the infinite as it is to be found within each of us. A psychology with a mythic or sacred base demands that we have the courage both to release the limitations brought about by old wounds and toxic bitterness and to gain access to the undiminished self with its vast inner storehouse of capacities. We can then use these capacities to prepare ourselves for the greater agenda—becoming an instrument through which the source may play its great music. Then, like the hero or heroine of myth, we may, regardless of our circumstances, become an inspiration for helping culture and consciousness move toward its next level of possibility. At this we startle, we shake. The scope of this dream demands that we live out of our true Essence, which is always too large for our local contracted consciousness to contain. I find that it requires many mythic adventures of the soul to reloom body and mind. But such is necessary if we are to return to everyday life with knowledge gained in the depths that can be put to use to redeem what T. S. Eliot called the "unread vision of the higher dream" inherent in both self and society.

Myths have such power because they are full of archetypes. Archetypes are many things—primal forms, codings of the deep unconscious, constellations of psychic energy, patterns of relationship. Our ancestors saw them in the heavens, prayed to them as Mother Earth, Father Ocean, Sister Wind. They were the great relatives from whom we derived, and they not only gave us our existence but also prompted our stories and elicited our moral order. Later, they became personified in mythic characters and their stories—the contending brothers, the holy child, the search for the beloved, the heroic journey. As major organs of the psyche, archetypes give us our essential connections, and without them we would lose the gossamer bridge that joins spirit with nature, mind with body, and self with the metabody of the universe. Archetypes are organs of Essence, the cosmic blueprints of how it all works. Because they contain so much, archetypes frustrate analysis and perhaps can only be known by direct experience. Thus, in the journey of transformation, we participate in these symbolic dramas and actively engage in archetypal existence. We form a powerful sense of identity with the archetypal character, and this mythic being becomes an aspect of ourselves writ large. Symbolic happenings appear with undisguised relevance, not only for our own lives and problems, but also for the remaking of society. Working with myth and archetype, we discover that we are characters in the drama of the *anima mundi,* the soul of the world. In this discovery we push the boundaries of our own human stories and gain the courage to live mythically and to help heal our world.

It is June 1985. Joseph Campbell and I are giving a seminar together in Santa Barbara. He has just been showing how in any civilization, myth serves four major psychological and social functions.

First, he tells us, myth brings us into communion with the transcendent realms and the eternal forms.

Second, myth gives us the art, the music, and the poetry to express the realization that we are members of a larger universe and that there is meaning and purpose behind it all. Myth, he says, provides a "revelation to waking consciousness of the powers of its own sustaining source." He shows many glorious slides to illustrate this point.

Third, myth tells us that wherever we are in time, space, or culture, the rituals of living and dying have spiritual and moral roots. When the rituals no longer work, a pervading sense of alienation from society often ensues, followed by a desperate quest to replace the lost meaning of the once-powerful myths. People become mean-spirited and withdrawn, even ready to comply with totalitarian regimes when all else fails. Wholesale leaps into one or another variety of fundamentalism reduce consciousness to a limited though comforting notion of the way things work. Often, people replace an outgrown mythology with one that belongs to a still earlier worldview. Then society is in danger of making a U-turn to the past.

The fourth and most important function of myth, Campbell says, is to "foster the centering and unfolding of the individual in integrity" with the self (the microcosm); the culture (the mesocosm); the universe (the macrocosm); and the pan-cosmic unity, the ultimate creative Mystery, which is "both beyond and within himself and all things."

Joe then turns to me and asks, "Jean, what to you is the nature of myth?"

I tell him and our listeners, "Well, Joe, to me a myth is something that never was but is always happening."

"Well then," he replies, "let's make it happen!"

In the twenty years before his death, Joseph Campbell and I gave a number of seminars together dealing with myth, archetype, symbol, and psyche. He would tell the stories of the gods and great myths, and I would devise processes so that the students could experience these myths and realities within themselves—the logomen, *the things told, followed, as in ancient times, by the* dromenon, *the things done or danced or played.*

Campbell was always astonished at how close at hand these experiences were, how effulgent with myth and archetype was the psyche of the most ordinary person.

"Whenever I work with you, Jean," he'd tell me, "I see the masks of the gods emerge in the faces of everyone in our audience. How can this happen?"

"How can it not?" I'd reply. "Besides," I'd add, looking at him meaningfully, "I had a great teacher."

On this occasion Joe decides to tell the story of Parsifal and the quest for the Grail. I follow his marvelous telling with my own agenda—active engagement with the myth as a transformational journey with the possibility of healing self and society.

Whenever a society is in a state of breakdown and breakthrough—what I have called whole-system transition—it often requires the new social alignment that myth can bring. The myth does not have to be new; it can be a very old myth seen in ways that mediate and refocus the issues of the time. So many of the problems that we see outside ourselves can be solved only by answers we find within. Since myth contains inner solutions in storied and dramatic form, it opens the gate to this disclosure, giving us pathways into the future. Over the past decades, there has been a rising tide of interest in the old Arthurian tales. Reams of scholarship, a stream of novels, plays, musicals, movies, television series, esoteric societies, and now computer games are filled with versions of these stories. Why is this so? Because the tales of Arthur and his knights appeal to our sense of wonder, evoking our memory of something that never was but is always happening. Even more significantly, they give us clues to means of greening the wasteland. Perhaps that is why Joseph Campbell wrote and spoke about these stories so often.

Within the Arthurian canon is an episode of particular interest, the story of Parsifal and the mysterious malady of the Fisher King who held the secret of the Grail. It was not the king alone who suffered; everything around him was falling into ruins, crumbling away—the palace, the towers, the gardens. Animals no longer bred; trees and plants bore no fruit; springs were drying up. Many physicians had tried without success to cure the king. Knights arrived at the court day and night, each asking first for news of the king's health. One day, a young knight named Parsifal was riding along looking for a place to spend the night, when he saw a man lying on his side in a boat fishing. The man directed him to a castle where he could find shelter. At first Parsifal could not find the castle and suspected that the fisherman had played a trick on him. Suddenly, he was enveloped in a numinous atmosphere, and the castle appeared before his eyes. He was greeted as if he had been expected and was led to the king, who was, of course, the fisherman he had seen. The king's wound in his upper thigh caused him so much suffering that all he could do was fish.

Parsifal was the honored guest at a magnificent dinner. He wondered at the beautiful chalice, or Grail, carried in procession by a gracious maiden; all through the evening she bore the Grail back and forth from the banquet hall into an adjoining apartment. From it streamed such brilliant light that the luster of the many candles was dimmed. Parsifal was aching to ask about the Grail. As a newly made knight, however, he was mindful of his teacher's admonition that a good knight does not ask too many questions. When he retired for the night, he determined that he would find someone the next morning to ask about the chalice he had seen. But when he awoke, he discovered his armor laid out for him and no one around to assist him in putting it on. Anxious to ask his question, he ran through the halls, banging on doors, "Please, can you tell me about the Grail?" But there was no answer; the castle was empty. Parsifal ran into the courtyard, jumped onto his horse, and galloped toward the drawbridge, which began to rise as he sped across it. Urging his horse forward, he just managed to leap to land. Reining his mount, he turned back toward the castle, pleading, "Is anyone there? There is something I must ask you!" But there was no answer.

As a result of missing his opportunity, Parsifal fell into despair and spent years doing knightly things with no passion. One day, after much experience and many acts of courage and kindness, he returned to Grail Castle, led by the ugliest but wisest of women. Paying no heed to courtly custom, he made straight for the king, addressing him without preamble, "Where is the Grail?" or, in some versions, "Who serves the Grail?" He was immediately shown the chalice and, turning to face it, he knelt to pray for the end of the king's pain. Arising, he turned to King Anfortas and asked, "Uncle, what ails thee?" In that very instant, everything was transformed. The king leaped up from his bed of pain, completely healed, and a strange and glorious luster was seen to come over his flesh; as the poet described it, "No one whose beauty is from birth ever equalled that of Anfortas coming out of his sickness." But it was not only the king who was healed. Springs began to flow again, trees and flowers to bud, animals to breed, and a great joy awakened in the hearts of the people. Those few words of Parsifal were enough to regenerate the whole of nature, and the wasteland became the green land.

In asking, "Where is the Grail?" Parsifal was asking, in essence, "Where is the supreme reality, the center of life, the source of existence, the creative potency, the holy kingdom?" No one there had thought until then of asking that central question, and the world was perishing from lack of imagination and absence of the courage or desire for reality. The wasteland world that resulted is, on an allegorical level, sadly similar to our own. We look about us and see the hazards of mass destruction through nuclear and biological weapons; threats to privacy and freedom; overpopulation; the savaging of women and children; exacerbated unemployment. Everywhere we find an encroaching wasteland of air, noise, water, and land pollution and the depletion of the Earth's resources; the overload of information and our vulnerability to collapse and breakdown; the dehumanization of ordinary work; the decline of the family. The wasteland looms in the proliferation of institutional megastructures that have created a vast chasm between public and private life, such that the political order is seen as detached from the values and realities of individual life, and the individual gives neither moral sanction nor legitimacy to the political order. In these ways the Parsifal myth illumines our present time. But the myth also offers powerful, soul-charging ways of healing the wasteland in ourselves as well as in our society. For we are all the wounded Fisher

King, each one of us is Parsifal, and every human being is a Grail of the most sacred life.

In working with this myth, my method is to have people embody all the parts. When they become the Fisher King, they look at their woundings, raising their pathos to the level of myth, revisioning a time of personal loss and tragedy as a potentially transformative event. I might invite my students, for example, to work in pairs, asking each other a series of questions: How were you wounded? What were the consequences of this wounding for good or ill? In the light of the wounding, what do you want? Then they are asked to tell the story of their wounding as a myth. Such telling does not erase past trauma but rather remythologizes it to reveal its deeper meaning. As a result, students often find that they are able to "fish" in the cosmos of the psyche, "catching" meanings and perspectives that nurture their understanding of the larger story of their life.

Playing Parsifal offers other insights. The name *Parsifal* can mean "total fool," while its variant spelling, *Percival,* can be interpreted as "piercer of the veil." In his name is Parsifal's story. He is the fool, the great innocent, who lumbers along through adventures and follies, never quite getting it, and getting caught as a result in a passionless life. Finally, he collects enough experience to ask the right questions and to become the piercer of the veil of reality. Thus I lead exercises to invite reflection on one's experiences and on opportunities taken and not taken. As Parsifal, students make the classical journey from mindlessness to mindfulness through exercises designed to increase the amplitude of what they are able to hold in consciousness. They begin by walking and becoming increasingly aware of the feeling tones of each bodily part. At the same time, they scan their emotions and hold those feelings in consciousness. Then they are asked to count forward and backward from one to twenty without stopping and without losing their bodily and emotional awareness. They are then instructed to hold as many perceptions as they can of the room and the people in it. Certain complex ideas are suggested for them to think about without, of course, losing awareness of the previous material. Through this method, many participants reach a new state of lucidity, which they describe as being "more awake" than they have ever been. In many ways, the experience mirrors Parsifal's journey to full consciousness that allows him to find his way back to Grail Castle.

Playing the part of the Grail gives participants the opportunity to sound depths upon depths of their inner spirits and to discover the truth of the saying from the Upanishads that "abundance is scooped from abundance and still more abundance remains." I lead at this point spiritual exercises aimed at finding the interior castle and the Grail that lies within. The process ends with a celebration and "grailing" of one another by the participants. One person in each pair kneels before a standing partner, and while music plays (I like to use a recording of "The Rose"), the one standing holds up his or her arms and becomes a grail, receiving the spirit of the sacred chalice, becoming a receptacle of divine life. As the song continues, the person brings the arms down very slowly and places his or her hands on the kneeling partner's head, saying, "I give you the fullness of your being." The music ends, and the partners change roles, each experiencing being the receiver of grail life and the giver of that larger life.

In mythic journeys such as Parsifal's, the shadow plays a large role. In psychological terms, *shadow* refers to the repressed, disowned, and unacknowledged aspects of self. When these shadow qualities are recognized and reconciled, a person often experiences a movement to greater maturity and depth of personality. Since time out of mind, myth and mythic knowing have served to balance shadow and light in individuals and in cultures. We waste our substance and dampen our spirits by insisting on seeing our shadows as negative, rarely looking at the trapped energy that they contain. When liberated and allowed its higher intention, this shadowed energy can be the fount of our very finest qualities and the taproot of our Essence.

To exemplify the power of the shadow in a most dramatic way, my associate, Peggy Rubin, and I sometimes perform in our seminars another story from the Arthurian canon, based on a fifteenth-century poem, *The Weddynge of Sir Gawen and Dame Ragnell*. There are several versions of this marvelous story, and we adapt ours from different texts, taking a few liberties with the original. However, the basic story is archetypal. We act all the parts, and as Peggy is a spectacular comic actress and I'm not too bad either, audiences have been known to laugh mightily as we tell and playact the following tale:

One day King Arthur is out hunting with his men and his favorite nephew, Sir Gawain. Sir Gawain is a true and perfect knight, loyal and courageous, clean in thought and word and deed. He rescues damsels in distress, takes care of old ladies, rights wrongs, and brings justice and comfort wherever he can. He is also tremendously handsome, with a great sunburst of golden hair. On this day, as they ride through the forest, the men are without armor, dressed only in their greens. While chasing a stag, Arthur comes to a place in the forest, some say to a ford in the river, where he is unable to pass, for looming in front of him is a giant knight by the name of Sir Gromer Somer Joure.

The huge fellow says, "Ah, Arthur, and Gawain too. I've had it in for you since you got that piece of land away from me. All right, now you're going to have to fight me. Enough of this Camelot baloney. I'm going to kill you, cut you into smithereens. Come on, fight me. There's only one of me and two of you."

"Now, just wait a minute," says King Arthur. "You are a knight, isn't that so?"

"Of course I'm a knight. Can't you tell?"

"Well, no true knight would ever fight unarmed men."

"Oh, shucks," says the giant. "All right. Then I'll offer you a challenge. You have a year from today to find out the answer to a question."

"Oh, we like challenges," says King Arthur. "What's the question?"

"The question is . . ." The huge knight sneers in anticipation, drawing out the suspense. "The question is, 'What do women really want?' "

"Oh, no," say Arthur and Gawain simultaneously.

"And a year from today, if you don't have the right answer, then you have to fight me, and I'll surely kill you. I'll turn you into dog food. And it will be quits forever for this Round Table drivel. . . ."

As he continues to rave on, King Arthur and Sir Gawain get away. Sir Gawain has a good idea. He suggests that they go in opposite directions, visit strange lands, and put the question to everyone they meet, especially women. Then each should put all the answers they gather in a large book and meet and compare notes before the time is up. For nearly a year they poll the female populace with the same question.

"Excuse me, madam, what do women really want?" Sir Gawain inquires of a likely matron in a market town.

"Well, what I really want is a nice fur coat and an even nicer furry man to go with it."

"Little girl, what do women really want?"

"What I'd like is someone to beat up my brother."

"Hello, there, old dame! What do women really want?"

"Oh, now, young man. What I'd really and truly want is for someone to bring an onion roll and a little hot soup to me in the morning, and to do the dishes, milk the cow . . ."

Coming at last to the red light district of Camelot, Sir Gawain sees the comely Margarita. He asks her the question, and she rolls her eyes and says, "Oh, sonny, do you think I could ever really tell you?"

"Oh, dear," says the good knight, and rides off to the convent, where he meets the sainted Mother Hildegard.

"Mother Hildegard, blessed lady, what do women really want?"

The holy woman looks pensive, her hands steepled in prayer. Finally she sighs and says, "Oh, my son, do you think I could ever really tell you?"

Sir Gawain makes his way to the court and asks the question of Queen Guinevere, to which she replies with a broad grin, "Ask Lancelot. He knows!"

The two men meet again in the eleventh month, just before the day they are sworn to return with the answers to Sir Gromer Somer Joure. As they compare their findings, they grow more and more worried. Somehow they know that they do not have the right answer. Finally Gawain says that he has heard that in the forest of Inglewood there is a woman who sits by a well; she is wondrous wise but wondrous strange. In the day that remains, he will seek her out and ask the question.

He enters the dark forest and journeys until he sees huddled by the well a shape that he ascertains is vaguely female. He taps the shape on a protruding hump and asks, "Excuse me. Madam? Madam, what do women really want?" Suddenly the shape turns around, and there before him is the ugliest woman he has ever seen. She has little rat eyes, warts with their own warts, a red, red face, steely wires for hair, and eyebrows so long that they are braided to the top of her head. She boasts many hairs around her mouth and one tusk of a tooth going up and another going down. She also drools.

"My, aren't you a pretty fellow," she cackles as she ogles the handsomest of men. "Well, I know the answer to your question, but what will you do for me if I tell you?"

Gawain gulps. "On my honor as a true and perfect knight, I will do anything that you ask."

Dame Ragnell, for that is her name, hoots with pleasure. "Will you marry me, then?"

Gawain pales, but, valiant knight that he is, he agrees.

"Now, I mean a wedding in a beautiful dress in front of the whole court, a high mass to celebrate it, and a bountiful feast—not one of these hole-in-the-corner affairs?"

Gawain agrees.

"Don't look so unhappy. Though I be foul, I be merry. Now, since you've agreed, I'll tell you the answer. What women really want is—sovereignty. They want not to be subject to men, but to have their own power of choice."

"Yes, madam, that sounds right. I'll arrange for our marriage, madam."

The next day King Arthur and his nephew meet with Sir Gromer Somer Joure. They hand him the two books, and he peruses them with growing contempt.

"What's the matter with you guys? Don't you even know how to ask a question? These answers are as ridiculous as you are. So now you have to fight me. Come on; let's to it."

Just as the giant is about to strike off his head, King Arthur interrupts with, "But we have one last answer. What women really want is—sovereignty."

"Ohhhhh. You've been talking to my sister! The wretch, may she burn in the fire. Well, have a nice day." And with that, Sir Gromer Somer Joure goes glowering into the forest.

The wedding proceeds on schedule with the ugly Dame Ragnell dressed magnificently in white and the handsome Sir Gawain a vision in green and gold. Dame Ragnell blows kisses to everyone as she goes down the aisle, but so offensive is her breath that people faint as she passes by.

At the altar the priest asks, "Do you, Sir Gawain, take this . . . creature for your lawfully married wife, etcetera?" To which the fair Sir Gawain answers, "On my honor as a true and perfect knight, I do."

The priest then asks, "Do you, Dame Ragnell, take this poor, poor Sir Gawain as your lawfully married husband, etcetera?"

"You better believe it, Tootsie. Now let's eat!"

The wedding banquet is a typical medieval feast: a stag stuffed with a boar, which is stuffed with a deer, which is stuffed with a woodchuck, which is stuffed with a partridge, which is stuffed with a hummingbird. Dame Ragnell is beside herself with gluttony. Drooling, she gnaws, gnashes, gobbles, and inhales food, tearing at it with her long dirty fingernails and long tusks. People throw up watching her eat. But no matter, for she finishes everyone else's portion as well.

"Now, it's time for bed!" she announces merrily. Everyone at table groans.

In bed, she is suddenly shy. Sir Gawain lies there with his eyes tightly shut and his hands crossed across his chest like a dead knight in a stone sepulchre. Dame Ragnell finally says, "Well?"

"Yes, madam?"

"Aren't you going to do something?"

"Like what, madam?"

"Well . . . you could give me a little kiss, maybe."

Sir Gawain blanches but proves a true knight. "Yes, madam. I will do that, and I . . . I will do more."

"More? Oh, I like the sound of that 'more.' "

His eyes still closed, Sir Gawain leans over and gives Dame Ragnell a little peck on the cheek. Then, girding up his courage, he reaches out a hand to touch her hair and then her face. But where there had been steely greasy wires, her hair is now soft and lovely to the touch. And her skin, where are the warts? Where did this velvety skin come from? And where is the hairy boar's snout that was her nose? Sir Gawain pulls back and opens his eyes to the most beautiful woman he has ever beheld. He says, "Wh-where is she? Where is Dame Ragnell?"

The beautiful woman replies, "Oh, my sweet husband. I am Dame Ragnell."

"You sure don't look anything like Dame Ragnell!"

"That's because I have been ensorceled by my wicked stepmother and turned into a hideous hag until the best knight in England would marry me and kiss me. But, my dear, I am afraid that I am still half-ensorceled, and you have a choice. I can be beautiful for you at night and ugly for all the others during the day. Or I can be beautiful for all the others in the daytime and ugly for you at night. Which would you have?"

Sir Gawain thinks about the alternatives and finally says to her, "You choose!"

Dame Ragnell throws her arms around him, saying, "Ah, well then, courteous knight, you have broken the spell by giving me sovereignty, so now I can be beautiful all of the time." And then as the poem tells us, "itt passyd forth tylle middaye" that they made joy out of mind.

In this imaginative tale lie the answers to many of our deepest worries as well as some solutions for dealing with our shadowed selves, the ugly Dame Ragnell that each of us contains. It begins with a state of vulnerability. King Arthur and Sir Gawain are in their unarmored "greens," in no position to confront the world in their usual way of knightly combat. We, too, vulnerable and unprotected, go forth to hunt down the truth about ourselves. Soon we face the implacable giant who stops us on our journey. Is it a boss, a family or religious tradition, or even some aspect of ourselves that looms large and will not let us get on with our lives until an essential challenge or question has been answered? This question or challenge takes us to people and places that we would not ordinarily approach—in Gawain and Arthur's case, to the women of their own and neighboring kingdoms. The great question calls us forward like a giant lure of becoming: What do women really want? What is the meaning and purpose of my life? What is the source of happiness? Is this all there is? By asking our question in the ordinary way, looking through endless bookstores, taking courses, reading newspapers, talking for hours to our friends, shopping, traveling, being of service to others, we hope that somehow the right answer will sneak through. And, when we feel our time is running out, we run right smack into our shadowed self, the Dame Ragnell who sits at the well of wisdom. She has the answer, but who is she and what does she want with us?

She often makes her appearance through what we think of as our own worst quality. In my seminars I talk about my own Dame Ragnell, hypersensitivity. I am in the all-time wrong profession for someone who is hypersensitive, facing, as I do, as many as a hundred and fifty thousand people a year. Some of these people will project onto me, send venomous letters, or in the case of a number of fundamentalists, make death threats. You cannot be in my line of work without becoming a symbol upon which some people will project their resistance and their fear. My idea of a fine life is living quietly somewhere, perhaps in a cozy cave, playing Bach on a harpsichord, translating ancient Greek poetry, and raising Airedales. But my daimon will have none of it. What then do I do with a classic case of thin skin, brought on, I am told, by having been born prematurely and never developing some of the neurological sheathings that protect most people?

The story of Sir Gawain and Dame Ragnell has been crucially important to me in reframing my own particular shadow. Yes, I am hypersensitive, but when I look at the deeper aspects of this condition, I discover the beautiful Dame Ragnell, which in my case is a high degree of empathy for others and a sensitivity to people, cultures, and ideas. If I focus on this aspect of my sensitivity, I acknowledge it as a quality that allows me my finest gift, my ability to do the kinds of work I do. The issue is one of focus. I do not lose my hypersensitivity; rather I shift lenses and see it also as the positive quality it always contained, my empathy for others.

To demonstrate how shifting lenses helps us see the beautiful Dame Ragnell hidden beneath the apparently ugly facade of what we deem our own worst quality, I sometimes perform a little demonstration. I ask for a volunteer to come forward and tell me his or her worst quality.

"Anger," the person might reply. "I explode too often with anger. I find myself getting angry over little things."

Then I step back, perhaps ten feet away, and try to sense the larger pattern that underlies the problem. I neither analyze nor psychologize but rather look for the light beneath the shadow, its hidden power and hidden beauty. Often, the answer is clear.

"I am sensing that your beautiful Dame Ragnell is emotionally brilliant," I might say. "You have a large emotional palette, which, like a painter, you could use to express all kinds and subtleties of feeling. Because you have limited and constricted this wide range of feeling, it explodes as anger. If you give sovereignty to your anger's deeper and more beautiful quality, it may grow and enhance your life. You may even find that as you express a wider range of feelings, your episodes of anger will become fewer. Does this seem right?"

I then analyze with the group the patterns of possibility that might emerge around a negative quality, as if the shadow brings with it a certain signature of grace. The archetype announces itself symptomatically and, when sought, proves to be radiant. For instance, those who name fear as their darkest shadow quality often have a very adventurous spirit that has been so squelched that it has surfaced as a fear of life. Those who speak of being judgmental frequently have as their beautiful Dame Ragnell a high aesthetic sense. They are keepers of the high pattern who sense the harmonies between things, be they arrangements of furniture or moral design. With no job opportunities available for this sense of proportion, they narrow their sights and end up criticizing and carping over details. Those who claim jealousy as their bête noir often prove to be great appreciators of others. Within their shadow lies a large generosity of spirit and the ability to recognize the qualities and skills of other people. Curtailed, appreciation sours into envy.

Procrastinators, people who simply cannot get around to the things they feel they are obliged to do, often prove to have an acute sense of timing, of *kairos*, of the right or most beneficial time to act. They are given to reveries in subjective time, traveling all over the world in several minutes, which may seem to be many days or weeks or, going the other way, enjoying the circadian passing of days and seasons as if they were but little whiffs of time. Seen in their true light, procrastinators are really time masters, with the ability to stretch, contract, and even collapse time. They can rehearse skills in subjective time, so comfortable are they in the inner worlds of time that objective time may lose its reality. By not employing their genius of orchestrating time—and this is where their shadow lies—they resent and betray everyday time and its commitments. If procrastinators would only grant sovereignty to their capacity for working and playing with time, they would soon find that they have "plenty of time" to meet their obligations and commitments.

Perhaps the most poignant of all Dame Ragnells is a sense of inadequacy and a resulting habit of constantly putting oneself down. Sometimes what I sense from such a person is a revelation so mysterious that it strains the power to express. I can speak of it only in metaphor, as I warn those for whom it is relevant. It is as if at some point in their lives they agreed to be the vehicle of a holy child, the bearer of a glory that they needed to protect in order to bring to term. Doubting their adequacy to bear so great a charge, they became hypervigilant, denying that they are "enough" and not taking any initiative that might hurt the Godseed that they carry. Unfortunately, somewhere along the line they also forgot the wonder that they contain and began to focus only on the inadequacy they feel and its resultant passivity, which they experience as a failing. Then feelings of guilt and unworthiness stream up from the unconscious and act in such a way as to confirm their negative feelings about themselves. If they would but grant sovereignty and full awareness to the holy child, who by now is possibly quite grown and ready to help them, they would be able to appreciate and celebrate the ways of the inner daimon and their connection to the holy child that is their guiding archetype. Not only would their lives move on to another track, but they would be able to deal with the shadowed self as an ally, a stimulus to continuing to refine their being and purpose.

None of this is to deny traumatic events that have played into and affected—indeed, reinforced—our shadowed selves. But, unlike traditional psychologists, I believe that these causes are secondary, the sorcery of circumstance, and that they can be released when we grant sovereignty to the higher, often mythic, quality within.

It is October 1986. Joseph Campbell and I are giving a seminar in a new skyscraper hotel on the outskirts of Washington, D.C. The hotel has many unresolved problems in its plumbing, dining service, and electrical system, and so several times throughout the night, everyone is awakened by the fire bell and plods down the many flights of stairs to the lobby, only to be told again and again by the hotel staff that they can't find the fire.

On one of these occasions I catch up with Joe, who like me is in pajamas and bathrobe. "There's no fire down there, Jean. Let's just sit on the stairs awhile until they give the all clear."

"What are you working on now, Joe?" I ask.

"I've finished a new book. It's called The Inner Reaches of Outer Space. *I try to show how the metaphors of mythology are universal and can't be pinned down to any time or place. I hope it will serve as the basis of a new mythology, one that transcends our puny local worldviews."*

"And this new mythology, Joe, will it be of the whole human race?"

"The whole human race, the clusters of galaxies, and the start of it all some fifteen billion years ago."

"It will be the ultimate Whodunnit, and Where do we go from here?"

"Yes, something like what James Joyce in Finnegans Wake *called 'The Hereweare-again Gaieties.'"*

"But we're not, are we, Joe? I mean, now that we know that we are sluiced from stars, it's a whole new ball game. We can venture into outer space, consort with pri-

mal cosmic forces. And at the same time we are spiraling into the microcosm, which will allow us to play at Second Genesis, rewriting the genetic script like some young god going for a Ph.D. in world making."

"Hermes Trismegistus said it first, my dear: 'As above, so below; as below, so above.' We are now at the point at which we can fathom scientifically the vastness expanding in both directions. Maybe this will give us a metaphor rich enough to restore our spirits. The German poet Novalis predicted this when he wrote, 'The seat of the soul is there where the outer and the inner worlds meet.'"

"Looking at the Earth from outer space shocked us back into a mythic mode, don't you think, Joe? Once we could look back at Mama Gaia, we were invested with the charge to be her partner. And to do this, we must agree to live mythically and realize that our lives are every bit as mythic as those of the old cultural heroes or heroines."

"To live mythically, yes, but also to regrow the myths, so that they reflect the current situation. This is where the mystery is, Jean. Because there are a whole new set of images and events out there—"

"—like the ones I talked about this morning—the coming planetary civilization, women in full partnership with men, the world connected though media, the new understanding of human capacities, the ability to play God. . . ."

"Yes, but these things will not become myth until they are transformed by the imagination and receive new orders from the archetypal ideas of inner space. Only then can we have a mythology that works, and until we agree to all these new things, we fall further into chaos until finally we self-destruct out of a sense of meaninglessness."

"The meaninglessness of having no myth?"

"You could say that, yes," Joe replies.

People continue to move past us, ascending and descending the stairs in the confusion of a mythless manor. Sitting next to Joe, I begin to think of these shadowy folk as Everyperson on the stairs of reality, or even as allegories of the rise and fall of civilizations. What a stupid, predictable, two-in-the-morning thought! "Joe, I wonder whether we can ever create or even direct the course of a new myth."

"No more than we can direct the course of tonight's dream, that is, if we ever get to sleep again in this hostile hostel. You know, I had to wait two hours for my steak and Scotch! No, Jean, I think that if anyone can catch the content of this new myth, it will have to be those who are awakened to the imaginative life. It will have to be the artists and the poets, and certainly the dancers." Joe smiles as Jean Erdman, his glorious wife and one of the great dancer-choreographers, joins us.

"What you mystics forget," she says laughing, "is that in order to know the universe, you've got to have a craft. The way of the mystic and the way of the artist are related, except the mystic doesn't have a craft."

"You are certainly right, my darling. The dancer's craft joins her to the world, whereas the mystic can get lost in indifference. That's why the poet says, 'There is only the dance.'"

The bell rings and everybody returns to bed . . . perchance to dream.

5

✦

OF BUTTERFLIES
AND ESSENCE

It is March 1984. I am taking a large group of my students on a trip through China. We are accompanied by the woman who is the chief communist bureaucrat in the Chinese tourism agency. We are not sure why this stiffly formal woman in her Mao jacket and forbidding manner has come along, but we suspect that it is to keep an eye on the political correctness of the other Chinese guides. They are clearly afraid of her, and whenever I am lecturing on Chinese history, philosophy, and art, they look over to her to see what their response should be.

What they do not know is that late at night she comes knocking at my door to discuss in her excellent English the philosophical issues I've raised in my lectures. She tells me that she is deeply drawn to the intellectual traditions of her people and regrets that the political climate in which she was raised did not permit her to study them. I ask her why, then, the government and the Bureau of Tourism have allowed me, a Westerner, to lecture publicly on these subjects, and not just to my students but to select groups of English-speaking Chinese officials and professionals. Even though I have been a professor of Asian philosophy, I am still embarrassed to find a growing number of Chinese in attendance as I speak of Taoism, the Analects of Confucius, the I Ching, the Tao Te Ching, Tang dynasty Buddhism, the philosophy of Chinese calligraphy, and related subjects.

She responds with a sad smile, saying that it is because of the distrust and fear that exist between the Chinese people and the scholars who hold the knowledge of the past after so many years of purging that past.

"The Western teacher who lectures on ancient Chinese philosophies is more to be trusted?" I ask in disbelief.

She does not answer but looks down at her hands and then says, "I am very interested in what you were saying this evening about Chuang-tzu. Tell me again, please, what he said about dreaming he was a butterfly."

I recite for her the famous lines, "Once upon a time, I, Chuang-tzu, dreamt I was a butterfly, fluttering hither and thither, to all intents and purposes a butterfly. . . . Now I do not know whether I was then a man dreaming I was a butterfly, or whether I am now a butterfly dreaming I am a man."

"You talk now, please, on the meaning of this."

"Well," I begin in my best Socratic manner, "what do you think of when you hear the word butterfly*?"*

She makes little winglike movements with her fingers. "Very graceful, beautiful things . . . like so. But also change, how do you say? Transformation from ugly caterpillar to beautiful butterfly. Something that goes from crawling to flying."

"That is what we call metamorphosis—the change from an outworn body or concept of one's self or society to a new one that has more freedom, more grace and beauty." I realize that I am treading on dangerous political ground here.

She, however, is willing to go further. "Yes, but remember, please, that the butterfly is playful, while the caterpillar seems to be in a labor camp, having to eat all the time in the garden in order to make the fuel to make the butterfly."

It is clear that we both know what we are talking about. I ask her, "So you would say, then, that all of this labor and sacrifice is to make for a complete change of being?" She nods enthusiastically. "But now we come to the dream part. How would you explain that? Why the confusion between Chuang-tzu and the butterfly?"

"Oh, that is easy," she declares, clapping her hands. "The man is a higher stage than the butterfly. So he wakes up as Chuang-tzu, still confused, because he has been dreaming he belonged to a lesser stage. He is waking up from the old dream."

She gets up and goes to the door, turning to whisper to me, "Thank you for the political discussion, Doctor. It has been most helpful to me."

I have often wondered about the when or what that causes us to recognize our true Essence, our butterfly nature. Does the caterpillar look up from its munching and regard the butterfly soaring above the bush, then forage faster and farther down the leaf so as to hasten its own becoming? Do the daimons of time and nature afford us early glimpses of our possible selves so as to encourage certain paths to be taken and discourage others?

In my eighth year, I had two experiences within a month of each other that had the most profound effect on my life and work. They called me beyond the show-biz "Me too!" imprinting from my parents that was the stuff of my daily life. Quite simply, they lured me into my Essence.

My father had taken me with him to deliver a script to the ventriloquist Edgar Bergen, whose weekly radio show my dad was writing at the time. Bergen's chief dummy, Charlie McCarthy, a wisecracking little fellow in a tuxedo, was one of the best-loved characters in radio comedy and was featured in many movies as well.

When Dad and I entered the open door of Bergen's hotel room, we found him sitting on a bed with his back to us, talking very intently to Charlie and then listening with evident wonder and astonishment to Charlie's answers. Unlike their usual repartee on the radio programs, there was no flippancy here, no in-on-the-joke sarcasm. In fact, one got the impression that Bergen was the student while Charlie was quite clearly the teacher.

"What are they doing?" I silently mouthed to my father. "Just rehearsing," he mouthed back. But as we listened to what Bergen and Charlie were saying, we soon realized that this was no rehearsal, for Bergen was asking his dummy ultimate questions: "Charlie, what is the meaning of life? What is the nature of love? Is there any truth to be found?" Charlie was answering with the wisdom of millennia. It was as if the great thinkers of all times and places were compressed inside his little wooden head and poured out their distilled knowing through his clacking painted jaws.

Bergen would get so excited by the remarkable answers that he would ask still more ultimate questions: "But, Charlie, can the mind be separate from the brain? Who created the universe, and how? Can we ever really know anything?" Charlie would continue to answer in his luminous way, pouring out pungent, beautifully crafted statements of deep wisdom. This rascally faced little dummy was expounding the kind of knowing that could have come only from a lifetime of intensive study, observation, and interaction with high beings. After several minutes of listening spellbound to this wooden Socrates, my father remembered his theological position as an agnostic Baptist and coughed. Bergen looked up, his Nordic face turning red, and stammered a greeting. "Hello, Jack. Hi, Jean. I see you caught us."

"Yeah, Ed," my father said. "What in the world were you rehearsing? I sure didn't write that stuff."

"No rehearsal, Jack. I was talking to Charlie. He's the wisest person I know."

"But, Ed," my father expostulated, "that's your voice coming out of that cockamamy block of wood."

"Yes, Jack, I suppose it is," Bergen answered quietly. But then he added with great poignancy, "And yet, when he answers me, I have no idea where it's coming from or what he's going to say next. It is so much more than I know."

At that moment my skin turned to gooseflesh, an electric hand seemed to touch mine, and a fractal wave of my future activities crashed on the shore of my eight-year-old self. For I suddenly knew that we all contain "so much more" than we think we do. The image came to me of a house with many floors, and I saw that in ordinary awareness we live on a shelf in the attic of our selves, leaving the other floors relatively uninhabited and the basement locked. What furnishings and books, what interesting artworks and appliances, what family, friends, and pets are to be found in the rooms of the many-mansioned self? Treasure troves, to be sure, powers and potentials, archetypes and inner beloveds, but also grand dreams and dramas are always burgeoning within the interior castle. For it is here that the Dreamtime meets the conditions of the everyday, and the universe itself touches into the little local life. So potent is this place of meeting, so beyond ordinary comprehension its real estate, that one often requires guidance into its domain. In ancient times, the guide to the mysteries was Hermes, the trickster. Charlie McCarthy was Bergen's own Hermes, his guide to the house of many floors that is the mystery of the human condition. Some once-and-future self woke up in me then and knew that I had no other choice but to pursue the path of Hermes and invent a career that would discover ways of tapping into the "so much more" of deep knowledge that we all carry in the nested gnosis within.

That night I had the first in a series of dreams that I continue to have to this day. I dreamed that I entered a small wooden house. Inside was a single plain room with a single door in the wall. I opened that door and discovered that the house went on and on, each room utterly different from the other, some filled with statues and artifacts of incredible beauty, others with vast libraries with ancient manuscripts and yellowed pages of music. I want to read the books, play the music, enter ancient chambers, which I regard with both dread and fascination, but I always wake up before I can. I ask myself, am I Jean dreaming that I am in that house of many treasures, or am I the house of many treasures dreaming I am Jean?

One month later I was back in P.S. 6 in Manhattan, my favorite school, which I always returned to whenever we were living in New York. It held special classes in which many of John Dewey's recommendations for experiential education were still being followed. We would mix music with math, drumming numbers and dancing fractions. We would visit factories to see how things were made, take regular trips to museums, and occasionally be taken to meet a great elder who lived in the vicinity. I recall being taken across the river and put on the bus to Princeton, where we were introduced to Albert Einstein. I must confess that all that I remember about him was that he seemed very vague and had a great shock of unkempt white hair.

However, one day, our teacher informed us that we were going to meet Helen Keller, the great woman who had become deaf, blind, and mute before the age of two. In preparation for our trip, Miss O'Reilly read to us the powerful passage from Helen Keller's autobiography that tells how, until she was six years old, Helen had no mental concepts. Little could break through the imprisoned flesh to the potential mind within. Little existed in her world but body functions and rage. Her teacher, Annie Sullivan, tried in vain to help her understand words through hand tappings. Finally, in desperation, Annie pulled Helen out to the ivy-covered pumphouse and held her hand under the water while she tapped out repeatedly into the other hand *w-a-t-e-r, w-a-t-e-r, w-a-t-e-r.*

Helen writes that her whole body became still. Suddenly she understood what Annie was communicating to her. That word *water* broke into her sealed mind like the sun into a frozen winter world. It was her mental awakening, and she learned the names for thirty things by the end of that day. Helen Keller, of course, went on to become the great educator, champion of the disabled and disadvantaged, and friend and inspiration to so many people the world over.

After this preparation, Miss O'Reilly took us to the Cosmopolitan Club where Miss Keller would be meeting us. Miss Keller was led out by her associate and companion, Polly Thompson. She was in her late sixties at the time, a large woman, quite tall, I remember, and utterly radiant. Her eyes saw nothing and yet were seeing everything. Her smile was a beneficence welcoming the world. I had never seen anybody so full of presence and joy in my life, even though I had been exposed throughout childhood to professional comedians who were always laughing. Helen Keller's joy was of another order entirely.

When she began to speak, I heard the voice of a prophet, a pythoness, whose strange inflections and pronunciations were those of someone who had never heard speech. After she had finished, I was so deeply moved that I knew I had to speak to her. Mind you, I didn't know what I wanted to say, but I knew I had to speak to her nonetheless. When Miss Thompson asked if anyone had a question, my classmates squirmed and looked sheepishly at one another. But I found myself raising my hand and going up to her.

Miss Keller placed her entire hand on my face in order to read my question. Her fingers read my expression, while the center of her palm read my lips. Still I did not know what I was going to ask. Her hand did not move from my face. Finally I blurted out what was in my heart: "Why are you so happy?"

She laughed and laughed, laughter rising from another dimension of sound—the laughter of a sequoia or a whale.

"My child," she said, her voice wandering between octaves, "it is because I live my life each day as if it were my last. And life in all its moments is so full of glory."

As her hand lingered on my face for a moment, I felt as if I were lifted into her radiance and that some kind of charge passed between us. When, years later, I lay on my back looking up at the ceiling of the Sistine Chapel, I understood the nature of that charge. For there on the ceiling was the famous painting by Michelangelo of God touching the outstretched hand of Adam. In my case it had been the touch of the blind Goddess to the little Eve.

These two events, along with my experience of trying to see the Virgin Mary in the closet at six, were the occasions that most deeply impressed me with my future tasks. In observing Bergen talking to Charlie, I saw how deep—shouldn't we say endless?—are the wells of the mind, and in meeting Helen Keller, I saw the unobstructed universe shining so brightly through the lens of a person apparently disabled but present as well as prescient beyond all others. Miss Keller, in mind and body, had spun new webs of connection where old ones had fallen away.

These experiences helped me turn a corner into what I was and was meant to be. From that time on, something within me saw it as my essential task to call people into greatness, regardless of their situation, circumstances, or prospects. Whether it be a poor woman in Bangladesh with seven children whose husband has just turned her out or an account executive in an advertising firm who hates his job and his life and is contemplating suicide, I always try to see beyond circumstances into an individual's essential self. Such deep seeing makes life move again. I believe that what we think of as greatness is something innate to humans seeking to move beyond a limited or outmoded condition and pushing us beyond our old edges. Then, whether out of frustration, madness, or yearning, we quest beyond the failings of our culture or circumstance, seeking to regain the taproot of the self, which leads us down to the very seedbed of reality and then, beyond that, into the Mind of the Maker.

The communist official has returned. This evening she is curious about how I got started in the work of "raising human butterflies." I tell her about my two experiences when I was eight. She seems both intrigued and disturbed.

"Excuse me, Doctor, the talking puppet I can understand. We have actors here in China who put on masks and costumes and become superior beings. But what you tell me about the blind and deaf lady does not seem possible. How could she learn to fly with such damaged wings? She must have had a selfless comrade who accompanied her. I feel that there is much pain and struggle in this story that you are not telling me."

I agree and tell her that the glory that was Helen Keller came about through an incandescent partnership with her comrade and teacher, Annie Sullivan. Helen and Annie met because of their incredible woundings, and both became vehicles of grace through their devotion to each other and then to the larger world that met them. In their story we see glimpses of the larger intention and possibility of ourselves when we attune to our own Essence.

But it was no easy path; in fact, it was the hardest path of all, the path of moving from darkness into a darkness illumined and transfigured. And in the midst of the illuminations, lest we think we can cross a bridge into unstoppable glory, there is life more abundant and more filled with challenge, chaos, catastrophe, and sheer human worry and concern. Helen and Annie, after their triumph resplendent with spirit, in-

herited the whirlwind: accusations of fakery, plagiarism, infestations of mean spirits; forms and fears of victimization by con artists; promises of support and then subsequent withdrawal of support; incessant and voracious appeals for help; fevers and congestions, rheumatisms and lumbago, and the increasing desperate frailty and blindness of Annie; marriage and shattered hearts; the lecture circuit; promises of movie riches; the need to turn to vaudeville for money to support themselves and then being made objects of ridicule for working between jugglers and trained pigs; accusations from conservatives about Helen's support of the Woman's Suffrage movement, the Civil Rights movement, the Socialist Party; betrayal or seeming betrayal by close friends; endless fund-raising for programs for all disabled people; and almost always, especially in the earlier years, worry and concern about how they were going to support themselves and where the next piece of money for them to live on was going to come from.

I tell the communist official that the miracle is that through all of this, Helen's spirit kept growing brighter, more sensitive to the possibilities of others, more appreciative of the sheer, staggering glory of being alive, living each day as if it were her last.

She nods solemnly. "Yes, that is a good story, a true story. I like the fact that Helen was a socialist fighting oppression. But I wonder, Doctor, if she would have become so great a woman if she had not had so many handicaps and so much suffering. In this she is like China. We have had so many troubles, and we are so handicapped in our resources, that like Helen we must seem blind and deaf to the rest of the world. But you will see; like Helen we shall triumph. We call people like you here to remind us of our magnificent culture and all the things we have accomplished in the past. This feeds us in our present cocoon and helps us to become butterflies."

There is a name for that transformation, I tell her. In the West, we call it a renaissance.

It is fascinating to note that the incidence of human greatness increases during one or another of the cusps of social change—during a renaissance, for example, when the culture is being so newly reimagined that it necessitates a rebirth of the self. However, the reverse is also true. A renaissance, with its accompanying rise of images and archetypal symbols, happens because the wall to the human soul has been breached, the door to the psyche unlocked, and a flood of new questions released as to who we are and what we contain.

The European Renaissance was such a golden time when internal and external realities flowed together. In the midst of vast social and religious upheavals, a miracle occurred. Ideas and images were excavated from their Greek, Roman, and Hebraic origins, forgotten texts were translated, esoteric attitudes became more widely available. A treasure trove of the Western world's past thoughts and dreams was excavated, and the horizon of what it meant to be human was greatly extended. Thus Shakespeare's lines of pure Renaissance exaltation:

What a piece of work is a man! How noble in reason! how infinite in faculty! in form, in moving, how express and admirable! in action how like an angel! in apprehension how like a god! the beauty of the world! the paragon of animals!

But something else was happening, too. The human psyche itself was growing, and the imaginal worlds of inner space were budding and flowering into the external world in a phenomenal growth of science, art, music, literature, and statecraft. The internal world knew the cosmos for its own, and the external world became "psyche-tized."

I believe we are in a similar period of cultural and personal expansion today. We are experiencing not just the revival of ancient images, but also the harvest of all the world's cultures, belief systems, ways of knowing, seeing, doing, being. For some, the richness and variety of world culture is just the press of a button or the touch of a computer key away. Fiber optics, interactive television, global computer networks, and other information superhighways make the world available to all who have access to these tools. This world network, along with increasing opportunities for travel, portends a renaissance of renaissances. In many ways, it has already begun—this higher renaissance that arises from the collaboration and cross-fertilization of cultures. Coextensive with this development is the virtual breakdown all over the globe of traditional ways of being, bringing with it the breaching of the soul and the rise of content from the inner world. I think of a conversation I had recently in Taiwan with a schoolteacher who had been brought up in a traditional Chinese family. "I am aware every day of so many new desires, many many new ideas, many new ways of learning," he told me. "I feel like I have inside me a sleeping dragon who has just woken up. I want to go flying everywhere and see what's what. And somehow I know that I must find a way to do it. Otherwise the dragon will devour me."

All over the world psyche is now emerging, larger than it was. What had been contained in the "unconscious" of many of the peoples of the world over hundreds and thousands of years is up and about and preparing to go to work. This is the news that rarely makes the headlines, and it will have consequences greater than anything we might imagine. Already we can see daily the negative consequences of this revivifying of hidden content: violence, oppression, the explosion of old fears and hatreds in countries that for decades had been contained under the lid of totalitarian regimes, the frequency of alcohol and chemical addictions, especially among those who feel that they have extra life to kill. "Thank God, our time is now," poet Christopher Fry says, "when wrong / Comes up to meet us everywhere, / Never to leave us till we take / The longest stride of soul men ever took." This stride of soul must carry us through every shadow toward an open possibility, in a time when everything is quite literally up for grabs. We can do no less. The psyche requires its greatness, as do the times.

Now, greatness not only demands and acts upon opportunities at opportune times but seems to also require that we become entrepreneurs of the possible, vehicles of change in the time wave. A friend, Sister Bridget McCarthy, is chief executive officer of the Mercy Hospital system in California, a huge organization that tries to deliver optimal health care to tens of thousands of people a year. Sister Bridget, born and raised in Ireland, and blessed with the brogue, has both the spunk and vision to do the impossible. Daily she meditates and prays to discover the ways of making a better health system. Daily she dips into her own Essence to find new ways of being, helping, doing. Realizing that the times demand that health care become proactive rather than reactive as well as patient centered rather than doctor or nurse centered, she has introduced a procedure in which all hospital employees—from top administrators and physicians through those who scrub floors and empty bedpans—participate in seminars and learning experiences that provide for continuous personal growth and professional development. By living out of a vision of becoming capable of passionately responding to the needs of the vulnerable, Sister Bridget and her staff have become entrepreneurs of a whole new era of health care, a teaching-learning organization that liberates while it heals, that breaks boundaries while it creates bridges, and above all empowers the patient with privacy, autonomy, information, and support to make appropriate decisions.

And then there is Robert, the son of a friend of mine, whose whole life has been a search for Essence. A lanky, balding man now in his midthirties, he knew early on that he had to pursue his destiny and break with all the molds. From the time he was a little guy, he was adamant in his desire to learn from experience. It greatly bothered him that what he was told in school did not mesh with what he learned in observing people and environments. By the time he was thirteen he had developed keen skills in both outer and inner worlds; as a mountain climber in the Cascades he learned a great deal about placing the body in space, and through a serious pursuit of meditation he learned to explore internal realms of Essence and spirit. At Evergreen College he became fascinated with the ways in which Eastern philosophy and medicine dealt with health and the energetic patterns of connection between body systems. As a student of tai chi, he observed how subtle physical movements affected both thinking and learning. He became an accomplished acupuncturist and then studied extensively in China, where he was one of the few Westerners admitted into advanced training in both tai chi and Oriental medicine. The tai chi masters would take only someone who could watch them perform over a hundred complex movements and immediately be able to repeat all of them in sequence. Robert found that the body could learn the movements faster than the mind could, but only if one could attune to the essence of the body—the *chi* power. Always looking for new avenues to opening his awareness further, he discovered that the process of learning was more important than the subject taught. I am honored to say that I have been one of his teachers. And, in the process, he has taught me much.

Returning to his home in Washington, he set up a practice joining Eastern and Western disciplines to help patients and students to better health and functioning. In this he has been a leading exemplar of the Essence of our era wherein the genius and discoveries of different parts of the world are brought together in a new synthesis. But the most important thing he conveyed in teaching students and patients was to help them learn the truth about who they are and who they are not. Maybe it is the purity of the man that allows people to release old patterns of false identity and seek instead the essential reality of the self. Many referrals began to come from traditional physicians who had either given up with patients or were worried about the side effects of standard medications. Thus he has been able to heal or greatly improve the quality of life of those suffering from chronic pain and joint disease and even people with terminal illnesses. His remarkable success came about not just through a judicious blending of Eastern with Western methods, but, most critically, through his insistence on education into Essence.

Then suddenly Robert was afflicted with a continuously growing benign tumor on the brain stem. Two operations removed large parts of the tumor, but it continued to grow into the brain. The effects of the third operation were devastating, as parts of the cerebellum had to be removed. Robert was left with extreme ataxia—loss of motor coordination—as well as paralysis on the left side, loss of hearing in one ear, and speech impairment. He who had had the finest and most sensitive use of his body was now confined to a wheelchair. However, there was no loss of intelligence and cognitive functions, and his spirit, like Helen Keller's, remains strong, surprising, even luminous. This has greatly astounded the hospital psychologist, who once said to him, "I would like to know your secret. With one operation you have lost your fiancée and your profession, and you are physically disabled. Why are you not depressed or suicidal?" Robert wondered if, given the questions, the psychologist could understand his answer. Simply, he had learned patience without anger. He could accept what is without giving in. His Essence had not changed or his belief in what he could yet create out of that Essence.

Robert asks himself, "What can I now do to create the future I want?" He reminds us that to get from here to there, first you have to be totally here. And so daily he performs a long series of physical and mental exercises. Exploring every kind of therapy that can conceivably help, he is making remarkable progress and astonishing all physicians who have studied his case. With all this, he continues to work, giving courses by computer, writing for the disabled, distributing alternative health products and acupuncture supplies, and continuing to see patients. He has become keenly aware of nonverbal communication and has gained other capacities: as his physical senses have changed his psychic senses have become more acute, and he is able to help people with a subtlety and prescience he never had before. "I have learned to invest in loss," he says, "and now it is becoming an asset."

"And what have you discovered, Robert?" I ask.

"Spirit has no limitation," he replies.

Such are the men and women about whom it could be said that their very Essence corresponds to the changing Essence of the time, for an era has its own particular Essence as much as a person does.

I once coined a word to describe the Essence of our era. *Kairos* in Greek means "the loaded time," for the most beneficial opportunities. To this I added *Eros,* or "passion" to make *kairotic*—the passion of the loaded time. Ours is a time when greatness should be rising—a time of dissolution and reconstruction—but we may find ourselves kept from greatness because our Essence is bound up in the culture and psyche of an earlier, nonkairotic time. The question then becomes for each of us, how do we achieve our own *kairos* and with it our own renaissance of mind and spirit—in a word, our own greatness?

Greatness may take the form of a great endeavor, or it may manifest as a fullness of life—a living out of one's Essence self. When I ponder the nature of greatness, thinking over the many truly great people I have known, I conclude that what they shared was a potent sense of their own Essence. Margaret Mead, Buckminster Fuller, Joseph Campbell, Clemmie, an old black woman in Mississippi, the Trappist monk Theophane Boyd, actress Ellen Burstyn, my oldest friend Gay Luce—all were able to live out of Essence for longer periods of time than most of those around them. This ability helped them use their gifts and capacities to a fuller extent. From this it follows that we must examine the nature of Essence and discern our own if we are to achieve our greatness.

Essence is not a place or a time, an insight or a state of mind. It is the deepest part of our nature, an actual presence that is innate and inborn. Sometimes it wears a personal face and a form and manifests as an image to our mind's eye. When it does, some call it a daimon, others an angel. Still others think of it, in its incorporeal form, as the soul. Ironically, Essence does not develop with education or with living for many years. It is beyond symbols and is, therefore, neither archetype nor angel, neither wise old man or woman nor divine child. These symbols point the way to Essence, which has been called in a number of traditions "the diamond body" to suggest the crystalline nature of this inner reality. Essence is so real, so substantial, that it exceeds all symbols, images, and language. Symbols and images can provide, perhaps, flashes of insight about Essence, but not its living embodied experience. Language fails in its attempts to describe Essence or denote its activities and capacities. Essence, we must conclude, can only be experienced. As Sufi philosopher A. H. Almaas says in his remarkable book *Essence:*

> This level of experience is so deep and profound, so full and packed with a live significance, so moving and so powerful that it is not possible to communicate it in words. Words can describe some aspects of the experience, but they fail actually to deliver the whole impact. Words can communicate the experience to somebody who already has had it or is right on the verge

of it. But not to somebody who does not know. (York Beach, ME: Samuel Weiser, 1986, 78)

It is hardly surprising that in these kairotic times, a bevy of popular recent books try to describe the experience of Essence and to encourage its cultivation, for example, Thomas Moore's *Care of the Soul,* Clarissa Pinkola Estés's *Women Who Run with the Wolves,* Gary Zukav's *Seat of the Soul,* as well as books by James Hillman. These writers wrestle with the concept of Essence because it may be the most important requirement for our emergence as full human beings. When we have lost our sense of Essence and with it the sense of our potential greatness, the call or lure of our own hidden being, we feel horribly incomplete. If we are going to survive our time and help make the changes that cosmos and history require, we must stop going on as half-light versions of who and what we really are. If we are to become in reality stewards of the Earth, cocreators in the great enterprise of an expanding reality, we must democratize greatness and do remedial work in Essence. The Sufi poet and mystic Jalalludin Rumi expressed our situation magnificently:

A basket full of bread sits on your head but you beg for crusts from door to door. Up to your knees in the stream's water and you seek a drink from this person and that.

Would that you could know yourself for a time! Would that you could see a sign of your own beautiful face.

Wretched human! Not knowing his own self, man has come from a high estate and fallen into lowliness. He has sold himself cheaply; he was satin yet he has sown himself onto a tattered cloak.

If you could only see your own beauty—for you are greater than the sun! Why are you withered and shriveled in this prison of dust?

Why not become fresh from the gentleness of the heart's spring? Why not laugh like a rose? Why not spread perfume?

Why is your Jacob deprived of the lightning of your beautiful face? Hey, O lovely Joseph! Why remain at the bottom of the well? (Rumi, Mathnavi II, trans. by R. A. Nicholson; London: George Allen and Urwin, 1950, 149)

When we finally do climb out of the bottom of the well, we experience Essence as a strange and beautiful country of the soul, a landscape of our greatness. Indeed, when we touch into Essence, latent actions and skills suddenly jump into life. A gestalt of qualities rises and fans out to a network of enterprises for those who are many-minded, or comes to life with a laserlike focus on a specific project for those who are single-minded. This explosion of energy and possibilities demonstrates that Essence has many more capacities than does the local self, which is carved out of the conditions of day-to-day existence. These capacities belong to the field of mind; they are very subtle and can be easily overlooked. Though they gather information from the physical senses, the extraordinary human capacities linked to Essence also have access to "news from the universe." In a state of Essence, all knowing is direct knowing, which goes beyond space, time, and personality; all senses and all systems are "go." In a state of Essence, you know with such a simultaneity of knowings that you can be said to have grasped the whole of anything or anybody. Such knowing brings a certainty, a clarity, and a precision that seldom come from reasoning, intuition, or insight. Quantum physics would say that the knowledge linked to Essence is knowledge of both the particle and the wave. Thus the deepest values, purposes, and patterns for life, the richest potential coding for existence, the source level of creative patterns, innovative actions, and ideas become known to us. From the perspective of Essence, the power and action of Gandhi is explicable; the sheer genius of perception and of rewriting the world of Emily Dickinson makes marvelous sense; the ability of Thomas Jefferson to study societies and then to reinvent them seems elementary; and Helen Keller's goodness, perseverance, and social activism in spite of immense obstacles appears to be a natural calling and way of being. The compassion of the Buddha, of Christ, as well as of the valiant unsung contemporary bodhisattvas who give over their lives to helping humanity are entirely understandable in the light of living out of Essence. We call such men and women great because they are in touch with the moral flow of the universe. We call them great because they live out of the very stuff of what is trying to emerge into space and time, the continuously creating universe.

Writing of Essence as *soul,* Gary Zukav suggests that being in this state

leads us to another kind of power, a power that loves life in every form that it appears, a power that does not judge what it encounters, a power that perceives meaningfulness and purpose in the smallest details upon the Earth. This is authentic power. When we align our thoughts, emotions, and actions with the highest part of ourselves, we are filled with enthusiasm, purpose, and meaning. Life is rich and full. We have no thoughts of bitterness. We have no memory of fear. We are joyously and intimately engaged with our world. This is the experience of authentic power. (*The Seat of the Soul,* New York: Simon & Schuster, 1990, 26)

What Zukav describes is similar to what I call the experience of the *entelechy,* a Greek word meaning the dynamic purpose that drives us toward realizing our essential self, that gives us our higher destiny and the capacities and skills that our destiny needs for its unfolding. It is the entelechy of an acorn to be an oak tree. It is the entelechy of a popcorn kernel to be a fully popped entity. And it is the entelechy of a human being to be . . . God knows what!

Seen in this light, my eight-year-old experience of witnessing the "conversation" between Edgar Bergen and Charlie McCarthy followed soon after by my meeting with Helen Keller can be seen as fractal signpoints pointing the way toward my entelechy, my essential unfolding. Walking backward through our lives, each of us can identify similar small moments in which we experience a prescient shiver of knowing who or what we will become. When such moments are accompanied by profound joy, by a sense of blissful and almost supernatural felicity, we can assume that we have touched into Essence. We enter then into a mythic domain in which the extraordinary is ordinary and reality conspires to bring us to our fullness. Once we have such an experience, we never again doubt that we have the capacity to be extraordinary, and this knowledge spurs us on to actualizing this potential.

I once asked Joseph Campbell if he had ever known the raptures of touching into Essence. After all, he had written extensively about high mythic moments. Surely he knew the experience firsthand? His answer was unexpected, for it had nothing to do with heroes' journeys or legendary encounters. He told me of a time when, as a very young man at Columbia College, he was on the track team. Always a superb athlete, even up until he died at eighty-three, during this particular meet he entered a state of perfection. He became, he told me, the ultimate runner and knew that condition of Essence in which he was at once the runner, the running, and the run. In this ecstatic state he left all other competitors behind and won the race by a remarkable margin.

I knew just what he was talking about, for when I was about fourteen, I had similarly experienced the power of identity with Essence while engaged in a sport. I had been training regularly for some years as a fencer. I regularly won at fencing matches and was being encouraged to train for the Olympic team a few years down the line. Fencing, for me, was poetry in action as well as a kind of intellectual sport. One needed to maintain high style; in my case, my fencing master, Frederick Rhodes, was a Russian who had studied with a French master who had studied with someone who had studied with one of the great masters of the eighteenth century. So the tradition I learned was the elegant and courtly form of another era, with salutes that looked as if one were signing the signature of God in the air with one's foil. At the same time, one was required to respond rapidly, anticipate the opponent's next move, and score points, while maintaining a sense of the style of the old French court. I loved the challenge, and it seemed that fencing was a sport bred in my bones.

One day I was participating in a round robin—a match in which you fenced with one opponent after another until you were defeated. My opponents, both men and women, included some of the city's leading fencers, all much older and more experienced than I. As I began to fence, I suddenly found that I was "in the zone." I was no longer just a pretty good fencer. I had tapped into the Essence of fencing. I was the sport, anticipating all moves, seeing all opportunities. I could not tire; endless waves of energy filled me. There was no possibility of besting me, and, one after another, twenty opponents came up and were defeated. *Quart, six, parry, advance, ehhhhhh la!* Strike to the heart. On and on it went, my Essence and the Essence of the sport in rapturous union of movement and esprit. A gallant élan filled me. I was all the great fencers who ever were—Scaramouche, Cyrano de Bergerac. I felt as if their spirits were joining with mine for one last great bout, until, after six hours of continuous fencing, the match was stopped, and I was declared the winner.

Why was it fencing that evoked my sense of Essence? Could it be genetic? On both sides of my family I come from generations of generals, warriors for whom swordplay was the highest art, learned in childhood. Was this then my ancestral skill looped into my chromosomes and casting a long arm into my own as I advanced and parried with the foil? Or could it be that fencing was a sporting fractal of my Essence, which takes on situations where I must make fast and accurate moves in order to get to the heart of things, be they corporations or cultures that require internal change or individuals who are seeking higher personal development? In all cases, I find myself within a formal context in which I must appear to play by the rules in order to reach the heart of the matter, to pursue the way in past the blocks and the parries confronting me. Or perhaps my warrior quality derives from a higher source, the archetypal face my Essence generally wears, that of the goddess Athena who, in later versions of her story, was born from her father's head fully armed, brandishing a sword.

I firmly believe that all human beings have access to an alternate or archetypal energy system that allows vital energy to mutate into extraordinary capacities and powers. Judging from the reports of enriched perception and knowing, such as accounts of mystical experience, heightened creativity, or exceptional performance by athletes and artists, we harbor a greater life than we know, one that informs our everyday functioning. This is the life of Essence, and reaching it, as William James told us, is "but giving your little private convulsive self a rest, and finding that a greater Self is there." In Essence we find ourselves hooked into perceptions and capacities that seem far beyond our own, and we gain access to knowings that transcend our given experience. In Essence we agree to relinquish those limited and limiting patterns of body, emotions, volition, and understanding that have been keeping us in dry dock, and we allow ourselves instead to become available to the extraordinary dimensions that we each contain for a larger life in body, mind, and spirit.

There is real science within this phenomenon of accessing Essence. The utter malleability of the body and mind, the psychosomatic complexity and polyphrenia of our natures, and the redundancy of many of our bodily processes make it possible for the transformational programs of Essence consciousness to work in various ways. When we tap into Essence, we unleash extraordinary abilities— rapid healing, overcoming pain, accelerated response time, and focus and endurance beyond our usual capacity. Then, too, consciousness has many levels beyond ordinary waking consciousness. The laws of local identity at one level of consciousness are not necessarily the same at other levels or, put another way, different domains of the psyche have different laws of form and function. This also explains why people in altered states of consciousness can often do things that they would not even think of doing in so-called ordinary states, such as extraordinary feats of strength and courage, as well as very rapid learning and productivity. Unexplored continents, entirely new geographies lie within our minds and bodies, with unique cultures and capacities. Traveling to these places with adequate maps, recognizing them as our soul's domain, and returning with their treasures is the active pursuit of Essence.

Essence is often activated by a particular geographic spot, as if Essence has for each of us a recognizable home place. I know the home place of my Essence. It is Greece. Each visit seems to render me available to an inner geography that calls me home. Two recent visits in particular were palpable experiences of Essence. The first was on my birthday, May 10, 1981, when my friend Gay Luce and I were leading a tour in Greece for about seventy of our students. We had come to Epidaurus, the site of the ruins of the Asclepian, the most important healing center of ancient Greece. The air was washed in brightness, and when we came to the place of the Abaton, where those who in ancient times needed healing gathered together to incubate their dreams, suddenly I was happier than I had ever been in my life. I knew this place, and it seemed that it knew me and welcomed me back. Something that was far older than my chronological years, older perhaps by thousands of years, called me for its own. Here, in Epidaurus, I was in Essence and Essence was in me. Then, when I thought it was impossible to know greater joy, Gay Luce came up to me knowing my state, for she was in a similar one. She and I had always felt that we knew each other of old and that meeting in the 1960s was merely taking up again a very ancient acquaintance. When we looked at each other in this place, it seemed as if space and time hurtled past us, and we were back then, thousands of years before, in classical Epidaurus, although some part of us had not left the present. We were suffused with "a sense sublime," a joy so great we had to step outside normal categories to be able to contain it. Indeed, it was many hours before either of us was able to speak or function at all, for that matter. We had joined a larger life, a longer life, and we had not yet learned how to use its organs. We had returned to an essential reality that for a few glorious hours opened the door to a world beyond calendars or precincts.

The following month, Gay and I created the ritual of the modern Asclepian and its dream incubation, hoping to restore for others the Essence of what was. In this extended process, which is always a part of my longer seminars, the participants don ritual clothing, dance, jest, create art and make music, perform dramas and tell tales, and spend the night together in sacred space having invoked a healing dream. In the morning, one or more of these dreams becomes the basis for the enacting of a rich and complex interpretation, which then often leads to a collective ritual of healing. *Kaire Asclepios!* (Hail, Asclepios!) we all chant in celebration of the healing power of this ancient form. In creating the modern Asclepian, Gay and I seemed to be recalling and reapplying from our collective memory what had occurred in the sacred temples at Epidaurus—a means of attaining not just a healing but a "wholing" as well. As happened in the ancient Asclepian, we seek to quicken the making of new connections between brain, body, mind, and spirit so as to bring one's entire self to a higher integration. These Asclepian rituals also were the roots of my creating in 1984 the Mystery School.

My second experience of knowing Essence in a place occurred, again on my birthday, in 1987, and again in Greece. My friend and associate, Peggy Rubin, and I were on a ferry traveling to Odysseus' home island of Ithaca. It had been raining heavily on the trip through the Ionian Sea, and the other islands appeared as looming ghosts in the heavy mists. I stood on the very front of the ferry, oblivious to wind and weather, as a sailor called out the names of the islands we were passing, "Zakynthos, Cephallonia, Ithaki!" As we rounded the corner into the main port of Ithaca, the sun suddenly broke through the rain and mist, hallowing everyone—me, Peggy, the sailors, and Ithaca herself in golden shafts of light. The incendiary air seemed part of some great ceremony, light sent by Hyperian as an investiture. Almost immediately we saw the sign in the small island within the harbor:

EVERY TRAVELER IS A CITIZEN OF ITHACA.

Again, my happiness was as bright as the air around me. I had come home at long last, like Odysseus. All those wanderings, meanderings—being blown off course, meeting monsters of recalcitrance and angels of opportunity, feeling surprised by joy and shocked by unspeakable circumstance, and too often caught for a long time on the island of frustration, and finally, finally called home to Essence, to Ithaca. Later, when we walked its streets, climbed its hills, sat over retsina and shish kebab in its cafes, watched its olives being pressed, its goats being milked, and its young girls dancing the ancient round dances, and when we investigated the places sacred to the memory of the school of Homer as well as to Odysseus and Penelope and the goddess Athena, I knew that those wanderings had all been worthwhile. I had been ferried back to my own inner home. Ithaca is a state of being.

These experiences taught me that some places are so strongly part of our existence that Essence returns to us there. Essence itself does have a locale apart from, though frequently primed by, these places sacred to our souls. Essence exists in a geopsychic realm that is within us, yet of a different order than the body. Essence grants an extended body and mind to the one who recognizes or wakes up to it. Then self-realization begins to happen naturally and spontaneously, like cooking on more burners. In this, Essence is not unlike David Bohm's notion of the primary implicate order of being that holds all things enfolded within it. Essence is your own special implicate nature. It is a radiance that changes and transforms everything it flows into. It contains the coded energies of change and evolution.

Essence invites us into an extraordinary partnership that becomes a dance, as music plays between the external and the depth selves, evoking our true nature from the welter of possibilities in the inner world. Nietzsche's query is essential: Where do these wise and creative things come from? The answer is the apparent chaos of the depth self. The music of Essence plays over this chaos, pulling patterns up from the depths.

How, then, do we rediscover our Essence and, through it, our greatness? In the wonderful book of conversations and letters exchanged between psychologist James Hillman and author Michael Ventura entitled *We've Had a Hundred Years of Psychotherapy—and the World Is Getting Worse* (San Francisco: HarperSanFrancisco, 1992), Hillman directs our attention to a large painting that Picasso did when he was ninety-one, the year before he died. The name of the painting is *Le Jeune Peintre*. It shows the artist, with an impish boyish face under a wide floppy hat, holding a palette board and brush in his hands. It is a haunting picture because, as Hillman says, it is a self-portrait of the deeper self of Picasso. It is the portrait of the daimon who haunted and inhabited him all of his life. We might think of the daimon as the ego of one's entelechy, the personification within one's psyche of the higher presence, which we have been calling Essence. Just a year before the end of Picasso's life, his daimon showed itself. "Here," it said, "this is who you are. Picasso, you are me, the ever-young painter. I am the clown, the innocent, fresh eye, the dark eye, the quick-moving Mercurius, the sentimental, bluish melancholy, the little boy. I am your ghost. Now you see who drives you, what has kept you fresh and eager, and now you can die." Hillman comments that *Le Jeune Peintre* is a portrait of the acorn painted by the oak. Or, to put in other terms, it is the portrait of the seed of the entelechy painted by the fully realized self. Hillman extends the idea by suggesting that Picasso's painting of his potentiating self confirms Islamic scholar Henri Corbin's notion that it is not my individuation but the individuation of my angel or daimon that is the main task; or, put another way, it is the entelechy self and its unfolding into Essence that is of primary importance. My local self is in service to my daimon, setting up my life so as to help in its becoming.

We can relate this notion of life's higher purpose to the images found in the depths of our psyche—images that provide important clues as to who or what within us is orchestrating the show. Corbin connects his interpretation of the daimon to the idea, drawn from Sufi mystical literature, of the *ta' wil*—the art of reading life. In doing *ta' wil*, Hillman quotes Corbin as saying, "we must read things back to their origins and principles, their archetype. . . . In *ta' wil* one must carry sensible forms back to imaginative forms and then rise to still higher meanings; to proceed in the opposite direction [to carry imaginative forms back to sensible forms] is to destroy the virtualities of the imagination."

Corbin's insight speaks to how we might view our lives more creatively. Just as the painting *Le Jeune Peintre* portrays a daimon who entered the world of space and time and found his individuation through the human being Picasso, so we can create our own unique image of ourselves and, in so doing, rediscover our daimon and its nature. Why is this so? Because as Jung and Hillman suggest, and I concur, the psyche consists primarily of images, and the primary activity of the psyche is imagining. We humans are essentially acts of imagination. Budded from the matrix of psyche, we bloom out of imaginal worlds from which we arise coded in myth and symbol. These imaginal and mythic worlds of the psyche operate continuously. They never sleep, which is why people often find their finest creations in dreams, when they are more closely in touch with their own ongoing creative source levels. Like the Aboriginal peoples of Australia, we live in the Dreamtime, the place where physical and metaphysical realities converge. Shakespeare said it best: "We are such stuff as dreams are made of. . . ." If at our core we are images, then our lives are the actualization, the out-picturing over time of the entelechy's image, what Michelangelo called the *imagine del cuor*. This core image is the ultimate sponsor of each person's life. Thus all the things that happen to us in the course of personal unfolding are secondary to the essential givenness of the image in the heart. Following upon Hillman's suggestion, you are not necessarily caused by your history, by what your parents and siblings did or did not do, by your schooling or the events of your early life. These serve to reflect and refract the primary image but did not create it. Before you were ever history, you were imagination. The image is the seed that contains both the psychic DNA and the motivating forces that shape the fully bloomed flower that you become.

How do you go about glimpsing this guiding daimon, whose special needs— some may even call them symptoms or idiosyncrasies—direct your life toward its possibilities? You don't start with the child and his or her particular traumas and woundings. Rather, you start with who and what you are now in your full maturity; you look at the leaves and the fruit and then work your way back to the roots—and not just any old roots, but often the gnarled and distorted ones that gave you your unique and peculiar shape. In these gnarled roots you may find the foreshadowing of the larger, more mature person.

Often the foreshadowing is found in a symptom. Manolete, the greatest and bravest of bullfighters, was so timid and terrified of everything as a child that he chronically hid behind his mother's skirts. Later, when he became a toreador, he took up the great red skirt of his cape and confronted and mastered raging bulls. Winston Churchill, whose golden tongue and equally golden pen forged a bridge of hope in a world darkened by war, was dyslexic, stammered until late adolescence, and was considered academically obtuse. Traditional psychology would say that each of these men compensated enormously in later life for their earlier problems. But to say so is to deny the greater mysteries of the psyche and its daimon, which are at play here. Hillman suggests, and my own studies of remarkable people agree, that in early life the daimon or angel knows the possibility for the adult life and acts to protect that possibility through symptomatic behavior so that it does not emerge before the person is ready to carry the genius that he or she bears. Thus the literary and linguistic genius of Churchill was shored up in dyslexia and a speech defect, while the immense courage of Manolete was preserved and protected behind an initial timidity. The talent can then grow undisturbed and unchallenged in other levels of the psyche, in the Dreamtime, as it were, for no one—sometimes not even the person who has the talent—is yet aware that it exists. It burgeons like a night mushroom beneath a protective cover of fallen leaves that look sickly and forlorn. The leaves are the symptoms that protect and in some strange way nourish the spores of the hidden genius so that it may arise at the right time, possessed of its own unique and unadulterated powers.

When I meet a child troubled by one or another inability, I always take it as a guiding principle not just to look at the symptoms, but also to focus on finding the child's guiding daimon and, thus, the child's potential abilities. As Hillman says,

> Psychology starts with an upside-down premise, that childhood is primary and determining, that development is cumulative, a kind of organic evolution, reaching a peak and declining. The early scars become suppurating wounds or healed-over strengths, but not necessary prunings for the shape of the tree; a shape ordained by the seed itself. Not only is childhood thus overvalued, but again is trapped in an organic, and melancholy model.
>
> Rather than developmental psychology, we should study essential psychology, the structure of character, the unalterable psychopathologies, the innate endowment of talent. (Hillman and Ventura, *We've Had a Hundred Years of Psychotherapy*, 68)

Like Hillman, I think it is important to begin by placing our roots in heaven, in the realm of creation and the archetypal patterns. Then we examine our lives to discover this pattern and its face, not only in childhood, but throughout our lives. Thus we start with what we are and read backward to what we already were as children—and to the daimon that was guiding the entire process. Margaret Mead used to say to me that by the time she was four years old, she was completely what she was. All that was added were the details. We have so overvalued childhood in America, and so overblessed that problematic inner child, that we have lost the power and purpose of the deeper directive force and image of our life, of which childhood development is only a small part, not necessarily the cause of who and what we are.

To find this deeper directive force, we turn again to archetypes. The word itself refers to the "first types" or "primal patterns" from which people derive their sense of Essence and existence. Quintessentially, archetypes are about relationship. It is easiest, perhaps, to understand this in psychological terms. Standard interpretations describe archetypes as the primary forms and constellations of energy that govern the psyche. Carl Jung observed that when archetypes are repressed—whether within one person or in an entire society—we are cut off from nature, self, society, and spirit. The mechanistic view of the world that we have inherited infects us with a split between subject and object (mind and body, inner and outer realities), between individuals and their relationships, and between the world of human culture and the natural realm of biophysical processes. Archetypes, in their finest sense, serve to heal these splits. As inhabitants of the We Are realm, archetypes bridge spirit with nature, mind with body, and self with universe. They are always within us, essential elements within the structure of our psyches. Without them, we would live in a gray, two-dimensional world. That is why even when archetypes are repressed, they bleed through into other realms of human experience, showing up in dreams, religious knowings, visions, artwork, ritual, love—and madness.

Unlike the daimon, which we have been discussing as the personal image or face our entelechy may wear in our consciousness, archetypes are shared constructs. We might think of them as greater daimons, which stand behind and inform the personal images of many individuals. Sometimes the archetypes manifest in their archaic forms as gods or goddesses or as legendary heroes or heroines of earlier cultures, but always such timeless beings ask to be seen in new and fresh ways; they ask to be regrown. Sometimes they show up as symptoms, because often we need the full shock of pathology in order to take them seriously. Seen from this perspective, the early symptoms of Manolete or Winston Churchill were also the announcement of the archetypal presence that was going to play out throughout their lives. Whenever they move into our awareness, both personally and collectively, archetypes and the old and new stories that they bring with them announce a time of change and deepening. I deeply believe that such is happening all over the globe. Because I travel so much, I have occasion to witness firsthand the changing of the archetypes as society changes.

Recently I found myself in a village in India on a Sunday. Everyone was coming in from the fields, tying up water buffalo and parking goats in order to sit around the village's one television set. In many of the over six hundred thousand villages in India, there is one television, which is watched by all. On this day, as on previous Sundays that year, all of India stopped whatever it was doing in order to watch the dramatization of the *Ramayana*. Prince Rama (an avatar of the god Vishnu) and Princess Sita (an avatar of the goddess Lakshmi) are the perfect traditional Hindu couple. He is handsome, noble, blessed with great strength and valor, while she is beautiful, virtuous, subservient to her husband, obeying him in all things. Due to a trick by one of Rama's father's wives, the couple is banished to a life of wandering and living in a forest for fourteen years. One day Sita is abducted from the forest by the demon Ravanna and carried off to his palace in Sri Lanka. With the help of an army of monkeys led by the sainted simian Hanuman, Rama is eventually able to defeat the demon and rescue his wife. He takes her back, however, only after he is convinced of her virtue and of the fact that she never succumbed to the wiles of the demon. Not a minute goes by in the Hindu world when this story is not enacted, sung, performed in a puppet show, a Balinese shadow play, or a stage or screen performance. It is the key myth of the Hindu psyche.

As we sat on the ground together watching the drama, I was greatly moved and entertained by the magnificence of the costumes and music, the great style of the performers and dancers, the beauty and munificence of the production. Why couldn't we have something like that? I asked myself. The villagers were as entranced as I, for this was religion, morality, and hopping good musical theater all in one. Suddenly, the elderly Brahmin woman who owned the television set and who was sitting next to me on the ground turned to me and said in lilting English, "Oh, I don't like Sita!"

"Pardon?" I was aghast. This was like a Sicilian Catholic saying she doesn't like the Virgin Mary.

"No, I really don't like Sita. She is too weak, too passive. We women in India are much stronger than that. She should have something to do with her own rescue, not just sit there moaning and hoping that Rama will come. We need to change the story."

"But the story is at least three thousand years old!" I protested.

"Even more reason why we need to change it. Make Sita stronger. Let her make her own decisions. You know, my name is Sita and my husband's name is Rama. Very common names in India. He is a lazy bum. If any demon got him, I would have to go and make the rescue."

She turned and translated what she had just said to the others who were sitting around. They all laughed and agreed, especially the women. Then the villagers began to discuss what an alternative story, one that had Sita taking a much larger part, might look like. It was a revisionist's dream listening to people whose lives had not changed much over thousands of years actively rethinking their primal story. It was like sitting in a small town in southern Mississippi, listening to Christian fundamentalists rewrite the Bible. Stunned and bemused, I suspected that I was seeing an early stage in the changing of a myth. No matter that it was ancient beyond all knowing; it belonged to an outmoded perception of women, and it had to change or go.

The beautiful production ended, and, following the commercial interlude, the next program that all of India was watching was the prime-time soap opera of several seasons ago, *Dynasty.* My hostess saw my chagrin at the comparative paucity of American television and, patting my arm said, "Oh, sister, do not be embarrassed. Don't you see? It is the same story."

"How can you say that?"

"Oh, yes, indeed," she continued, her head wagging from side to side. "It is the same story. You've got the good man. You've got the bad man. You've got the good woman. You've got the bad woman. You've got the beautiful house, the beautiful clothes, the people flying through the air. You've got the good fighting against the evil. Oh, yes, indeed, it is the same story!"

Thus are myths and metaphors recast, redesigning the human fabric and all our ways of seeing. It is our privilege and our particular challenge to witness and assist a new story coming into being. As actors in this new story, we are seeing the rise of new archetypes or, perhaps, the further evolution of old ones. Perhaps what I have described as Essence is what inspires such change over time, finding its expression not only in the transformation of great stories like the *Ramayana* but in the biographies of real men and women.

Such musings lead me to speculate that if Essence transcends our local lives, it may thread through a constellation of lives, as a kind of guiding oversoul that orchestrates One Great Life lasting for aeons but bubbling up from the cosmic womb in a series of incarnations. I am often asked what I think of reincarnation. Have we lived before? Will we live again? Or is this a sunlit journey to a sunless shore? Every year I receive a number of manuscripts from people assuring me that they are the reincarnation of some well-known figure and then, in endless prose, trying to prove it. I have received to date four manuscripts from Mary Magdalene, seven from Jesus Christ, an even dozen from Merlin, but none from the Buddha. (He evidently moved on to another plane.) I always reply that I think that the universe is so complex and diverse in its alternatives that to limit our continuity to just reincarnation is to do the universe a grave injustice. I suspect that many of our "memories" of other lives have other explanations, not the least of which is that we catch the fractal waves of similar folk in the field of our own particular style and history. We may be similarly quickened by the dominant Essence that comprehends the family of which we are a part.

Take me, for example. On the surface of it, I would seem to be an excellent candidate for claiming an earlier and very specific incarnation. One morning when I was about twelve, I woke up with a curious rhyme going through my head: "Hocus pocus, where is Proclus?" I had never heard of Proclus but resolved to find out. The information in my encyclopedia was scant. He had been a fifth century C.E. philosopher of the Neoplatonic school and one of the last directors of the Platonic Academy. Translation of his extant voluminous writings was difficult to find, and I didn't try. As the years went by, the name *Proclus* would recur occasionally upon awakening or drop into my mind out of the blue. I never pursued any formal study of his work, even in graduate school. Something seemed to keep me from it—a shadow around the name, something familiar and yet forbidden.

Then, several years ago, Peggy and I arrived in London, exhausted from giving seminars in Europe. As is our wont when we are in a city that has theater, we had planned to attend as many plays as we could, but I had a terrible cold and fever contracted in Germany and took to my bed. However, as an inveterate book buyer in the kingdom of bookstores, neither cold nor fever nor chills nor pains could keep me from my appointed task. Leaning on Peggy, I walked from the Great Russell Hotel to Dillons, a bibliophile's heaven. As soon as we got there, Peggy went upstairs to engage her penchant for British mysteries, while I stumbled around on the lower floors. My fever was mounting, and reality was becoming liminal. Nothing seemed either real or solid as I wandered, semi-hallucinatory, among the shelves. Finally I collapsed and lay on the floor. The British, being what they are, politely stepped over my supine form, as if nothing out of the ordinary had happened. I tried to get up but was so weak that it wasn't worth the effort. Instead I cast my gaze over the shelf by which I had fallen. The books facing me were Marianus' *Life of Proclus* and a study of Neoplatonic interpretations of Homer, with a very long section on the philosophy of Proclus.

I pulled out the biography and began to read. I was so astonished at what I found that I refused to get up even when Peggy found me and tried to take me back to the hotel. My life and that of Proclus seemed to be ancient and modern variations on the same pattern. He had traveled much, starting when he was quite young; had early shown considerable flair for oratory, philosophy, and theology; had been taken up by well-known scholars; and had become a teacher and, one gathers, a giver of seminars. His schedule was filled to overflowing with writing (he required himself to write two hundred lines a day), teaching, counseling, spiritual practices, and friendships. He made a study of many different religious traditions, honoring them and celebrating their rituals and gods, but he was especially devoted to the goddess Athena. In fact, when the Christians pulled down her giant statue in the Parthenon, he had a dream in which the words occurred, "The Lady will come and live with you." His home was within the environs of the Asclepian on the slopes of the Athenian Acropolis, so he was always close to the practical as well as the spiritual healing methods of the followers of Asclepios. He ran into trouble all his life with the more zealous of the Christians, who were always trying to close the Platonic Academy and the other philosophical schools of Athens. He was very active in community life, trying to help create a more ideal society for Athens. By invitation, he traveled to many cities in the Greco-Roman world, lecturing and advising on social and human development. He ranged widely and deeply in his studies, not only through philosophy and theology, but also through mathematics, physics, languages, theurgy (working with gods and archetypes), medicine, cosmology, poetry. He tried to integrate these studies and see the pattern connecting one to the other. He also had a gift for taking a great text, especially the *Dialogues* of Plato, and writing a commentary that allowed him, while giving an exegesis of the text, to amplify his own thought on many matters. He essentially ran an ongoing mystery school, and people from all over came to it, creating a bonded community of fellow seekers into the nature and practice of a richer reality.

Well now, I felt like saying, here we are again—the eternal return of the same person in a different form and time. *Plus ça change, plus c'est la même chose!* You'd think at least that they would give us a different scriptwriter: try my dad, now that he's in comedy heaven. The ruse, however, is in the very repetition. Rather than seeing my life as a repeat performance with the same old soul doing the same old things with a few variations, I would put forward a more cogent explanation. I propose that archetypes link individuals through time and space into an Essence family or, more broadly, an Essence party. For example, people like Proclus and myself who do the kinds of things we do might belong to the family or party of Athena. What Proclus and I call Athena may be the archetypal source of the Essence of similar incarnations. In other words, we of the family of Athena are being spored with similar energies and styles to help this archetypal person or greater daimon with "her" unfolding in the world of space and time. That is, one's local daimon, which I have called the ego of one's entelechy or life purpose, may itself be nested in a greater daimon or guiding archetype. One's individual entelechy is the bridge between the local life and the greater life that is its inspiration. Thus, I was spurred on to unfold my life in the way I have by an entelechy or purpose designed to bring me as close as possible to the high wisdom, compassion, and service personified by the greater daimon, "Athena," whom I share with Proclus.

Everyone, I suspect, has a relationship to a "field" or family of an archetype or greater daimon. Christianity would generally gather together most who profess to be Christians within the family or field of Jesus Christ, although in Catholic tradition, as in Hinduism, the family connection can be found through a special devotion to a saint or a god or goddess. In Hinduism, and especially in Buddhism, this devotion becomes the richly evocative practice of deity yoga, which is the spiritual path of the present Dalai Lama. One feels oneself partnered by an archetype and in one's meditation and life knows oneself to be the exotype in time and space of that archetypal being beyond time and space. Thus in deity yoga, one incarnates in one's spiritual practices the qualities and then the actual Essence of the spiritual personage. This one does by first dissolving into one's essential nature and then, in this emptied state, connecting and communing with the archetypal partner.

However one reaches them, archetypes may prove to be realities that our world of growing complexity requires for its sanity.

The communist official has asked me an impossible question. "Explain please, Doctor, exactly what an archetype is."

I bumble through a series of inadequate explanations. While she listens, she studies her own hands. It seems that she is making a cocoon with them. She speaks softly, and is that a tear coursing down her face?

"When I was very small, and we still had the old religion, I loved Kwan Yin with all my heart. Then, after the revolution, we broke with all the old ways and I had only the party and Chairman Mao. But that, too, is passing away." She opens her hands into a butterfly. "I know where the new archetype will come from. China is the great cocoon for the birth of the new archetype."

"Will it come from your political system?" I ask.

"Oh, no. It will come out of our hearts when they break open. Then the dream will become real, and the new archetype, the butterfly, will fly all over the Earth."

6

✦

BUDDY, CAN YOU PARADIGM?

It is August 1988. Virginia Satir, the luminous family therapist, "people-maker," and all-around facilitator of self-esteem and awareness, has recently been diagnosed with terminal pancreatic cancer. We talk each day—sometimes twice a day—by telephone from our homes at respective ends of the continent. Although we have long appreciated the other's work, we really don't know each other and have met on only a few occasions. Now, in extremis, she has reached out to me, since mutual friends told her they think I might be able to help her.

At first we share similarities: we are both tall, strong women with Texas in our backgrounds. We have both been educators and empowerers, both trying to see the larger story in the lives of those who come to us as students or clients. Both of us have given the world the illusion that we are extroverts, hearty and dramatic in our handling of people and events, although the truth is that we are very private people, much given to spiritual reflection and practice, and not as revealing as we let most people think. Each of us travels a stupendous amount, Virginia absent from her home giving

seminars around the world as much as 352 days of the year. Each of us is an enthusi-
astic appreciator and feels called to help people reconnect with their essential selves,
see a larger story, be part of a deeper life. But where Virginia's calling is essentially a
therapeutic one, mine remains focused on helping to shift the paradigm of who we are
and what we may yet become.

"That's just what I need now, Jean," Virginia says to me one day. "I know the emo-
tional factors in the growth of cancer. I know the family origins of it—after all, both
my mother and my aunt died of this same cancer at seventy-two, which is how old I
am. But I also know that this lovely body can continue to live. There are so many cases
of people going into remission; some of them have even been my patients. Help me
heal, Jean. Help me find my wholeness, so that I can turn my immune system around!"

At the age of fourteen, my life was blown open by grief, and I, too, was desperate
for some kind of healing. My father had been spending more and more time away
from home, which in the past would not have been unusual, since he had a studio
where he would often go to write, but now he rarely came home even at night. He
complained that our New York apartment was too crowded with Sicilians, my
grandmother and aunt having moved in with us. And there were other matters as
well; late at night I would often hear my parents arguing bitterly. Some years before, my father had met Polly Ferguson, and now he wanted to divorce my mother
and marry her. My mother was devastated, and when I found out I was, too. Dad
was my best friend and most interesting comrade. What would happen to the *Jean
and Jack Show*, which had been running almost continuously for fourteen years?
My wounding was a double one, my grief compounded by shame over my parents' divorce. I even tried to hide it from my classmates. They began to get suspicious, though, when they came to the apartment to see me when I was sick and
my father dropped by. My friends would remark that he acted like a visitor, not
like someone who lived there.

As if this was not enough sorrow and humiliation, I had just been "asked to
leave" New York's Performing Arts High School. I was considered a bad influence
on the student body, since I was always preaching about the purity of the artist.
These were the early great years of the school (the subject of the movie and television series *Fame*), when Clifford Odets taught playwriting, Sydney Lumet conducted the acting class, and Stanislavsky was God. Method acting, with its
emphasis on the "truth" of one's feelings and the development of sense memory,
seemed to me a sacred calling, so I was appalled by the way my fellow students
were taking on the personas of elderly thespian decadents like Tallulah Bankhead.
Like a very junior Jeremiah, the holiest of the holier than thous, I roared and in-
veighed against this worship and imitation of false goddesses and gods, convincing many of the girls to stop wearing the thick makeup they plastered on their
faces each morning, speaking of acting as a new priesthood that brought the
parishioners or audience to the truth of their souls, and generally making a nui-

sance of myself. Nor was I accepted at Brearley, then the apogee of girls' private schools. I had been asked during my interview what I thought was the highest ethical virtue and who I thought was the most important figure in history. When I replied, "A sense of comedy and Akhenaton, because he was the world's first theoretical monotheist," the interviewer blanched and told me that she thought I would be happier elsewhere. Of course, I had also flunked the math exams.

I then entered the only school that would take me, the Julia Richman Country School, and found there the best education I had ever had. Julia Richman was a huge stewpot of girls of every color, nationality, conceivable background, and experience. Puerto Rican gang members sat side by side with Jewish refugees from Dachau and Auschwitz and compared lives. Wealthy New York debutantes of suave voice and manner (the ones who also couldn't get into Brearley) played basketball with tough Irish and Polish girls who screamed encouragement in shrill and nasal tones, "TROW DA BALL OVAH HERE, YA JOIK!" A fractal loomed, and I loved it. Here was the world that both had preceded and would follow me throughout my life, a mix of cultures and styles, a great hodgepodge of human types—the full range of experience, all crammed into one school on 67th Street and Second Avenue.

I was accepted there immediately and soon was also given the opera *Martha* to direct. It was thrilling to be taught by wonderful teachers, especially the elegant and Athenalike Mabel Finnegan, my Latin teacher, who introduced me to the joys of ancient languages as well as to Homer's *Odyssey*. The *Odyssey* became and remains my favorite book, so much so that I later wrote my own book about it, *The Hero and the Goddess: The Odyssey as Mystery and Initiation.* Even back then, the story seemed to hold a deeper meaning for me but one that I was both too young and too full of my own youthful adventuring to encompass. I, too, had ended up on many islands full of unexpected challenges, had met strange beings who represented a spectrum of weird and wonderful archetypes, was shipwrecked with my family in nameless towns with no money, and, like Telemachus, the son of Odysseus, was waiting for my father to come home. Where, I wondered, was my Athena, who would persuade the other gods to let that happen?

Though I had not been much of an actor at Performing Arts, being more interested in preaching, I became a pretty fair performer at Julia Richman under the training of our English teacher, Catherine Jones, who became a lifelong friend. She entered me in a national Shakespeare contest; playing Viola in Shakespeare's *Twelfth Night,* I came in second out of thousands of entrants. Underneath and despite all of this, I was still seized by enormous waves of grief over my parents' breakup. I had read somewhere that running would help dispel anguish, so I began to run to school every day down Park Avenue, trying to race, like Odysseus at sea, ahead of the storm clouds of my grief.

One day, on 84th Street and Park Avenue, I ran into an old man and knocked the wind out of him. This was serious. I was a great big overgrown girl, and he was a rather frail gentleman in his seventies. But he laughed as I helped him to his feet and asked me in French-accented speech, "Are you planning to run like that for the rest of your life?"

"Yes, sir," I replied, thinking of my unhappiness. "It sure looks that way."

"Well, bon voyage!" he said.

"Bon voyage!" I answered and sped on my way. About a week later I was walking down Park Avenue with my fox terrier, Champ, and again I met the old gentleman.

"Ah," he greeted me, "my friend the runner, and with a fox terrier. I knew one like that many years ago in France. Where are you going?"

"Well, sir," I replied, "I'm taking Champ to Central Park. I go there most afternoons to . . . think about things."

"I will go with you sometimes," he informed me. "I will take my constitutional."

And thereafter, for about a year and a half, the old gentleman and I would meet and walk together as often as several times a week in Central Park. He had a long French name but asked me to call him by the first part of it, which as far as I could make out was Mr. Tayer.

The walks were magical and full of delight. Mr. Tayer seemed to have absolutely no self-consciousness, and he was always being carried away by wonder and astonishment over the simplest things. He was constantly and literally falling into love. I remember one time he suddenly fell on his knees in Central Park, his long Gallic nose raking the ground, and exclaimed to me, "Jeanne, look at the caterpillar. Ahhhhh!" I joined him on the ground to see what had evoked so profound a response.

"How beautiful it is," he remarked, "this little green being with its wonderful funny little feet. Exquisite! Little furry body, little green feet on the road to metamorphosis."

He then regarded me with interest.

"Jeanne, can you feel yourself to be a caterpillar?"

"Oh, yes," I replied with the baleful knowing of a gangly, pimply-faced teenager.

"Then think of your own metamorphosis," he suggested. "What will you be when you become a butterfly. *Un papillon, eh?* What is the butterfly of Jeanne?"

What a great question for a fourteen-year-old girl, a question for puberty rites, initiations into adulthood, and other new ways of being. His comic-tragic face nodded helpfully until I could answer.

"I . . . don't really know anymore, Mr. Tayer."

"Yes, you do know. It is inside of you, like the butterfly is inside of the caterpillar." He then used a word that I heard for the first time, a word that became essential to my later work. "What is the entelechy of Jeanne? A great word, a Greek word, *entelechy*. It means the dynamic purpose that is coded in you. It is the entelechy of this acorn on the ground to be an oak tree. It is the entelechy of that baby over there to be a grown-up human being. It is the entelechy of the caterpillar to undergo metamorphosis and become a butterfly. So what is the butterfly, the entelechy of Jeanne? You know, you really do."

"Well . . . I think that . . ." I looked up at the clouds, and it seemed that I could see in them the shapes of many countries. A fractal of my future emerged in the cumulus nimbus floating overhead. "I think that I will travel all over the world and . . . and . . . help people find their en-tel-echy."

Mr. Tayer seemed pleased. "Ah, Jeanne, look back at the clouds! God's calligraphy in the sky! All that transforming, moving, changing, dissolving, becoming. Jeanne, become a cloud and become all the forms that ever were."

And there was the time Mr. Tayer and I leaned into the strong wind that suddenly whipped through Central Park and he exhorted me, "Jeanne, sniff the wind." I joined him in taking great snorts of wind. "The same wind may have once been sniffed by Jesus Christ (sniff), by Alexander the Great (sniff), by Napoleon (sniff), by Voltaire (sniff), by Marie Antoinette (sniff)!" (There seemed to be a lot of French people in that wind.) "Now sniff this next gust of wind in very deeply for it contains . . . JEANNE D'ARC! Sniff the wind once sniffed by Jeanne d'Arc. Be filled with the winds of history."

Filled with the winds of history, and eccentrically empowered by Mr. Tayer, I was becoming quite a celebrity at Julia Richman High School, where I was running for president of the General Organization. What Mr. Tayer with his French mind meant as metaphor, I with my American literalism took as fact. I would wake up in the morning and take great sniffs of Joan of Arc, Shakespeare, Charlemagne, Madame Curie, and George Sand, the great French woman novelist whose novels Mr. Tayer had suggested I read. (Years later, the fractal wave of this suggestion brought the actress Judy Davis to several of my seminars to study my movements and demeanor, some of which she integrated into her characterization of George Sand in the movie *Impromptu.*)

With all these beings inside of me, and feeling remarkably polyphrenic, I had taken on a huge variety of activities. In athletics, I was teaching swimming, playing basketball (badly), and fencing (well) on intramural teams. I was directing and starring in school plays, selling Girl Scout cookies, participating in school debating forums, being a monitor for whatever needed monitoring, heading various academic and service societies, and occasionally doing my homework. After I won the presidency of the General Organization, my activities increased to include endless school government meetings, column writing for the school newspaper and magazine, involvement in citywide meetings with other G.O. presidents, and reading the Bible in school assemblies. As I told Mr. Tayer about all these activities, he would shake his head and say, "*Incroyable!* Jeanne, you are trying to do all the stages of evolution all at once. I wanted you to become a butterfly, not a continent."

Mr. Tayer himself was fully present to every moment; being with him was attending God's own party, a continuous celebration of life and its mysteries. He was so full of vital juice that he seemed to flow with everything. He saw the interconnections between things, the way that everything in the universe, from fox terriers to tree bark to somebody's red hat to the mind of God, was related to everything else and how all of it fitted into one great story. He wasn't merely a great appreciator, engaged by all his senses; he was truly penetrated by the reality that was yearning for him as much as he was yearning for it. He talked to the trees, to the wind, to the rocks as dear friends, even beloveds. "Ah, my friend, the mica schist layer, do you remember when . . . ?" I would swear that the mica schist would begin to glitter back. Mica schist will do that, but on a cloudy day? He treated everything as personal, as sentient, and addressed everything as *thou*. And everything that was *thou* was ensouled with being and *thou*-ed back to him. When I walked with him, I felt as though a spotlight was following us, bringing radiance and light everywhere. Even the poem that he inspired, "Rolling River," became golden. My English teacher, Miss Jones, submitted it to *National Scholastic Magazine,* where it won the gold medal for the best poem by a high school student in 1954.

I remember another occasion when he stood quietly by as a very old woman watched a young boy play a game. "Madame," he suddenly addressed her. She looked up, surprised that a stranger in Central Park would speak to her. "Madame," he repeated, "why are you so fascinated by what that little boy is doing?"

The old woman was startled by the question, but the kindly face of Mr. Tayer seemed to allay her fears and evoke her memories. "Well, sir," she replied in an ancient but expansive voice, "the game that boy is playing is like one I played in this park around 1880, only it's a mite different."

"How is it different?" Mr. Tayer asked.

"Well . . . I'd have to show you," she replied.

We noticed that the boy was listening, so Mr. Tayer promptly included him in the conversation. "Young fellow, would you like to learn the game as it was played many years ago?"

"Yeah, sure, why not?" the boy answered. Soon the young boy and the old woman were sharing old and new variations on the game—as unlikely an incident to occur in Central Park as could be imagined.

But perhaps the most extraordinary thing about Mr. Tayer was the way that he would suddenly stop and look at you with wonder and astonishment—a whimsical regarding of you as the cluttered house that hides the Holy One. I felt myself primed to the depths by such seeing. Evolutionary forces were called awake in me by such seeing, every cell and thought and potential palpably changed. I felt greened, awakened, and the defeats and denigrations of adolescence and even the departure of my father seemed partly redeemed. I would go home and tell my mother, who was still a little skeptical about my walking with an old man in the park, "Mother, I was with my old man again, and when I am with him, I leave my littleness behind." One simply could not be stuck in littleness when held in the lustrous and loving field of Mr. Tayer.

One day Mr. Tayer stopped suddenly in our walk down the street toward the park. He turned to me and asked, "Jeanne, what to you is the most fascinating question?" A long moment passed, and then I knew the answer. "It's about history, Mr. Tayer . . . and destiny, too, I think. I just finished reading that book you told me about, *Human Destiny* by Lecomte de Nouy." In fact, I'd been reading many of the books that Mr. Tayer had casually mentioned, Alfred North Whitehead's *Adventures in Ideas,* Henri Bergson's *Creative Evolution,* Plato's *Republic.* "How can we take the right path in history so that we even have a destiny? My friends at school all talk about the H-bomb, and I wonder whether I'll ever get to be twenty-one years old. And yet, Mr. Tayer, you always talk about the human future, as if we had a future. I want to know what we have to do to keep that future coming."

"We need to have more specialists in spirit who will lead people into self-discovery. Perhaps, Jeanne, you will be one of them."

"What do you mean, Mr. Tayer?"

"We are being called into metamorphosis into a far higher order, and yet we often act only from a tiny portion of ourselves. It is necessary that we increase that portion, but do not think for one minute, Jeanne, that we are alone in making that possible. We are part of a cosmic evolutionary movement that inspires us to unite with God. This is the lightning flash for all our potentialities. This is the great originating cause of all our shifts and changes. Without it, there is nothing but struggle and decline."

"What do you call it?" I asked. "I've never heard of it. Could it even have a name, something so great as that?"

"You are right. It is impossible to name."

"Try to name it, Mr. Tayer," I challenged. "I have heard that once things are named, you can begin to work with them."

The old man seemed amused. "All right, I'll try," he said. "It is the demand of the universe for the birth of the ultrahuman. It is the rising of a new form of psychic energy in which the very depth of love within you is combined with what is most essential in the flowing of the cosmic stream. It is Love."

I did not really understand what he was saying, but I nodded sagely and said I would ponder these things. He said he would also.

One day, toward the end of our time together, Mr. Tayer began talking to me about the "lure of becoming" and how we humans are part of an evolutionary process in which we are being drawn toward something he called the Omega Point, the goal of evolution. He told me that he believed physical and spiritual energy was always flowing out from the Omega and empowering us as well as leading us forward through love and illumination. It was then that I asked him my ultimate question, the one that haunted and continues to haunt me all the days of my life: "What do you believe it's all about, Mr. Tayer?"

His answer has remained enshrined in my heart. "*Je crois* . . . I believe that the universe is an evolution. I believe that the evolution is toward Spirit. I believe that Spirit fulfills itself in a personal God. I believe that the supreme personality is the Universal Christ."

"And what do you believe about yourself, Mr. Tayer?"

"I believe that I am a pilgrim of the future."

The last time I saw Mr. Tayer was the Thursday before Easter Sunday, 1955. I brought him the shell of a snail. "Ah, escargot," he exclaimed and then proceeded to wax ecstatic for the better part of an hour on the presence of spirals in nature and art. Snail shells and galaxies and the labyrinth on the floor of Chartres Cathedral and the great rose window there, as well as the convolutions in the brain, the whorl of flowers, the meanderings of rivers, and the circulation of the heart's blood were taken up into a great hymn to the spiraling evolution of spirit and matter.

"It is all a spiral of becoming, Jeanne." He looked away, his wan face seeming to see into futures that I could not. Minutes passed. Finally he spoke. "Jeanne, the people of your time toward the end of this century will be taking the tiller of the world. But they cannot go directly"—he used the French word *directement*—"but must go in spirals, touching upon every people, every culture, every kind of consciousness. It is then that the *noosphere*, the field of mind, will awaken, and we will rebuild the Earth." He took my hands and looked at me intently. "Jeanne, remain always true to yourself, but move ever upward toward greater consciousness and greater love! At the summit you will find yourself united with all those who, from every direction, every culture, have made the same ascent. For everything that rises must converge. Ah, so much I wish I could live to see it."

"See what, Mr. Tayer?"

He didn't hear my question. Instead, he seemed already to be seeing something else, in ecstasy. He began to speak in faltering but eloquent spasms. "All around us, to the right and left, in front and behind, above and below, we have only to go a little beyond the frontier of sensible appearances in order to see the divine welling up and showing through. See, over there, in that cherry tree, in that rock, in that child. By means of all created things, without exception, the divine assails us, penetrates us, and molds us. We imagined it as distant and inaccessible, whereas in fact we live steeped in its burning layers."

Mr. Tayer continued to speak about everything—war, pain, beauty, death, rebirth. He told me the present chaos was not the end of the world but the labor pains of a new Earth and a new humanity coming into finished form. At the end, his voice dropped, and he whispered almost in prayer, "Omega . . . Omega . . . Omega . . ." Finally he looked up and said to me quietly, "Au revoir, Jeanne."

"Au revoir, Mr. Tayer," I replied. "I'll meet you at the same time next Tuesday." For some reason, Champ, my fox terrier, didn't want to budge, and when I pulled him along, he whimpered, tail down between his legs, looking back at Mr. Tayer.

The following Tuesday I was waiting where we always met at the corner of Park Avenue and 84th Street, but he didn't come. The following Thursday I waited again. Still he didn't come. The dog looked up at me sadly. For the next eight weeks I continued to wait, but he never came again. It turned out that he had died suddenly that Easter Sunday, but I didn't find that out for a long time.

Years later, when I was in graduate school, someone handed me a book without a cover called *The Phenomenon of Man*. As I read the book, I found its concepts strangely familiar. Occasional words and expressions loomed up as echoes from my past—*metamorphosis, noosphere*. When, later in the book, I came across the concept of the Omega Point, I was certain. I asked to see the jacket of the book and looked at the author's picture. I recognized him immediately. Mr. Tayer was Teilhard de Chardin, the great priest-scientist, poet, paleontologist, and mystic. During that lovely and luminous year, I had been meeting him outside the Jesuit rectory of Saint Ignatius, where he was sometimes living. I like to think that just as I partially replaced my father in my companionship with Teilhard, perhaps he saw in me the daughter he never had, the one he could talk to, even though he was being crucified by his church. For those were the years when he was forbidden to publish anything of his giant spiritual and scientific vision, could not teach, mentor other priests, or discuss his larger work.

About twenty years ago, as one of the founders and vice president of the American Teilhard de Chardin Society, I told the story of my walking the dog with Mr. Tayer to a group of elderly Jesuit priests. One old man came up to me and said, "I know all about you!"

"You do, Father?" I responded. "How does that happen?"

"I was Father Teilhard's housemate at the Jesuit rectory in those years, and I used to ask him where he was going on those afternoons when he came back from working at the Wenner Gren Foundation and immediately went out again. He told me he was meeting with this jolly large young girl, and now I see that she was you." Thus I met my earlier fractal self.

When I reflect on that girl who was me, I realize that adolescence is a time of natural paradigm shift. One has left the nursery culture, feels deeply, waxes poetic, knows intensities of emotion, drowns in despair, rises in ecstasy. To have an elder call one forth in such a time of confusion is to stay awake and not shut down, as so many adolescents do. Because Mr. Tayer gave me friendship and stretched my mind, it stayed open at a time when it might have diminished or scarred over from grief. Adolescent rites of passage traditionally involve ordeals and rigors that result in physical or psychological wounding. With these wounds, however, come also the secrets of the culture—the elder mentor offering the young initiate rare knowledge into the nature of things. In its ideal form, the natural wounding of adolescence serves to break open the crust of childish habit. Under the aegis of a wise elder, the wounding, instead of devastation, becomes a doorway through which one can be called forth, as I was invited by Mr. Tayer to envision my butter-fly state. The seeds of destiny were awakened, and my entelechy was called to the front of the room of consciousness. I never forgot this experience, and I have tried over the years to establish programs for rites of passage in schools and clubs so that real wisdom teaching is imparted along with the initiatory dramas of adolescent transition.

More than anything, what Mr. Tayer taught me was to join the potentials of my local life to the potency of the larger life that dwells within us all—to see the universe as miraculous and, in so doing, become miracle literate. Seen through his eyes, what the world deemed extraordinary became the wonderful ordinary, and the numinous extended universe took up residence in human hearts and homes. To Mr. Tayer, humans were ubiquitous with stars and galaxies, Christ and Caesar, all minds, all hearts, all memories. He had access to the great connecting pattern. The hound of heaven that woofs at our heels, urging us onward, never goes away, because we belong to an extended universe that resides partly in heaven, partly on Earth. Woof woof, the hound seems to say. Remember the other part of yourself; remember where you also live. And so we are always driven to ask: Where do I come from? What is my place in the scheme of things? How do I serve a larger purpose? Why do I feel that I am constricted in this time, place, and body; where is my larger time, place and body; and how do I get there? Or, as Francis of Assisi put it, "What we are looking for is who is looking." We gaze into the mirror and start. "Who dat?" And who is looking beyond the eyes of that reflected who?

To see the miraculous in everyday life, however, requires training. It demands that we no longer fall into what Thoreau called the "profanity of the trivial" or what William Irwin Thompson refers to as "the collective cultural trance" that prevents us from seeing the basis of our divinity. Thompson writes in *Evil and World Order*,

> We are like flies crawling across the ceiling of the Sistine Chapel. We cannot see what angels and gods lie underneath the threshold of our perceptions. We do not live in reality; we live in our paradigms, our habituated perceptions, our illusions, the illusions we share through the culture we call reality, but the true . . . reality of our condition is invisible to us. (New York: Harper & Row, 1976, 81)

Why can some people like Mr. Tayer more readily see these cosmic connections, these points of entry into a larger universe, a fuller possibility? Perhaps it is because they have shifted paradigms, not just in thought, but in a way that affects their entire body-minds, thus affecting everything and everyone around them. Recently, speculative science has offered opinions about how and why such shifts happen. One view, from quantum mechanics joined to consciousness studies, holds that there is always a spectrum of probabilities concerning any event or happening. Normally, the mind-brain system expects a certain train of probable outcomes with regard to fortune or misfortune, health or disease, even happiness or unhappiness. These expectations are held as patterns of electrons moving toward certain ends. Make another decision, however, or hold a different expectation with intention, and the electrons bound up with the usual probability wave collapse. This permits new vectors of energy to emerge, which themselves are guided by the mind's new belief, and a new pattern of probability emerges.

Another popular current explanation for the paradigm shift draws on the arcane mysteries of hyperspace. The universe is redolent with many dimensions, or so hyperspatial physicists and mathematicians like Michio Kaku tell us. The fireworks that attended the Big Bang opened up a plenitude of frequency domains. However, interacting with other dimensions would require velocities faster than the speed of light. Thus space-time warps, whimsically called "wormholes," would be needed in order for objects (or us) to take a quick tunnel trip through adjacent dimensions. Finding such wormholes would be quite a job, requiring the services of a galactic Columbus, *Star Trek* notwithstanding.

Now, although our bodies may not be able to participate in other dimensions, our minds may well be omnidimensional. I believe that consciousness has the innate capacity to tune and modulate to different domains. Implied here is the notion that there are tunnels or psychic warp spaces and times within the field of consciousness through which different universes can be connected. Does this mean that the mind has the means to travel in time, to visit the time and place in ancient Israel when Christ delivered the Sermon on the Mount, to be present in consciousness at the signing of the Declaration of Independence? Is the past still present, nested in the many frequencies that make up the Mind of the Maker?

I have often set up exercises for my students in which they claim to have experienced these things. Is this just suggestion, the ravings of an altered state, or is it something else? I am not willing to close my accounts with reality and say it is "nothing but," for nothing but is never so. What seems to be true, however, is that by changing consciousness, we can experience more profound patterns of the universe. I find, for example, that when we are in mythic or spiritual levels of consciousness, we become citizens of a larger universe with regard to perception, time, space, dimensionality, and possibility. It is then, too, that our psychological makeup is less traumatized by past experience, is more capacious and capricious, and we feel extended into a multidimensional universe.

Perhaps that is why many myths tell of doors leading to other worlds. When we are living mythically or enacting an archetype, we seem to pass into a reality in which what had been latent becomes overt. As we have seen, myth seems to provide a wormhole into larger spheres of being, to uncode latencies for richer perceptions and ways of knowing. What we think of as paranormal phenomena may belong to another system within the universe, one that is mediated by archetypes. Archetypes bring larger patterns of possibility, evolutionary cadences, and a wider spectrum of reality into conscious knowledge and experience, and we feel these larger patterns as an influx of creative potency and sometimes even as paranormal experience. Rapid healing, for example, can be the result of the healer dissolving his or her local self and being filled with an archetypal or sacred image (not I but Christ through me does the work). By bridging oneself between here and the greater there, one enters into archetypal dimensions that may contain the blueprints of greater possibility, the primal stuff for social and creative change. Archetypal space-time may also contain the optimal template of a person's health and well-being. The job of the healer is to call that template back into consciousness so that it can work upon a malfunctioning body or mind, tuning here, correcting there.

People with the passion for paradigm shifts have also embraced the thinking of Nobel physicist David Bohm. He believes that the universe is constructed along holographic principles, wherein every part is related to every other part—indeed, contains at some level every other part. On the basis of quantum theory, Bohm suggests that there are two principal orders of reality. One is the primary order, which is implicate, enfolded, harboring our reality in much the same way as the DNA in the nucleus of the cell harbors potential life and directs the nature of its unfolding. This is an order of pure beingness, the grand frequency that contains all the other frequencies and dimensions. I find it consonant with the realm of Plato's forms or Whitehead's primordial nature of God. Buddhist and Hindu philosophies have similar metaphysical systems and psychologies to account for this primary order of pure potentiality. At this level of reality, there are no things or movements as we understand them. All is an undivided totality, an energy sea that transcends specification and knows neither here nor there. I see it as the realm that is at once the coalescence of all pattern and the living source of all caring. Along with Teilhard, I see it as the source of love and organicity, the lure of evolution, and the Mind that is minding. Thus I think of the primary order as the place from which the forms of reality are engendered. It is the order pervading all our processes, prompting our paradigm shifts, and potentially always available to us.

The eternal part of our consciousness is forever contained in this implicate order, but the greater part is caught up in Bohm's second-generation reality, that which is explicate, unfolded, manifest in space and time, filled with kittens and quasars and the need to connect with others. We all have it in us to travel back and forth between the two orders, for our brains seem to serve both as gates into God and holographic reducing valves that render God-stuff into structure and form. I have trained my own reality to be very fluid, moving back and forth between ordi-

nary and extraordinary realities, local and archetypal worlds, implicate and explicate domains.

My old friend botanist Rupert Sheldrake brings all this speculation together
when he states the very basis of paradigm shifts: things are as they are because
they were as they were. The laws of nature are not absolutes; rather, they are accu-
mulations of habits. A law like gravitation, for example, is a pretty well-fixed
habit, probably owing to the trillions of beings throughout the universe who give
it general assent. Yet yogis, swamis, and more than a few Catholic saints report
that in deep meditation or spiritual rapture, they have been known to bump their
heads on the ceiling, for rapture is nothing if not a paradigm shift. Laws change,
habits dissolve, new forms and functions emerge whenever an individual or a society learns a new behavior. This is because we are all connected through what
Sheldrake calls "morphogenetic fields," organizing templates that weave through
time and space and hold the patterns for all structures but that can be changed according to our changing thoughts and actions. Thus the more an event, pattern of
behavior, or skill is duplicated, the more powerful its morphogenetic field becomes. We know, for example, that people in the twentieth century learn to ride
bicycles and to use machines more quickly and effectively than people in the nine-
teenth century. Similarly, today's children and adolescents learn to use computers
and to write programs in ways that seem beyond the competence of their parents.
Or, as an adult friend once said when he couldn't get a computer program to
work, "Let's call in an expert. Get the kid next door."

Beneath the collective surface crust of consciousness, a new paradigm is growing, a paradigm so subtle, albeit pervasive through many lands and cultures, that
we do not yet know its name. Is it the no-name organic lure of evolution, the implicate God becoming incarnate in ourselves? Is it a convergence between what is
here and what is there on a grand scale, one that will shake the foundations of reality—the big shift itself? Cosmos emerges from chaos, as scientists tell us, and
present breakdown may be the plowing of the old order so that the seeds of new
becoming can be planted—at least, I dearly hope so.

*Virginia and I are working with healing imagery. Our mutual friend and student
Barbara Jo Brothers has offered me words and images that she feels would speak to
Virginia in a very deep way. Many of the images are rural, Virginia having grown up
on a farm; some relate to family, since Virginia holds families accountable for many
of the besetting problems of the human race.*

*"Virginia," I say over the phone, "this is not your cancer; it is your mother's. She
did not know how to let go of it, but you do. She did not know she had another choice.
You, however, are the champion of making choices."*

"I truly do believe that, Jean, and I choose life!"

*"Then, Virginia, let us go to a life-giving place. I want you to find yourself in a
cornfield. Breezes are rustling though the husks. Can you feel it?"*

"I certainly can!"

"Then feel the wind blowing away the chaff that is the cancer. Let the spirit of the wind sweep away the wild, uncontrolled growth. And let the cells that don't need to be there fall away. Ah, here comes a plow. Can you see it?"

"I not only see it, I'm the one who is doing the plowing. It's an old-fashioned wooden plow from the last century like we had in the field. I can feel the smooth wood of the handles."

"Virginia, tell me, what are your favorite concepts?"

"That's easy, Jean. Reconstruction and congruence."

"Then plow the cancer cells under the ground, so that they can serve as manure for your true growth, the kind that is congruent with who you really are. Let the matter that is these cancer cells be reconstructed into the blaze of greening, loving energy that can sweep you into your new form. . . . Now tell me what is happening to you, Virginia."

"I sense my essential self as a seed planted in this freshly plowed field, waiting for spring's warm moist light. Ah, now I feel the morning light pour deep into me like the morning sun. New life, good life is beginning in me. Now I must think about how I will use that life."

"Attend and listen carefully. You are safe now. You are deeply loved. You are being reconnected with your essential health."

Over the phone I hear Virginia give a little cry.

"What is it, Virginia?"

"I just felt a shift go though me, Jean. Something changed. Life moved in."

And so it goes, day after day, a cornucopia of healing images pouring back and forth across the telephone wires.

Life moves in, or if not, we court it, wallow in it until we feel the shift. During my fifteenth year, I was moved by my encounters with Mr. Tayer to try my hand at some adolescent mentoring, with wild and woolly results. During summer months of the years I was meeting with Teilhard, I was sent to Texas to visit my grandmother, Viola Bell Anders. As a result of my parents' divorce and my friendship with Teilhard, I was beginning to plunge more deeply into spiritual literature, and I arrived in Texas loaded with *The World's Greatest Scriptures*, the complete works of Thomas Aquinas, Plato, and Thomas Paine, and a variety of New Thought pamphlets. I was prepared to spend the summer reading and contemplating.

My grandmother had other ideas. She had me doing the laundry every day for the genteel boardinghouse that she ran. That was a lot of sheets and pillowcases. When I countered that I had more important things to do with my time, such as searching for new outlets for my "mind's evolution," she accused me of putting on airs and thinking myself better than I was. She herself had a brilliant mind, far more parochial than Mr. Tayer's expansive one, but full of surprising leaps and deep crannies of factual knowledge. Her friends assured her that had she been born a little later, she probably would have been governor of Texas. I have no reason to doubt that, for she surely had political genius and ran the town of Commerce, Texas, the Baptist church, and most of the women's groups, including the DAR, with an iron fist. She was the Boss Tweed of east Texas, and few candidates could get elected without her support. A woman of striking appearance, almost six feet tall, she had natural platinum blonde hair and an hourglass figure, was a splendid pianist, had a wide and deep acquaintance with literature, and was considered the finest hostess and conversationalist for miles around. Elegant and extremely feminine, she was also as strong as a horse and only recently passed away at close to a hundred years old. But then she was in her prime, a woman of many gifts and shadows; we called her "Mud."

She had divorced my grandfather, Jasper Houston, a man of kindly but low-keyed disposition, while he was convalescing at a TB sanatorium and gone on to marry one of the richest men in east Texas, Curtis Anders. She placed my father, then only seven years old, with her parents and visited him sporadically. Dad told me that whenever she would arrive, he would run up to her, arms open; instead of embracing the little boy, she would immediately turn him over on her knee and give him a thorough thrashing. She told him that the punishment was for all the bad things he would do until she saw him the next time. All his life my father tried to please his mother, writing her long interesting letters weekly, sending her presents, visiting whenever he could, but she rarely responded to his overtures. This scarred his soul and made it difficult for him to value his own accomplishments. I was aware of all this that first summer I stayed with her and was very angry about how she continued to treat my father.

My war with Mud began the day I arrived, when she took me walking through the streets of Commerce to show me the town and introduce me to her friends. She suddenly spotted her black maid who was just turning the corner, sheepishly trying to hide the pail she was carrying.

"Beulah, what is it that you've got in that pail?" Mud asked.

"Nothing, ma'am," the frightened Beulah replied.

"Beulah, show me right now what's in that pail!"

Beulah reluctantly took out a potato.

"You stole that potato from me, didn't you, Beulah?" Mud charged.

"Yes, ma'am."

"Then you are dismissed from this moment." With that, my grandmother fired the woman after many years of service.

"You can't do that, Mud!" I exclaimed, incensed. "You can't take away a person's job just because of a measly old potato. Why, I bet you don't even pay her enough to keep body and soul together."

"You keep quiet, girl," she admonished. "You're just a smart-aleck Yankee Eye-talian who knows nothing about how to treat the Negras. Furthermore, if you feel so sorry for her, you can just start doing her work, Miss Eye-talian Smarty Pants."

That's how I got to do the laundry.

Between fights, we had deep and thoughtful conversations on spiritual and psychological subjects. Mud was capable of a most remarkable display of intellectual fireworks, and I would reciprocate as best I could. About the middle of that first summer, I finally earned some grudging respect, and one morning she called me down to say, "Jeanie, I see that I can never change you. You are what you are, and I think it wise not to stop you from becoming whatever you are, as I was stopped when I was your age. So I will give you your freedom to do whatever you wish, if you get your chores done."

Given that release, I prepared myself to metamorphose into whatever it was that I was becoming. I arranged to do the laundry and the ironing starting at four every morning. That way I would be finished by nine and could sneak out to meet the boys of my gang. In my spare hours, I had met a group of teenage boys who had nothing much to do after they finished their chores. It was too hot for sports, and most families didn't yet have television sets, so they just moped and hung out, waiting for someone to give them something to do. I had first met them when I was passing the movie theater. They were standing bunched together and hooted at me as I walked by.

"Hey, Yankee girl, how come you talk so funny?"

I stopped in my tracks. "You think I talk funny, do you?"

"You sure do."

"Well, I can talk even funnier than that." I proceeded to regale them with several dozen jokes from my father's collection. After that, they were mostly hooked, and somehow over the remaining weeks, I became their spirit leader, the one who came up with ideas for what to do next. I had found a motorbike in the garage, and as motorbikes were big that year, we would all take off together on bikes and hit the towns around Commerce. When I returned the following year, we graduated to motorcycles, and I began my career as a teenage messiah.

As I recall that summer, it unfolds before my inner vision like a foray into virtual reality: I am standing on a rock exhorting my followers, now a larger group of boys—twelve, as a matter of fact. I am wearing white shorts and a white shirt held together by a big black belt with a silver steer's head on the buckle. My outfit is completed by a battered pair of black cowboy boots and a cowboy hat. My hair is very long and not styled in any particular way—sort of hanging all over the place (as it still is).

"Are you with me, guys?" I exclaim.

"You bet. Sure are. Hee Haaa!" they respond with enthusiasm.

"Okay, then, we'll get on our motorcycles and go from town to town. We'll stop at the farms and the ranches, wherever there're people who need us. God will guide us!"

Foster John Higgins, the doubting Thomas of our group, interrupted. "Our money will run out pretty fast, Jeanie. What will we do for food?"

"We'll do odd jobs. Then we'll share our prosperity with the poor and the hungry. Every day, all along the way, we'll meet people in despair—people who will change because we'll see them differently than they see themselves. My friend Mr. Tayer, back in New York, looks at folks that way, and I can teach you all how to do it." (Even then I was into shifting paradigms, although this one may have been an uphill battle—shift one, slip back two!)

This notion did not seem to interest the boys much, but the idea of traveling certainly did. Dick leaped from the ground in a wild burst of enthusiasm, "They'll hear our motorcycles; they'll see our fires at night."

I continued on the same bent, "We'll increase their joy; we'll recharge their rundown hopes!"

My sort-of boyfriend, Floyd, chimed in, "Wherever we've been, they'll tell stories about us."

"We're gonna be famous, Floyd," I informed him matter-of-factly. "You've got to expect that!"

Then LeRoy, the biggest boy in the group, sixteen years old and 240 pounds, stood up and announced, "We'll b-b-be le-le-legends."

I rose into rapture. "The kindness and goodness of our actions will reverberate through history. What we have done and who we were—the happiness we have brought—will become eternal in the telling. Our deeds will multiply, and people will be comforted and transformed by our example."

"Everyone will imitate us," Floyd whooped. "The world will be renewed."

Suddenly the boys began to leap for joy, wrestle, and dance in an all-out cross-cultural puberty rite. It looked like a mixture of the Zuni rain dance, the Irish jig, and the Twist. Indian war cries and rebel cheers were freely interspersed with shouts of "real cool, Daddy-O" and other mantras of the fifties. Finally, they collapsed on the ground, grinning at the sky. Cap Holiday summed up everybody's feelings when he sighed, "It gets more and more exciting every time we talk about it."

My sort-of boyfriend, Floyd, abruptly sat up, his mind suddenly filled with strategy, "But now we gotta start doing something about it. Ya'll been earning money after school during the summer with your jobs, and it looks to me like we oughta be ready to go in three weeks—just before school starts."

"Meanwhile," I said enigmatically, "we can start practicing."

I walked over to the big tree under which we had parked our motorcycles. I took out a rag and began polishing the dilapidated but still-running Harley one of the boys had loaned me.

"What do you mean, Jean?" Billie Bob asked.

The other boys fell in behind him. I continued polishing. "I figure that tomorrow we'll get on our motorcycles and go over to the fair at Greenville and see what we can do for the folks over there. We'll set up"—I made a great flourish and snapped the dirty rag—"a saving booth!"

"Hey, that's a great idea."

"What does she mean by a save—?"

"That's a crackerjack scheme, Jean."

"I always wanted to sit behind a saving booth."

"What'll we do at a saving booth?"

"Hey, Jean where do you get your marvelous ideas?"

"I have insights," I said laconically, while returning to my polishing. "I have insights," I repeated with studied nonchalance.

LeRoy cut in in his slow but steady way, "Yeah. I s-still c-can't get o-o-over the ins-s-s-sight y-you t-told me b-bout last w-w-week. How y-you're the re-in-car-na-na-tion o-of J-J-Je—."

"LeRoy!" I shouted, trying to stop this little divine revelation.

"Huh?"

"You're getting bigger and stronger every day, LeRoy. Let's see, come on up here on the rock." I climbed up after him and bent his arms into a classic muscle-man pose.

"Why, do you know you're as finely muscled as a Greek god? Why, I imagine if you'd lived in ancient times, you would have been an Olympic victor with a laurel wreath wrapped around your head. Odes would have been written to your physique. Kings and conquerors would have come across the seas to lay praising poems at your feet."

"Gee, th-that w-w-would have b-been s-s-s-swell."

"Tell us, LeRoy," I commanded, "tell us how you achieved your strength."

"The j-jersey calf. I got it b-by l-l-lifting the j-jersey c-c-calf. Ev-e-very day since it w-wa-was a little b-b-b-biddy th-thing. Ev-very day I'd g-go in th-the l-lot and l-l-lift it. And wh-wh-while it g-got heavier, I r-r-reckon I g-got s-s-s-stronger, c-c-c-cause of . . . c-c-c-c-cause it g-got h-heavier, uhh, and n-now it's a b-big old th-thing, and I c-c-can s-s-s-still almost p-p-p-p-pick it up off th-th-th-the g-g-g-ground."

"Splendid, LeRoy," I crowed. "That's what I call self-discipline."

"Th-thank you, Jeanie. Thank you v-v-very much."

"But splendid as that is, there is still something greater lurking in your spirit."

"Uhh . . . uh . . . w-what is th-that?"

"*Mens sana in corpore sano*," I quoted, remembering Mrs. Finnegan's Latin injunctions. "A strong mind in a strong body."

"Jeanie, that will never be," Foster John objected. "LeRoy's pretty near kin to that cow, in brains, anyway."

I turned to the laughing boys with a surprised and hurt look. Their laughter died away, and they became embarrassed and self-conscious under my stare. Quietly I said, "LeRoy is in many ways the nicest among us. LeRoy, would you do me a big old favor?"

"Sure w-would, Jeanie!"

A positive-thinking tract by Emmet Fox that I had just read popped into my mind.

"A seven-day mental diet. That's the secret to your success, LeRoy. Just like with that calf. You apply yourself every day to putting muscles on your brain by studying for two or three hours. If you can fall into that pattern for seven days, you can do it for the rest of your life. Pretty soon you will be as smart as any of us."

I had another idea, drawn from my talks with Mr. Tayer.

"And I want you to think about something else. What is the butterfly of LeRoy?"

"Bu-bu-bu-bu-butterfly?"

"Oh, never mind." My mood changed abruptly as I remembered my plan. "But back to our original proposition. Our motorcade to the distressed multitudes, our caravan of comfort!"

My voice rose as I felt myself inspired by who or what I did not know, but I felt I'd better keep it orthodox for the boys. "I can do all things through Christ who strengthens me. Oh, fellows! Our destiny mounts surging, pounding, the mysteries of the universe, the Omega Point—uh, the mysteries of the universe become our nerves and sinews, and we . . ."

The boys moved in close. One of them, Joe MacLibby, punched Floyd's arm. "Floyd, she's onto it! Go ahead and ask her!"

Another boy agreed. "She knows, Floyd, go ahead and ask her."

Still up there on the rock, I looked down at Floyd. "Yes, Floyd, go ahead and ask me. You think I don't know what's in your minds. I know what you want to ask me! And it's true! *I can heal!*"

I'd been keeping this under wraps for a long time, since my father always laughed over my forays into healing bugs, curing turtles, and attempting to raise hair on his balding head. Actually, I had been trying to develop healing hands since I was a small child. Now seemed to be the moment to try something big and to try it in public.

From the boys came an outcry of animal noises, groans, grunts, choking-on-a-bone kinds of sounds. That didn't faze me. I was riding a tide of new feelings. I remembered the performance I had seen Katherine Cornell give as Shakespeare's Cleopatra, especially the moment when she stretched out her arms and said, "Give me my robe. Give me my crown. I have immortal longings in me." I too stretched out my arms and said, "Something is happening to me. A power! A power! I must reach out."

Behind my closed eyes, I heard a wail, a voice like a beagle baying at the moon, "Le-Roy! *Leeee-roy!*"

I opened my eyes to see Miss Mary Maude drifting into the lot wearing her old housedress, her stockings rattling around her ankles, her ancient mangy dog, MacDuff, tottering a few steps behind her. A sudden shudder went through the boys, a well-deserved frisson, for Miss Mary Maude was thought to be more than a bit "tetched." She had been a schoolteacher for many years but also had become the repository of the town's secrets. In the past she had been closemouthed and responsible, but now, in her eighties, no barriers remained between her mind and her mouth. When she spoke, skeletons would fall out of closets. She would mutter horrible secrets, make known weird alliances, publicize sins and suicides. What was worse, she was mantic, oracular, her dreamy eyes filled with strange knowings. She had gained a curious vision of tomorrow, as well as a sense of *kairos*, the loaded time when things could change or open up for people and places. Such was the case as she glided toward LeRoy, his huge form looming over her frail one. Lifting her hand up to touch his face, she said, "Where is your tongue? Go find your tongue, LeRoy."

She then pointed to me and said, "There it is. It's right there in her hands. Go on. She's waiting for you, boy."

My knees turned to water, but there was no doubt about it; my hands were tingling. "Miss Mary Maude, I-I don't . . ."

"Your time is here, Jeanie," she announced. "It's all around you. You feel it, Jeanie? You feel the tingling?"

In confusion, I lifted my trembling hands, only to discover that not just my hands were shaking but my whole body as well. A thought went through my mind. Was this method acting at its best? Had Performing Arts really gotten its hooks in me, or was this real? "Come on, body, stop shaking!" I told myself, but it wouldn't stop. "My God, this is *real!*"

I backed away from the group in bewilderment. I needed to get away. I knew I was at a threshold, and I wasn't sure I wanted to cross it. Seeing my motorcycle, I jumped on, started the motor, and began to take off. Miss Mary Maude called after me, "No use in running away, Jeanie. Your time will always catch you."

I tore through Commerce, Texas, as if the Furies were after me. Looking over my shoulder, I saw the boys following me in twos and threes on their bikes. Last to follow was a reluctant LeRoy. Through that hot, dusty August afternoon, we raced toward a destiny that we didn't know. We roared through tiny, dusty villages and mesquite-covered hills, kicking up the red earth as we passed through towns with names like Dot and Bugtussle.

After a while we stopped at our regular eating place, The Tortilla Flat. LeRoy was first through the door. He shoved a coin into the jukebox, pushing any button as he collapsed on top of the plastic sphere. I remember the music; it was Carl Perkins singing "Blue Suede Shoes." The boys piled in and crammed themselves into a couple of booths. I went to sit away from them at the end of the counter. LeRoy rose from the jukebox, breathing heavily, and slowly made his way to the other end of the counter.

The waitress took the orders. "Your usual, LeRoy?" she asked. "Your usual, LeRoy?" she repeated. No response. "Well, I'll just get you your usual, LeRoy." She brought him the Sky-High Tortilla Special.

I ordered nothing; I couldn't eat. LeRoy and I stared at each other, eyes on a direct line across the curving counter. We became at that moment the haunted and the hunted. LeRoy, famous as an eater, pushed away his plate of oozing tortillas. The boys were watching us all the while, trying to eat their food but growing more and more distracted by the drama at the counter. The energy between LeRoy and me was higher than any tortilla special, more crackling than any nacho chip.

The waitress came over to LeRoy. "C'mon, LeRoy, eat your food. I put extra hot sauce on it for you." She gave the plate a little shove toward his ample belly.

LeRoy looked at the food in revulsion, leaped up, went over to the jukebox, and began to dance a solo lindy hop. I went over, took his arms, and we began to dance together, fast at first and then, when our eyes connected, winding down until it seemed we were dancing in slow motion. At that moment, there was no one left in the world except me and LeRoy and the strange destiny to which we were both being called.

Floyd got up and left. The boys piled after Floyd, the food on their plates mostly uneaten, LeRoy and I following reluctantly behind. The power was building up between us, and we had to let it lead where it would.

Back on the bikes, we went racing toward the setting sun, the road uncoiling like a snake with a purpose. The dust in our throats caused us to stop briefly at a filling station, where the boys bought a couple of Cokes apiece, each guzzling down one with his right hand while his left hand held the other in wait. LeRoy began to drink his bottle of Coke but then stopped while I tilted mine in libation to the Earth. Why I was doing this, I did not know. It was just happening. Both of us watched in fascination as the droughty red Earth drank up the Coca-Cola. When the Earth had swallowed its last slurp, LeRoy and I hooked in again. Now it seemed our eyes were meeting at another level, a level in which anything was possible, an open moment.

Climbing onto the bikes again, we rode until we found a grassy mound, brown parched but waiting, on the property of a Methodist summer camp. It seemed to me the kind of place associated with fairy dances and spirit convocations. The light had changed to an end-of-the-day kind of light that promised an opening between the worlds. I climbed the hill, the boys following, LeRoy straggling behind. Bathed in the westering sun, I turned to LeRoy and said softly, "Come here, LeRoy."

The boys backed away. LeRoy was scared. A tear coursed down his cheek. He tried to speak but could only make stuttering sounds. I became stronger. "Come here, LeRoy!"

Floyd got behind him and gently pushed him forward, "Go on. Go on." This time I held out my hands to him. "*Come here, LeRoy!*"

LeRoy gave me his hands. I held them very tightly. A very faint thought still coursed its cynical way along the back of my mind. Was I acting? Was this real, or was it showbiz? If Dad were here, he would laugh the whole thing away. But Dad wasn't here anymore. Suddenly, I exploded in agony, shouting, "God, God!" and broke into violent sobbing. It was as if a world was choking its way out of me, and I could not stop it. The boys were shattered at this sight, as was my own inner observer. I rarely, if ever, cried and then only at the death of animals. But this was something else—almost like giving birth—autonomous, unquenchable, its own unique creation. Slowly I came out of it and, looking up at LeRoy, said weakly, "Talk to me, LeRoy. You can talk to me now."

"What do you want me to say, Jeanie?" he asked. Then loudly and triumphantly, he proclaimed, "*What do you want me to say?*" He ran his tongue around his upper lip several times. "I don't stutter. *Listen!* I don't stutter anymore. I'm healed." Then, speaking with great deliberation, he announced, "I can say anything I want to, and my tongue won't get twisted."

LeRoy looked around, his eyes blazing, searching for something to say. It was as if all the bottled-up talk, poetry, passion, and yearning, all the things he could never have said but now could, would soon be pouring out of him. Every one of us was entranced, watching, waiting. I knew, and I thought the boys knew too, that the first thing LeRoy would say would be the words of our destiny, the true speech giving us our true path, our orders from Spirit.

LeRoy must have taken three full, endless minutes to decide what he was going to say, and when our tension and expectancy were at its highest, he finally proclaimed with the power of revelation, "YOU CAN BE SURE IF IT'S WESTINGHOUSE!" He added a further insight: "Pepsi-Cola Hits the Spot, Ten Full Ounces That's a Lot." He ran around to each of us, declaiming. Wild, truculent, he unleashed a cascade of commercials, a catharsis of advertisements: "If I only have one life to live, let me live it as a Clairol blond. Winston tastes good like a cigarette should. The little old winemaker me. Good to the last drop. A little dab'll do ya." The stores of his mind continued to unload themselves through his galloping mouth. "It's what's up front that counts! Does she or doesn't she? Double the flavor, double the fun, doublemint, doublemint, doublemint gum. Mutual of San Antonio puts the sure in insurance. Use Ajax, boom, boom, the foaming cleanser. Shut the door to the pimple problem. Friends, would you like to win a free trip to Paris?"

The boys were horrified and began to move away, backing off toward their motorcycles. Finally, only LeRoy, Floyd, and I were left at the mound.

LeRoy was unstoppable. "Have gun will travel. Protects all day without irritation. The breakfast of champions. No more ring around the collar. See the USA in your Chevrolet. L & M has got the secret that unlocks the flavor. Indescribably delicious. New York's a great place to visit, but I wouldn't want to live there. Sing along with Mitch. Mickey Mantle. I dreamed I went to the opera in my Maidenform bra."

Finally, Floyd shouted in front of his nose, "LeRoy, if you don't stop talking, I'm going to jerk a knot in your tail!"

LeRoy threw back his head and hooted in glory. "Gollee bum! I gotta show my mama." Slapping my hand as he went by, he said, "See you later, alligator."

"After a while, crocodile," I added limply.

LeRoy went back to his bike, yelping and yahooing all the way. I followed briefly and then collapsed against a tree. "Where is everybody?" I asked.

"I guess they're gone, Jeanie," Floyd told me.

"Why?"

"You healed him, Jeanie. I guess they never saw anything like that before!"

"But God's grace was in me. I wasn't acting. I was so full. Why did they leave?"

"LeRoy's reaction was . . . uh, sort of unexpected."

"But there was so much love. Where is it now?"

"I love you, Jeanie," Floyd said.

I touched his shoulder, smiled weakly, and started to walk aimlessly through the woods. Floyd followed me. After this last admission, he was embarrassed, and for a while he couldn't say anything. Finally, he explained. "Jeanie . . . don't . . . don't be sad. You did a great thing, Jeanie, really you did. I was so proud while it was happening. I was scared, too, because it was holy, kind of. Hey, Jeanie, I have a great idea. Tomorrow we get you to start practicing. We'll go over to Miss Mary Maude's house, and you can heal her dog MacDuff of the mange. Then the next day, I take you over to my uncle Jimmy Joe's, and you cure him of the shingles. Jeanie, I figure by the time September comes, you'll be up to where's you can raise the dead."

"Shut up, Floyd," I responded. At that moment I decided to leave my career as a traveling teenage messiah and become something more controllable—an intellectual.

LeRoy may have been the most outlandish fractal of my career as a healer, but, looking back, I realize that I have always known that I had a gift for healing. I persist in thinking it a natural talent given to all human beings, and certainly to a number of cats and dogs, and I have taught thousands of people to think the same and to go about the business of healing as a normal and natural phenomenon.

One of the most reliable techniques that I teach is actually the simplest. I ask the healer and the one to be healed to sit or stand together. The healer asks the one to be healed, "What is wrong, or what hurts, or what is the nature of the discomfort?" After she is told, the healer asks, "On a scale of one to ten, with one being normal and ten being as bad as it can be, where are you?" The person may reply that she has a headache and finds the pain to be about a seven. The healer than asks the person with the headache to think of a healing archetype. This could be many things—an actual sacred personage, like Jesus or Buddha; some god or goddess; some well-loved person, past or present; or it could be something from nature, like a waterfall, a cool and flowing stream, a magnificent tree, a sunbeam. The healer will also hold a healing archetype in mind and gradually move into a sense of continuity or even identity with that archetype. I use the great archetypal physician of the ancient world, Asclepios. Holding this archetype moves awareness away from the place of discomfort and connects it to a working, creative force, whose only desire is to heal. One moves, therefore, from the This Is Me of local pain and illness to the We Are, where the discomfort can be mediated and redeemed by archetypal energies that are themselves larger than the illness.

This done, the healer then places her hand about an inch above the open palm of the person to be healed. She asks her partner to tell her when she senses the special click signifying that the energy fields of the two have connected. It is a very palpable thing, this sense of interacting fields, and can be as subtle as a whisper or as strongly charged as an electrical current. We know from the studies of Harold Burr and Leonard Ravitz at Yale over many years as well as from work by Robert O. Becker in Upstate Medical Center, New York, and Victor Inyushin in Russia that energetic fields—shells of electromagnetic resonance or a pattern of plasma flow— surround each living organism. When an organism is in a weakened state, the weakness can be detected in the field and the field can be strengthened at that point. I explain to my students that what we now call vibrational healing may well be an important part of medicine in the next century. But for now, we must rely on the ability of one human being to act as a battery charger for another.

After the sense of connection is made, the healer, reminding the one to be healed to hold on to the image of the archetype, places her hand about a half-inch above the area where the discomfort is being experienced. The healer becomes aware of herself as a pure flow of energy that is serving to bring a more optimal frequency into the field of the other. She can even say words like, "As your field is being re-energized, so your brain is now being activated and knows exactly what to do to send healing as well as to restore your body to its best possible function- ing. And that is happening now." Often the healer will feel certain spikings of en- ergy, and at that point, it is generally the case that the field has been restored in that area. From long experience, I have discovered that these surges of current in the healer's hands are felt in the one being healed as moments when there is a dy- namic change for the better. Every so often, the healer asks the person being healed, "Where are you now on a scale of one to ten, remembering that ten is ter- rible and one is feeling just fine." In most cases, the person will report a drop in numbers from, say, seven to five to three or even lower. The healer keeps working until the person gets as close to one as possible. Then I suggest that the healer tell the person being healed to take a brief walk for about a minute or so around the area in order to establish the healing throughout the body. As a final action, the healer may want to do a more global healing of the whole body, placing her hands about an inch above the body and speaking words such as, "I am now giving stronger confirmation to this healing throughout your entire mind and body, and in touch with your archetype of healing, you will continue to improve as the day goes on."

Regardless of where in the world I teach this technique, the results are the same. People feel better and, in most cases, continue to improve. Often I make the exercise one of mutual healing, the healer and the one to be healed changing roles so that each can have the experience of being the healer. This strengthens the process and makes it more natural. What had been thought to be extraordinary becomes ordinary, and another barrier to human possibilities has been breached. But it is also important to know when the healing of the body cannot take place, when the life is ready for transition and the issue is really one of healing the soul and bringing peace and reconciliation.

It seems for a while that Virginia is improving. She feels she is. She reports renewed energies, less discomfort. She has even taken to painting flowers in her garden. But she also takes a variety of radical alternative therapies, some of which, like coffee enemas, I find appalling.

She begins to ask for another kind of healing. She seems to be making other kinds of choices as to what she will do with her life. She asks for soul work. She wants me to help her mend old wounds of relationship with family and reconcile with her two former husbands, both of whom are deceased.

Together, we enter the Dreamtime, and I guide her to that eternal place where history is still fluid and the drama can be rewritten. I take her into a very special garden, the garden of all realities.

"What do you see there, Virginia?"

"It is so beautiful here, and, oh, there is a stream. People from my life arise from this stream like fountains—many fountains, many people I have loved."

"And are all of these fountains the same?"

"No, some of them are stronger than others. Some rise high, some low. Some have brilliant colors; others you can barely see, they are so wispy. And then there are the ones that spurt mud. I think I'd better go check them out."

Virginia goes over to a mud-spouting fountain. It turns out to be one of her husbands. There is no sound coming from the other end of the phone. Finally I say, "Hello, hello, Virginia, are you still there?"

"He has no self-esteem," she remarks with disgust. "And that's a hard thing to get past."

"What's past is past, Virginia, and what's now is forever. Let's use some of your own techniques. Let's call up yourself when you were married to the guy and have her stand in front of him."

In the course of her seminars, Virginia would often bring people up and introduce them to each other. In her gifted presence, peoples' Essence came through, and they felt ennobled and richly seen. When she did this with families or people in relationship, the results were often astonishing; years of trauma and projection would fall

away in a few hours. Now she attends to the most difficult task of all, her own trau-
mas and projections. She does not want to leave this world without giving and receiv-
ing forgiveness.

"Virginia, you have not been afraid to take risks on your own behalf. Take the risk
of feeling the full range of your feelings."

"I see myself as hiding behind my strength when I am with him. She, myself, is
afraid that he will hurt her delicate core, and so she puts on a mask of superiority. It
belittles him, and she is made less as he becomes so."

"Then speak to him of his essential strength," I say. "Recognize his true power, his
own fragility, and do for him what you have done for so many: call him back into his
own unique wonderfulness."

Virginia does this and then moves on to other fountains that need cleansing and
reconciliation. One is her younger sister, Edith. There had been a lot of strife in her
family. Virginia was the eldest, the partner of her mother, but felt edged out after
Edith was born. To make matters worse, while her mother was giving birth, Virginia
was suffering from peritonitis following a ruptured appendix. She began to think of
the baby as a distraction that almost killed her, and the sense of low-key hostility to-
ward her sister had been present for most of her life.

As there was still considerable anger toward her sister, I thought that we should
take an indirect approach. I had her meet me in the garden, where I became one of
the fountains along the stream. I asked her how she felt toward me.

"Vulnerable, trusting, and absolutely open and available," she answered.

"Well, look who is standing behind me."

"Could it be . . . is it really Edith?" she asked and then entered into communion
with her sister. Afterward she said, "How could I have mistaken all that scatteredness
for hostility? Thank you, Jean, I see her whole and I see her beautiful soul. You have
helped me love my sister again. You have no idea how important that is to me."

At its best, healing is actually "wholing," calling people to become who and what
they are because one sees them as whole despite all appearances to the contrary.
Those who train themselves to drop their local prejudices of percept can achieve
certain states of mind in which, quite simply, one sees the other as God-in-hiding.
True, this God-in-hiding may still be in a fetal state and may require some midwifery to be drawn forth. Being a midwife of souls is a delicate matter, for it requires both a sense of timing to know when the gestation is complete and a
willingness to be available during the entire birthing process. It also requires providing sufficient nurturing for the early stages of development. But mostly it demands that one see in the other his or her entelechy, the Godseed ready to emerge
from the womb of time that gives each being its uniqueness. Since I am given to
seeing people in this way, I am thought by some a foolish optimist or, at best, a
total innocent—an opinion my husband shares. And yet I continue to act and feel

"as if" the person before me, regardless of apparent deficiencies in ability or behavior, is a holy child, the worth of which is inestimable.

Such was the case with Aaron Schwartz, a butterfly who, to all the world, seemed caught in a damaged cocoon.

I live not far from a center for mentally disabled adults. Some years ago, the center put on a yearly show, often a shortened version of a Broadway musical. All the parts were sung, and there was virtually no speaking or dialogue. The time I went, they were doing *Fiddler on the Roof*. The people in the chorus were clearly retarded, but with the principal actors it was harder to tell. The man who played the leading part of Tevye, the dairyman, seemed to me to be simply too good, too full of dramatic fire and theatrical juice to be disabled. I turned to the friend who accompanied me and said in a disgusted voice, "What a fake! What a fake! That is an out-of-work, off-Broadway actor playing the part of Tevye, using these handicapped people as foils to make himself look good. I'll bet he's got a number of New York agents sitting in the audience."

My friend perused the playbill and said, "No, Jean, that's not so. It says here that all the parts are being played by the residents in the home."

"Listen, Louise, I'm the professional, and I know!" I said in a full display of my prejudice. "That is an out-of-work actor, or else he's a doctor who should have been an actor."

"But it says here that—"

"I'll prove it to you after the show."

After the performance, we both wandered backstage, and in one of the dressing rooms, I found the leading actor sitting with his false beard hanging half off, staring into space.

I addressed him in a jaunty, knowing manner.

"Hi, there. You were really very good. What was the last play you did off-Broadway?"

No answer. The man continued to stare into space. I began to get nervous.

"You're a doctor, then. Aren't you a doctor?"

Still no answer. The man turned my way with a blank look. Suddenly I was so appalled by my own tactlessness that I was shocked into doing the right thing. I took the man's hands in mine and began to sing and dance to the music of the title song of *Fiddler on the Roof*, "My name is Jean Houston . . . and I certainly enjoyed your show. . . ."

The man's eyes lit up. He stood up and began to sing back to me, "My name is Aaron Schwartz . . . and I'm glad you found me out." Dancing now as well as singing, he continued following the same melody, "Oh, when I am singing and I'm dancing, then I know who I really am. For when I am singing and I'm dancing, I can find myself."

Singing now in rhyming words, he told me that when he tried to communicate as others did, it was as if a curtain fell in front of his mind, but when he was singing and dancing, the curtain lifted, and the world moved into meaning. He would pause now and then to invite me to enter the song and sing about my life. I tried, but I was incapable of keeping up the rhyme.

The following day I was able to check out some of his history. It seems that Aaron had grown up in an orthodox Jewish family in which singing and sing-songing were common forms of communication. A simple phrase like "Oh, Hymie, pass the pastrami . . ." was often sung rather than just spoken. Aaron's inability to think or act in nonmusical form went largely unattended. When his parents died and he went to live with cousins, it was found that he could not learn or talk or interact unless he was singing. When tested under "normal" conditions, he was deemed mentally deficient and eventually ended up in this center in Rockland County, New York.

By chance, shortly afterward, I found myself talking to a rabbi friend who was close to the producers and artists of one of the last remaining Yiddish theaters. I told him about Aaron Schwartz, and he became fascinated with the idea that our singing man might find his true life on the Yiddish stage "where most of it is singing anyway. And for the speaking parts, Jeanelah, you can teach him plain-song, so he sounds like he's talking on one note."

And that's what happened. Aaron took on small parts in the theater and, of course, was at his best when singing in Yiddish or Hebrew. The only problem was after the play was over, when the actors and the rabbi would go to a nearby Jewish deli for matzo ball soup and corned beef on rye. Aaron would place his order with a song.

"Rabbi," the actors would ask, "why is it that Aaron never stops singing?"

"Ach," answered the rabbi, looking up to heaven, "that is because Aaron is in tune with the Master of the Universe, blessed be He, and as the commentaries tell us, He is singing all the time. So stop worrying and eat your soup." Then, addressing Aaron, the rabbi continued, "Now what were you saying, or rather singing, Aaron?"

I have ample proof that such healings of body and spirit can have lasting effects. Not long ago I was stuck in a Southwest Airlines flight that was puddle-jumping between cities in Texas. A major storm had come up, and we were circling an airport, unable to land. It was quite late, and I was exhausted and sick with bronchitis, trying desperately to get some sleep. In the seat behind me, however, a man was talking endlessly in a loud and cheery voice. Every so often he would give off huge guffawing laughs that seemed to shake the plane. Finally, I couldn't stand it anymore and turned around to ask him to please be quiet.

It was LeRoy! A gargantuan LeRoy spilled over the seat, his personality and certainly his voice box equaling the size of his body. He had become a successful insurance salesman. I know, because to shut him up I bought an accident policy before we finally landed.

Virginia is leaving us. Her sister has come to her bedside, and Virginia has smiled and squeezed her hand. All is well between them.

I am able to have a last conversation with her. She is barely able to speak, so I tell her something of what she has meant to the world. I tell her of an Australian Aboriginal community that I have encountered that uses her work and words to recreate the power of their culture, restore their self-esteem after two hundred years of denigration, and rediscover the sacrality of their relationships to nature and each other. I recall my meeting with Taiwanese psychologists who are helping to release Chinese families from centuries of repression by incorporating her methods of truth telling and appreciation. I remind her of cycles of hatred that have been broken, families that have been mended, and of people drawn together in teaching-learning communities of peacemakers and pathfinders. They are the firstborn of the heart in a new civilization, and she is their mother. I speak to her of the many groups all over the world that she has seeded; so many and so deeply nurturing have they become that it may well be that the world has turned a corner because she has lived.

"Dear Virginia, I invite you to meet yourself. I invite you to know how you have changed the world."

Her final words to me come slow but with a strangely joyous certainty. "Then . . . I . . . have . . . done . . . what . . . I . . . came . . . to do. . . ."

7

✦

ALTERED
STATES

It is September 1979. Before me, stretched out on the floor of an inn in Easton, Maryland, are several hundred government officials. I have put most of them in trance and am guiding them to travel to a future "possible society" and bring back descriptions of what they find there. As president of the Association for Humanistic Psychology, I have worked with the Department of Commerce to create this four-day conference entitled "Policy Alternatives for the Decade Ahead." Jimmy Carter is in the White House. There is fresh thinking in Washington—a cautious willingness to explore means to better society and the people in it.

Looking over the bodies on the floor, I see the heads of national agencies, undersecretaries and assistant secretaries of government departments, representatives from the White House. The working government of the United States is here and in an altered state. Of course, getting them to this point has been a considerable journey; many arrived at the inn in a more familiar altered state—tense, combative, and extremely skeptical. When they came in, I wanted to confiscate their bulging briefcases, but I knew that was a lost cause.

"This is No-Man's Land for the New Age," says one of my worried copresenters. She adds, "Government bureaucrats spend their time rearranging the deck chairs on the Titanic. They're not going to listen to us."

"You're probably right," I reply. "So we'll have to alter their consciousness."

"How?" she asks.

"With jokes," I answer.

My brain is larded with my father's legacy of jokes and gags; dendrites and ganglia all end in punch lines. For me laughter is the ultimate altered state. At the peak of roaring laughter, one exists, as in midsneeze, everywhere and nowhere, and is thus available to be blessed, evoked, deepened. In the bag of tricks I have used over the years to bring people to other states of mind, I still find that for most, laughter remains the easiest way to begin moving beyond that half-awake state we call "normal waking consciousness." So I open this august gathering with ten minutes of stand-up comedy.

Much laughter and rib nudging later, I look out over the audience: no more glacial stares or supercilious smirks. Good, they are ready for the next part, something familiar—substantive but inventive speeches on social and economic reconstruction with the aim of building a people-centered society. This is followed by George Leonard leading exercises in aikido, to show in martial arts terms how to disarm an opponent without causing injury and even to allow for win-win situations. I note with satisfaction that the bureaucrats have no problem with this. Grounding ideas in the body is always a good way to increase flexibility of mind and bonding of community.

When it is again my turn to speak, I demonstrate methods of enhancing creative processes and of increasing the brain's flexibility and functioning. I show them ways of taking any problem or work-related issue and running it through multiple frames of mind—thinking in images, thinking kinesthetically with the whole body, seeing an issue in musical or rhythmic patterns, finding the pattern that connects one pattern to another, drawing it, singing it, drumming it, embodying it.

I am surprised to discover that quite a few of these bureaucrats are remarkably skilled at imaginative thinking. When I ask them why this is so, they respond that they are so used to dealing with the absurdities of government that paradoxical and fantastical images are but a tiny step from their everyday fare. When we move into small-group, think-tank sessions, however, their old habits start to reassert themselves. They resume the intellectual jousts in which they have become expert—point, counterpoint, rebuttal, and sophisticated name-calling.

After fifteen minutes of shticks and stones, we presenters suggest an alternative. After stating a point, switch sides and argue for an opposing view. Only after all have spoken from multiple perspectives can they return to their original argument and see how it has grown in richness and depth.

The atmosphere thickens, becomes charged. The government officials alternate between processes that enhance their physical and mental well-being and sessions of work on major policy issues. This schedule is mixed up with a lot of music and dance, entertainment, and always an undercurrent of jokes and folly.

By the fourth day, most participants are in an open, even ebullient, state. People up and down the government hierarchy, who normally would seldom speak to each other, are freely exchanging names and addresses and planning to get together for "transformational lunch bunches." Ideas and plans for interagency projects are in the air. Everyone senses that if this freewheeling atmosphere of personal growth and creative intensity could be sustained, America could turn a corner.

But what corner and to where? That is why I have put these policy makers into an altered state. In visiting a future America, they hope to discover the what and the where of it all.

It seems that one way or another, I have always lived in the Altered States of America. When I was about four, my mother took me to the Hal Roach Studios to test for one of the final productions of the *Our Gang* comedies. Mr. Roach sat in the audience and asked me to go through a door, close it, then come back through and tell everybody my name. As soon as I walked through the door, I saw that it led to a blank wall. I shot back through the door immediately and told Mr. Roach that I wouldn't close it. When he asked me why, I replied, "Because there is nothing on the other side. And if I stay there, I'll become nothing, too."

"Well, tell us your name."

I thought for a while, but my name was lost, swallowed up in the world beyond the door. Finally I explained, "I don't remember, because in the nothing place I have no name."

"Wonderful!" said Hal Roach. "Sign her up!" But before the contract could be signed, my father got another job a thousand miles away, and we were off.

I continued to think about the world beyond the door and whether nothing was really no thing. I began to be fascinated with what lay beneath the surface of things. I started to peek under tree bark, pull up clumps of lawn to discover what lay under the grass, look under rocks. I became a voyeur of vegetables, peeling off layer after layer of onions, carving out doors in peppers to peer endlessly at the great green cathedral within. Thus even at a very young age, the mysteries that lay within consciousness called to me. Of course, at first it was only the consciousness of crawdads, but many great enterprises have small beginnings.

We were traveling across the country and stopped to pick up my dad in New Orleans where he had been working on a show. As the train started to pull out of the station, we saw Dad running for the platform holding a suitcase in one hand and a large bucket filled with what appeared to be miniature lobsters in the other. He tossed the suitcase to my mother and pulled himself and the bucket up onto the train. Halfway out of the station, the train stopped for minor repairs.

"I've just learned how to pull off one of the greatest wonders in natural science," my father announced breathlessly.

"What's that, Daddy?"

"Hypnotizing crawdads. I've got a whole bucket of Louisiana crawdads here, and I'm going to put every one of them under my spell. You just watch."

My father plunged his hand into the bucket and pulled out a small malevolent pincer. "You are growing verrrry sleepy. Your eyelids are growing heavier and heavier, and you are sinking into a deep and peaceful sleeeeep." With that, he upended the crawdad and placed it so that it was balanced like a tripod on its head and front claws, like a person doing a yoga exercise. In this position, the creature seemed to be possessed of a tranquillity and inner peace seldom if ever achieved by crawdads.

Clearly, at this moment, my destiny loomed before me. "Oh, Daddy, let me try, too."

"Sure, Jeanie! I tell you what. Let's have ourselves a crawdad hypnosis contest. Here, we'll each put a suitcase on the floor and see how many crawdads we each can hypnotize on top of the suitcases. The one with the most hypnotized crawdads wins. Okay?"

This turned out to be a game demanding enormous skill and imperviousness to pain. We were constantly nipped, and when we finally succeeded in setting up a line of entranced crawdads, we discovered the awful truth of the domino theory. If one fell over, they were all likely to go. We kept catching collapsing lines of crawdads and standing them on their heads again, until finally, for one glorious moment, we each had a field of mesmerized little monsters balanced on our suitcases. Dad had twenty-eight, while I had twelve. It was a testament to human ingenuity and the trance capacities of crustaceans. Then, with a mighty lurch, the train started, and forty irate crawdads went scrambling all over the compartment, bent on mayhem.

From that moment on, I was hooked on hypnosis. I would try it out on everybody—my friends at school, the dog, people I met on the train. Once when I was about eight or nine, we rented an apartment from a woman who dabbled in spiritualism, and I found her library to be a wonderful source for tips of the occult trade, including an entire course on conducting seances. There was no denying the wild card talent I exhibited early in life for bringing people into states of Dionysian frenzy—witness the excesses of the congregants at the Kid Preacher church—or making them fall into trance without even trying . . . much.

"Time and space go warp around you, Jean," Margaret Mead once told me. "You must be living in several worlds simultaneously."

"No, I'm just trying to get beneath the surface crust of things, Margaret," I told her.

"Oh, fiddlesticks!" she protested. "You wouldn't want to get there unless a large part of you were there already! You are chasing yourself down the rabbit hole."

And indeed my life has had an Alicelike theme running through it. Always I look for the looking glass that carries us further into the unknown worlds within. While I was in graduate school, a most remarkable looking glass presented itself and invited me to enter. It was called LSD.

The varieties of my psychedelic experience began in my friend Michael Corner's fourth floor walk-up in Greenwich Village. Michael was finishing his doctorate in neurophysiology and had introduced me to several psychiatrists and physicians who had a special license to do LSD research. They had asked me to think about joining them in the study of the effects of the drug on human personality because of my familiarity with myth and symbol, aspects of which were always recurring in their research subjects and which their medical education had not prepared them for. They wanted me to help guide research subjects through the arcana of the psychedelic experience. First, however, I had to experience the drug myself.

After the initial physical sensations (a very mild nausea and stiffness of the neck) had passed, I began to notice that the wooden floor had started to ripple. I walked across the floor, climbing up its steep waves and sliding down its inclines. Occasionally, I would catch one of its oaken crests and ride it to the wall in much the same way that a surf rider travels on the waves.

I looked first at the guide, whose appearance was unchanged, and then at Michael, also under LSD, who was sitting in the lotus position. His well-fringed face was alternately shifting from Christ to Pan, then back to Christ again. He opened his eyes and came out of his private nirvana for a moment to say to me, "Well, this is *it!* What more is there to say?"

I directed my attention toward the room, and suddenly everything was holy. The stove and the pottery and the chairs and the record player and the soup ladles and the old bottles—all were touched with sacrality, and I bowed to each in turn and worshiped. One pot in particular was so endowed with divinity I dared not come closer to it than four or five feet lest I be burned to ashes for my unclean lips and impure heart. But a godly peach proved friendlier and accepted my adoration with kindly beneficence, radiating on me the preternatural light of its numinous fuzz. I bowed my gratitude and moved on, transfigured by the deity of things.

I remember looking at a finely detailed photograph of the Swiss Alps. I had admired this photograph before, in my pre-LSD days an hour or an aeon ago, but now its precision became reality; the temperature plunged, fine crystals of snow whipped across my face, and I circled like an eagle above the crags and snowy summits of the mountaintop. An expedition of climbers waved up at me, and I lifted one talon to wave back.

I was called back to the room in Greenwich Village by what seemed to me an obscenity. A sound, a chant, lascivious and brutal, a whining pornography assaulted my ears and left me furious with moral indignation. "How dare you say things like that to me!" I said to the disembodied chant. It suddenly ended, as quickly as it had begun, and I saw Michael removing a record, which he explained to me contained fertility mantras directed to the goddess Kali. A Bach toccata then was put on the phonograph, and the music of the spheres left their archetypal abode and took up residence in the walk-up on Bleeker Street.

At this time I closed my eyes and experienced a vision of the future that unfolded in vivid colors before my closed eyes, accompanied by voices that were audible only inside my head. I found myself and the rest of humanity standing together on the foothills of the Earth, being addressed by two splendid and luminous figures many hundreds of miles high. They could be seen plainly in spite of their height. They told us that they were the Elders of this particular part of the cosmos and had lost their patience with the human creatures of Earth. The recalcitrance of greedy, warring, barbarous humanity had reached new peaks, and now that nuclear power had been discovered, the outrageous breed evolved on our planet might yet try to subvert the whole cosmos. And so it had been decided in the Council of Elders that unless humanity could find something in its creations with which to justify itself, it would have to be destroyed.

Having heard this message, we earthlings scattered and searched our libraries, museums, histories, and parliaments for some achievement that might be seen as a justification for our existence. We brought forth our greatest art objects, our Leonardos, Michelangelos, Praxiteles, but the Elders only shook their heads and said solemnly, "It is not sufficient." We brought forth our great masterpieces of literature, the works of Shakespeare, Milton, Goethe, Dante. But these also were deemed insufficient. We searched in our religious literature and offered the figures of religious genius—Jesus, Buddha, Moses, Saint Francis, but the Elders only laughed and said, "Not sufficient."

It was then, when destruction seemed imminent and all had given themselves up to their fate, that I came forward and offered to the Elders the music of Johann Sebastian Bach. They listened to the entire corpus, and great silver tears of incredible brilliance shimmered and trickled down the lengths of their luminous bodies, after which they were silent. On and on this silence extended, until they broke it to say, "It is sufficient. You of the Earth are justified." Then they went away.

For a period of time that I had neither capacity nor wish to measure, I pondered this vision. It seemed to have resonances of something always known, a mythic substrate coded in the interstices of the human mind. Then, when the music had ended, I lay on my back and looked up at the ceiling where a kaleidoscope of images from ancient civilizations flickered rapidly before my eyes. Egypt and Greece, Assyria and old China sped across the ceiling. Flickering pharaohs, fluttering Parthenons, and a palpitating Nebuchadnezzar all contributed to this panorama.

And suddenly—destruction! The air was thick with the ammonia smell of death. Noxious vapors stung the eyes and choked the throat. The stench of the apocalypse rose up with the opening of the graves of the new and old dead. It was the nostrils' view of the Night on Bald Mountain, an olfactory *Walpurgisnacht* rite. The world had become a reeking decay. Then I heard Michael rebuking someone with the words, "Christ, Timmy, couldn't you have used your sandbox?" Timmy was the cat, and the apocalyptic smell had issued from a single turd he had deposited in the middle of the floor.

I turned my attention from Timmy's tangible residues to Timmy himself. He stretched himself with infinite grace and arched his back to begin the ballet. Leaping through time and space, he hung like Nijinsky, suspended in the air for a millennium, and then, drifting languidly down to the ground, he pirouetted to a paw-licking standstill. He then stretched out one paw in a tentative movement and propelled himself into a mighty spiral, whirling into cosmic dust, then up on his toes for a bow to his creation.

He was a cat no longer, but Indra, the primeval god, dancing the cosmic dance in that time before time, setting up a rhythmic flux in nonbeing until, at last, it attained to life. The animating waves of the dance of creation pulsed all around me, and I could no longer refuse to join the dance. Before I could allow myself more than a cursory leap into the cosmic fray, a great flame erupted somewhere in the vicinity of my left elbow, and I felt obliged to give it my attention. The guide had started a fire burning in the hearth, and the fire commanded that I concentrate upon it to the exclusion of all else.

It was a lovely fire. Mandalas played in it, and so did gods—many hundreds of beings, known and unknown, rising in El Greco attenuations for one brilliant moment, only to lapse again into nothing. I fell into musing, and after aeons had gone by and worlds within worlds within worlds had been explored, I looked up and spoke to Michael. In an attempt to define our relationship at that precise moment, I said, "You and I, we are ships that sometimes pass one another on the seas but never meet."

"Bullshit!" said Michael, and my vast, rippling reflections were shattered in an instant.

"Let's get out of here," I said.

"Where to?" he asked and seemed to find his question very funny. "Where to?" he asked again, convulsed with laughter. At last he managed to add, as if there were no other *where* or *to,* "Where to, Bruté?" Still howling, Michael and I, along with our guide, headed for Rudy's Buddha Shop, which was on the ground level.

We began to descend the four flights of stairs. They never ended. Down, down, down, down, down, down, down—into the bowels of some ultimate cavern, into the center of the Earth, no doubt, or perhaps into nowhere, we descended the stairs, forever and ever. "Will they ever end?" I asked, starting to panic. Only one more flight, I was assured. And then, an infinity of stair steps later, we arrived and entered the shop, and everything brightened.

The room was a cacophony of Buddhas. Screaming gold Gautamas seared the eye from their sunspot satoris. Seething stone saviors revealed a Buddha-to-come in each of their granular particles. Wooden hermaphrodite Lords of the East reconciled all opposites, all dualities, all dialectics. "Yin, yang, Jung!" I cried and dragged Michael toward another room with a balcony just over the street. But the journey was long, and I felt like Alice when she had to go twice as fast in order just to stay in the same place.

From the balcony, the crowded street leaped up to greet us, and it seemed we had only to reach out to touch the passersby. A painted elf skipped past us, and I looked after him in astonishment. "Just a fairy," Michael explained. "I thought it was an elf," I said, for all double meanings were lost on me. A decrepit old gargoyle tottered by. "Poor old gargoyle," I remarked. "He can't find a flying buttress on which to perch." And suddenly I felt very sad, for the whole of life became explainable in terms of people losing their potentialities by default and decaying into gargoyles who could be happy again only if they could find their proper niche, their own flying buttress, overlooking eternity.

Continuing to observe the scene below from the balcony, I felt as if my consciousness were projected downward so that I saw the people passing by as if I were standing on the sidewalk and confronting them. From this perspective, they became an animated waxworks, escapees from Madame Tussaud, who bit their wax nails, clutched their wax newspapers, and knit their wax brows as they thought waxen thoughts. I kept wondering how long they could keep up this charade before they melted down into puddles and oozed away along the pavement.

But then, as I looked down on the scene below, it seemed as if I were viewing it from a very high place. I chanced to observe a particularly rough square of pavement, and what I saw there caused me to cry out to Michael to come over and share in this latest wonder. For there below us in that square of pavement lay all of Manhattan—its canyons and skyscrapers and parks and people laid out beneath us in miniature. The proportions, the infinite detail were perfect. We could have been in an airplane flying low over the city. But here it all was, in a common block of pavement, the city within the city.

Holding on to each other, Michael and I decided to leave the shop and enter the endless reality that was the streets of New York. It seemed that a horde of people came bearing down upon us. Tides of gray automata threatening to engulf us. "Don't worry," I counseled Michael, "I shall be Moses." As I raised my arm, the crowd parted, and we were free to enter the Promised Land.

People continued to stream toward us and past us. I focused on an old woman in her late seventies, a dowdy pathetic creature dressed in shabby black and carrying impossibly huge shopping bags. As she made her way heavily toward us, I saw, no longer astonished, that she began to lose years. I saw her as an Italian matriarch in her sixties, then in her fifties. As she continued to bloom backward in time, she entered her portly forties and, after that, her housewifely thirties. Her face softened, her body grew more shapely, and still the years kept on dropping away. In her twenties she was carrying a baby, and then she was a bride and carried orange blossoms. A moment later, she was a child who, in turn, shrank into a newborn baby carried by a midwife. The umbilical cord still uncut, the baby let out a howl of awakening life.

But then the process was reversed, and the baby grew back into childhood, became again a bride, passed through its thirties, forties, fifties, sixties, and was the old lady in her seventies I had seen at the beginning. The old woman blinked, her eyes closing for a fraction of a second, and in that instant I clearly saw her death mask. She passed us by and had moved a little down the street when I heard from the direction she had come, a baby's howl of awakening life.

I turned my head, expecting to perceive afresh the same woman but saw instead the vortex of a crowd streaming into the giant doorway of an immense building. The vortex atomized into points of energy. Radial lights and shimmering vortices converged into a single solar concentration that seethed in thermal fury to explode at last in a kaleidoscopic burst of falling jewels. A golden shovel crunched into a mound of opals near which was a sign that bore the incomprehensible words, "Dig We Must for a Growing New York." An ironclad tympana bruised the ears with a raucous counterpoint of jackhammering. Construction or destruction or something more profound was in process, and two protean tractors loomed before us, large and living. In the cabs of these vital creatures sat little robot mannequins, absurd toy trinkets that were undoubtedly wound up every morning to mimic the motions of life. How proper it all seemed—the man-machine playing at noblesse oblige with the machine-man. Between themselves, the living tractors maintained an uneasy truce.

But then their clanging vituperations took on a primeval resonance. Voices screamed from an early swamp, and I saw that the warring tractors were warring dinosaurs, their long necks driving and attacking in sinuous combat. "Too much," I thought, and with what seemed a great effort of will, I returned through the centuries to regard the street.

I noticed how unspeakably profound was the action of people getting on and off of this bus. On and off. On and off. The eternal return. Pagan yet Christian. Circular but linear. The bus plunged ahead along the route of its manifest destiny then stopped a short distance down the street, while people kept climbing aboard at intervals to catch its life force, only to be deposited unceremoniously along the byways of their all-too-partial life segments. But where was the bus going? Toward what ultimate destination? Heaven? Fort Tryon Park? Utopia? Perhaps it was a million years away. We, too, got on the bus to discover what destiny it would lead us to. Suddenly I knew. "It's Fifty-seventh Street, Michael! That's where the bus wants us to go."

Getting off the bus on 57th Street, we found ourselves at a store specializing in handicrafts from Czechoslovakia. Soon I was transfixed before a wooden statue. It was a rough folk carving of Jesus sitting with his legs crossed, leaning his face in his hand, waiting. Just waiting. And I knew what it meant. He was waiting, just like I was, for his destiny to catch up with him. Poor old Jesus. Poor old me. We shared the same dilemma of waiting. I burst into nonstop laughter, and Michael had to pull me from the store, as the customers and salesclerks were getting nervous.

And so it went—a millennium of adventures condensed somehow into a few brief hours. It all ended very suddenly for me, when a parking meter I was watching abruptly flipped its red time-expired flag, and I knew it was over.

What had begun, however, was my research guiding several hundred people through LSD journeys over the next three years. It proved to be the best possible education in the nature of mind and consciousness. To prepare for becoming a psychedelic guide, I reviewed the ancient precedents of this role. Priestess and shaman were the first purveyors of its techniques. Seer and sibyl had mapped the cosmos of its domain. But for me, the most instructive of precedents was found in the figure of Virgil in Dante's *Divine Comedy,* a work that had fascinated me since childhood.

In the first canto of the *Divine Comedy,* Dante is lost in the dark woods, haunted by strange sounds and shapes. When his confusion is at its greatest, he is met by the figure of the master poet Virgil, who tells him, "I shall be your guide to lead you hence through that eternal place. . . ." Virgil then leads Dante through the vast tapestry of the medieval universe. With time suspended and all of life at hand, Dante perceives past and present, grandeur and corruption, history and legend, tragedy and comedy, humanity and nature. Virgil introduces him to the dramatis personae of extended reality, figures from mythology, fantastic demons, gods and godlings, symbolic animals, allegorical personifications, mighty archetypes. As we read, we, too, are led by Virgil through an enhanced reality in which everything is bound up with everything else in a pattern both absolute and universal. We are links in the great chain of being, in which the hierarchy of the human body parallels the hierarchies of the nature, the state, the cosmos.

I soon discovered that the richness and variety of Dante's journey were strikingly similar to the psychedelic experience. As my research subjects crossed the threshold of altered consciousness, they were flooded with a kaleidoscopic vision of extended perceptual fields and psychological insights, a visionary torrent of cultures and contexts, myths and symbols, remnants of what appeared to be racial or transpersonal memory—an infinity of the components that constitute our being. Like Dante in the dark woods, they could easily have lost their way in the labyrinth of strange byways and unknown paths—an all-too-frequent occurrence in unguided psychedelic experiences. My task, then, was to lead my research subjects through this terrain and to elicit, without too much prompting, what they saw and knew there. Finally, I would try to guide my subjects, much as Virgil did Dante, to experience the interrelationship of this material within themselves. To do this I had to help the subjects select out of the wealth of perceptual and conceptual phenomena the most promising opportunities for heightened insight, awareness, and integral understanding.

During this time I sought my own Virgils, too. I went to the great theologians with whom I had been studying, Tillich and Niebuhr, and told them how a secretary who had scarcely ever left Brooklyn experienced within her visions of death and resurrection, wise old men and women, rituals of passage, epic mythic journeys, a panoply of gods, and even a powerful sense of union with the One. I told them about a stevedore who spent his days taking crates off ships but who had revealed in his psychedelic experience that within his consciousness lay an entire encyclopedia of mythology, a cauldron of spirit, and a theological knowledge that was equal to anything I had heard in seminary. I told them of the unitive bliss of an advertising man, the Homeric inner journeys of a waitress, the transcendental experiences of a housewife. What would they make, I wondered, of an army officer whose revelations paralleled those of Saint John of the Cross, with similar language and detail? To all this they answered, "These are merely cases of somatopsychic depersonalization. They have nothing to do with the reality of things. For that, you must yearn and strive and pray. What you are reporting are illusions."

Needless to say, I was disappointed by their cavalier dismissal of the psychedelic experience. With no outward Virgil to guide me, I would have to discover the poet of consciousness within myself. Holding this guiding archetype, I soon chanced upon an itinerary of the domains of the psyche that seemed as true a passage as Virgil's had been for Dante. It was based on observing a recurrent pattern of "descent" to four levels in the drug experience that seemed to correspond to four major levels of the psyche. I came to term these levels the *sensory,* the *psychological,* the *symbolic,* and the *integral* or *spiritual.*

At first, as the psychedelic drug took effect, my subjects experienced primarily an altered sensory awareness of their body and body image, accompanied by spatial distortions and changes in perception. Time would be altered, a few seconds seeming to last a long time. If subjects tried to persevere in their old predrug frame of reference, they were usually in for some unpleasant moments. I would try to acclimatize them by directing their attention to the heightening of color and forms of well-known objects—especially seashells, stones, flowers, plants, and vegetables. I would open a door into the glorious cathedral within a green pepper. Or I would surround my subjects with a cornucopia of fruits and vegetables and ask them to enter into a friendly relationship with them. I would augment this experience by playing Beethoven's *Pastoral* symphony. The surging notes of this hymn to nature combined with my subjects' growing botanical bliss to produce a euphoric mingling of sight, touch, smell, and sound. Then, when the climactic symphonic moment arrived, I would slowly peel back the husks of an ear of corn, and my subjects would know that they had witnessed a mystery. I borrowed this last idea from the *epopteia,* the revelation at the end of the Eleusinian mysteries. After all, it had worked for the ancient Greeks.

I would then encourage my subjects to close their eyes and watch their inner visionary theater. The initial stages of the sensory level revealed mostly light shows with random color flows, checkerboards, vortices, and other constructs of the eye's pattern-making abilities. Imagery would gradually become more specific, with pictures, scenes, and faces, but it was often disconnected and without any particular meaning.

Several hours into a session, my subjects would pass into the second or psychological stage of experience in which content was introspective, with emphasis on recalling and reflecting upon their existence. This level and the previous level of sensory experience make up what I have come to call the This Is Me realm. Here my subjects would study their past, their problems, and their potentialities, often with a good deal of emotion. Memories would surge into consciousness, providing a greater quantity of materials with which to work. These materials could be sifted, analyzed, and ordered to enhance self-knowledge or confront problems in a new way. The visual imagery on this level seemed to promote a greater concreteness of thought and also a more intense than usual flow of imagination and fantasy. At this level I saw subjects map out novels they wanted to write, solve engineering problems, and come up with all sorts of inventions and new ideas. I came to realize why this was possible. Since imagery contains a great deal of information coded in symbolic form, images supply much more material than do words that can be used for personal reflection or problem solving. At this level I found that I had to remain silent for long periods of time so as not to interrupt the process. Only if my subjects were caught in a circular rut in which some no longer useful theme would repeat itself over and over would I assist them. I always had to remind myself that Virgil was not Dante's psychiatrist, although he effected considerable therapeutic change in the poet. I saw my main responsibility as helping my subjects enlarge their worldview, increase their aesthetic appreciation, and widen their enjoyment of the multiple realities within reality. When they were able to consider the enormously rich and varied experience available to them, it seemed wasteful if not destructive to limit their exploration to a specific psychological problem. I found it necessary to sensitize myself to my subjects' experience so that I could anticipate what they were sometimes seeing or feeling. However, I never took the drug along with them. In fact, I only took LSD three times myself, a dubious record for a psychedelic researcher. Instead, I meditated and availed myself of a variety of nondrug consciousness-enhancing exercises before beginning any session.

The third or symbolic level of the psychedelic experience consisted of powerful and often archaic dramas. I saw that each of us is on a continuum between the personal-particulars of our lives and the personal-universals, which we each also contain. Beyond the surface and the literal seems to lie the self's larger vision and comprehension of itself. This larger vision makes itself known as an entelechy, the dynamic purposefulness and full capacity of a person that is contained almost as an autonomous self within the self. An individual's entelechy self can be liberated or activated by participation in symbolic dramas, which is why it often appears clothed in the symbolism of the mythic form or figure. As an inhabitant of the We Are realm of the psyche, which itself is undifferentiated as to space and time, the entelechy, like the mythic drama itself, contains the universal codings and reagents that allow the local self to mature and deepen in the milieu of the universal self and the universal drama carried in the myth. The discovery of the symbolic or We Are realm became the basis of a great deal of my later work in archetypal and sacred psychology, in which I use myths and legends as the stage upon which individuals as well as cultures rediscover and deepen their genius and possibilities. It also served to orient my work toward mythologizing rather than pathologizing.

Observing the panorama of imagery reported by my subjects, I had a front row seat on the greatest theater of the mind ever produced. Here the symbolic images were predominantly historical, legendary, mythical, ritualistic, and archetypal. I felt like an archaeologist unearthing the treasures of the planetary psyche. The gold of Troy, the mask of Agamemnon, the iconic beauties and mysteries of ancient pantheons, the inscrutable sphinx, the divine bestiary—all were there for the seeing. My job was to discover the techniques that would allow my subjects to uncover these masterpieces beneath the detritus of ordinary life. My own passion for history sometimes took over as I invited my subject to walk along the Piraeus with Socrates or witness a battle in the Thirty Years' War, to participate in the bull leaping at Knossos or help in the building of the Great Pyramid. I would send my subjects forth to gaze over the shoulder of that Cro-Magnon human as he or she painted the great bison in the cave at Altamira. I would urge them to join in the thrust westward of the army of Genghis Khan, witness a performance of *Hamlet* in the Globe Theater when Shakespeare himself played the Ghost, or mingle with those present at the court of Louis XIV.

In addition to housing the dramas of history, the We Are realm holds archetypal and mythological beings of all times and all cultures. My subjects would often find themselves acting out myths and legends internally and passing through initiations and ritual observances that appeared to be structured precisely in terms of their own most urgent needs. So vivid would be the experience of living out the life of the mythic figure with whom they were identifying that subjects would report they had moved into far more profound aspects of their own nature.

The deepest level of experience was the integral or spiritual, which I judged only a small number of my research subjects ever reached. At this stage, subjects experienced psychological integration, illumination, and a sense of fundamental and positive self-transformation. They named it a religious experience, for on this level, ideation, images, body sensation, and emotion were fused in what was felt as an absolutely purposive process culminating in self-understanding, self-transformation, spiritual enlightenment, and possibly mystical union. This experience corresponded to entering what I have described as the I Am realm of being. Here my subjects experienced what they regarded as a confrontation with the Ground of Being, God, Goddess, Mysterium, Noumenon, Essence, or Fundamental Reality. The climate of this level was always intensely emotional, and I noted how this intense affect served to bring about a lasting positive integration of the restructured organization of the psyche.

As I followed over many months and even years the development of those who achieved the spiritual or unitive level, I found that behavioral patterns that subjects had regarded as damaging or ineffectual seemed to have been effaced or cut through, and a deeper, more evolved pattern emerged out of the *wokwoom*. I also observed that after this experience, subjects felt strengthened, energized, more serene and spontaneous. There was a heightened sense of harmonious relationship to other people and to things, indeed, to the world in general. Aesthetic response was awakened and, with it, a higher sense of the pattern that connects and a commitment to creative production. So connected were these two that I began to see spiritual experience and creative experience as existing on the same continuum.

As for my participation, I found that my guiding activity stopped at the threshold of the spiritual level. Just as Virgil had to leave Dante at the portals of the "realms of bliss" and could not enter paradise with him, so I as guide could do no more than bear witness to the culmination of the process I had launched. I hoped and, indeed, in some cases perceived, that an inner Guide belonging to a deeper realm would take up the task of guidance, as Dante was met by the divine Beatrice who assisted him in the final vision and ecstasy in which he saw "the love that moves the sun and all the stars."

The government officials seem to be moving deeply into the possible society they are visiting in their minds. I ask them to remain in their inner state but to raise a hand if they are experiencing something they would like to share. A number of hands go up, and I make my way toward them with the microphone, stepping over bodies as I go.

An official who is in charge of almost three million employees says, "I find myself in a country where government is very small and officials rotate through a variety of jobs. No one is allowed to stay in a government job for very long. I have left the government and have a new job as an actor."

I place the mike near the mouth of a woman in the Office of Technological Assessment. "Small is beautiful in the society I find myself in," she tells me. "Technology is natural and even elegant. There is much use of solar and wind power, and gas engines are found only in museums. People go about on bicycles, and there are gardens everywhere, even in the cities. I am on my way to a concert in an outdoor theater."

I move next to a black woman in the Department of Health, Education, and Welfare. "This is a fine place for the family. Old and young all live together. If you're having problems with your mama, you just go visit an auntie for a while or a third cousin or somebody's motherly friend. Many juicy cultures here, and lots of music. I think I'll just stay awhile. Don't bother bringing me back."

Visions of changing the world for the better were, of course, the lifeblood of the 1960s. Today, we think of that era not only in terms of righting social wrongs but also as the supreme epoch of youth culture—free speech, antiwar protests, radical student organizations, flower children, sex, drugs, and rock 'n' roll. However, current nostalgia for the good old days of "tune in, turn on, and drop out" and "don't trust anyone over thirty" neglects to mention that many of the ideas embraced by the young came in fact from people then in their late sixties or seventies.

In those heady days, I found myself suddenly very popular. I had been lecturing about my LSD work at such places as Harvard Theological Seminary and publishing my visionary findings in academic journals of religion and philosophy.

These activities—and the fact that I was one of the few people in New York with a legal supply of LSD—earned me a certain reputation for eccentric originality and gave me the opportunity to meet a number of the old men who were pioneers of expanded consciousness. What I learned from them was formative and has continued to influence my life's work.

I had received a call from the eminent Gestalt psychologist Fritz Perls asking me to visit him in his apartment on Central Park West. I arrived in a state of nervous anticipation. Why would so great a man want to speak with someone so young and ignorant? I was greeted by a formally dressed gentleman in a gray pinstripe suit with a diamond stick pin in his Sulka tie. He seemed to be the very model of an elegant Viennese psychiatrist. He bowed over my hand and led me in to his tasteful and book-lined apartment. Perls's equally elegant wife Laura served us tea and little sandwiches. She seemed to find me a great curiosity and kept commenting on my extreme youth while casting inquiring looks at her husband. We discussed my LSD research, which seemed to interest them both.

Then Dr. Perls brought me into his study and closed the door. We sat facing each other a long time before he spoke. As the seconds ticked by and he continued to stare at me, I was certain that he was seeing right through me, reading my jejune soul and finding it wanting. Finally he spoke. "Miss Houston, I am a fake."

"Sir?"

"Yes, I am a fake, Miss Houston. I am much sicker than my patients, and it is not right that I continue to treat them. I have tried every kind of analysis. I even invented a new kind to take care of my own problems, but it is no good. So . . . I am wondering if you would be so good as to give me an LSD session. Perhaps LSD might get me past the catastrophic place I find myself in."

"Well, Dr. Perls, if you don't mind telling me, what is the nature of your problem?"

Perls leaned back in his chair, closed his eyes, and began to recount a Grand Guignol of the psyche. I felt like Alice in the Underworld as Perls took me on a guided tour of the sufferings and humiliations that he had inflicted on himself and others. He seemed a Minotaur at the center of the labyrinth of his own misery. His remorse was genuine, and he was desperate to find some thread that would lead him out. Could LSD be that thread?

"Please, Miss Houston. I can no longer live with what I am. Can you help me?"

I did not know what to say. I was shocked to the core at what I had just heard— a catalog of demons and deviance. Trying not to show this, I pulled myself together and said in my most clinical manner, "Dr. Perls, from what I have seen of the LSD experience, I believe it to be contraindicated in your case. LSD tends to bring on an amplification of the contents of the psyche. Judging by what you have just told me, I don't think that you want that kind of magnification."

Perls interrupted, "But surely, Miss Houston, you see that I can handle anything."

"Yes, Dr. Perls," I replied, "but I cannot. I am twenty-two years old, and I simply do not know enough to handle a psyche as complex as yours."

"You are very honest. But I think you can."

"I grew up as the daughter of a professional comedy writer who is, at the same time, a great innocent. I am afraid that I am also. I see comedy where others see neurosis. I am fascinated by the depths of the psyche, but I find story and allegory where others find madness and mayhem. I mythologize where others pathologize."

"But that would be perfect, Miss Houston. I need to find another way of viewing my life. I have been stewing in the soup of pathological explanations for too long. Please, can you lead me out of the soup with an LSD trip?"

Still I refused and insisted that LSD would pose a very serious threat to his condition. I begged him not to take the drug with anyone else. He smiled sadly and said he understood. Before he showed me out, he gave me his last copy of his book *Ego Hunger and Aggression.*

Some years later I was at the Esalen Institute in Big Sur. There in the cafeteria I saw Fritz Perls, gone gloriously to seed. He was dressed in dirty, torn overalls, his beard was long and unkempt, and he seemed wonderfully happy. I learned that after I left his apartment, he called Timothy Leary, who provided him with ample opportunities to take LSD. I went up to Perls and whispered, "You didn't follow my advice."

"No, thank God," he bellowed and fell into raucous but telling laughter.

I went on to read much of Perls's later work. He had become the wise old man of Gestalt therapy, helping patients uncover the entire reality or gestalt behind any issue in their psychological lives. His genius at having them play all the parts of the self, incarnating many aspects of any situation, became for me a deep learning in attending to the demands and knowings of the multifaceted or, what I later called, the polyphrenic self. The power and subtlety with which Perls guided this complex self and called forth its attributes and healing laid the basis for some of my own later work. Fritz Perls was a deep-rooted blossomer, and if some of those roots lay in a psychic hell, his soaring branches brought many closer to heaven.

The early sixties provided many such encounters and vignettes of transformation. Nineteen sixty-three was a banner year for altered states and an extraordinary one for me. In January, I hosted another old man, the writer Aldous Huxley. His books on psychedelic experience, *The Doors of Perception* and *Heaven and Hell,* as well as his recent utopian novel, *Island,* had become scripture for me, so I was quite prepared when I opened my door to discover a man who looked like an archangel. Very tall, with eyes misted over from surgery, he seemed to be gazing into other worlds. He had the most sensitive face I had ever seen and, when we sat down to talk, the most sensitive mind as well. He was courteous to a fault. Someone had given me a six-foot stuffed panda for Christmas, which I had propped up in a chair in the living room. Because his vision was so poor, Huxley would address remarks to me and then to the panda. I didn't have the heart to tell him the truth about the silent guest.

We began by discussing what happens when one looks at flowers in the psyche-delic state. In *The Doors of Perception*, reflections on his mescaline experiences, Huxley described how the experience of three ordinary flowers flung open doors into the very heart of the universe. He asked me to read to him the relevant passage. I brought the much marked book from my shelf and read aloud:

> I was seeing what Adam had seen on the morning of his creation—the miracle, moment by moment, of naked existence. [It was] a bunch of flowers shining with their own inner light and all but quivering under the pressure of the significance with which they were charged. . . . What rose and iris and carnation so intensely signified was nothing more, and nothing less, than what they were—a transience that was yet eternal life, a perpetual perishing that was at the same time pure Being, a bundle of minute, unique particulars in which, by some unspeakable and yet self-evident paradox, was to be seen the divine source of all existence. . . . (*The Doors of Perception*, New York: Harper & Row, 1963, 17–19)

I closed the book. "Reading this again I understand why in so many of the world's myths and scriptures, we find that God began by making a garden."

"Ah, yes," he said, "but where is this garden?"

"In paradise," I responded, and then to show him I knew my way around mythology, I added, "which is itself a Persian word meaning 'enclosed garden.'"

"Quite so. But according to many scriptures, paradise moved away after the fall into spiritual dimensions. And there it still is to be found by traveling to the antipodes of the mind in trance or prayer or meditation or by means of psychedelic substances. When one crosses into the other worlds of the mind, one discovers divine horticulture. Preternaturally brilliant flowers bloom abundantly in most of the other worlds described by visionaries and mystics, and they bloom not just with luminosity but with meaning for the one who beholds them."

"Are you saying that what is seeded in us for our further blooming is already coded in these flowers met in the mind's antipodes?"

"Of course. When you bring flowers to an altar, you are not just making a beautiful offering. You are returning to the gods the things they know in the other world. Flowers can be the bridge between here and the beyond, for they exist in both realms."

"So the flower that one sees with the inner extended eye is the one that grows in the visionary paradise. It offers its image to the brain but at the same time leads the soul back to paradise. But can this experience be had only through a deliberately altered state?"

"No, of course not," Huxley replied. "Whatever in nature or in a work of art resembles one of those intensely significant, inwardly glowing objects encountered at the mind's antipodes is capable of inducing the visionary experience, if only in partial or attenuated form."

As we continued to talk, we were no longer a young woman and an elderly man. We were comrades in speculation, co-adepts in the mysteries of visionary vegetables. We spun out fantasies of galaxies, stars—even of our universe itself—actually being flowers opening. I told Huxley about my encounter with Tillich and the *wokwoom,* and we speculated that the Big Bang might have been the bursting of a great pollen bag, the seeds of which moved out in radiant waves to fertilize the ovum of the void, creating an abundance of stars and planets, which themselves burst out to fertilize new forms of life in a great and continuous botanical wave of flowering.

Feeling emboldened by Huxley's wonderful conversation and generous manner, I questioned him about *Island,* his last published book. He had created in this novel a society based on optimal education and enlightened human relationships, fertilized by the occasional sacramental use of moksha, a visionary vegetable—a utopia that stood in absolute contrast to the dystopia he had earlier created in *Brave New World.* More a brief for Huxley's later ideas on education and social reconstruction than it was literature, the book inspired much of my own later work in educating the possible human and creating a possible society. At the book's conclusion, however, the ideal society is destroyed, taken over by fascist military forces. Try as I might, I could not contain my resentment over this ending.

"Why, Mr. Huxley, did you permit the book to end that way? It's an impossible ending; it could never happen that way. The *Island* society is built on education. The people in it are so highly developed that they would always find a way to bring their culture back. You can't just wipe them out with the stroke of a pen on the last page."

"You are right," said Huxley.

"I am?" I said, surprised that the great man would agree with me. I expected at least a recondite explanation.

"Yes, I am afraid you are, and my wife agrees with you. You see, I had originally written a longer book with an ending that would have pleased you. But a terrible fire in my home in California destroyed all my manuscripts, including the one for *Island.* And you see, well . . ." Huxley paused, wondering whether to go on. Finally he said, "I haven't been feeling well recently, and I wanted to get the book out. I am afraid that I rewrote a shorter book in which the ideas were more important than the plot or literary development."

Before leaving, Huxley took my hand. "I have so much enjoyed our conversation. You must come out this year and stay with my wife Laura and me. I have been very fortunate in my marriages. After my first wife Maria died, I married Laura Archera. She's Italian—a virtuoso violinist and a psychotherapist. She is quite wonderful, and I do not know what I would do without her. You and she would be good friends."

I never saw Aldous Huxley again. He was indeed very ill and died later that year of cancer. But he showed me much—the doorway to an unobstructed universe, a playful conjunction of the scholarly with the speculative, the aesthetic with the spiritual. From Huxley, too, I gained the idea that societies could be remade and that education had to be. The wise and luminous Laura Huxley and I later became friends, and I have lectured at her conferences on several occasions, as well as delivering an address in 1994 in honor of the hundredth anniversary of her husband's birth. Her work on what she calls "our ultimate investment," the optimal education of children from prebirth on, both stands as a formidable contribution in its own right and continues the vision of Aldous Huxley in *Island*.

A few months after meeting Huxley, I was introduced to his great friend and colleague, Gerald Heard. If anyone could be called the father of the human potentials movement, it is he. Renaissance man, scholar, scientist, author, novelist, mystic, prophet, and poet of ideas, he like Huxley could talk intently and without a shred of condescension to a woman fifty years his junior. His extraordinary versatility in science, psyche, and spirit and his luminous conversation made him friend and evocateur not only of Huxley but also of Christopher Isherwood, Stephen Spender, W. H. Auden, Henry and Clare Booth Luce, Ray Bradbury, Michael Murphy (the founder of Esalen), and many other innovative thinkers and doers. He was as at home in Eastern philosophy as he was in Western thought and had guided several contemplative schools in spiritual development.

Under the name H. F. Heard, he had also written a number of mysteries and theological fictions. One of his novellas, *Dromenon*, told the story of a medieval archaeologist who ventured into a cathedral, walked the labyrinth of the dromenon incised on its floor, followed with his eyes and psyche the same pattern carved in the walls, and through this was brought into a psychophysical state of ecstasy and spiritual awakening. The story impressed me so deeply that I adopted the image of the dromenon labyrinth on the floor of Chartres Cathedral as the symbol of my work.

I had been given a manuscript of Heard's latest work, *The Five Ages of Man*, to review. Reading it, I felt as if I had been restored to a forgotten gnosis. Here was human history seen through the eyes of an Olympian, the human soul known by a guide to its mysteries, and history and soul interwoven like the caduceus of Asclepios. Joining the principles of phylogeny and ontogeny to the social and personal history of humankind, Heard proposed that human consciousness, in its personal as well as its species development, had evolved through five stages. The preindividuality of the infant corresponded to the developmental level of the early human; the individuality of first adulthood corresponded to modern consciousness; and the postindividual stage of the wise elder corresponded to postmodern society. Heard not only charted the psychological journey of each stage but also showed the specific crises that arose to impede or traumatize the full potential of each. What were strikingly original in the book were the psychophysical methods and therapies, more in the order of complex initiations, that he offered as modern ways of surmounting the crisis of each stage and thus of entering more fully into the next level of development.

Heard's approach was meat and drink to me, for I was discovering that for all their ability to open the doors of inner and outer perception, psychedelics could not provide the psychospiritual and psychophysical growth and training we require to develop beyond our habits and cultures. Heard and I would walk through the New York streets, his long artist's hands carving arcs of ideas, his eyebrows like great wings rising and falling to the music of inquiry. He was a man of remarkable aesthetic appeal, fired by boundless curiosity, elegant playfulness, and a passion for discovery. In these walks and talks he gave me keys and clues to ancient and modern methods of enhancing the spectrum of human possibility. Years later, I wrote a book honoring and further developing his premise of five stages of human development, *Life Force: The Psycho-historical Recovery of the Self.* To my mind, Gerald Heard was one of the great souls of the twentieth century and the wellspring from which arose the movement to heal and enhance consciousness on this planet.

Despite these remarkable encounters, I did not spend all my time with elderly gentlemen. I began to think that it was time I had a marriage partner. None of the young men who kept calling me for dates seemed appropriate, and I suspected that they were really more interested in my legal supply of LSD. I began to meditate on the possibility of meeting someone new, hoping to see with my inner eye the face of the man I would marry. Instead I saw only ancient Egyptian statues. Naturally, I took this as a sign that I would meet my future husband in the Egyptian collection of the Metropolitan Museum of Art. So I began to spend my mornings there, striking up conversations with any presentable looking man. I saw a lot of antiquities and had a number of weird conversations, but my husband-to-be was not among the mummies.

Several weeks later a new friend, Arthur Ceppos, publisher of the Julian Press, decided that I was much too prudish for my own good. "I am not prudish," I protested, "I am simply half-Sicilian!"

"Yes, but I think for your own education, you should read some of the books I've just published on sexuality by a young man I've brought here from Arkansas, Robert E. L. Masters."

"Oh, I've read books on sexuality," I said blithely. "Why, I've read Herbert Marcuse's *Eros and Civilization* and Norman O. Brown's *Life Against Death.* Yes, I think I have a grasp of the subject."

Ceppos was clearly trying to keep from laughing. "Well, Bob's books are considerably less conceptual. They are more an anthropology of sexual behavior: *Forbidden Sexual Behavior* and *The Cradle of Erotica.*"

I took the books home and tried to read one. I got through about twenty-five pages before I gave up in dismay. I handed them over to my friend Michael Corner, who enjoyed them immensely. "People actually clutter their minds up with this kind of material?" I asked Ceppos on the telephone. "The author should be ashamed of himself. I'd like to give him a piece of my mind."

"Well, you can do that tonight," said Ceppos. "My wife Pru and I are having a small dinner party, and Bob will be there."

When I was introduced to Bob, I saw a very attractive young man in his midthirties with a shy manner and a boyish Midwestern face. He seemed quite startled to see me and kept looking at me as if I reminded him of someone. Later he told me that as a child, when he was falling asleep, he would frequently find himself in a closet where he would push back the clothes to find a door. Opening the door, he would go down some stone stairs and climb into a boat where there was always a grown-up princess who would take him on wonderful journeys. He said that he was bowled over by the fact that I looked and sounded exactly like the princess of his childhood.

We never got around to talking about his books. It turned out that for many years he had been doing research on peyote and mescaline, and with my LSD studies, that was all we could speak about.

Ceppos, trying to change the subject, finally interrupted with, "So how have you been spending your days in New York, Bob, when you're not writing books for me?"

"Well, I write in the mornings and in the late afternoons into the evening. In the early afternoons lately, I've been visiting the Egyptian section of the Metropolitan. I've been especially drawn to the statues of the goddess Sekhmet."

I turned white and took another look at Bob. Maybe he was the one. Maybe we had been missing each other because of the different hours we visited the museum. He seemed intelligent and interesting, and there was no question that I was drawn to him—but a sexologist?

"How exactly did you start to write about sexual behavior?" I finally asked him.

Bob then told us that in his teens he had informally studied philosophy in Paris at Le Tabou and similar cafes with Jean Paul Sartre and his friends Albert Camus, Simone de Beauvoir, and Jean Cocteau. They were often joined by Americans John Steinbeck and Erskine Caldwell. Then he went on to Marburg for further studies and an attempt to translate Heidegger's *Sein und Seit* (Being and Time) into English. Finally he finished his education at the University of Missouri, where he also taught philosophy. However, the academic life soon paled, and he got a job as editorial writer for the *Houston Post* and later for the *Shreveport Times*. During this time he began to collect curiosa and accounts of unusual behavior culled from the annals of natural history, anthropology, sexology, and medical history. He also wrote seven books—two novels, a book on aesthetics, several books of poetry, and several more on natural history. Sartre had told him to accumulate many manuscripts and then to make a big splash by publishing them all at once. That is what Sartre had done, and the critics were so in awe that his reputation was made.

With this goal in mind, Bob took his life savings, bought many reams of typing paper, and arranged to go and live in a cabin in Springdale, Arkansas, for two years to finish his books. He put the copies of his manuscripts and many of his collected curiosa under the canvas tarpaulin of a truck, while his typewriters, some of the anthropological material, and the sexology collection went into another vehicle. A friend drove the truck. When they stopped in Waldron, Arkansas, Bob and his friend exchanged hostile words with a local who regarded them as city slickers from Shreveport. As they were pulling out, the man threw a lighted cigar onto the tarpaulin of the truck. They did not smell the smoke or see the flames behind them until they were outside of Waldron. Bob's friend escaped the truck just in time, for after the gas tank ignited, the fiery column rose so high that it burned through telephone wires many feet overhead. Bob's manuscripts and notes were destroyed, as were most of his library and collections. The only thing that survived was the sexology collection, which was not on the truck.

Surprisingly, instead of feeling anguish and loss, Bob found himself curiously free and very light. Now he could begin his life over again, with no daily job to go to and two years to write whatever he wanted. He decided not to try to rewrite the seven lost books but to start fresh. He began with the sexology and anthropology material, since that is what remained. When Ceppos accepted the first two books, Bob moved to New York to try to make up for lost time by writing as many books as he could in as short a period as possible. Working around the clock, except for his excursions to the museum, he produced something like eight volumes in two years, a record even Isaac Asimov would have envied.

It was seven months before I saw Bob again. In late February, I fell very ill with what the doctor diagnosed as influenza. He left a few vitamin pills on the night-stand.

"Such a wonderful physician," said my mother, who was by this time well into Christian Science. She had been drawn to the positive thinking aspects of New Thought after my father's departure, perhaps to deal with her own despair. "He doesn't prescribe any medication. Here," she told me, "read this wonderful passage by Mrs. Eddy about how illness is only an illusion."

I could hardly read or think or speak or do anything that required effort. Turning over to one side was a major accomplishment, and flipping onto my stomach was a Himalayan adventure. Before dawn each morning, my temperature would soar, and with it would come a most interesting altered state of consciousness. Even though I was very sick, I still took a researcher's interest in the hallucinations that accompanied the rise in temperature. One morning at 3:00 A.M., my delirium took the form of a group of women in flowered hats who identified themselves as recently deceased Westchester matrons who had been heads of their garden clubs. Perhaps the women's flowered hats and horticultural interests were the result of my conversations with Aldous Huxley on the mystical nature of flowers!

My mother had moved a bed into my room to take care of me during my illness. The women looked over to her sleeping form and said, "Jean, wake up your mother and tell her to give you the blood test that's given to alcoholics."

"Go away," I moaned. "You're just my lousy fever."

This infuriated the women. "Don't patronize us, young lady, and don't tell us what we are. We know what we are, though we doubt that you know what you are. Now, wake up your mother and tell her to give you that blood test."

"But I never have more than one glass of wine a month," I protested, knowing even through my high fever that these hallucinatory women were over the top. The women persisted until I finally called out weakly to my mother to get me . . . a hot chocolate, since I couldn't bring myself to deliver their ridiculous message.

"Now why did you do that?" the women fussed. "You know we are just going to keep after you until you do what we ask."

After about an hour of this ghostly barrage, I finally capitulated and said, "Mother . . . could you get me . . . maybe . . . the blood test that's given to alcoholics?"

"Why, yes, Jean. I'll do that first thing in the morning."

I was stunned. Never had my mother been so compliant when it came to standard medicine. Later she told me that when I awakened her the second time, she had been dreaming about Nana, her dead mother, who was holding a dead chicken in her hand and telling her in some anger that the doctor was an idiot.

The blood tests revealed that I had a serious case of hepatitis. There is a reasonable explanation for the women in the flowered hats. They were, I believe, my collective body wisdom, somewhat whimsically attired but bearing critical information that was unavailable to my conscious mind but able to reach me in my feverish altered state. From that experience I began to develop procedures using less radical altered states, generally trance and guided imagery, to help students contact their own innate body wisdom. Often I lead them to call forth a personification of this wisdom as a being whom they are invited to call "The One Who Knows Health." The personification makes it possible for their inner knowings to assume recognizable form and to communicate with the conscious mind as directly and unambiguously as possible. Quite graciously, the Other World had sent me some allies in my crisis.

The Other World also sent me at this time an enigma that has continued to perplex me. One night I woke up around midnight in my usual feverish state and discovered that I was someone else. My name was Miguel de Hidalgo, and I was a physician who lived in Barcelona, Spain. I got up out of bed, hugely shocked to find myself in a sick female body. I turned on the light to discover that I was in a strange bedroom lined with bookshelves. The books were in English, a language I had little knowledge of, so I could barely understand the titles. I looked in the mirror and did not know the woman who looked back at me. Panicked and confused, I went over my own life's history. I reviewed my childhood in Spain, the schools and medical college I had attended, my marriage, and the names of my two children. Everything about my life as Miguel de Hidalgo was fresh and clear, but what had happened to my body, and where was I? Even my thoughts were in Spanish, for that was my language. Miguel de Hidalgo might still be caught in another body but for the fact that he noticed on the nightstand a vase filled with anemone flowers that a friend had brought Jean Houston earlier that day. At that moment, through the good graces of the flowers, Jean Houston came back into her own body and, hopefully, Miguel de Hidalgo went back to his.

What in the world of altered states was going on here? Could it be, as many ancient traditions suggest, that the soul wanders in sleep and that Miguel de Hidalgo and I got caught in each other's fields? Or did our coming together happen because we are all in a seamless web of kinship anyway, and my high fever just gave me leakier margins with which to receive that part of my kinship that was a dreaming, wandering Spanish physician? Or was it just a dream? *La vida es sueño,* the Spanish say, and in this case the dream was as real as life.

By the fall of the year, Bob joined me in some of my research and served as a subject for my studies of altered states. We worked well together and saw a great deal of each other, but I had no idea he was interested in me and not my legal LSD. Bob, however, wrote me an eighty-page epic poem of love and devotion and proposed marriage. When he was away on a vacation, I could sense some archetypal presence urging me to accept. So what else could I do? We were married in May 1965 and spent our honeymoon writing our first book, *The Varieties of Psychedelic Experience,* which recounted our mutual and separate studies. The book was featured on the front page of the Sunday *New York Times Book Review* section under the headline "Psychedelicious or Psychedelirious?" It was a cautious but congratulatory review, and I found myself sought after as a speaker on the college lecture circuit and a guest on many talk shows.

The spirit of the sixties was by now in full swing, the age of Aquarius having dawned in a blaze of psychedelic colors. LSD had become a *cause célèbre,* and people were uncorking their minds with Berkeley-spawned bathtub-gin varieties of the substance. I spent much time on the road trying to put out some of the resulting conflagrations. People often ask me why Bob and I have no children. I explain that during the years when I would have considered having children, say, 1966 to around 1972, I felt it my duty to offset the horrendous aftermath of so much irresponsible drug taking. In 1965, Bob and I had started the Foundation for Mind Research to study nondrug ways of exploring human consciousness. Around 1966, due to controversy generated by both scientific disagreement and media madness, the Food and Drug Administration withdrew most of its licensing for research with psychedelics. With research and therapy stopped, the black market boomed.

A typical week for me in those days included teaching philosophy all day at Marymount College in Tarrytown, New York, coming home to our New York City apartment to run nondrug studies of altered states in the evenings, and then on the weekends traveling to one or another college to deliver a lecture dissuading students from using drugs. Often the pattern was that, following a campus lecture by Timothy Leary on the glories of the psychedelic experience, pushers of LSD-laden sugar cubes would peddle the drug on campus at about eight to ten dollars a cube. (A dose of LSD cost about two cents to make.) Inevitably, some students would enter into bizarre and sometimes psychotic states, and the frantic college president would call me to come and "do something." I would arrive on Friday night and lecture to a packed audience.

I knew that there was no point in intoning a litany of horror stories, so instead I would try to give a reasonable description of what psychedelics could and could not do. I was careful to explain that in unprepared settings and with the poor quality of LSD sold in the schools, there was always a possibility of "bad trips." I would speak to the untapped treasures of the mind that were waiting to be released without drugs. Then I would often stay on for several days to help create a program for the college in which students could learn ways to "turn on" their minds and senses using alternate methods. The exercises Bob and I devised for these students were later published in our book Mind Games: The Guide to Inner Space, which later inspired the John Lennon song.

One evening in 1969, while lecturing at Fitchburg State College, I noticed that the first three rows filled with what could only be described as failed hippies. Paint was haphazardly slapped on their faces; they wore bent feathers and wilted flowers and seemed unacquainted with showers or baths. My lecture on psychedelic drugs, including the question and answer period, was carried live on the radio to the surrounding region. As I concluded my remarks, one of the hippies languidly raised his hand and asked, "How come if I mix purple smash with angel dust, my head feels so funny?"

I decided that the only approach to take was the macabre. "Oh, purple smash, that's atropine. Angel dust is a pig tranquilizer. Together they unknit the dendrites in your brain as well as shoot your blood pressure sky high. Do you feel like your head is exploding? Yes? Well that's because it is. Next question, please."

A young woman dressed as a shaman who had fallen on hard times raised her hand. "When I mix green turkey with zombie gray and add some Jim Beam to it, my stomach hurts. What should I do?"

I explained sweetly that her stomach was acquiring holes from the mixture, as were her liver, pancreas, and kidneys. "But don't let that bother you," I added, "because soon you will be able to have little windows open on all your major organs and observe the fascinating sight of their crumbling away."

"Far out!" said the girl.

I then launched into a stern lecture on the dangers of random drug taking, to which the first three rows grinned amiably and offered the comment, "Really weird, man."

At the end of the program, I was told that I had a phone call in the dean's office. After I identified myself, I heard a voice filled with intonations that spelled Mafiosa. It said, "I'm from the local. You know what the local is?"

"*Sì,*" I responded, my speech pattern now congruent with his, "I know what the local is."

"You've been talking too much to the schools in our area, and you're hurting our business. So we want you to know that if you keep on doing this, we're going to cut you up."

I responded, in perfect Sicilian, with a phrase I learned from my sainted grandmother, "*Eh, stronzo! Di spero ou diablo te caccio ouchu e te kaka indo purtusso!*" Cleaned up a bit this translates as, "Hey turd! May the devil scoop out your eyeballs and relieve himself in the sockets!"

The voice on the other end seemed shocked, even moved.

"*Eh, paesana?*" he asked.

"*Sì, io sono paesana,*" I replied.

"Good-bye," he said.

"*Ciao,*" I agreed.

I don't speak much Sicilian, but the little I do is perfect, since the accent is bred in the bone and only a Sicilian can pronounce it properly. I later learned that the local drug Mafia had been using some students in the college as distributors of drugs to colleges in the northeast. In return, they were supplied with the latest brain-eating garbage; thus the three rows of failed hippies.

I also did stints in Haight-Ashbury, the famed district in San Francisco where kids arrived wearing flowers in their hair and street acid in their brains. Whenever I visited the district, I was busy trying to guide kids down from bad trips and persuade those who were selling or even giving away the stuff to stop distributing their goods. One young couple was especially known for the jazzed-up acid that they sold or gave away. The young man had long bushy red hair and a beard, while his girlfriend wore her hip-length hair in many braids and danced and sang along the street with her large breasts bouncing under her braless tank top. The two were known as Sunshine and Red Wing, the Psychedelic Kids, and they seemed immune to all my persuasions, enticements, and threats. They regarded LSD as a religion and wanted to put huge quantities of it into every water reservoir. They assured me that this was the only way to world peace, happiness, and a new age for the human race. "Like, it's the sacrament, you know? Like, it turns us all into Jesus and Buddha. It's like, you know, soul medicine."

I would have lost sight of the Psychedelic Kids but for the anomalies of neighborhood. My New York home is only a few miles from one of the largest concentrations of Hasidic Jews in the United States. One day my secretary and I were driving near Monsey, and I commented on the many Hasidic men and women and children who were out walking that day. Suddenly I shouted to my secretary to stop the car. I jumped out and ran over to a very sober, even solemn Hasidic couple. There was no mistaking the red hair and beard, although the male half of the former Psychedelic Kids was now dressed in the long black coat and wide-brimmed hat of a Hasid. His wife was wearing a black wig, dark matronly clothes, and clunky shoes. She was very pregnant and pushing a baby carriage with three other small children trailing after her.

"Sunshine!" I shouted to the man. "Sunshine Katz! And Red Wing!"

"I am called Abraham now," he said, looking around nervously to see if any of his religious brethren were noticing this meeting. "And my wife is called Hannah."

"You, of all people, owe me an explanation!"

"Yes," he answered somewhat reluctantly, "I suppose we do. You see, we went too far out on acid. We lost all boundaries and burned out completely. When we got back to New York, we knew we needed something that would take us higher than LSD but give us boundaries. We met some former acid heads who had converted back to Judaism, and since we were Jewish, we did the same, only we needed a more rigorous community than Conservative or Orthodox ones."

"And are you happy, Sunshine, I mean, Abraham?"

"I am happier than I have ever been in my life. When I am sitting at the rabbi's table and studying Talmud, or when I am dancing with the Torah, I know true bliss, far beyond anything I ever knew with drugs. I have found what for me is the true way."

"And Red Wing, I mean, Hannah?" I asked, looking her way. She had all this time refused to look at me, her eyes either cast down or absorbed in attending to one of her children.

"For Hannah, it is not the same. Women have different roles in Hasidic life. I'm sorry, but it is not right that I be seen talking to you. *Shalom aleichem.*"

"*Aleichem shalom,*" I said to their departing figures.

With the ending of the psychedelic drug research, Bob and I turned our attention to discovering other means, both ancient and modern, to explore consciousness. We constructed in our apartment laboratory a sensory deprivation chamber in which our research subjects could lie without sight and sound and, suspended as they were in foam, also without touch. Because the brain requires a certain amount of stimulation in order to maintain its usual processing of the world, when deprived of sight, sound, and touch, our subjects would begin to hallucinate, projecting their own internal sights, sounds, and feelings. "Where is that music coming from?" they would ask. Or, "How did you get a movie projector in here? And how can it be showing movies from my life?"

We also went to the other extreme and created an audiovisual overload chamber. Our research subjects sat surrounded by a curved screen on which as many as twelve slide dissolve units projected a flowing phantasmagoria of abstract imagery as well as polarized slides. Music that matched the images was piped through headphones. The artists and engineers who helped us design and build this chamber, like light artist Don Snyder, also helped create the great multimedia discos of the sixties, the Electric Circus and the Fillmore West. Being in the chamber stimulated imagery centers in the brain. After a while, the subjects seemed to enter into an unconscious partnership with the forms and colors flowing in front of them and to project their own internal imagery onto the screen. Then we would ask the subjects to close their eyes and discover that the "show" was continuing in the form of eidetic imagery seen with the eyes closed.

At the same time, we also developed what became a rather notorious instrument to facilitate research into altered states and visual imagery. We called it the Altered States of Consciousness Induction Device (ASCID), and we got the idea for it from reading about the devices that witches had used to help them in their "travels." The witches' broomstick, we learned, was actually a kind of cradle or leather bag suspended from a tree, the movements of which affected the vestibular system so that the witch, who may also have augmented her journey with a dose of *datura stramonium,* felt that she was flying off to other realms. Our ASCID device was essentially a metal swing or pendulum in which our subjects stood upright, supported by broad bands of canvas and wearing blindfold goggles. We suspended this pendulum from a very sensitive device so that the subject's slightest movement sent the metal frame forward and backward, side to side, and in rotating circles. These motions, affecting the inner ear, induced a state in which our subjects lost their usual reference to space and time and eventually even to their own bodies. In anywhere from two to twenty minutes, they entered into a trancelike state and frequently descended through the four levels of imagery that I had observed with my psychedelic subjects. In the ASCID cradle, great journeys were taken, books written, inventions discovered, lifelong concerns seen in new ways—so much so, that some of our subjects began to refer to the device as the cradle of creativity.

We continued to use the cradle for years, and many other researchers adopted it for their use. Gradually we discontinued using it, for we found that people would get addicted to it and even refuse to explore their inner states without first taking a ride. However, using varieties of trance, hypnosis, guided imagery, meditation, and active imagination, Bob and I found that we could take people on journeys without drugs or machines.

From our studies of hundreds of subjects, we concluded, first, that the inner imagery process appears to be essentially creative, tapping into domains of the self that are available all the time. These other domains, generally corresponding to the four levels, offer vast reservoirs of unconscious knowledge and content to the creative process. The further into these domains one goes, the richer the solutions will be. For example, images observed long enough will cease to be random or disconnected and will organize into symbolic dramas, narratives, or problem-solving processes. Fiction and drama may be manifestations of this inherent tendency, which is why I often say that if novels didn't exist, the brain would have to invent them. We are storied and storying beings to our core. Certain Buddhist and Sufi disciplines, as well as the proliferating image therapies, owe their efficacy to the imagery coded in the domains of the self.

Second, we found that if our subjects prolonged their observation of their inner narrative imagery, they discovered increased motivation to do creative work as well as break through any blocks to creativity. Many blocks to creativity or to taking action are actually blocks within the imagery process. Change the imagery around the block, and in many cases the block is released. This is as true for cultures as it is for individuals. Much of my later work with cultures has focused on finding images buried in the myths and symbols of the culture that can release a people from self-denigrating attitudes or feelings of hopelessness.

Finally, in an altered state of consciousness, especially when imagery is central to the experience, the mind enters into a different domain of time, and processes of thought that should take weeks, months, or even years is done in hours, minutes, or seconds. In the state that I call Alternate Temporal Process (ATP), time is telescoped so that, for example, in five minutes of clock time, a person can in the inner world rehearse a piece on the piano in a way that yields as much improvement as if they had practiced in a conventional way for many hours. The same is true of using ATP with a creative process. The mind speeds over alternatives, selecting, synthesizing, putting together ideas and images. So-called creative breakthroughs may often involve ATP; the mind simply does not have the time to block the flow of the creative process.

My work with altered states of consciousness has continued over many years and in virtually every part of the world. I have peered into the inner worlds of Africans and Chinese, Peruvians and residents of Tierra del Fuego, Eskimo and Egyptian Coptic monks. From all this I conclude that there is no such contrast as ordinary consciousness versus an altered state of consciousness. Consciousness is always altering, and that is its very nature—to expand, contract, exalt, depress, go inward, go outward, and even ride a flat line into nothingness. The task, it would seem, is to learn how to self-orchestrate along the continuum of consciousness, and that is what I have tried to teach people to do. Then one never needs to seek strong drink, visionary drugs, madness, or, as in the case of Rimbaud, the conscious disordering of one's senses in order to visit the many worlds that each of us harbors. Within the realms of our minds, we contain different personas, skills that we never thought to have, audacious inventions, and even the beloved of the soul. We are such stuff as consciousness is made of, and our little world is larger than we think.

The government officials are coming back to full waking consciousness. They stretch, look at one another, giggle, and then all talk at once. They are full of plans at once idealistic and feasible. Each has discovered a heart's desire for a future America, many societies within the one Great Society. The one theme that runs through virtually all of them is that the ideal society will be rich with theater and music.

Of course, what they did not know is that their next president indeed would have a theatrical background—in the movies. However, as is the antic way with altered states, he may not exactly have been what they conjured while lying on the floor in visionary America.

In recent years I have met quite a few of these people, some still in government service, many not. Several head foundations devoted to improving the lives of the needy; others work in corporations trying to create a culture of excellence. Some have gone into private agencies to protect the environment, and more than a few have become writers, novelists, artists, professional chefs, and one even a teacher of African dance.

"Why African dance?" I asked her.

"Lying there on the floor, I saw it all," she replied. "We have to change the rhythm of society if we are going to change anything at all. And listen, honey, when you had us all there in that altered state, you may have thought nothing much would come of it, but you're wrong. What we learned down there just went underground for a while during the eighties, you know what I mean? And now it's popping up all over the place."

8

✦

Schooling Godseeds

It is April 14, 2020, and I am visiting an elementary school in Ames, Iowa. I am known as Granny Jean. As I approach the school's grounds, I am astonished at the variety of buildings that comprise the learning centers—simple huts made of mud and wattle, an Indian tepee, a large geodesic dome, a walk-in space station, even a pennant-flying medieval guild hall. A group of children is busy building a log cabin, while others are spraying liquid cement into fanciful shapes for a new kind of building. All these structures are set amid trees and meadows.

In the near distance I see a soccer game in progress, but I turn when I hear someone call out, "Embrace tiger, go to mountain." It is a class in tai chi, and I marvel at the delicate but controlled poetry in the children's movements. I move toward the guild hall and prepare to enter, thinking that this is the administration building, but when I reach the door, I bump into nothingness. The seemingly ancient structure is a hologram.

I hear giggling behind me and turn to be met by my hosts—two children, around ten years old, one of whom is in a motorized wheelchair that he appears to run by thinking the direction he wants to go. They introduce themselves as Tony and Lakshmi.

"We fooled you, didn't we, Granny Jean," says Tony, as he moves his chair closer to me. "That's my science project—creating holograms of buildings and placing them around the meadow."

"And what's your science project, a dinosaur theme park?" I ask the girl, thinking back to a movie I enjoyed in my salad days.

"Oh no, I'm doing an integrated study of fifteenth-century Florence, the time of the Renaissance. I'm trying to understand how it happened, why it happened, and I'm looking into the work of Michelangelo and Leonardo da Vinci. I'm learning Italian, taking a course in sculpting, getting the math I need to measure the Duomo and compare it with Calvary Lutheran, and cooking green bread and weird stews like they ate back then."

"And how do you like your study, Lakshmi?"

"Great, it's real raga, you griff my high?"

I remind myself that I must find the time to catch up on young people's vernacular. "Watch out for the Satori Hole," she cautions, as she steers me around a sudden cavelike opening in the ground, where I later learn that children crawl in to meditate or just enjoy some solitude.

"Let's take her to see the little kids first," says Tony as he points his chair in the direction of the learning center for younger children.

"This is a wonderful school, Granny Jean," Lakshmi tells me as we follow Tony, "because everyone here is special."

"Do you mean that the children here have special talents or special problems?"

"Oh no, nothing like that, although we have every kind of kid here. No, it's just that we all treat each other as having all kinds of wonderful possibilities. We're all marvelous, and we're all different. In a million years there's never been anyone like me or Tony."

"It sure wasn't like that in my day," I mutter as I catch up with Tony.

He joins the conversation. "My mom tells me that long, long ago, like when you went to school, someone like me with cerebral palsy would have to go to a school for disabled children. We still have some schools like that, but here I'm just a special case of being normal. Here are the little kids."

We enter a room that is a riot of color, shapes, music, and even smells—a child's garden of the senses. I feel that I have passed through the looking glass into Alice's world, for dancing around the room are young children, each of whom is carrying a large plastic letter that is almost as big as the child carrying it. Each child is making the sound of her or his letter: "Ah-ah-ah-ah! B-b-b-b! M-m-m-m! Ca-ca-ca-ca!"

The teacher is pounding away at the piano and calling out words to spell. "Let's put together a HAT!" Immediately there is a mad scramble as the H, the A, and the T find each other and arrange themselves to form the word. The teacher notices us and, without missing a beat, signals Lakshmi to take over. Lakshmi starts to play and calls out "SNAKE!"

The teacher, a tall black woman, comes laughing toward me. "We have a saying around here: If you want to hold it in your head, you'd better hold it in your hands. I'm Jenny Jefferson. I'm glad to meet you."

"Does that mean that the children touch everything they are learning about, Jenny?"

"Everything, as well as running it through the other senses as well—all two hundred of them." She leads me over to a table where three children are conducting a math experiment, figuring out how to divide an apple into three equal parts. In the process they are sniffing, biting, cutting, and measuring apples—and discovering fractions. Apple juice streams from their mouths; apple pieces are strewn all over the table.

A small child comes up chewing away on her fruit. "Ms. Jefferson," she says, "why does a third have to be less than a half?"

"What a wonderful question, Barbie," Jenny says as she goes over to the table and cuts an apple in half. "Now you tell me this. Can this half of an apple be more than this whole apple?"

Suddenly in Barbie's eyes appears that perpetual miracle so small and yet the essence of all discovery, "Oh, I see. . . ."

Just then the door opens and a bevy of children, all about eight years old, come running in. I notice that each is carrying a little book. "Story time," one of them yells, and the first grade comes bounding up to meet them. Soon each of the older children is reading from a book to several of the younger ones. "What's going on here?" I ask Tony.

"Oh that's the third grade reading the books they wrote to the first grade. You get to write and illustrate your own stories and then the computer helps you publish them. But you've also got to learn book binding at the art center. That way you have your own hardcover book. And when you read it to the little kids, it gets them interested in writing. Neat, huh?"

"Very neat," I say as I draw near to one third grader who is explaining her book to several younger children. The cover seems to be a drawing of old-fashioned farmers. "See, my mom and I found an old graveyard from the 1800s near where we live. So I did some research on the families who were buried there, and I made up a story about their lives."

"Read it. Read it," the children press her.

"Okay, here goes," she says and turns to the first page. "It was a dark and stormy night. . . ." The kids nestle in closer.

Before I was twelve years old, I must have attended close to twenty schools. From Brooklyn to Pismo Beach, from Teaneck to Tarzana, I hit every kind of school system that America in the forties and early fifties had to offer. In the course of a year,

I might have moved from the friendly drone of a one-room schoolhouse to the lock-lipped terror of a "religious" school to the rowdy exuberance of a "progressive" institution (where you never learned to read but the finger painting was great) to Miss Prigg's bluestocking establishment for young WASPs to a school for army brats where the war in the classroom nearly matched anything the daddies were up to.

Needless to say, my real education took place on the train. My mother believed in the classical dictum that the mind's muscles are built up through memorization and that the great intellects of the past owed their gifts to the reams of saga and scripture they committed to memory while they were children.

"Jeanie," she said to me one day shortly after my third birthday. "We're going to put biceps on your cortex. Now repeat after me, 'To be or not to be. . . .'"

"Be not be. BUZZZZZZZZZ. Look, Mommy, I'm a bee. BUZZZZZZZ. I'm gonna sting you."

"That is the question," my mother persisted.

"What is the question, Mommy?"

My father often interrupted these sessions by encouraging me to memorize— not the immortal lines of the Bard but a slew of original efforts he and I composed together. One unforgettable ditty, made up, I believe, somewhere between Pittsburgh and Terre Haute, ran as follows:

> I have a funny daddy who walks here and there with me,
> And everywhere that Daddy goes, there Jeanie's sure to be,
> And everything that Daddy says, that Jeanie's sure to tell,
> You may have heard my daddy's jokes; I hope he fries in hell!

Fortunately, my mother insisted on having me commit to memory passages of somewhat higher literary quality. By the time I was ten, I had been made to learn by heart whole scenes from Shakespeare's plays, sheaves of poems, mostly of a style that could only be described as nineteenth-century heroic, great chunks of Dante's *Divine Comedy,* and (from my father) all sixty-seven stanzas of "The Face on the Barroom Floor." We also sang a great deal of Italian opera together, especially the arias of Verdi and Puccini. The rest of my education went apace. I was always on a collision course with history, and geography was something that sped by at eighty miles an hour.

"Jeanie, quick, look out the window. There goes the continental divide, and it was there that Chief Stony Foot captured the traveling minstrel show and put them to work tanning buffalo hides."

Learning to read and write was a unique experience. My father sat me down next to a radio, turned on some comedy show, and ordered, "If you hear anything funny, write it down."

"I don't know what's funny," I whined.

"What do you mean, you don't know what's funny? You're my daughter, so by God you better know what's funny!"

So by age five I was stealing jokes for my father, which he would rewrite and present on another show.

Between train trips, I actually went to school. Dad insisted that I enroll wherever we stopped for more than several weeks. He thought that the experience would be good for me, even though we rarely stayed in any one place long enough for me to learn much. This was a source of constant contention between my parents.

"School isn't for learning," I heard my father tell my mother one day. "Heck, Mary, you can teach Jeanie more than any fool schoolmarm can. No, if Jeanie goes to school, it's for an entirely different reason. School is for politics."

"But, Jack, the poor child never has time to have any period of adjustment."

"You're right, Mary. So the only way for her to avoid the problem of adjustment is to take over! If she gets to be president of the class every time she changes schools, then she won't run into any of the ornery treatment the new kid generally gets."

With my father as my campaign manager, the technique of taking over soon was refined into a science. The campaign began immediately upon moving to a new town. "Jeanie," my father might say as we carried our belongings into a newly rented house, "tomorrow morning you get enrolled in the fourth grade at the Riverside–Van Nuys Elementary School. Start thinking about what you can do to begin Phase One."

"Phase One: get them interested," I repeated to myself. "I know, Daddy. I'll start with my rodeo rope tricks. They went over great in that school in Biloxi, Mississippi."

The next day I was introduced to class 4B by the teacher, Miss Rosenbloom. I heard a titter from the front rows and instantly spotted my enemies. They were the same all over the country. Wherever I went, they wore the same tight ribbons and shiny patent leather shoes. They had clean fingernails, wore rings with semiprecious stones, and had names like Roxanne, Jeanette, Paula, and Lillian. They were the elite girls in the class, the social butterflies, the stuck-ups, the Nasties. They knew how to create a magic circle of power and prestige, and they ruled supreme in determining who was in and who was out. I knew them, and by their smirk I knew that they knew me.

I cast my practiced eye around the room in search of my buddies. There they were—the dreamers and the tricksters, scratching their necks and shuffling their feet, ready for anything or anybody that could show them something different to be or do. And there, in the last row, with no one sitting near him, was my special friend, the class outcast. Whether he was the poorest kid in school or the class weirdo, he was almost always my best friend. He was generally more interesting than the rest of the kids, and what's more, both my parents seemed to like him best. If I sensed I was in for a landslide, I generally tried to bring him in as vice president.

As the teacher drilled us through arithmetic and spelling, I noted that class 4B that day was at a level that my mother called "California so-so." This contrasted with "Southern slow" and "New York speedy," the level she tried to keep me at. Since I had had so many different teachers, I recognized Miss Rosenbloom's style; she was a "sleeper." There were also "screamers," "shamers," "stand-over-ers" (they hovered over your desk while you wrote), and "spitters" (when they yelled at the class they sprayed the front row). Of course there were nice ones too—the ones who tried to invent interesting ways to help you learn new subjects. I thought about Miss Murray, who had us make up our own songs as part of music appreciation; of Mr. Horowitz, who taught mathematics and shop and joined the two together to teach us basic geometry while we made tables; and of course my dad, who had us inventing new machines with odds and ends we found around the neighborhood or at the city dump.

As Miss Rosenbloom droned on, I looked around the room and noticed that about half the class had died. "Pay attention, children," she admonished. "Otherwise, you won't be able to pass the test." Oh oh, I thought, she's one of those who teach for the test. I won't be learning much here. Years later, I understood that people's long decline into psyche-sclerosis of the mind started in classrooms like these. At least Miss Rosenbloom and her ilk taught me what not to do with a child's mind!

I am sorry to say that little has changed in the wasteland of teachers lecturing out of textbooks and bored children responding to directives in workbooks. And although the state of the art in educating the child's whole mind and body is presently quite high, the application of these findings, except in special schools and cases, is shockingly low. In fact, of the thirteen thousand hours spent in school from kindergarten through high school, something like 75 percent of all classroom instruction is still centered around textbooks and has little to do with life as She is lived! Policy makers fear real-life experience and absolve themselves by loading on more course work and longer school hours and by cutting out art and music and other glories that speak to the beauty of the mind and spirit. No wonder the National Commission on Excellence in Education has said, "If an unfriendly foreign power had attempted to impose on America the mediocre educational performance that exists today, we might well have viewed it as an act of war." Occasionally Miss Rosenbloom would break the tedium by asking a question, and always the same kids held up their hands to answer. The Nasties, especially, waved their hands in the air. "I know, Teacher. I know. I know!"

Finally, recess came, and as the children bounded out to freedom, I sought out the outcast and asked him his name.

"Coo Coo, Coo Coo, Coo Coo!" he screamed at me in a frenzied imitation of a cuckoo-clock bird. "Coo Coo Fanny. That's my name."

"Yes, but what's your real name, the name your mom and dad gave you, not the name that the kids gave you?" As a veteran observer and boon companion of crazy kids, I was in familiar territory here.

"Charles Longbotham," he replied, somewhat more soberly, "but everybody's called me Coo Coo since second grade."

"Why?" I asked.

"'Cause they say I'm crazy."

"Are you?"

He nodded.

"How?"

"Well, they tell me that every so often I jump out of my seat, get stiff as a board, spin around a couple of times, and then pass out. When I come to, I predict things, like which team is going to win the baseball game or that the principal is going to break her leg, which she did. I never remember afterward what I said, and that's why they call me Coo Coo."

"Listen, Longbotham," I replied, "a prophet is never without honor except in his own country. That's the way it was with Jesus, and that's the way it is with you. You're not cuckoo; you're wonderful! You have a great talent. I tell you what, you stick with me, and we'll take over the class."

Obviously, I realized even back then what I tell my students today—that many people labeled crazy by contemporary standards are, in essence, creative or spiritual geniuses. Think of what many formally trained psychologists would make of the curious practices and visionary knowings of a Teresa of Ávila, a Saint Francis of Assisi, an Emily Dickinson. I seriously doubt that any of them would have gotten to their teens without being put on some tranquilizer or psychoactive drug. We do such great originals a disservice by labeling them as pathological. When we see them in their fullness—mythologize, rather than pathologize, their visions and special gifts—we enrich ourselves and bring evolutionary insights into the world.

With my new friend in tow—I, for one, could recognize his genius—I took my lariat and went out to the playground. I strolled over to the dead center of the schoolyard and began spinning the lariat over my head. Soon kids were beginning to notice and to gather around, except the Nasties, who stood clustered together and giggling over by the fence.

"Hey, what's your name?" called out one of the members of the admiring circle that now surrounded me.

"Jean."

"Hey, Jean, do you know how to lasso things with that rope?"

"Sure," I replied. "What do you want me to lasso?" I looked around for a post or something, but my eyes landed on the Nasties still bunched over by the fence pretending I didn't exist. Then it dawned on me. Here was a perfect opportunity to launch Phase Two of my dad's carefully worked out plan of conquest: turn the world upside down. This meant bringing the people who were at the bottom up to the top and letting the people who were at the top enjoy a little humility, for a change, and in general shaking up all the usual habits and expectations. I moved closer to the fence and let fly with my rope. Soon many hands were helping me haul a gaggle of furious girls toward the center of the playground. Though I knew I would pay for my triumph, I had won the first round.

"Boy, are we going to get back at you!" said Lillian, the leader of the Nasties. "We're going to tell the teacher and have you put in the class for special problems."

"No you're not," I replied pleasantly, "because if you do, I'm not going to invite you to the best and most fun party you'll ever go to in your life, which I am having next week. I am inviting the whole class. We're going to play the game that everybody is playing in New York City. It's called Juby Juby Ding Ding, and I'm the only kid in California who knows the rules." Actually, the only place this game existed was in my head. But Lillian was hooked, and she knew it.

As we trailed back to the classroom, I noticed Coo Coo struggling along by himself. "Would you like to carry the lariat, Longbotham?" I called out to him.

His face lit up, and he came running over. "Sure, thanks," he said and carefully took the rope from me.

"His name isn't Longbotham," a little girl named Gigi Getz advised me. "It's Fanny—Coo Coo Fanny."

I could see Longbotham's face fall. "No, it's not," I retorted. "It's Long-both-am, Charles Longbotham, and anyone who calls him Coo Coo Fanny can't come to my party. And you shouldn't be mean to him, 'cause he's special. He's a prophet just like Jesus."

"I'm Jewish," said Gigi. "I don't believe in Jesus."

"Well, like Moses, then. Come on, Longbotham, predict something."

Longbotham sucked in his breath, shut his eyes very tight, hammered on his head with his fist, and said, "I predict that Lillian and her friends are going to try to get you into lots of trouble. And I predict that we're going to have lots of fun."

Longbotham proved to be a true prophet. During the rest of the week, the Nasties tried their hardest to humiliate me. Later that week, I asked Miss Rosenbloom for a monitor's job, hoping that I'd be made blackboard monitor, which would have given me opportunities to show off how high up the board I could reach and how much chalk dust I could raise and to perform other feats calculated to arouse voter interest.

Unfortunately, Roxanne, one of the chief Nasties, was the keeper of the class assignment sheet. Still smarting from being hog-tied on the playground, Roxanne smiled sweetly and offered me the post of bathroom monitor. Her suggestion was greeted by hoots of laughter from my classmates. My dilemma was clear. If I accepted the job of bathroom monitor, I would not only have to give up part of my lunch period three times a week to guard the bathroom, but I would sink to the level of class leper—somewhat on a par with Longbotham. But to refuse would have been a greater humiliation—to admit defeat and to sink into classroom anonymity. Then I remembered my father's sage political advice, "It's okay to let yourself appear at first to be the underdog. That way everybody has sympathy for you. It's the old log cabin to the White House routine." With that in mind, I accepted the appointment.

On the having-fun side, I also scored a few victories, such as the great show-and-tell caper. Show-and-tell time was my personal province. I used to think it was invented just for me. It was the bedrock of my political strategy and afforded me many hours of free publicity. On the day of show-and-tell, I wore my trick sleeves to class, intending to demonstrate my prowess at sleight-of-hand, another educational must my father imposed on me. "How can you possibly have a successful life and not know magic tricks?" he reasoned sagely. When my turn came, I got up and said, "Today I'd like to show everybody a mysterious magical marvel that I learned from a wise old Indian chief. What I do is say some powerful magical words over somebody and then I pull out of his head his secret nature. That's right. I pull out something that tells what you're really like. Now, who wants to go first?"

Every hand in the class shot up, except for the Nasties. I called on the class baseball nut first. "Okay, Donald, you come up and sit down right here in front of me." I waved my arms over his head intoning, "Abracadabra, Capilly capike. Tell us what Donald really is like!" Then I reached into Donald's ear and pulled out a miniature baseball and bat, purchased the day before at the five-and-dime. "That's you, Donald," I said, handing him his secret nature. Donald was delighted.

"Who's next?" I asked and chose Longbotham out of the sea of waving arms. He sat down in front of me and I chanted, "Azarec, pazarec, moxi pan-dessence. Tell us the nature of Longbotham's essence!" I gave my sleeve a shake, and suddenly about fifty gold stars, the kind you get for good marks, appeared in Longbotham's hair. "Congratulations, Longbotham. You're made of gold stars."

A beaming and bemused Longbotham went happily back to his seat picking stars out of his hair.

"Okay, let's have a girl now. How about you, Lillian?"

"Yeah, Lillian. Go ahead. Go find out what you're really like."

Lillian got to her feet reluctantly. "I know what I'm really like," she whispered to me with the knowing smirk of one professional to another as she sat down in front of me. "And you're going to need about a thousand gold stars."

"We'll see," I said. "The magic never lies." Waving my arms in my most impressive manner, I chanted, "Gezzam and gozzam and ho hum and diz. Tell us who Lillian actually is." I reached down into her hair and, with a jerk, produced a horrible shrunken head from the Amazon, which I had demanded and gotten for a Christmas present. "Here's Lillian's secret nature!" I hooted, and pandemonium broke out.

Lillian ran screaming to the back of the room with me hot on her trail, swinging the shrunken head by the hair. The head must have had some truly magical properties, because the classroom reverted to a kind of primitive chaos. Kids fell into wild, convulsive laughter, more than a few wet their pants, and the head was sent whizzing through the air from hand to hand. All this was climaxed by Long-botham's spinning like a top, keeling over, and then sitting up to chirp, "President Coo Coo, President Coo Coo."

After that episode, Miss Rosenbloom barred me from show-and-tell forever, but that, of course, didn't stop me. In my seminars and workshops, I am always using stunts to help my students get in touch with their Essences. We wear cos-tumes and masks, give gifts to each other and dance our dreams, spin like derv-ishes, dissolve into laughter, and create a magnum of mayhem—all in the service of discovering our "secret nature," the Godseed hidden in each of us. Orchestrat-ing all of this as chief show-off and impresario has, I guess, always been part of my Essence, even in the fourth grade.

Lillian, of course, retaliated as soon as possible for my show-and-tell triumph. On the day of my party, which the kids had begun to call the "world's greatest party," I showed up ten minutes late for bathroom monitor duty because I had been trying out some of my father's better jokes with the lunchroom crowd. When I pushed open the swinging door, I discovered that the bathroom had been sabotaged. The cubicles were festooned with streamers of toilet paper, water was cascading to the floor from sinks that had been stoppered and left with the faucets running full blast, and the toilets were packed with wads of paper towels. And to underscore this debauchery, someone had even scribbled on the mirror in lipstick, "Where is the bathroom monitor?" For my dereliction of duty, Miss Rosenbloom made me stay after school to write one hundred times on the blackboard: "I will always be on time at the bathroom."

When I finally got home, my party was in full swing. My father, who had been voted the most popular boy in the class when I was in third grade, had scarcely noticed my absence. As usual, he had completely taken over and, by now, held my classmates completely in thrall. As I went through the front gate, a strange appari-tion bounded past me in a gorilla mask and an orange fright wig and wearing huge clown feet ending in bright red toenails. He was followed by a boisterous, yelping stampede of my classmates. Every so often, my father would stop in his tracks, scratch himself monkey-style, and burst into a torrent of gibbering. The kids quickly caught on and began pelting him and each other with bananas and peanuts that had been artfully strewn about the lawn earlier in the day.

As the merriment reached epic proportions and my dad clambered up a tree to recover Gigi Getz's Star of David, which had somehow ended up dangling from a branch, the Nasties arrived.

"Who is that?" Roxanne asked.

"My father," I replied apologetically. "He's King Kong."

As with one mind, one voice, one collective sentiment, the Nasties began to sing-song, "Jean has got a monkey for a faaaa-ther! Jean has got a monkey for a faaaa-ther!"

I plucked at my father's sleeve. "Daddy, please take off your mask. You'll ruin everything." With a great deal of reluctance, my father complied. I knew I had to do something quickly to take back control of my party. After all, I was the one running for class president, and for once in my political career, I wanted the kids to vote for me, not for my father.

"What are we going to do now?" Gigi asked me.

"I've got a great idea," I said brightly, playing Lady Bountiful. "I'll make everybody ice cream sodas."

"Oh, no!" my dad objected. "These kids don't want to have ordinary ice cream sodas. What these kids want to do is play Sodas and Ladders. Who wants to play Sodas and Ladders?"

"Me, me, me, me, me, me, me, me!" came a chorus of replies.

My heart sank. Sodas and Ladders was a messy little game of skill that my father had used many times with contestants on his stunt shows. Each boy is stretched out on his back with a large paper cup taped to his forehead. Each girl stands on a stepladder and tries to make an ice cream soda by dropping scoops of ice cream, chocolate syrup, ginger ale, whipped cream, and a cherry into the cup below. The first pair to complete an ice cream soda is the winner.

Kids being kids, the point of the game soon changed to a contest of decorative skills. Roxanne had Coo Coo looking like an early Picasso, and Robert, under Gigi's ministrations, took on the appearance of a banana-split psychosis by Van Gogh. The boys were lapping it up, however, and Chickie, my dog, happily slurped away on pistachio ice cream noses, whipped cream ties, and chocolate shirts complete with cherry buttons.

Amid the mess, a strange kind of frenzy gripped the students in class 4B. There were no more clean clothes. There were also no more inhibitions. The games got wilder and faster. Dad would no sooner finish one game than he would launch another. He convinced the fattest boy in class to allow a board studded with tacks to be strapped to his broad posterior. Paula, one of the Nasties, was chosen to be "it." She was sent out of the room while the kids agreed to concentrate on one of an unlikely collection of objects my father had taken out of a closet for the occasion, including a jar of pig's feet, a trombone, a container of chicken fat, and the umbrella "used by a dear old lady to beat the living tar out of the only man who had ever kicked Lassie." When Paula returned, she moved toward each of the items in turn, guided by cries of "hot!" and "cold!" from the class. On each cry of "cold," Paula was to spank Tubby with a net full of balloons. The game continued until she guessed correctly or all the balloons were popped.

Perhaps the more jaded of my readers might think that my father was skirting perilously close to the shade of the Marquis de Sade in these games of his, but I beg to differ. My father was the original innocent; moreover, he understood the kid mind. As the founder and chief gamester of the Mystery School, which I often describe cheerfully as the longest-running adult kindergarten, I was trained by the best.

Of course, the game of Hot and Cold deteriorated as well. Soon balloons glistening with chicken fat were sailing through the air like a greasy armada, and the kids were taking turns playing golf with the pigs' feet. In a last attempt to turn the tide of attention toward myself, I cried, "Let's play Juby Juby Ding Ding." But my suggestion fell on deaf ears, as the mad-eyed throng flowed like lava after my father.

My father was a shoo-in for president. I had to stop the party. But how? At this point only some extreme and drastic measure could command their attention. But what? A line of poetry kept humming through my head, "The boy stood on the burning deck. . . ." What did that mean? Then it dawned on me—the burning rope trick. Of course, I'd never done the trick before, but there had to be a first time. I went off to the garage to find the fire-making materials. A few minutes later, I was back on the lawn setting a match to my gasoline-soaked lariat.

Nobody noticed as it caught fire. Class 4B was reeling and squealing mindlessly.

"Hi ho Silver," I sang out and spun the burning rope sideways so I could jump through it. I sprang with my Mary Jane shoes and passed through the circle of flame.

"Show-off! Show-off! Show-off!" The Nasties had noticed me.

"Hey, look at Jean." So had everybody else.

I leaped again and again, back and forth through the spinning fire. It was a perfect moment. I could do no wrong. The rope and I were joined in some mystic fiery circle of understanding. The fourth grade was standing around me, openmouthed in wonder. The Nasties were prickling with jealousy.

Vaguely in the background, I was a aware of a note of dissonance. My father had at last noticed what I was up to. He lunged for me, but at that moment I raised the rope in a circle over my head and took off across the lawn. Little shreds of burning rope began dropping around me, and something nearby began to smell suspiciously like smoking chicken fat. It was my pinafore. The kids kept a respectful distance, but one ventured a bit of advice.

"Hey, Jean, I think you're on fire."

"Show-off! Show-off! Sets herself on fire," the Nasties chanted like a Greek chorus.

"The boy stood on the burning deck . . ." I intoned while slapping at my pinafore. Seeing my father hurtling toward me, I threw the rope behind me and made a flying leap under the house where I knew he couldn't reach me.

"Fire!" I heard somebody yell.

I wriggled out of my hiding place long enough to catch sight of the miracle of the burning bush, California style. Evidently, my rope had landed on a dried-up banana tree that was sitting on our lawn like a mummy looking for a handout. I closed my eyes tight, stuck my fingers in my ears, and held my breath to the count of sixty, hoping it would all go away. About four of these later my walled-off eardrums insisted on picking up the muffled clamor of a fire engine. A wet nose touched mine.

"Go 'way, Chickie," I said without opening my eyes to what I thought was my dog.

"I'm not Chickie. I'm Coo Coo. I thought you'd like this nice cold bottle of Nehi Orange."

He thrust it into my face again.

"The cop is here," he told me. "So's the fire department. So are a lot of kids' parents. It was the best party I ever went to," he added respectfully.

In the days that followed, I rode the crest of popularity. My father had become a legend to the whole school, and I was honored as the living proof that he really existed. Even the big kids in the sixth grade buttered me up and asked if they could come over and meet my dad. Of course, we couldn't have any more parties. My mother said that the insurance wouldn't cover them, and anyway, our house had been declared off-limits by any number of irate parents.

As if this wasn't enough to ensure my election, Coo Coo, who as my best friend had also seen his status rise, sealed the victory. On the morning of the election, he spun around, got stiff as a board, fell down, and began to speak in a prophetic voice. To the amazement of the assembled voters, he announced, "God just told me that he wants Jean to be president of this here class!" How could anyone say no to that?

That afternoon, I was elected president of the class, with Coo Coo as my vice president. I held the post for exactly two days. Dad got a call to do a show in St. Louis, and we had to leave immediately. In my absence, Mr. Charles Longbotham became president of class 4B.

Jenny, Lakshmi, and Tony take me into the geodesic dome. In the middle of the room is the art center, while many banks of computer terminals line the perimeter of the space. Children of every age are busy at keyboards and graphics interface terminals. Their skills seem professional, but of course they've grown up with computers, and for them operating a computer is as normal as riding a bike.

Some children have their screens ablaze with multimedia projects; others are browsing the world's libraries, while still others seem to be speaking with children in other countries. I notice a tiny television camera positioned on each screen. One boy tells me he is discussing a science project with an Egyptian boy also in the fourth grade in Giza. They have been studying the effects of acid rain in their areas by measuring the pH levels of the soil and comparing their findings with other children online around the world. Jenny whispers, "These kids are doing real research in tracking environmental pollution. Their findings will become part of an international data bank. That's what we try to do here—make learning real and give the children opportunities to use more of themselves in authentic ways, creating knowledge that is of value to the world."

"How right you are," I reply. "What has always turned kids off was having to learn things that seemed to have no point."

Lakshmi joins us, telling Jenny, "I led the class in their relaxation exercises and now the little kids are having their snooze." She turns to peer at the screen of a girl who seems to be conducting a survey. "Hi, Amanda, how are you doing with It Ought to Be a Law?"

As the girls talk, Tony explains that proposed laws are sent to the children by legislators in the statehouse. The kids visit or talk on-line to people in their neighborhoods about the legislation and give the lawmakers feedback about what their constituents think.

"Where is the teacher?" I ask Jenny.

She points to a young man wearing a T-shirt plastered with fractal art. "He's over there working on his own project. You see all those kids around him? He's helping them find the information they need for their projects. You see, with information at every child's fingertips, teachers are not the absolute holders of knowledge anymore. In fact, the kids you see here are learning to ask their own questions and then to find the answers. More often than not, they bring the curriculum to the teachers."

"My teachers are my coaches," Tony adds. "I bounce ideas off them."

"My favorite teacher is like a guide in the jungle," Lakshmi explains. "She knows a lot of paths to follow that she thinks I might like. And sometimes she lets me get lost so I can create my own paths."

"What about tests?" I ask.

Jenny jumps in mock horror. "We don't use that word around here. All those awful things ever did was measure recall on demand. And sensitive and creative children who thought in different ways too often felt themselves to be failures."

I thought back to the one-right-answer, true-or-false tests of my school days, as Jenny continued. "We try to give children a sense of the many variations and nuances that are possible in any answer. We offer them the capacity for complexity."

"How do you measure progress if there are no tests?"

"Through a much broader kind of assessment. Children keep portfolios and make videos of their projects. As you've seen, they do community projects as well and keep a record of those. They also keep records of their scientific and artistic experiments. The teachers review the portfolios so they can follow each child's ability to understand and apply what he or she is learning. Each child develops a personal electronic portfolio as well, a file of everything she or he has written, so that they can look back and compare their earlier writing with their present efforts. This way, each child is able to assess his or her own sequence of development."

We have moved into the art center, where children of all ages as well as a number of parents are busy making beauty and magic out of all sorts of materials. Looms, potters' wheels, paints, clay, and fabrics of all kinds are strewn in appropriate areas. The sounds emanating from this area are primal, happy ones—the slap of paint, the chip of stone, the rattling of the loom, the sloppy squish of God-only-knows-what. An *old Japanese woman about my age moves from station to station helping one and then another child. She seems to be mistress of all the arts, and as we approach, I sense a kind of fey mischief about her.*

"In the midst of all this high-tech, we need as much high-touch as possible," she says as she extends a paint-streaked hand. I think she is going to shake my hand, but no, she slaps a wad of clay into it. "Make something!" she commands, and I dutifully begin to massage the clay, remembering that I haven't played with clay since I had my Mystery School students model their archetypes in clay. "This is the place where we learn to use all the other parts of our brains. This is where we become creators!"

Lakshmi takes me over to her own art project, a half-finished sculpture of the hand of David. Her work area is plastered with blowups of details from Michelangelo's statue, which she studies somewhat querulously. "The problem is," she admits, "that you can't just study sculpting and then take a hunk of stone and make a hand. First, you've got to get inside the mind of Michelangelo. Isn't that so, Keiko?"

Keiko nods.

"And how do you do that?" I ask.

The art teacher smiles. "You let your mind go idle, breathe yourself into the stone, and then breathe yourself into Michelangelo's intention. When you have it, you pick up your tools and begin."

"Sounds like Zen to me," I respond.

Keiko winks.

Progressive schools are, perhaps, more alike than they are different. Aside from modeling in clay, the school that I have run for thirteen years now in upstate New York has much in common with the Ames, Iowa, grade school of the future. Through the Mystery School bulletin board on the Internet, for example, past, present, and future students work together on projects and breathe electronically into one another's intentions. But the Mystery School also owes something to the madness and mayhem that characterized my California fourth grade. Fractals quake and snicker from those days to my present life. In some sense, I have never stopped trying to give "the world's greatest party," and, unlike most politicians, I have never stopped following through on my campaign goals: get them interested, see the hidden potentials and possibilities in people and events, and turn society upside down so as to reinvent the world.

I began the Mystery School in 1984, and it has run continuously since then, both in a peaceful mountain setting near Port Jervis, New York, and in branches in the western U.S., Canada, India, and Holland. Mystery School is a community of ordinary, extraordinary people who come together to dream and scheme themselves into their highest human possibility. Nuns and corporate executives, health care professionals and artists, educators and homemakers dance and playact, create art and enact rituals. And up in front, there I am, still making up games for which only I know the rules, doing tricks designed to shake people out of their ordinary perceptions, telling stories and jokes, and pulling people's Essence out their ears in an ongoing theatrical show-and-tell. And back in the corner by the ladies' room, there are sometimes even a few of the Nasties, still glowering and chanting, "Show-off. Show-off." But this time, they're paying tuition for the privilege.

What is a Mystery School? It is my modern continuation of a community of seekers who have been meeting for millennia: in ancient Greece, Egypt, and Afghanistan; in the kivas of the indigenous peoples of the American Southwest; in druid circles in the forests of old Europe. Indeed, I make this connection plain on the opening night of the first weekend in February, when the New York Mystery School begins. Participants, who have committed themselves to attending nine weekend sessions in the course of the year, walk backward in space and time to be met by the mystery schools of the past. As I call each student's name, I give that person the name of a historical mystery school to remember for the year. One student might be charged to hold the energy of the mystery school of the Cathedral of Chartres; another might be given the school of Pythagoras or of Isis and Osiris or of the Eleusinian mysteries.

Then we plunge into the year's subject matter. Every month we focus on a different aspect of the year's central theme. For example, one year we studied and enacted the stages of the mystic path, using as texts Evelyn Underhill's *Mysticism* and William James's *Varieties of Religious Experience*. Each step on the mystic path was discussed in my lectures (I write a small book each month in preparation) and was brought to life by literature, music, drama, ritual, and story. Francis of Assisi became the exemplar of the stage of Illumination; Joan of Arc relived for us the stage of Voices and Visions; Don Quixote became the embodiment of the stage of Purification; the ancient texts and legends surrounding the feminine wisdom principle, the Sophia, served to illustrate the Dark Night of the Soul, and so forth. Other years we have delved into the world's great myths, spiritual biographies, science fiction and the myths of future times, extraordinary human capacities, and the Mind of the Maker as seen through a study of the world's great creative geniuses.

During the course of a Mystery School session, every sense is engaged, every habit shaken up. The body is stretched with psychophysical exercises, the alembic of mind quickened by the essence of ideas from many disciplines. I try to teach the things I love best—history, sacred psychology, music, theater, philosophy, theology, poetry, high and low comedy, the new science, cosmology, metaphysics. All this is larded with processes that engage people in a communal sharing of their own thoughts and life stories. Together they embark on visionary journeys in which they see their own lives as life writ large. Participants return year after year for the community such shared work creates; some form transformational friendships, others meet and marry, and virtually all find Mystery School to be the place in which they can finally be what they really are and become what they would be. Mystery School is for many a metahome away from home.

I created this school principally to help engender a passion of purpose and a deep commitment to live truly and beautifully in high service to others. I also wanted to put into practice the truth that I learned from Margaret Mead and from my early schooling—that recognizing people's hidden potentials and involving them in nontraditional teaching-learning communities is the best way to foster personal and social transformation.

We are walking outside, skirting an acre-sized map of the state of Iowa laid out on the freshly hoed ground. Children are planting corn, potatoes, wheat, soybeans, and other crops according to areas of the state where they are principally grown. Rivers and lakes are marked by little pools and runways for streams. The perimeter is being planted as a flower and herb garden, and the teacher is showing them how to garden biodynamically, so that plants having a mutual affinity are placed close together.

Nearby is a small barn where children are tending chickens and pigs and even milking goats. Cheese making, I learn, is very big this year. I notice that there are quite a few older people about; in fact, some of them are teaching as well as being taught by the children to do certain skills.

Jenny follows my gaze. "Folks of all ages are welcome to come to school here, to teach or learn or both. We even have an After Four program for people who work. The school programs continue until about midnight, and some children even live here if they need to. We want the children to think of school as an enduring and reliable refuge. In the evenings children bring their parents in to learn crafts or do computer work. And remember, this school is in no way isolated. It is hooked in to the local community college, the state university, and many other community organizations, so we are constantly changing in response to the needs of the learners and the community."

"My grandfather is giving a course in Sanskrit and Hindu philosophy here at night," Lakshmi chimes in. "My mother comes, too, and brings Punjabi snacks for all the students."

"It's a very popular course, except you've got to have a lot of water around for people who are not used to the curries," adds Jenny.

Suddenly I note a group of children dressed in buckskins and long calico dresses. We move toward them and watch as they demonstrate a variety of ancient skills— making soap, souring milk, sharpening a knife, and mending clothes.

"They just came back from spending a month in the eighteenth century," Tony explains.

"What?" I exclaim. "I knew that schools had progressed, but time travel, too?"

"In a way, yes," he laughs. "They go to a special colonial village as part of their internship and learn to live as people did in that time. They get to do all kinds of neat stuff, like you see, and also live in nature."

"They learn how to do complete processes from beginning to end, just like our ancestors did," Jenny adds. "They learn about the night sky, about living in all kinds of weather, about birth and death, and the means by which people survive and create

their world. We try to let them comprehend from real experience the ways of being human of thousands of years, so that they have real respect and humility for where we've come from and where we may be going."

In addition to challenging me to create my own school, my experiences as a schoolgirl launched me into a long-standing war with the educational status quo. When I began my own research and teaching, I came across too many children who were bright, curious, inventive little folk . . . until they went to school, where their genius was all undone. I sometimes think of traditional schooling as a systematic forgetting of everything we already know that is really important. I am convinced that there is no such thing as a stupid child. There are only incredibly stupid and brain-diminishing forms of education. What would happen to society and its citizens if school became a place of discovery instead of diminishment? For that matter, what would happen to the human race if each child was seen as the unique treasure that he or she really is? I received my own revelation about this in my experiences with Billy.

In October 1970, my husband Bob and I were the subject of a long article in the religion section of *Time* magazine. A former nun working as a reporter on the magazine came to our foundation to explore firsthand some of our methods for inducing altered states of consciousness. In her life as a nun, she had longed for but not ever had a mystical experience. Following my instructions during a guided meditation, however, she had a powerful breakthrough, which she wrote about rapturously in the pages of *Time*.

From that moment on and for about the next four months, we were bombarded by letters, telegrams, and phone calls. We could scarcely leave our building in New York City without being followed by someone pleading with us to take him or her into higher states of consciousness. The funniest call came from a man with a thick Jewish accent who said, "Listen, already. Me you want to work with. I'm a rabbi, I'm a Zen master, and I'm a Sufi master."

"That's wonderful, sir," I responded. "What is your name?"

"My name is Sam Lewis, but you can call me Master."

Gradually, the calls and letters abated—all but one. A woman in northern Michigan continued to call, write, and send telegrams insisting that I come to Michigan to speak to her women's club. She informed me that there was no honorarium available, I would have to pay my own plane fare, and I would have to come on Tuesday, when I was teaching. Intrigued by her chutzpah, I went.

It was clear from my opening remarks that the ladies of the club had little interest in what I was saying. They listened politely for a while and then turned their attention to each other and the chicken à la queen and Waldorf salad that adorned their plates. When I finished, there was only the continued mumble of their voices, until one woman clapped slowly and loudly and was eventually joined by a tiny shiver of applause.

"Well, thank you for inviting me; it was most interesting. I haven't had Waldorf salad in ages," I said to my hostess gingerly. "So, as it seems that it's about to snow, I'd better catch the next plane back."

"No, you can't go just yet," she said quickly. Then looking for some explanation she added, "You must come home with me . . . for coffee and cake."

Reluctantly, I followed her home and found myself in her chilly living room. There was a fire burning in the fireplace. I immediately moved over to the couch by the fire.

"No, you can't sit there," she admonished as my bottom descended to the couch. I straightened up, my eyebrows making question marks.

"You must come downstairs to the basement with me."

At that point I knew I was in the middle of an adventure, and as long experience has taught me, when you are in the middle of an adventure, the best thing to do is just go along with it. Following her, I descended a nearly vertical set of wooden steps and found myself in a small, cold, darkened basement room.

When the woman turned on the light, however, I was met with wonders that seemed to be a zany merger of *Mad* magazine and *Popular Mechanics*. The room was filled with crazy inventions of the kind that even my father would have been proud to create. Water ran down a chute, throwing a Ping-Pong ball into a socket, which caused a bell to ring and a miniature pig to spin, which turned an alligator's head into which you stuck your pencil to be sharpened. Other machines did practical things in similarly imaginative ways. There was a shelf holding common-looking objects that were captioned to make a mind-boggling difference. Here, for example, was a revolving goldfish bowl for tired goldfish. Some white paste was labeled "Easy-Off Whisker Remover." Directions written under the caption informed me that a man was to put this paste on his face at night, which would cause his whiskers to grow inward, so that the next morning, he could bite them off. It appeared that Rube Goldberg was alive and well and living in northern Michigan. I noted that a young and very shy boy had followed us down the steps.

I turned to the lady and said, "Now I know why you wanted me to come to Michigan. It wasn't to talk to your club. It was for us to talk about your husband's inventions."

"No, my husband did not invent these," she responded, smiling at the boy.

"You invented them?"

"I would have neither the imagination nor the skill."

"Then who?"

The woman pointed to the boy. "Billy invented and built them all."

"You invented these?"

For an answer he looked down at his shoes and nodded. I turned to his mother, "You must be very happy having such a brilliant child."

"Well, I'm certainly happy, and I'm glad you are. But his teachers are not. Billy is flunking all his subjects."

"How in the world is that possible?" I exclaimed, looking around again at wacky but wonderful examples of the boy's creativity.

"I'm glad you asked that, Dr. Houston," she said with an expression of having led me into the lair of a mystery. "You thought I asked you to come here to speak to my women's club."

"No, Madam," I demurred. "I was beginning to suspect that you did not."

"Well, you're right," she said. "I've been making quite a study of Billy and the way he thinks. I know that there are many children like him who are labeled unintelligent and are made to feel worthless in school. And I know that if we can make the proper scientific studies, there are wonderful things we can do to encourage and develop children like Billy. That's why I invited you here."

"I'm game," I said. "How do we start?"

"Let me show you something," she said, pulling a tape measure, a pad, and a pencil from a drawer. "Now, Billy, you remember how you learned in school last week how to figure out the area of a room?"

"Oh, Ma, do I have to?"

"Yes, Billy. You just go ahead and do it."

I watched as Billy took very careful measurements of the room, and then, already with a sense of defeat, addressed himself to the pad and pencil. He made many erasures, and I think a saw a tear course down his cheek. After a while, he handed his mother his pad with the answer he had so painfully arrived at. According to his calculations, the small basement room was about the size of a football field.

"Well, of course, that's wrong," his mother told him.

"Of course," said Billy.

"Now do it your own way, Billy."

Billy set to work cheerfully on his task. He looked again at the measurements he had taken, closed his eyes, and began to hum to himself, making strange little movements with his hands, as if he were constructing something. His head followed the movements of his hands, and every so often he would open his eyes and jot something down on the pad. Then he would close his eyes again for some more internal business, always matched with snatches of melody and the movement of his hands. Finally, he seemed finished, jotted down his answer, and gave it to his mother. Having worked out the problem myself in the traditional manner, I saw that it was the correct answer. Now I suspected what was going on.

"Billy," I asked, "what were you doing when you closed your eyes? Were you thinking in pictures?" For years now I had been studying people given to imagistic thinking and had noted that imagery often gave them access to rapid and effective problem solving.

"Yes," he admitted, "but it's other stuff, too."

"What kinds of stuff?"

"Well, when I close my eyes to figure something out, it's like a cross between music and architecture."

"That does it!" I exclaimed and called up Sister Margaret Mary, head of the philosophy department at Marymount College, where I was then teaching. I told her about Billy and my desire to see if something could be done about him at his school, concluding, "So, Sister, could you please teach my courses in Hegel and phenomenology, Neoplatonism and existentialism, and process philosophy for the next week?"

"Oh yes, Jean," she agreed sweetly. "Anything for the greater glory of God."

A nearby university had an excellent testing department, and I took Billy there to be given a standard IQ test. He scored 85, which is thought to be below normal intelligence.

"That's all right, Billy," I said brightly. "Now let's just take this test over again, and you do it in your own way."

"That's not possible," he replied.

"Why not?" I asked.

"Because, Jean . . . this test is made for people with your kind of mind. It's not made for people with my kind."

"You're right," I agreed.

All at once I had a great notion. "Never mind, Billy. We'll go through the test again, and at each question, you tell me how to ask the question."

"You mean, you'll ask the questions so I can answer them by doing the special kind of stuff I do in my head?"

"That's right, Billy. We'll just have to redesign the test together as we go along."

And that's what we did. He asked if I could turn the first question into music. I tried to comply, singing and dancing and snapping my fingers in some semblance of the question. "I've got it," he said and set to work. He asked if I could turn the second question into something that looked like a house designed by Frank Lloyd Wright. I did the best I could, shaping the air, mugging, and doing everything but standing on my head. And so the test proceeded, while the orthodox statistical psychologist who marked the test looked on with a superior smirk. At the end, when Billy had finished and the test was being marked, I was exhausted, having danced, skipped, sung, emoted, and generally run through the entire canon of human expression. After a short wait, the shocked psychologist came back with the test scored at 135, fifty points higher than Billy's previous mark. I believe that the score would have been higher still had I been better at asking the questions in an imaginative manner. As I have written of this experience in *The Possible Human*, "Here was a child, deemed below normal by the standard intelligence test, rewriting and reconceptualizing the test and then, more often than not, giving the correct answer to questions where previously he had failed. Even when he scored a wrong answer, his responses were unusually creative, and on some more enlightened test would have been acknowledged for their brilliance and originality."

The next day, armed with scripture—the IQ score—I visited the principal of the school Billy attended. We also brought along several wagons filled with some of Billy's inventions. The man who faced me across the desk looked like he had posed for the dour farmer in Grant Wood's *American Gothic.* Summoning my courage, I trotted out the inventions, showed him the IQ score, and gave a little homily on alternate styles of knowing and learning. The principal stared at me impassively. I tried another tack and addressed the fact that Billy might just be a genius and that the traditional sort of schooling was destroying him and children like him. No reaction. I kept on, scolding, appealing, dragging out of memory every paper I had ever read on the subject. Finally, when I was about to give up, the principal's face suddenly cracked like a piece of dropped peanut brittle. From the sounds coming out of his mouth, I couldn't tell whether he was laughing or crying.

"Is something wrong, sir?" I inquired, more than a little shocked by his outburst.

"You bet there is," he wheezed. "I was a student of the great educator John Dewey back at Columbia Teachers' College in the twenties. He used to tell us about children like this and the kind of teaching that would help them succeed in school, and I believed him. Wrote a paper on the subject myself, as a matter of fact. But then I bought into the system. Became a superintendent of schools. Did things efficiently. Kept the old ways going. Tried never to rock the boat or put things into the schools that I had studied about with Dewey." He paused and wiped his eyes. "What the hell. I'm sixty-five years old, and I'm going to retire soon anyway, so let's do it. Maybe I can do something before I go to justify myself to the memory of my old teacher."

And with that, he called in Billy's teachers. "Listen to this lady, and try to do what she says."

The first thing I did was have Billy show his teachers his inventions. They had never seen them or even known they existed, so private had Billy become about himself at school. They were bowled over. "This child, this (in a whisper) *backward* child, made these things?"

"He's far from backward," I answered. "Here, look at his IQ score."

"IQ score," they exclaimed. "Then it must be true."

"Oh, yes," I said, looking heavenward. "He thinks in a different way. Here, I'll show you. Bring me some of the exams he has failed."

"That's all of them," the teachers answered.

"Well, just bring me a few, then." They did, and Billy and I redesigned the exams on the spot, with the result that he scored a passing grade in each. When the teachers were properly astonished, I asked them to stay after school for the next week so that we could work together to discover ways of helping Billy and children like him learn.

Suddenly Billy interrupted, "Could I bring in Sally? Could I bring in George? I think that they think the same way I do."

Four of the teachers agreed to be part of the study. One refused, saying that he had never learned of this sort of thing in teachers' college, and it was so much baloney and probably against the teachings of his church.

The next week taught us all more about education than we had ever known, as the children helped us figure out ways of presenting information and questions so they could respond from varying arenas of their minds. I remember George saying to the history teacher, "Mr. Hayden, when you tell us about George Washington crossing the Delaware and you drop in all those facts, I can't remember them. So why can't you make it like *Star Trek?*"

"What do you mean?" Hayden asked.

"Well, why not have us close our eyes and picture George Washington crossing the Delaware while you drop in the date, and then I think I'll be able to remember it."

"Why, yes, " said the teacher. "I think I can do that."

"But, Mr. Hayden, " George persisted. "Why does George Washington have to cross the Delaware anyway?"

"Because he did."

"No," the boy continued, "why not have him drown, and then let us figure out what would have happened to American history if George Washington had died?"

"Well . . . yes . . . that's an awfully interesting way of presenting history, George. We'll try it . . . the invention of alternatives in history. A fine idea."

Just then, emboldened by George's foray into changing the nature of teaching methodology, Sally addressed the math teacher. "Mrs. Shumacher, I hate math. I throw up before every exam. And I was thinking, what if you made me queen of the planet of Math. Then all the figures and numbers would be my subjects, and they would show me how things work on my planet. And because I was their queen, they would love me. And if they loved me, then I would love them, and then I wouldn't hate math anymore."

It was all I could do to contain myself. This child was presenting one of the most profound ideas in educational psychology—lift a learning block by replacing it with a more powerful emotional construct. Hot dog!

Together with the children, we explored other ways of learning, the children teaching us much more than we taught them. I followed Billy's progress over the years and was gratified by the way he came out of himself and became more involved with school and friends. He continued to develop his crazy inventions but soon added more "useful" inventions as well.

What was surprising, however, was that throughout most of his junior high and high school, as well as his college career, he rarely got above a B or a B-minus average. Only when he went to graduate school in design engineering did he do well, graduating summa cum laude. Years later, when I asked him to explain this conundrum, he said, "Well, Jean, so many of the tests had multiple choice questions. You know, answer either *a* or *b* or *c* or *d*. I couldn't help myself, Jean. I would often see a more complex and interesting possibility and would put it down as *e*, and the teachers would sigh and mark me down."

Billy's case is legion, and many of the people reading this book might themselves be Billys or have children or know of ones who are. He is an extreme example, of course, for by the age of twelve, he was a highly developed visual thinker.

But there are so many children whose natural style tends toward visual or kines-thetic or even auditory thinking and who are penalized as a result. How many thinkers and creative spirits are wasted, how much brain and emotional and even spiritual power goes down the drain because of our archaic and insular notions of education?

By 1972, inspired by this and similar incidents, I was working with schools all over America to put art back into the curriculum and to develop teaching and learning strategies that allowed for many different kinds of learning so that no child would be left out. At the Mead School in Byram, New York, I worked with its founder, Dr. Elaine de Beauport, to develop a curriculum in which art was central to the learning process; in fact, the open art center was the first thing everyone saw upon entering the school building. Each child spent hours each week in the art center, learning painting, sculpture, design, book making, batik, collage, montage, weaving, and other artistic forms. They were encouraged to discover their own creativity as they developed their skills and know-how. Through this emphasis on art, children not only learned how to do entire processes, developed fine eye to motor skills, and became natural artists, but they also employed these same skills in learning mathematics through music and rhythm, science through sensory feeling, and chemistry through the creation of batiks and collages. Thus even "reg-ular" subjects used artistic means to amplify the learning process.

Students made covenants to gain mastery of specific subject matter each term—in math, reading, geography, ecology, or history. And in virtually every case, they did so, for learning had become freedom, joy, and the unfolding of who and what they were. Equally important to the success of the school, teachers and parents joined together in an ongoing learning process with the children, breaking down the sharp divisions between home and school, the teacher and the taught. As a result of these innovations, few if any children failed in this school, and when they took the standard tests, they scored much higher than many in traditional schools. The Mead School remains one of the great educational experiments in America and is still producing wonderfully creative and resourceful children who, together with their teachers and parents, form one the best continuing teaching-learning communities in America.

I have tried to bring this model to schools throughout the world with varying success. In Asian countries that were once part of the Raj, one first has to lift the prison gates of nineteenth-century British education (which the Brits themselves have long abandoned). I have tried to convince both teachers and government ad-ministrators that the old medium is no longer adequate to the new messages beaming at us from the world and time. At the cusp of the millennium, we can no longer be educated for the year 1926 or earlier. Yes, we must continue to learn to read and write and cipher, but we also need to embrace an education for liberating the ability to imagine, to dream, and to expand the limits of the possible. We re-quire education at its edges, education that guides us through the munificence of our capacities and inspires us to become stewards of this most critical time in human history. My life has been a search for the education that would nurture this goal and make it happen. Perhaps I will find it in the future.

We are coming to the end of our tour.

"There is one more room we need to show you, Granny Jean. It is our most special room."

"What's in it?"

"We can't tell you. You have to discover it for yourself."

The children lead me to the mud-and-wattle hut. Above the entrance is a sign: The Billy Room. I enter alone, and what I see so astonishes me that . . . I enroll as a student in the school.

9

✦

GRANDMOTHER HERSELF

It is June 1987. We are in a village in Kenya a hundred and fifty miles south of Nairobi. The village women have been up all night cooking a feast in our honor. Helping the people of this village has been a project of the ICA, the Institute of Cultural Affairs, with whom I have been working. The ICA has a long and remarkable history of helping villages in so-called Third World countries improve their social and economic conditions, work democratically, and move toward greater equality between men and women.

Before we sit down to eat the stiff porridge and stewed meats, the women dance and sing for us. Then they prop up the drunken mayor of the town, who good-naturedly welcomes us in slurred, besotted speech. The women tell him what to say in an audible whisper. They seem to be running the show, while he is a cardboard fixture. School children rush in, many of them young girls in neat school uniforms, all wanting to try out their English on us.

In this village we see how seemingly minimal changes can affect the traditions of hundreds and even thousands of years. The ICA had helped the villagers build a tank to hold water. Now the village women no longer have to spend many hours walking miles each day to get water. This one act has changed the society utterly, for now the women have the freedom and time to do other things, and their first concern has been bettering life in the village.

However, it also means that women's culture, the mobile culture that grew up along the morning walks to the water, has changed as well. The ambling culture of the water bearers focused on singing songs, telling stories, trading—gossip, healing knowledge, practical magic, powerful remedies. It was a side-by-side culture—nonfocused, languid, diffuse.

With the water tank in the village, the women found they missed their traditional walks and needed to find other ways of getting together. Moreover, spending more time in the village, they had become acutely aware of things that needed changing and now had the energy to do something about them.

"Sister," they had said to an ICA representative, "now that we women no longer have our side-by-side, we need a teahouse where we can meet. Help us build a teahouse."

My friends and I got some money together to help them build a teahouse, and when that was done the women found themselves facing each other for long periods of time over their beverages. Face-to-face encounters, with their inevitable discussions and meetings around issues and projects, replaced their former ambling relationship. This changed everything.

Now they continued to dance and sing, but it was to build up spirit for what they were intending to do to improve the sanitation, the school, and the lives of their men, many of whom were in Nairobi, ostensibly looking for work but more often than not drunk on palm wine. Gradually the women had taken the leadership role. Cooking and singing, they were remaking virtually every aspect of their society.

As the women lead me around the village, I notice things both little and big that reflect astonishing change. The flies do not cluster over children's eyes, and those eyes, unlike the impassive eyes of children I have seen in villages without hope, are seeking, darting, filled with laughter and curiosity. The ever-present dogs look well fed and even friendly. Where were the slinking, skeletal, feral creatures that had haunted the land? Even the beggars have vanished. Well-irrigated gardens flourish everywhere. Pipes are being laid down for sewage and drainage. Streets are swept. The school has been transformed from an ugly government-issued affair into a merry place daubed with paint and children's drawings—giraffes and elephants and wildebeests. One picture stands out, a crude but powerful rendering of an old woman, her hair a halo of white, sitting up in what looks like some kind of bed.

"Who is that?" I ask the teacher.

"That is the one we call . . ." The teacher pauses and confers with the women and children who are accompanying us. Everyone seems to have an opinion about how to

explain the old woman. Finally, the teacher turns to me and says, "That is the one we call Grandmother Herself! Would you like to meet her?"

As we walk together to the little house where the venerable old woman lives, I learn that she is the guide, the envisioner, the inspiration for the women of the village. As I bend and step through the low doorway, I know her immediately—the wisdom woman, good witch, mistress of herbs, brewer of healing drinks, speaker for nature, knower of the human heart, visionary seer, generatrix, withering wit, prophetess and pragmatic genius, social artist, avatar of the local goddess—Grandmother Herself!

Propped up on pillows, she laughs when she sees our white faces but then beckons us toward her. Someone gives us tea, the strong African brew with milk and tea boiled together, and we settle around her. We know we are in the presence of the One Who Knows. Sometimes she talks to us; sometimes she addresses spirits, invisible, but evidently available, the conversation moving between worlds with no apparent hesitancy.

"Listen," she says, "I do not have much more time here before I, too, become an ancestor. So listen. The world has gone too crazy. It is time for the woman ways to return. I talk to the ancestors. They advise me, and then I advise the women, and you see what has happened here." She looks past me to someone who is not there. "Yes, Grandmother, I will tell them that."

She takes my hand and brushes the skin as if to find some real color under all that paleness. "You all have new duties on this Earth, you women," she says after a sip of tea. "You have the responsibility to make the world work. The men are growing weak, and you are growing strong. Soon there will be balance. Soon the men will look to you as equals, and together you will grow a new nest, and a nest of nests. The spirits will help you, especially the Grandmother spirits. They have become very tough and powerful. But now you must support each other, work and pray and dance together. You must remember what the men have forgotten. You must remember how to have a society without war and palm wine. And you women of this village, you must stop cutting the rosebud!"

The African women seem shocked by this declaration. The old woman goes on to explain. "That belongs to old ways that are dying, old ways that hurt women." Cutting the rosebud refers to the practice, widespread throughout black Africa as well as in Egypt, of circumcising young girls, removing the clitoris as well as other genital parts so that they will not have sexual pleasure. The practice is performed by older women on girls of twelve to fifteen and has much ritual authority. It is also extremely dangerous, often resulting in septicemia, and makes childbirth especially difficult.

"And you white women," she continues, "you must stop cutting yourself off from your souls. I see your souls standing off in the corner, like children who have lost their mamas. Take your souls back!"

As we talk and listen, I feel myself present to two worlds; a remembrance of things past is congruent with the present scene. I am recalling a time almost nine years earlier.

It was November 1978. I was sitting at the hospital bedside of another old woman, Margaret Mead. Two weeks later she would die. She had been dozing as I had been reading to her. Suddenly she opened her eyes and looked across the room. She pushed herself up to a sitting position and said to the wall, "Get out of here. I'm not ready for you. Go away!"

"Margaret, there is no one there," I told her.

"You can't see them, but they are there all right!"

"Who, Margaret? Who is there?"

"Dead people. My mother, my father, and Ruth. They say they are here to take me with them. Please leave! Go away!"

Ruth was the anthropologist Ruth Benedict, who had been Margaret's most intimate friend and colleague.

They must have vanished, for Margaret lay back down and turned her attention to me. "Listen, I've got something very important to say to you. Forget everything I've been teaching you about working with governments and bureaucracies!"

"Now you tell me this?" I sputtered, looking down on my terminally ill friend.

Margaret seemed to find this funny. "Yes," she said. "I've been lying here being an anthropologist on my own dying—fascinating experience, by the way; there is no hierarchy to it—and I've had an important insight about the future. The world is going to change so fast that people and governments will not be prepared to be stewards of this change. What will save them is teaching-learning communities. They could come together in churches or businesses or even in families. They could meet weekly and do your kinds of exercises, especially ones that develop their capacities. There must be humor, laughter, music, games, and good food as well. That will keep the participants coming back. Then, when they feel ready, they will choose projects to work on to help their communities. The only way to have a possible society, Jean, is to develop the possible human at the same time. So, when it seems right, you go out there and make this happen."

"Yes, Margaret. I'll do that."

But that's not where the story begins. It begins at five in the morning in a Manhattan apartment near the American Museum of Natural History, where a small, feisty woman of seventy-five wakes up. She reviews her dreams and observes her mental images—vivid, prolific, teeming with memory and reflection. She begins to plan a critical speech she will soon give on the human uses of science. She remembers an appalling art exhibit in Copenhagen; a man tried to create human beings and instead made grotesques. Her body responded to the degradation of people treated as objects—"target populations," "human inventories." She recalls dozens of scientific studies that objectify the human condition. She thinks of her audience of scientists and sees them as strangely deficient in music and art, eyes veiled, ears stopped up. A sweep of Beethoven races through her, a sense of standing before Michelangelo's *David* and of looking up at the ceiling of the Sistine

Chapel. These images give way to pictures of early humans, pitiful, helpless, with their arms full of sticks; then to a memory of a New Guinean friend, primitive in 1928, intellectual in 1953. Images join images, words appear suited to form, and a complex and potent speech unfolds, her presidential address to the American Association for the Advancement of Science. The woman decides that it is time to get up and go to work on the typewriter. Her eyes open, and Margaret Mead climbs out of bed.

For some reason that I've mercifully forgotten, I was demonstrating a particularly exotic headstand in an elegant salon in Bath, England.

"Jean!" a voice commanded from the next room. "Stop walking around on your head and tell these people about your experiments with time distortion." I had only recently met Margaret Mead, and I did as I was told. She took notes in a small but fat red book, challenging me on fine points and nodding happily, her tongue darting between her lips as new information was added to her burgeoning storehouse of ideas.

The room became crowded and international. A well-known British don drifted over and informed Margaret in unctuous polysyllables that Western civilization was dead. "Rubbish!" she thundered.

The don was showered with concrete instances in which Western civilization appeared to be in its prime. Suspicion was cast on the perceptual powers of Oswald Spengler, whose major work, *The Decline of the West*, the don had been citing. The don backed away, sucking hugely on his unlit pipe. An old woman appeared, eyes bright and arms filled with flowers. She gave Margaret the flowers and launched into a poignant tale about her youngest son. Margaret listened intently, encouraging her with searching questions. The old mum left, looking as if she had been crowned. A Russian chess champion came over, babbling amiably and incomprehensibly. Margaret nodded and smiled and grunted back at him.

The college girls that Margaret and I had assembled in England for a conference on the future of women's education were still shy and even a little scared. They hung back in reverential circles, straining to catch pieces of the conversation.

"Come closer, girls," Margaret called. "I want your opinion on something."

"Our opinion?" a Radcliffe senior stammered.

"Sure. Now what do you think about . . . ?"

Throughout the course of that evening, Margaret Mead touched almost everyone at that party. She absorbed information about everything from the preservation of the ancient baths of Bath to the future banes of Britain. She sought opinions, made friends, and encouraged people of all ages, dispensing names and references for their convenience and education. She even wrote letters of introduction and prefaces for books on the spot. New networks were woven; old ones were widened. Grandmother Herself had come to the party, and everyone stood to benefit.

Nothing seemed to escape her. She observed the smells in the air, the wave-lengths of emotion. How something was said was just as important as what was said. She studied the spatial relationships of people in the room, the patterning and repatterning of groups and couples. "Look, Jean, over there. You see that cou-ple becoming bored with each other? All right, now watch. They are going to move toward that lone man in the corner, and it's going to become a threesome. And then that triad is going to form a double triad."

"How did you know that, Margaret?" I asked when that was exactly what hap-pened.

"I merely observed the kinesics, the body signals those people were giving out, and then saw how the spatial relationships in the room made it very probable that they would end up together."

Margaret demonstrated several other predictive examples of how people would rearrange themselves, and then, when one of her predictions didn't turn out as expected, she declared, "Now that's fascinating! Let's go over and find out why that didn't happen." As it turned out, one of the people in question had to ur-gently go to the bathroom.

"Humph," said Margaret. "I should have caught that one. I can generally always tell when someone has to go to the bathroom!"

That evening, while we walked back to our hotel, she reran the party for me, commenting on, among other things, the neck and head posture of chess players, the emotional style of certain English mothers born in the last years of Queen Victoria, the effect of bright red walls on general animation, the sudden resolution of philosophical arguments by the come-to-supper smells of just-grilled shish kebab. I found myself wondering, was Margaret doing cultural anthropology that evening, or was Margaret doing Margaret Mead, or was there any difference?

During the week of the conference, I had ample opportunity to observe her re-markable perceptiveness and the unusual ways her mind worked. Supremely well organized and a master guide through the byways of the small conference (which she, in fact, helped to invent), she exhibited at the same time a wild free streak of speculation, association, and invention coupled with a cast of mind that one gen-erally finds only in kindergarten or other outposts of the untrammeled genius of childhood.

She thought in images as well as in words, often, her whole body joining in the pursuit of some memory or association. I recall asking her about an obscure taboo among the Arapesh, a New Guinea tribe she had studied, and she replied, "Oh, yes. I discussed that with George Devereaux at the Breadloaf Conference of 1937, and he was wrong!"

A characteristic statement.

"How in the world can you remember a thing like that?"

"Well, when you asked me about that Arapesh taboo, I immediately found my-self in my mouth and thinking about food . . . bread . . . Breadloaf Conference of 1937!"

"You store images and memories in different parts of your body?"

"Certainly. It makes for much better recall." (I decided then that it wasn't that Margaret was fat; it was just that she was padded all over her body with information.)

One morning she came in complaining of having had a "murdered baby" dream. This meant, she told me, that her unconscious was reminding her of something she had not attended to back in New York. She frequently had these dreams when she knew there was something she ought to do that she had not yet done.

"Do you remember your dreams?"

"Many of them, most of the time," she answered.

"And do you dream true?"

"Ah, you are on to me," she beamed, her eyes sparkling behind her glasses.

We began to discuss how each of us as children had been greatly taken with the romances of George du Maurier's *Peter Ibbetson* and Rudyard Kipling's *The Brushwood Boy,* in which the principal characters are able to "dream true," meeting their beloveds in the dream world and having marvelous adventures together. As a child, Margaret had duly followed Kipling's prescription: "Clasp your hands behind your head and never stop thinking of the place you want to be, and when you go to sleep, you'll be there." If nothing else, this formula keeps you slightly alert as you fall asleep, and with this thread of consciousness comes some ability to orchestrate your dreams. "I am generally able to dream about anything I wish," she told me, adding that she routinely assigned the problems of the day to the dreaming of the night, waking up in the morning with a variety of solutions.

As the days progressed, I discovered that her many modes of thinking, learning, problem solving, imagining, memory retention, dream orchestration, and creative processing provided in one person a living confirmation of the latent human capacities I had seen over years of laboratory research. Many of these innate but little-used capacities were second nature to her, natural and normal practices in her everyday life. In her comfortable way, she had democratized greatness and domesticated the range of human potential.

Not that there were no shadows lurking in the range. For example, she did not suffer fools gladly, and her notion of foolishness was very wide indeed. "Rubbish!" and "fiddlesticks!" were her ultimate expletives, pronounced with such withering scorn that you would have much preferred a foul-mouthed harangue. Then, too, the drama and scope of her personality were at first meeting both appealing and appalling. I had heard that she was truculent, but this table-pounding, word-blistering warrior broke the mold. I found myself wondering, "This is Margaret Mead? This . . . child?" For, indeed, her behavior was childlike in its uninhibited display, uncensored emotion, and total expressiveness.

Margaret's free-wheeling attitude spread to others as well. All academic proprieties were dropped as Margaret and the elegant English science writer and historian June Goodfield lit into each other with Elizabethan fury. "You are totally wrong. This is an intolerable statement!" one would shout, while the other would roar back with a storm of argument and proof. The college girls looking on were stunned by the no-holds-barred passion of these two pillars of the intellectual establishment and were even more astonished when, after all this thundering at each other, they met in the middle of the room and hugged each other hugely. At the end of this session, Jacqueline Wechsler, then president of Hunter College and a former nun, raised her hands in a movement that could be described as liturgical, "Lord, students, mark you this! You have seen two women arguing passionately, without a shred of rancor, as men do all the time. We have not learned to do this, but we must."

Later that evening, while we were relishing a sumptuous meal at the best restaurant in Bath, Margaret turned to me and asked, "Jean, of the seven deadly sins, which is yours?"

"Well, obviously gluttony," I replied, forking down another mouthful of the gingered salmon mousse. "Which is yours, Margaret?"

"Greed," she responded with great emphasis, her lips drawn back to show a great many teeth. "Greed for new experiences!"

The next morning while we were consuming an English breakfast of porridge, eggs, bangers, bacon, kippers, mushrooms, tomatoes, beans, toast, and marmalade, I challenged her, "Margaret, how's your greed quotient today?"

"Very high, as usual," she answered, chewing lustily. "Good," I responded, "because I've got a new experience for you. You know, you've got the most interesting mind I've ever encountered. I'd like to study the way your mind works."

She laid her fork down and stared thoughtfully at her plate. I wondered whether I had offended her. After a few moments, she looked up smiling and said, "Let's do it. All my life people have been interested in what I think. You are one of the few who care about how I think. We'll do it!"

That was July 1973. In September she phoned me and demanded to know why I hadn't called her. I equivocated with the usual business about not wanting to intrude on her time, how busy she was, and so forth.

She cut me off with alacrity. "Jean! Don't you know that I expect people to initiate contact with me? I have to be the one who is pursued. Otherwise, life would be impossible."

Still, I am ashamed to say, I kept my distance. I was amazed at my reticence. Here I was in my early thirties, having achieved a certain recognition for research and writing, hardly shy, and deeply interested in pursuing actively the scope and range of Margaret's mind, a mind that seemed tailor-made for the studies I had, to some extent, pioneered. And yet, I could not call her. Was it her fame that stopped me? That seemed unlikely. With a comedy writer father, I had grown up in a milieu of hot-shot comedians and movie stars and had been blessed with knowing many of the great elders of my era. The wonderful walks with Teilhard de Chardin in early adolescence had been fractally repeated with Aldous Huxley and Gerald Heard in my early twenties. I had studied with theologians Reinhold Niebuhr, Paul Tillich, Paul Ricoeur, and Martin Buber in graduate school and, in my studies of psychedelic drugs, had regularly interacted with some of the most original crazies, mystics, and maniacs on the sixties scene.

It was as if somehow I knew that Margaret was of a different order of being, perhaps because she was a woman. In pursuing the mind of Margaret Mead, I was crossing a forbidden threshold, entering, it seemed, an area of women's mysteries in which silence was the rule and in which the usual rituals of mind and behavior were flouted and regenerated. I had been trained into conforming by some of the best male minds and the best male logic. I was even a key observer of the best male manias. But now circumstances were demanding that I transcend both the training and the conforming and attend to something that was too deep to be denied, too necessary to be negated.

Not that the feminine mind could have been evaded much longer by me or anybody else. The culture, both local and worldwide, had reached a level of complexity mixed with crisis that demanded a new approach. The tide of consciousness was rising, and feminine sensibility and potential were becoming critical to human survival, even as they upset and confused the styles and standards of many cultures.

There was no denying it. Fifty-two percent of the human race was about to become full partners in the business of human affairs. We were approaching the great divide at which humans would become either the neurons or the cancer of the planet. It is estimated that by the year 2010 there will be almost as many people on Earth as there are neurons in the cerebral cortex. If the Earth is a living organism, and if its human nervous system is nearly in place, then women's roles of necessity must expand beyond a preoccupation with childbearing to encompass all fields of human endeavor, to make women available to the complex requirements of the emerging planetary civilization. The noosphere or global mind field, foreseen by Teilhard de Chardin, is coming closer. And essential to its development is clearly the rich mindstyle of woman, now ready to emerge everywhere after centuries of gestation in the womb of preparatory time. Herstory, rich and fecund, is coming into the light. This emergence is perhaps the most important event of the last five thousand years, and its consequences may well have an unimaginable effect on cultural evolution.

As a new partnership develops between men and women to address the entire human agenda, it spirals back and gathers in the achievements of the earlier partnership culture of the late Neolithic age. As the remarkable, if controversial, work of Marija Gimbutas and others has shown, the culture of old Europe from about 7000 to 3500 B.C.E. was essentially an agrarian economy centering around the rites and worship of the Great Goddess. The findings of James Melaart in Çatal Hüyük in Turkey and of Gimbutas in southeastern Europe reveal civilizations of extremely complex and sophisticated arts, crafts, technology, and social organization. As Riane Eisler suggests, the evidence indicates that these early cultures were nonpatriarchal partnership societies, in which descent and inheritance passed through the mother and in which women played equal roles in all aspects of life and work. Every aspect of the culture reflected this. For example, the art of the period is nonheroic, without representations of conquests or captives. Instead, the art abounds with scenes and symbols from nature, with sun and water, serpents, birds, and butterflies, and everywhere shrines, votive offerings, images, and figurines of the Goddess. Though artistic evidence is seldom linear and is best interpreted on the meander and the spiral, implying the many turnings of the dance of life, the artifacts of this period suggest a gentle, high culture—nurturing, playful, and pacific. This partnership culture was exported to Crete, where it flourished in populous well-organized cities, multistoried palaces, networks of fine roads, productive farms, an almost modern system of drainage and irrigation works, a rich economy with high living standards, and the lively and joyous artistic style characteristic of Cretan life and sensibility.

These gentle civilizations, however, eventually perished at the hands of marauding raiders and nomads. The conquerors not only imposed their own rigid rules but also shattered the finely wrought symbiosis among humans, nature, culture, and spiritual realities. We might imagine that the invaders felt both drawn to and terrified by the gentle complexity of the high civilization they encountered and were both fascinated and frightened by the pervasiveness of its sensory and artistic brilliance. Thus, they muscled and armored themselves against the enticement of its sensualities. They feared, dreaded, and violated the places and persons who bore witness to the ongoing communication between the seen and the unseen orders, which they themselves had lost. They married their male gods to the Goddess and made her the docile wife or the holy terror. They did away with the ancient rights of women and destroyed partnership in favor of patriarchal rule.

But now history along with herstory has cycled back upon itself, and men and women prepare for new transformational partnerships. There is good reason to believe that such partnerships will help to release men from the old polarities of gender that forced them into limited and limiting roles, and qualities of intelligence will be added to the human mind-pool that will render most previous problem solving obsolete. Linear, sequential solutions will yield to the knowing that comes from seeing things in whole gestalts; constellations of knowledge will be prized rather than discrete facts. The emphasis may shift to affirming things that are true but not accurate rather than to giving assent only to things that are accurate but not true. Process itself will be as celebrated along with the pursuit of goals.

Cultures in which the feminine archetype is powerful emphasize being rather than doing, deepening rather than producing and achieving. Such cultures are almost always nonheroic; they tend to make things work, cohere, grow. If, for a hundred thousand years or so, you've been stirring the soup with one hand and holding the baby with the other, kicking off the woolly mastodon with one foot and rocking a cradle with the other, watching out for the return of the hunters with one eye and determining with the other on which cave wall you will paint a magical bison, then you are going to develop a very complex consciousness. This is a consciousness that is extraordinarily well adapted to orchestrating the multiple variables of the modern world and to negotiating the multicultural realities of that world.

In our culture's supreme dialectic between Logos and Eros, Logos has been assigned to men and Eros to women. Universally the feminine sensibility seems to tend more naturally toward Eros. Logos, the principle of ordering and mastery—traditionally a more masculine principle—is essential to the creation and sustenance of civilization. But Eros is of a different order; it is concerned with the interrelationship of psyche and nature. To the feminine mind, Great Nature is as important internally as it is externally. Joined by the principle of *unus mundus*, the unified reality stream, the inward realm has as much ontological status for women as does the external world. Thus the feminine principle expresses itself as an unfolding of levels of existence, not as a conquest of facts. Under the principle of Eros we become not systematic—the goal of Individual Man—but systemic, the province of the Postindividual, orchestrating our lives to mesh creatively with the finely balanced systems of nature. We become aware of ourselves not as encapsulated bags of skin dragging around a dreary and demanding ego, but rather as organism-environments engaged in fields of life—from a subtle awareness of the psychic weave between ourselves and others and the network that connects us to the larger social organism.

Today, as we advance to the stage of planetary society, we must avoid the domination of one principle by the other. If Eros is rising, it is as a necessary corrective to the tyranny of Logos. Dominated by Logos, Eros becomes stalemated in obsessive sexuality and desire. Dominated by Eros, Logos is stuck in dogmatic, habituated patterns of social order and ritual. Creating a new reality, both socially and personally, requires a new blending and rich interplay of Eros and Logos. Then Eros can become a deepening, unifying principle, granting us resonance with larger fields of life, leading us to become planetary persons, and bringing true global and psychic interdependence. Logos can become a more sensitive regulating principle, subtly guiding the interchange of psyche and social order toward the flowering of a world civilization that preserves human difference and wide variation in cultures, partners the planet, and engenders the soul.

Many of us in research and clinical psychology have witnessed in our research subjects and clients over the past several decades a remarkable activation of images of female principles—archetypes and goddesses. Because of my work with cultures all over the world, I can testify to the rise of feminine archetypes and myths of the Goddess on a global scale. This development, along with the proliferation of books, articles, and conferences on the Goddess, has great implications for culture and consciousness. The women's movement may be the outward manifestation of what is happening on depth levels in essential, mythic, and archetypal space-time. Perhaps the movement has evolved because the crisis of the external world is calling for the rise of the Goddess to restore the balance of nature or because the release of women into full partnership demands a similar release of its archetypal principle or even because, in the cosmic cycle of things, the time of the Goddess has come. But all evidence indicates that the feminine archetype is returning. The identification of the Earth by scientists with the name of the ancient Earth goddess, Gaia, is the signal that Herself and Herstory have come round at last.

Denied and suppressed for thousands of years or, what is almost as bad, sanitized and given only mercy jobs by wary male theologians, the Goddess archetype returns at a time when the breakdown of the old story leaves us desperate for love, for security, for protection, for wisdom, for meaning. We humans are yearning for nurturing and cultivation of our whole being, that we might be adequate stewards of the emerging planetary culture.

Back in 1973, however, when I encountered the feminine archetype in the formidable person of Margaret Mead, I was still asking myself what we were afraid of, what secrets we were trying to protect. Did we fear a mode of mind and consciousness that was too free in its associations and therefore prone to charges of sloppiness? Was it that the mind was not primarily linear, objective, and scholastic but rather circular, empathic, and narrative? Was it because the feminine myth was more of the order of Proteus, the shape-shifter, rather than of Prometheus, the stealer of fire from heaven? More, was it that the feminine face of God with all her prodigality of possibilities had the potential for turning the world upside down? Was it that once we agreed to the reality and validity of the feminine mind-style, there was in fact no turning back?

In stepping into Margaret, I was stepping into an abyss. I was agreeing to break a conspiracy of silence that had lasted for millennia and to tell tales once only whispered. The irony for me was that I had been a student of patterns of historical development, comfortable in contemplating abstract paradigms of cultural change. But now I was invited to take a front-row seat on the living emergence of a dynamic style of feminine mind and behavior, and the possible consequences were loaded.

Hegel once wrote about world-historical individuals, those richly endowed people whose personal interests, sensibilities, and passions correspond to the needs and turnings of their times. Out in front or behind the scenes, they are the impresarios of change, the orchestrators of culture and consciousness. Margaret Mead was such a person. For more than fifty years, whenever major or minor issues were called into question, more often than not Margaret was there, speaking at conferences, networking the thinkers, innovating, challenging, scolding, and, above all, making things happen. On questions of global pollution, intergenerational learning, or the benefits of breastfeeding, she was an expert in follow-through, without which civilization would quickly lapse into entropy. She knew how things worked. As an anthropologist and an intensive observer of culture and social process, she studied the forms of political and social order and used them to effect change and growth in even the most recalcitrant institutions.

Margaret, the woman, brought *anthropos* (a very male, patriarchal term) to the public domain. Often, she did this by looking at female concerns and structures in the societies she studied. She assumed a kind of rightful Mother-Mind joined to a personal momentum that was not about to be caught in anything that was going to stop the drive in her. Our culture often takes a cookie cutter, cuts a pattern from the protean dough of our possibilities, and pronounces us legitimate. Margaret Mead took the pattern and transcended it. She wanted six children, discovered that she was unable to have them (except for Mary Catherine Bateson, born in 1939), and took the whole world for her child. She decided that something needed to be done in her household—which was the world—and then did it. In graduate school she switched from psychology, the study of the psyche of the individual, to the study of *anthropos*, the whole of humanity. And she did it as if she were keeping house in a very poetic way, always going to the heart of the matter, taking care of people's spirits as well as their physical, emotional, and intellectual needs.

The public's notion of her helped, of course. Whether she was seen as the eminent anthropologist, the arbiter of common sense, or even as Grandma Herself, the consensus was that in her we had a national resource, like coal or oil, but much more interesting and far more dependable. She was small. She was sturdy. She worked around the clock. And she became one of the rare positive fixtures in the global mindscape—the happy warrior who brooked no whiny nay-saying—an ageless wise one who knew perfectly well that the emperor had no clothes but then went about finding him some, the priestess of pragmatic occasions.

In October 1973 she called me again. "You remember that mind of mine you said you wanted to study? Well, you'd better study it soon, because it's going very fast. I am making the strangest verbal transpositions, substituting nouns for adjectives. This morning, I called a typewriter a *ladder.* Perhaps there's something you can do for me?"

The following day I went to the Beresford, the building across from the Museum of Natural History, where Margaret shared an apartment with her friend and colleague Rhoda Metraux. She seemed anxious to see me and readily complied with the series of tests I gave her. They showed that she was indeed exhibiting unusual verbal, visual, and motor transpositions. I asked her to hold a Chinese plate and describe the scene painted on it. This she could do with no trouble, but then, as she turned the plate in her hands, she remarked that she could still see the scene right side up even though it was now upside down. It took several seconds for the original picture to vanish.

"Let's walk through your apartment, Margaret, and you tell me the history of some of the pieces that we see." She led me through her large, comfortably furnished rooms, her talk teeming with the memories and associations of more than seventy years of intense living. She pointed to a New Guinea mask and remarked, "Now that bicycle there I picked up in Manus when my second husband Reo Fortune and I went there with the help of Radcliffe-Brown to study—"

"Margaret," I interrupted, "you brought a bicycle all the way back from Manus?"

"Of course not!" she retorted angrily, and then, with a hint of terror in her voice asked, "Did I call that mask a *bicycle?*"

As I watched her standing there, a worried granny face perched on dumpling body, I had a hunch about the source of her problems.

"Margaret, can you remember the last time that you had any exercise?"

"Certainly, " she answered smugly. "It was August 15, 1964. I played shuffleboard on Doxiades' yacht."

"Margaret," I said, "It's not your mind that's giving you problems. It's your body! Apart from one game of shuffleboard and occasionally squatting in an interesting position to interview natives, you've had extremely limited body movement and—"

"That's not true. I walk," she retorted.

"Where? Across the street to the museum?"

"Well, yes, there, but also from the cab to the lecture room at Columbia, and then in airports, of course, to pick up my baggage, and then there's—"

"Margaret, you are inhibited."

"I am *not!*"

"You have accumulated a lifetime of muscular inhibitions, which are now finally being translated in your brain into cortical inhibitions. That is why you are experiencing some slippage in both perceptual and linguistic categories."

"Oh."

"Are you willing to retrain your brain and learn something radically different from anything you've ever learned before?"

"Always."

A few days later, she made the first of many visits to my home and research foundation in nearby Pomona, New York, to begin a course of psychophysical reeducation.

My father once described my home as a cross between a mausoleum and an explosion in a paint factory. It was built in a whimsical manner by actor Burgess Meredith with fifty-foot rooms, stages, and a three-story hexagonal tower. My avocation as an archaeologist and collector of antiquities means that it now houses an even more whimsical collection of ancient gods and artifacts. An Egyptian mummy case overlooks an intertribal calling drum from Kenya, which itself is beckoning to a Ming Dynasty ivory statue of an Immortal, who is looking into the open mouth of a Roman marble head of Tragedy, whose eyes gaze on a nine-foot intricately carved Balinese bird-god. And so it goes throughout the house, a gathering of the sacred flotsam of millennia interspersed willy-nilly with computers, biofeedback machines, psychophysical testing equipment, and other paraphernalia necessary for high-tech studies of human possibilities. All of this fights for space with a library of some sixty thousand volumes.

"Humph!" said Margaret, as she navigated her way around a fourth-century B.C.E. Egyptian mummy case. "Humph, humph!" she snorted as she passed a Spanish suit of armor, a Tibetan exorcism trumpet, and a two-thousand-year-old Mexican statue of a ballplayer, straddling a copy machine. But she was silent when she peered speculatively at a three-thousand-year-old bronze statue of Sekhmet, the Egyptian goddess of war and healing. For a while, it looked like a stand-off between Margaret and the lion-headed goddess. Clearly, one old warrioress was psyching out the other. "That statue has views!" Margaret said finally. "One shouldn't have such a statue in the house." One could practically see Sekhmet saying "Humph!" back to her.

"Such a strange place," she commented at dinner. "Nothing goes with anything, and yet somehow it all works. Like the inside of your mind, eh, Jean?"

Conversation turned to the psychology of hand gestures in seventeenth-century Chinese porcelain figurines (seemingly, a safe subject), when suddenly Margaret and my husband Bob were embroiled in a battle about the erotic quotient of Chinese people. My quirky Airedale, Oliver, glared balefully at Margaret and lowered his tail. Margaret was claiming with immense authority that the Chinese had no interest in sex apart from procreation, while Bob was taking quite another point of view. Bob is no slouch when it comes to belligerence, and he was giving as good as he got. The argument escalated crazily, voices hitting sonic boom levels. I wanted to crawl under the table. Then the Airedale nipped Margaret. His sensitive ears had had enough. I used his intervention to change the subject.

"Margaret," I began in my most placating, if muddled, manner, "suppose that there were people who cared about you and wanted you to have a good fifteen or twenty years more, not of deterioration, but of quality life, and they put in, not a mandate, but a strong plea and told you how. Would you do it?"

"No," said Margaret. "I would not." Then, noting my crestfallen face, she added, "However, since it is my responsibility to stay alive in this body at this time in history as well as I can, Jean, and if what you and Bob tell me to do will be a way, while I'm here, to make my brain work better, I'll do your exercises. Shall I take off my clothes now?"

Bob blanched. A few minutes later in a studio upstairs devoted to psychophysical work, Margaret (in long white bloomers and T-shirt) began the first of many bodywork sessions with Bob. He started her with gentle movements to loosen her joints and gradually increase the range of her arm and leg movements. As I watched him work, I noted approvingly that I had used a similar exercise the week before with a group of very ancient nuns who had had even less experience with exercise than Margaret. The gentle sisters had responded well and had been so grateful for their increase in flexibility, pressing upon me gifts of convent-made jellies and breads.

"Owwwwww!" Margaret bellowed.

Bob stopped, stunned. No one had ever reported feeling pain at his ministrations.

"No, please continue," Margaret ordered. "This is very useful."

Margaret's whalelike bleats of what—pain? rage? revulsion?—continued relentlessly throughout the session until I could not stand it anymore and crept cowering off to my office three floors below, stuck my fingers in my ears, and thought, "I am participating in the murder of Margaret Mead."

An hour later she came jauntily downstairs, white bloomers, walking stick (a shepherd's crook), and all, saying, "That was wonderful."

"Wonderful?" By this time, I was an emotional wreck. "You were screaming the entire time."

"Of course I was," she answered happily. "That's why I have freedom from load."

"Freedom from load" was a phrase much used by Margaret's crowd in the 1920s. It meant not dwelling upon or carrying around heavy psychological or emotional baggage. Judging by Margaret's behavior, it also involved having a catharsis on the spot whenever the going got rough.

Bob continued to work with Margaret, and she changed for the better. The lost words returned, she no longer made ellipses, and for the first time in years, she got her figure back. The people at the museum reported that she was really much easier to work with—not great, but easier.

From the fall of 1973 until her death in 1978, Margaret continued to come to our house, often spending many days with us as Bob worked on her and she and I worked on studying the mind of Margaret Mead. One day, after we had known each other for about six months, she announced, "You're just like me!"

"No, I'm not." I replied. "I am much nicer to people than you are and nowhere near as smart."

"No, you are like me. You think in patterns, are as eclectic as I am, seem to be afraid of nothing, have invented a new profession, and are dedicated to making the world work. Also you have memorized the same kinds of poetry that I have. Furthermore, I need another daughter, so that's probably you." Mary Catherine, who was my age, was living and teaching in Iran at the time, so I became Margaret Mead's second daughter. Thus I found the principal mentor of my life.

I was used to being adopted by elders. Perhaps because I was really interested in what they had to say, they saw in me a continuity for their feelings and ideas. With Margaret, however, a lot more was involved, a style of female mentoring that was at once a nurturing, a chastening, a weaving, and an apprenticeship in the sources of true power. One day while we were in the middle of studying her creative process, she offered me an enormous challenge. "I need for you to remember my life as if you had grown up with me, Jean. That way, you will not only understand my mind, you will come to understand how to make the world work." Margaret proceeded to paint such vivid pictures of her early life that I felt as if I were witnessing the making of the possible human.

I was amazed at how many similarities there were in our upbringings. She told me that after kindergarten, she was periodically educated at home because her family members, and especially her strong-minded, innovative schoolteacher grandmother, had thought so deeply about education that they disapproved of formal schooling. As my mother had done, her mother gave her a great deal of poetry to memorize, and her grandmother dispensed hardy maxims for her to take to heart while the grandmother brushed her hair. What an image! A grandmother imparts moral wisdom to the back of a young girl's head while taking out the tangles in her head space. Margaret learned basketry, carpentry, weaving, wood carving, and other manual skills requiring fine eye-to-muscle coordination. Testing her in her seventies, I found that her coordination in this regard surpassed nearly everyone I had ever tested.

Following a suggestion of William James, her mother exposed her to many sensory stimuli when she was still an infant—colors, textures, pictures of great works of art, and masterpieces of music, including an ancient Greek hymn to Apollo retained in the Byzantine Church. Margaret was encouraged to use all her senses in every kind of activity, even the most abstract ones. Dualisms were discouraged; she was trained to accept the unity of mind and body, thinking and feeling. If I asked a Texas relative where he existed, he might say, "Why, Jeanie, I exist right here," pointing to his head. If I posed the same question to a Sicilian relative, "Graziella, where do you exist?" she might point to her heart, saying, "Here, Gina." When I had asked the same question to a Chinese friend, he pointed to his solar plexus, his *t'an tien*. But when I asked Margaret that question, she responded matter-of-factly, "Why, all over of me, of course."

Of course.

Given this base of rich sensibility, Margaret acquired an unusual ability to store memories and learn abstract material rapidly. As an anthropologist, she also had the physical empathy to understand, through body sensing, the special skills of physical cultures. She could feel a complex fishing procedure in her bones and sinews or sense an intricate dance as a kinesthetic rhythm in her muscle fibers. She shared photographs of her in the field that showed her assuming some of the sensibilities of the cultures she was observing. She appeared soft in Arapesh, tense in Manus, unfocused and "away" or even in trance in Bali. From her I learned how to assume some of the characteristics of the cultures I would be studying and working in, which is probably why I have been accepted in cultures in which other

Westerners have been given a polite but cold shoulder. (It also helps that I often wear the clothing of the culture, sagging saris and all, as well as get a suntan and darken my hair with a rinse so as to look a little more like the people with whom I am working. There is nothing much I can do about my height, unless I am with the Watusis.)

Grandmother Mead also insisted that Margaret learn how to perform entire procedures from beginning to end. If she asked to learn to weave, she was required to help chop down the tree with which to make the loom. When she asked if she could help make cheese, she was told, "Of course, Margaret, but first you must watch how Bossie gives birth to her calf." My research indicated that this training may have been a major determinant in developing her keen intellect full of sensory feelers, her thorough and methodical way of working, and her adeptness with analogy in relating and explaining things. One had only to look at a few pages of her anthropological field notes to see a mind honed to the most acute capacity for observation, able to make useful applications to cultures half a world away. I discovered that this insistence on process, something that I missed in my more whimsical upbringing, meant that whenever she began or joined a project, she invariably followed it through to its natural conclusions—often, to a new beginning. This made for an extraordinary number of projects in progress at any given time.

Early in childhood, Margaret also began setting herself tasks and seeing how fast she could do them. She was inspired by witnessing her parents having a contest to see who could write the "Lord's Prayer" more times in an hour. Thereafter, whenever Margaret read a book, she would first estimate the time it would take to finish it, then try to do it faster. As she sped through the pages, she would add the handicap of trying to concentrate on the book while someone else in the room read aloud. This kind of self-imposed exercise led to Margaret's formidable mastery of time. Whenever she tackled a piece of work, she immediately alerted her senses, set an agenda, and began racing. Each minute had thrust upon it the contents of an hour, each hour was laden with a day, and from her birth in 1901 to the time she entered my life in the early 1970s, she had probably accrued the experiences of four or five lifetimes. Needless to say, she exhilarated anyone in her vicinity, and low-energy people tended to do their best work around her. When she sent me to interview her exhusbands, they all commented on this phenomenon. Talking with second husband Reo Fortune and his wife at their home in Cambridge, England, I was astonished when Mrs. Fortune said to me, "Would you please ask Margaret to come and live with us? Reo produced so much work when he was living with her." Third husband, Gregory Bateson, told me that her speediness had led some anthropologists to cast doubt upon her work. How could anyone "do" a society so quickly and then produce a book about it the following year? Bateson explained, "The reason people didn't believe her was because they had never seen how fast she worked." He also told me that he had never produced so much as when he was married to her.

Much research, including my own, indicates that thinking need not be limited by the slow pace of our physiological being or by the linear inhibitions of our verbal thought. In high-level creativity, the mind races over many alternatives, picking, choosing, discarding, synthesizing, sometimes doing the work of months in minutes. Join to this Margaret Mead's multimodal techniques, discipline, and organized self-orchestration, and you get a performance that felt normal to her but looked to the rest of us laggards like runaway acceleration. When I pointed this out, she said, "Nonsense, Jean, I'll get you up and running. I want a twenty- to thirty-page report from you by the end of this week on the latest research in stress." And thereafter, she would set me almost weekly tasks (which generally had to do with helping her in her work and research) that in pre-Margaret days I would have thought impossible within the given time. Under Margaret's eagle eye, I somehow managed to complete them. She raised the nature of the possible in me, a phenomenon that was tantamount to the breaking of the four-minute mile. There is no question that I owe the prodigality of my present output to Margaret's training. In addition to my other tasks, I research and write a small book each month that is the basis of my Mystery School lectures; prepare and deliver other public talks; and, many weekends, plan and lead a three-day seminar. Along with this is constant traveling; answering some of the mail; phone calls; books to write, review, and write prefaces for; radio interviews and other media projects; volunteer work; home life, including keeping my husband and dogs happy; keeping up with my wide circle of friends; and being the family cook. How do I do it? I get up very early, live in accelerated time, avoid self consciousness (which takes up an awful lot of time and energy) and worrying about what others will think, and let myself be sponsored by an image of what I want to create or achieve that day, that week, that month, or that year. Having a friendly support system also helps immensely.

Margaret and I also discovered that very early in our lives, our families treated us as full persons. When she was about four, Margaret's grandmother enlisted her help in looking after her parents, and she began to think of adults as her children, needing care and protection. While still very young, she was moved deeply by the image in "The Ballad of Sir Patrick Spens" of the young moon holding the old moon in its arms. This became a seed image for her that flowered as she grew up into thinking of the whole world as needing care. She was the first global midwife, building community wherever she went, and she passed that responsibility and that title on to me. Now there are many of us, men and women alike, but many of us began out of Margaret's inspiration.

I once gave Margaret a Rorschach test, and, not surprisingly, she scored right in the middle between fantasy or inner life and action in the world. There is no doubt that the richness of her inner life provided the momentum, the ideas, and the charge for her outer activities. Thus she virtually legislated her own success. Able to mobilize inner and outer with equal force, versed in the forms and practices of many cultures, she could turn ideas into realities with amazing speed and effectiveness. She told me that one must always learn the forms and laws of a culture, be it another country, an institution, or a corporation, and learn them better than its constituents. Then one knew how to initiate change without being a victim. "You must sidle into an organization like a crab, Jean," she once told me. "I would never enter an agency whose prime interest is economics through the front door as an economist. I come in from the side as an anthropologist. That way they can't attack me. And because I know its forms better than those on the inside, I can play with those forms. Insiders are often stuck in their own rigidities, but me, ha, I know the other levels of the game and how to invent new ones. That's how you change the world, Jean. That's social artistry!" In a world in which most projects fall afoul of the principle of entropy, she worked on a different principle, one I have tried to emulate—that we are dynamic participants in a participatory universe. Thus she taught me that it was important to challenge people at odd moments and in unlikely situations. That, she said, would throw them off base and get them moving and thinking again.

In testing her sensory imagery, I discovered that Margaret also enjoyed very developed olfactory and tactile abilities. She could always smell fear and anger (an acrid odor); her nose also told her when someone she knew had been in a room. Long after the fact, sometimes fifty years or more, her skin would recall someone holding her hand with loving pressure. Moreover, she was capable of synesthesia, or cross-sensing. A synesthete can hear color and see sound, taste time, and touch aromas.

She readily demonstrated this ability. I asked her once to describe for me the taste of our living room. She replied, "Ah, this room tastes like a room in which spices were placed last week." I then asked, "Margaret, what is the sound of Bob's face?"

"Bob's face? I hear a symphony."

"Really, Margaret, you hear a symphony? Is it a good symphony?"

"It's different."

"Margaret, what is the touch of my voice?"

"Well, Jean, your voice is a brush. Not a brush made of pig's bristles, but also not as soft as a silk brush that you use on a baby's hair. It's somewhere in between."

"Not nylon, I hope!"

"No, not nylon! It's something alive."

In the course of our friendship, which was both intense and familial, she forced me to find out things about myself that I never could have known without her not-so-gentle prodding. One day, when I was visiting her in her office, she discovered that I was hypersensitive to a degree that bordered on the ridiculous. I had received a letter attacking me and was about to throw over all of my work, since my attacker obviously knew what a nincompoop I really was.

"Fiddlesticks, Jean. Hate mail has many remarkable uses. Here, I'll show you. You commented earlier on how tired I seemed, and you're right. I am. But watch!" She went over to a file and pulled out a letter from ten years earlier. As she read, her face turned scarlet with anger, and her breath quickened. "Aaarrrgh!" she raged, as she finished.

"Are you all right, Margaret?"

"Certainly I'm all right. I got my energy back, didn't I?"

I keep my hate mail, too, but I don't reread it as often as Margaret did.

From that point on, she involved me in many of her projects, as I did her in mine. The most interesting of our projects was with our mutual friend Robert Schwartz, who owned and ran the Tarrytown Executive Conference Center. Margaret believed strongly in sapiential circles, groups of strong-minded people who meet regularly to share ideas, develop projects, and more often than not, make things happen. The Tarrytown Group, as we called ourselves, met for some years for a weekend each month to discuss and, wherever possible, solve critical issues facing the world. Treated royally and fed extravagantly at Schwartz's luxurious conference center, we called upon experts who knew about the subject of the month to join us in our reflections. What ensued were some of the richest conversation and exchange of ideas I had ever known, with Margaret challenging, scolding, evoking, bringing us to the thresholds of our minds, and then pushing us over. Whether it was developing the strategy for surveillance systems in the Sinai or working with E. F. Schumacher on applying his "small is beautiful" projects or even designing model cities in natural settings where grandparents would be educators, we spurred each other on to high inventiveness. Generally, we came up with cogent and creative methodologies that Margaret, in her unique way, would send forth to the appropriate authorities. I remember that after one particularly splendid session, when we were all quite proud of what we had accomplished, Margaret rushed to the phone, dialed the White House, and said, "Now, Jimmy, I think we have the solution to that problem we were speaking about. Now what you have to do is . . ." So, for a few short years, I felt that I was helping to run the world.

But there was more. Margaret decided that I was part of her continuity. Our meetings became more frequent and, I now realize, more feminist. She took me into companies where women were coming into leadership positions so that we could "practice cultural anthropology in the corporation." Often we saw women who were modeling themselves along male lines in order to get ahead. "A stupid thing to do," Margaret complained. "They are becoming second-rate men, and they'll stay in second-rate jobs!" Then she encountered a woman executive who worked differently. With the executive's permission, we followed her around and observed her style. "Look how she braids her work, Jean. She is attending both to

the process of how things are done and to getting the task done." Indeed, the executive, who was overseeing the production of the company's quarterly report, was
sensitive to the environment of feelings among her employees. She noticed who
was feeling left out, who was not voicing an idea. Later over lunch, Margaret, the
executive, and I spoke about how women all over the world were challenging the
most sexist institutions, from the medical establishment to organized religion,
and replacing them with a new social order. Education, career, marriage, recre-
ation, business, investments, government, and religion were changing as a result.

"You'll see," said Margaret. "Within the next thirty years, women will be both
priests and presidents. Why? Because women's resourcefulness and resolve increase as circumstances become more difficult."

"I see this with women business owners," the executive added. "They are more
likely to succeed, because women admit they need allies and partners and thus
surround themselves with good people. Also, women don't need to work in pyramids or hierarchies of power. I'm trying out a new way of forming clusters of people from every level of the company in order to look at issues as a whole, not just
in the old segmented way."

"Is it working?" Margaret asked, her eyes twinkling behind her glasses.

"Yes, I think so, or it will," the executive replied. "The men are a little wary, but
they are catching on. And it makes for much livelier meetings when everybody
feels they have a chance to participate."

"But what about sexism, violence against women, backlash? They're bound to
increase as women become more powerful," I added, bringing up the shadows that
I always see lurking behind any innovation.

"Of course they will increase," Margaret said grimly. "You can't turn around
the social order of thousands of years in a few decades without expecting a backlash. I wish I could live to see it. I'd know how to fight the backlash. It's a matter of
transforming our values and priorities. It's a matter of midwifery." With that mantic statement, she left for a doctor's appointment.

That was November 1977, and although I didn't know it, it was the prelude to the
most terrible thing that ever happened between us. In December, Margaret was
diagnosed with incurable pancreatic cancer, a disease that had recently killed her
younger brother. Despairing of orthodox treatment, she began seeing a great
healer, Carmen di Barrazza, almost daily and, by the summer of 1978, had already
lived months beyond her expected time. By then she had lost almost a hundred
pounds and was on crutches because she had tripped on the hem of her sagging
pantsuit, refusing to alter her clothes since she believed she would soon get well
and resume her comfortable heavy weight.

She had called a conference of her "best beloveds" at Chautauqua, the quaint
nineteenth-century town that each summer becomes a vast symposium of lec-

tures, concerts, and plays performed before large audiences in classical settings. The idea was that each one of us would "sing for our suppers" by giving lectures and then meet with Margaret from seven to ten each evening for discussion. It was to be Margaret's final sapiential circle. And so there we were—her favorite former husband, Gregory Bateson, Erik and Joan Erikson, her daughter Mary Catherine Bateson, George T. Land, Don Michaels, and myself. Margaret was too ill to attend our dinners together at the refectory where the conversation sizzled and sang. After dinner, when we adjourned to meet with Margaret, our conversations were desultory. Margaret was clearly dying; we were all upset, and our ideas were caught in anguish. We tried talking about the new paradigm—a new way of understanding process and reality—but we couldn't make much progress. Each evening, however, we bravely continued on until the grandfather clock tolled ten.

The morning of the last day I was there, I was sitting on the 1870s porch with Margaret, sewing up her pants and doing quite a poor job of it. Joan Erikson, a master weaver and craftswoman, came by, looked at my work, and said, "You don't do that very well, do you?"

After a period of silence, punctuated only by my grunts when I pricked my finger with the needle, Margaret suddenly began to rail at me. She blamed me for the decline and fall of the United Nations, the nutritional problems of Native Americans, and the current oil crisis. As she went on and on, ranking me with the goddess of chaos, I found that in spite of my hypersensitivity, I was not offended. On the contrary, I found it all very interesting, and there was always a tiny grain of truth to whatever she said. I was working with Native Americans; I had been involved with the United Nations; and I had missed an important meeting because of the long lines at the gas station. As her harangue continued, she got jollier and jollier, and I noticed that her wan and withered cheeks were filling out and becoming rosy. "You seem to be getting very happy with all of this," I remarked. "In fact, you don't look like somebody who is dying."

"You're right," she responded. "I am not going to die. Do you know why? Because you people need me. Remember last night when you and Erik and Gregory were talking about the new paradigm? Well, I helped create the current paradigm, and I'm one of the few people who understands how it works. As long as that paradigm is working, I am needed, and I cannot die. I will die only when a newer paradigm comes along that I do not understand."

I looked at my watch and saw that it was time for me to deliver my lecture on the possible human at the outdoor amphitheater. As I went down the stairs, Margaret called out sweetly, "Good-bye, darling. Have a good lecture."

That evening we all sat together again having our usual conversation that went nowhere. At five minutes to ten, something happened to me. It was as if I was seized by history. I was myself, and yet I was no longer myself. I was on this Earth, and yet I was part of a much larger universe. It was not unlike my six-year-old experience of understanding everything, only the focus now was on the emerging new paradigm. My insight was so enormous that I could barely get the words out of my mouth. I remember saying something about how we were not unlike deciduous trees, with periods of leafing and flowering and absorption. As I continued to stutter out the immensities I felt, I noticed that Gregory Bateson was leaning his six-foot-six-inch frame toward me, as was Erik Erikson. "Yes . . . yes . . . go on, Jean," they encouraged me. "You really are on to something."

At that moment, Margaret picked up her crutch and began banging it on the floor. "Stop! Stop! Stop! Stop! Stop!" she shouted.

"I will not stop," I said. "This is the most important thing I have ever known. I've got to get it out."

Gregory Bateson said, "Yes, Margaret, dear. Let her continue in what she was saying. It's very important. Go on, Jean, please go on."

And so I began to voice it again, the huge revelation tying up my tongue. And again Margaret banged away on the floor with her crutch, "*Stop! Stop! Stop! Stop! Stop!*"

"I cannot stop. This is so important!" I said, tears of rage leaping from my eyes. Yet even as I said and felt this, another part of me was observing and appreciating the high drama of the occasion.

"What you are saying is of no importance whatsoever," Margaret shouted. The clock began to strike ten. "Furthermore, you are corrupting the minds of everyone here."

"Me, corrupting the minds of Erik Erikson and Gregory Bateson?" I sputtered.

"Yes, you are. Furthermore, it is ten o'clock. The meeting is over." And with that, she pulled herself up on her crutches and made her painful way out of the room.

We all sat in silence for a while. Then Gregory Bateson came over and, without speaking, took my hand, held it for a moment, and left. Erik Erikson placed his hand on my shoulder and also walked out. He was followed by his wife Joan, who looked down at me and said in her candid, wise-woman manner, "You lost, and that is why you won." Mary Catherine collapsed, crying, in my arms.

I knew what had happened. Margaret lived in a world that knew other aspects of time. Because she had conquered linear time, she was no longer bound by it. So many times I had seen her know things one day that would happen the next. And so it was that in the morning she had raged at me because some part of her already knew that in the evening I would try to put forth something of the newer paradigm, the one that condemned her to death should it enter the world. That was why she tried to stop me from speaking. As it was, she was entirely successful. So shocked was I by the drama that the paradigm was lost from my consciousness, and I have spent the intervening years trying to recover it. Perhaps one day, when I am a very old woman, a bright young woman will come and tell me about the newer paradigm, and I will not stop her but die happy.

I had a prefigural fractal of this when I stood attendance on Margaret's dying several months later. "Margaret," I asked her, "was it because you thought I was going to come up with the newer paradigm that you were so angry with me that night?"

"Yes, darling," she answered in her quiet, dying voice and then added something that she rarely said: "I'm sorry."

After Margaret's death, I found myself haunted by questions that she had seeded in our years of working together: How do you grow a world or green a dream? How do you speak to the hopes of millennia in the midst of the futility of millions? How do you reseed a society that is but a few seasons away from wasteland and toxic dread?

On her deathbed, Margaret suggested to me that the answers lie not with economic or political initiatives but with a deepened citizenry. We can transform the world only by transforming ourselves, for what threatens our survival is not weaponry or technology but the people who use them. Our tendency to blame weapons or governments is a symptom of the powerlessness we feel in ourselves. Unlike Margaret, who played her own capacities like a symphony, most of us do not participate sufficiently in the music of our minds to orchestrate the challenge of change in our complex modern world. That is why we bring to bear on our many-layered social and economic problems technically complex but short-term solutions. Because of their simplistic psychological base, these attempts generally lead to long-term failure. When thinking and doing are largely linear, analytic, hierarchical, and lacking in the feminine dimension, and when the self that does the thinking and doing is insular, fearful, manipulative, and overly masculine, our best intentions in problem solving become a crazy-quilt patchwork of Band-Aids.

In 1984, George Orwell wrote of a society that was the horrendous embodiment of these trends. As we approached that much mythologized year, Margaret's admonition to me in her final days to create teaching-learning communities became a personal imperative. With the help of my friend Elsa Porter, who had been Assistant Secretary of Commerce during the Carter administration, I proposed in that election year to run not a candidate but an alternative vision, one that would take democracy seriously. With so much shadow around the year 1984, the times demanded some sunlight as well. Trusting in that vision of light, Elsa and I created a process that empowered people to engage actively in the re-creation of their local societies—to trust the fire in their bellies though it had been banked very low and to provide contexts and situations in which this fire could be raised to the red heat of action. I had always been a latency lifter for individuals, calling forth the possible human; now I wanted to lift the social latency in calling forth the possible society.

The organization we launched was, in fact, called The Possible Society. Beginning at the Press Club in Washington, D.C., we brought to some seventeen cities in the U.S. and Canada a series of weekend-long celebrational teaching-learning events for large groups of people—the possible humans—who could grow beyond their shrunken aspirations and achieve a larger freedom to think, to dream, to experience, to share, and, finally, to do. In the course of the seminars, people were given both inspiration and practical demonstrations of their extended capacities. The weekends were joyous, pulsing, musical events, in which participants learned the high arts of deep acknowledgment and mutual empowerment. Because the groups were large, from 700 to 1500 people drawn from all levels of the community, the weekends amplified the transformative experience, stimulating both personal and communal growth.

Most of the organizers of these events were students in the 1984 Mystery School. They were taught to mobilize involvement by community groups like the Girl Scouts, the Red Cross, the Elks Club, the Rotary. We kept the cost of the seminars very low and offered free attendance to those who could not afford the nominal fees, often only thirty-five dollars for the weekend. Most of the organizers, including myself, donated their services, and publicity was accomplished by word of mouth.

After the first few seminars, we realized that there was simply so much information to give that we had to code it within a story. I chose the great secular American myth, *The Wizard of Oz*. Set in the center of the country, in a time when the land is wasted and the peoples' hearts depressed, the story looks forward in its portrayal of the Emerald City to the technological golden age of the immediate future. Taking its structure from the mythic hero and heroine's journey, it tells of the genius of the child, Dorothy, unrecognized and unnurtured in dreary, gray Kansas, who discovers the way to the Oz of her own extraordinary nature.

In my lectures, I described Dorothy's companions on the journey as symbols of human disempowerment—disempowerment of mind (the Scarecrow), of heart and feelings (the Tin Man), and of courage and will (the Cowardly Lion). Within the mythic magic of this well-loved story and using songs and dances from the movie, we interwove talks and processes that redressed each disempowerment. Speaking to disempowerment of the mind, I called attention to the range and variety of human intelligence and guided brain exercises and processes in which people explored different styles of problem solving, such as thinking in images and thinking kinesthetically. For the disempowered heart, participants shared their joys and sorrows, their vulnerabilities, and their dreams. Aided by the music and the genius for opening the heart of contemporary composer and musician Robert Gass, participants became tender and trusting, and many new and lasting partnerships of the spirit formed. When it came to courage, participants explored their fears and envisioned what they would do if they were given the gift of courage. In the end, they challenged each other to generate courageous intentions for themselves and for society and to form groups of mutual support and empowerment to put these intentions into action. Most of Sunday afternoon was devoted to organizing participants into working groups around particular themes, such as education, environment, health care, and other social issues. In many cases, these groups grew into ongoing teaching-learning communities with programs to sustain the inspiration and personal and social development begun during the weekend. Projects that were undertaken and carried out included cleaning up the beaches of Santa Cruz, delivering good dental care to the elderly and indigent in Oklahoma City, and creating "green dollar communities" in British Columbia in which a portion of the profit from the sale of certain items remained in the community to be channeled into development. Thousands of social projects, many of them quite innovative, grew out of these weekends, and many of the groups begun in 1984–85 continue to meet.

Personal miracles also abounded. In Indianapolis, two men working together as partners in an exercise felt a deep meeting of soul and began a rich and supportive friendship. The exquisite irony of the pairing, which they enjoyed greatly when they discovered it, was that one man was the president of one of America's great foundations and the other a janitor in one of the foundation's buildings. In Sacramento, with fifteen hundred people in attendance, a young man spoke to me at lunch about a great teacher he had had as a child in the Midwest and how he had modeled his own teaching after hers. Later that day, while performing a process in which people danced through the room with eyes closed until, at a given moment, they found a partner and opened their eyes to discover the wonder of the unknown other, the young man could be heard shouting with excitement, for the older woman that he beheld when he opened his eyes was the very teacher he had spoken of, whom he had not seen for twenty-five years. I had my miracle as well, for it was also in Sacramento that I met Peggy Rubin, who was to become my closest associate.

After these seminars, I felt prepared to begin answering the many calls I was receiving from development agencies around the world to serve as a kind of global midwife to teaching-learning communities. In spite of Margaret Mead's mentoring, I am no anthropologist, but I have tried to follow her example in helping cultures to preserve themselves while they explore ways of becoming valuable members of the planetary community. I endeavor to guide communities to discover not only the genius of their given culture, but how this genius can grow and develop in a world of so many changes. I have learned that what often appears to be chaos is really cosmos in its most literal sense—world making and remaking.

Through the auspices of the Institute of Cultural Affairs, UNICEF, and other local and international developmental agencies, I have worked with cultures that have scarcely changed since the time of Christ and others that are medieval in structure. I have also given seminars and training programs in so-called First- and Second-World societies. I have become aware through all this that we are living in the midst of the most comprehensive cultural transition the world has ever seen and, with the rise of women, we cannot even begin to determine where it all is going. As a woman, I myself am called into ventures that would have been impossible to my female forebears. Yet when I wake up in the middle of a jet-lagged night in Burma or Bangladesh, I still wonder what I am doing and why.

I remember one such sleepless night in January 1991 in Yangon, Myanmar, formerly known as Rangoon, Burma. Rolf Carriere, the director of UNICEF for Myanmar, had brought Peggy Rubin and me there to give seminars on human development for Burmese leaders. I tossed with anxiety until morning came. What could we possibly do that would be of any value?

As we drove to the college where the seminar would be held, we passed golden-roofed Buddhist temples and stupas as well as military compounds. Barbed wire was everywhere, and the streets were filled with what appeared to be the largest segments of the population—soldiers, and monks and nuns. Rolf pointed out a crumbling family home where Daw Aung San Suu Kyi, the leader of the Burmese democracy movement, was under house arrest. Later that year she won the Nobel Peace Prize for her nonviolent campaign to bring democracy to her homeland. The previous year, even though she was detained, her party, the National League for Democracy, had won a landslide victory over the ruling military government. The military refused to recognize the results and arrested most of the party's leaders to protect the nation from "dangerous subversive elements."

Why, I wondered as we drove, had we been invited? Surely our views on the possible human and the possible society made us subversive as well. However, we were courteously greeted by several hundred people representing health, education, welfare, and religion. The heads of Buddhist orders were in attendance, including an elderly monk who entered upon each process with great gusto and good humor. He was, we learned, the leading abbot of Theravada Buddhism and one of the founders of the worldwide Vipassana meditation movement. Several military officers were also present; they seemed uncomfortable with our philosophy and exercises and did not stay until the end. Everybody else, however, was remarkably responsive. We followed a main tenet of my work, weaving the processes and exercises through stories germane to the culture, in this case Buddhist stories and legends well known to most Burmese.

This group turned out to be different from any I had worked with. The air itself bristled with awareness. I was struck by the aliveness of these people, many of whom had experienced the harshest of political realities. Each person was in danger at any moment; each dreaded the knock on the door in the middle of night; each was aware that others might be informers. And yet they remained gentle, wise, attentive to their spiritual practices, and, in spite of painful circumstance, committed to change and new life. When I asked participants to find a place to stand somewhere in the room, I was startled to see them instantly form into perfect rows. Yet they learned with alacrity to open the inner and outer doors of perception, use the kinesthetic body to enhance body awareness and to improve skills, and master the intricacies of reordering subjective time. In spite or, perhaps, because of war and repression, their imaginative faculties were stupendous. Rarely had I seen any group come up with so rich a range of ideas, so original a palette of poems and essays, feelings and perceptions. It was as if I were watching an Eastern garden bloom after decades of drought. In potent dormancy beneath the soil, the Burmese were ready to germinate, waiting only for the first opening in government policy. I realized that we had been brought in by UNICEF to stir the soil and to announce the spring, to help midwife the emerging culture with its intermingling of ancient and new strands of cultural DNA.

When we concluded the seminar, the abbot, who had learned his superb English while growing up under British colonial rule, came up and, in a whisper, paid Peggy and me a most intriguing compliment: "These exercises have opened a new chamber in my mind. My own practices have been so different. You teach us to use so much of ourselves, so many capabilities. I think this kind of work can be very important not only for Burma, but for Buddhism." Raising his voice, he asked with a merry twinkle, "Tell me, how did you come to the business of reinventing the world?"

I thought of Margaret Mead, and I smiled.

The old African woman looks at me curiously. "You have a Grandmother behind you. She is short like me and fat like me, and like me she carries a stick. She is not black like me, but we understand each other. When did she become an ancestor?"

I cast back in my mind and remember. It was several days after Margaret Mead's death. We were in the General Assembly chamber of the United Nations at a memorial service. I had just delivered a eulogy honoring Margaret and her life. I was to be followed to the podium by Buckminster Fuller. Before the service began, nervous U.N. officials, knowing of Bucky's penchant for delivering talks that lasted many hours, asked me to persuade him to be brief. With tears in his eyes, Bucky rose and said, "Margaret always told me that I talk too much. Margaret, we love you." And with that he sat down.

Juliette Hollister, a wonderfully original and free-spirited friend of both Margaret and me, had brought a cage full of doves that she wanted to loose to fly around the august chamber. This, she felt, would symbolize the peace that has been sought in this famous room as well as the freedom of Margaret's spirit. I feared that the doves would perish in the intricate metal latticework that covers the lighting fixtures high above. I gesticulated in Juliette's direction, "No! No! No!" Reluctantly she put the latch back on the cage.

Behind me, I sensed Margaret's presence, still holding her stick and saying, "Humph. Enough of this. Let's get to work."

10

THE ROAD
OF TRIALS

It is the fall of 1986. My father, very ill with leukemia and soon to die, has written me a letter about the direction my life and work are taking. In it he says,

> *My father (and mother) used to tell me that comedy writing was "just a bunch of foolishness"; they pleaded with me to get into "something worthwhile" such as sawmill work, a return to chiropractic, or even selling bread from a truck. Believe me—I know how it feels to have a parent tell one to change jobs late in life. Therefore, it will require much tact to give you the following advice:*
>
> > *The myths of Homer—and others—are interesting and appear to be of utmost importance to you. But when you lectured on the workings of the brain, there was intense interest and there were always overflow crowds. You can hold audiences with your discussions of the brain; certainly the brain is appealing to all of us; we each possess one. If you should decide to switch from myths to scientific facts about the brain, your expertise will attract and hold the interest of*

millions of TV viewers. If you can prove to the world that you are an expert on even one subject—the mysterious brain—your life will not have been lived in vain. . . .

My father had recently attended a seminar I had given on the Odyssey for the students and faculty of a Lutheran college in California. Although the students had appeared to enjoy it very much, some of the faculty had been disgruntled by my treatment of the myth as a source of spiritual meaning. With an ear finely tuned to criticism, my dad had listened in on faculty dissension, remembering that when I was giving seminars on mostly scientific subjects, there was generally nothing but wide-eyed approbation. After all, who could argue with science? After the seminar was over, Dad had wanted to drive me to the Los Angeles airport. He said he had to talk to me about something extremely important. By this time, in his weakened condition, his driving had become so erratic that my instincts told me that it would be dangerous, especially since he seemed in so emotionally charged a state. And so, much to my lasting sorrow, I refused, and it was then, after he turned away, his feelings deeply hurt, that I caught the last glimpse I would ever have of him—painfully thin, shoulders hunched in illness and regret, a dying man. And at that moment, I knew I would never see him again.

A week later the letter arrived. I plunged into a mixture of despair and ambivalence. Did he really think my entire life had been in vain? His mother had continually expressed disappointment in the way he had turned out. Was this the inevitable fractal wave of family history? As my progenitor, he perhaps really did know what my true calling was and how I had royally botched it. Yes, but as a writer for show business, he thought only in terms of how many were in the audience and how loudly they applauded and whether or not you were known to the media. As an agnostic, he could never understand my forays into myth and sacred psychology. And yet he always attended all of my seminars on the West Coast, was the acknowledged resident clown and cutup, took copious notes, flirted with all the women, and generally had himself a fine time. But these were words from the end of a life and therefore Olympian, oracular, telling it the way it is. And most important of all, my dad, my greatest friend and ally, had concluded while nearing his conclusion that my life had been in vain. At that moment something very palpable began to die in me as well. Perhaps one would have to call it self-value.

In the weeks that followed, my father called me every few days, asking that I come out and visit him, but I was too busy giving scheduled seminars and promised him a date in December. Finally on December 8, he called me, saying, "I feel like the car meter when the red flag has flipped over saying 'Time Expired.' Please get here fast. We've got to talk about your work."

"I'll be there next week, Dad," I replied. "Starting tomorrow, I've got six hundred people in a New York ballroom."

"Great, what's the subject?"

"*The* Odyssey."

Silence on the other end. "Well, get here when you can."

What I didn't know is that an hour later he was rushed to the hospital for major surgery because of internal bleeding.

Several days later in that New York ballroom, I had reached the point in the Odyssey where Odysseus and his men are punished by the gods for an excess of hubris and are blown off course to wander through a road of trials for the next ten years. Just then the sponsor of my seminar interrupted me, saying that I had an urgent phone call. It was Polly, my dad's wife, telling me to catch a plane immediately as my father was dying. I told the seminar participants that I had to leave and that my superb associates Robin van Doren and Sarah Dubin Vaughn would give the seminar until I returned.

As I ran our of the auditorium, a young man came running alongside me. "Listen, I've got to quit this seminar. It's not what I need."

"What do you need?" I asked, still running.

"I need something grounding and realistic, and this just doesn't cut it."

I wondered whether these were my father's final words to me.

"We'll give you your money back," I shouted over my shoulder as I ran blindly down the escalator, tears streaming from my eyes.

The woundings of our lives can cause the withdrawal of our substance, the leaching of our spirits. Or we can choose to see them as the slings and arrows that fortune provides to gouge us sufficiently full of holes that we may yet become holy. "Wisdom through suffering," Sophocles said, and millions have assented to this cold if accurate comfort. For it is in the trials of wounding that all our immature or shadowed parts rise to meet us, never to leave us until we are either flat-out defeated and ready to begin the path of wisdom or willing to take steps to redress our lesser selves.

When I graduated from high school, my lesser selves—jubilant and inflated from a star-strewn adolescence—were just about ready for a spectacular fall. For me high school had been pure bliss, a constant fanfare of teenage ambitions and dreams, but soon I moved into the hell of college. My college career began in one of the heavenly antechambers but then proceeded gently downward, with occasional slight upturns, until it plunged headlong into the most complete misery I had ever known. From this nadir, I rose again to a safe harbor in purgatory, until I finally graduated into a kind of redemption, which, for me, was graduate school. But not before wounding had taken a considerable toll.

Due to my extracurricular activities, I had done poorly on the college entrance tests. The night before the SAT exam, for instance, I had organized and run a high school dance that lasted well into the morning hours and ended in a riot, and so I arrived at the exam in a spent and sullen state. The questions on the examination sheet and the contents in my brain seemed to have nothing to do with each other, and the simplest of problems posed a vast mystery. As a result, I was turned down by all the colleges I had applied to—Radcliffe, Smith, Duke, Cornell, and thirty-four others. The principal of Julia Richman High School, Miss Marion Jewell, wrote to her alma mater, Cornell, telling the admissions officer that he had made a terrible mistake in turning me down, but he wrote back that regardless of how noble and valuable she felt me to be, my scores indicated that I was not suited to intellectual work.

Ultimately, I was put on the bottom of the waiting list for Barnard College and managed to squeak in. Barnard occupies a portion of Broadway in New York City between 116th and 119th Streets. It is part of the Columbia University complex and shares many activities and courses with Columbia, the then men's college, as well as with the other schools and institutes within the university. Yearly, Barnard put on a ritual event known as the Greek Games, in which freshman and sophomore teams, dressed in ancient costumes, march, ride "chariots," race each other across hurdles, and hurl the discus. After hurling a discus through a windowpane, I was selected to be high priestess of the games that first year. I greatly enjoyed learning to chant and emote in ancient Greek as well as wearing the glorious vestments and coiffure of a priestess. My dramatic gestures and intonations brought me to the attention of the drama department, and I was invited to try out for a part in Jean Giradoux's magical play, *The Madwoman of Chaillot*.

I read for the part cold, having never seen the play before. But while I was reading, it seemed that I had always known the role, that I was the Madwoman. In playing her I found the fractal of the elder I would become and the mad sanity that would guide my life. The play tells of evil lurking in Paris in the form of greedy capitalist prospectors who want to dig for oil under the lovely historic streets of Paris. Aurelia, the Madwoman of Chaillot, gets wind of the plot and conspires with her fellow madwomen to lure the evil men into her cellar by convincing them that its stairs lead to a hidden wealth of oil. When they have begun to descend steps that go endlessly down, she seals the cellar door behind them. With the world rid of evil, the deaf-mute sings and all wrongs are redressed. Although the role of the fantastic elderly Madwoman should by rights have gone to a senior, the faculty director, Dolph Sweet (later of movie and television fame), gave it to me.

The rehearsals were marvels of creative mayhem, since the most talented and eccentric young actresses and actors at Barnard and Columbia found their way into the production. It was one of those rare occasions of utter theatrical joyousness, in which everything—set design, costumes, acting, directing, fed by the ebullience of the play and the originality of the players—became champagne.

In those rehearsals I felt my soul truly flame forth. The great speech of the Madwoman, in which she expresses her philosophy of daily life, became my extended mantra, the code by which I would live. Aurelia is addressing a despairing young man who has been pulled out of the river Seine, explaining why life is so glorious. Here are her words and, in italics, how I take from them a blueprint for life richly lived:

To be alive is to be fortunate, Roderick.

That's right, I say to myself, constantly celebrate the joy and opportunity of being alive! And if you don't feel that way, at least try to act as if you do.

Of course, in the morning when you first awake, it does not always seem so very gay. When you take your hair out of the drawer, and your teeth out of the glass, you are apt to feel a little out of place in this world. Especially if you've just been dreaming that you're a little girl on a pony looking for strawberries in the woods.

Acknowledge my shadows, my incompleteness, and the fact that I often seem to remember a better world just beyond the veil, but then, having offered my complaint to the gods, get on with it!

But all you need to feel the call of life once more is a letter in your mail giving you your schedule for the day—your mending, your shopping, that letter to your grandmother that you never seem to get around to.

Have a plan, a creative intention that I advance bit by bit, day by day. And, above all, hold to my big dream.

And so, when you've washed your face in rosewater, and powdered it—not with this awful rice-powder they sell nowadays, which does nothing for the skin, but with a cake of pure white starch—and put on your pins, your rings, your brooches, bracelets, earrings and pearls—in short, when you are dressed for your morning coffee—and have had a good look at yourself—not in the glass naturally—it lies—but in the side of the brass gong that once belonged to Admiral Courbet—then, Roderick, then you're armed, you're strong, you're ready—you can begin again.

Adorn myself in the awareness and delight of my own potentials. Do my spiritual exercises and practices and know that the usual criticisms that I will get from the world do not reflect my real being. Try to see that being in the inner mirror of my mind. So charged, renewed, and refreshed, feel ready for any challenge.

After that, everything is pure delight. First the morning newspaper. Not of course these current sheets filled with lies and vulgarity. I always read the *Gaulois,* the issue of March 22, 1903. It's by far the best. It has some delightful scandal, some excellent fashion notes, and, of course, the last-minute bulletin on the death of Leonide Leblanc. She used to live next door, poor woman, and when I learn of her death every morning, it gives me quite a shock.

Allow myself a stimulus, a morning reading or conversation, the brisk and bitter tang of media and newspaper, the shock of new and old, to prime my circuits, get my blood racing.

Then Roderick, I begin my rounds. I have my cats to feed, my dogs to pet, my plants to water. I have to see what the evil ones are up to in the district—those who hate people, those who hate plants, those who hate animals. I watch them sneaking off in the morning to put on their disguises—

to the baths, to the beauty parlors, to the barbers. But they can't deceive me. And when they come out again with blonde hair and false whiskers, to pull up my flowers and poison my dogs, I'm there, and I'm ready.

Always have friends, relatives, and projects that I check up on, following their progress, being part of their lives. Be open to their hurts and pains, their enemies from within or without, and be ready if called to do something about it. Take some part of the universe as my special care, some chronic evil that I regularly try to redress, be it the local apathy to the autistic or to Indian Point, the nearby nuclear power plant that is so dangerous it could blow up this part of the world.

All you have to do to break their power is cut across their path from the left. That isn't always easy. Vice moves swiftly. But I have a good long stride and I generally manage. Right, my friends? Yes, the flowers have been marvelous this year. And the butcher's dog on the Rue Bizet, in spite of that wretch that tried to poison him, is friskier than ever.

Fool the expectations of the naughties and the haughties of the world. Break their power through paradox and laughter and come up with solutions that leave them far behind. Above all, celebrate life in the face of their morbid decay. ("The Mad Woman of Chaillot" in *Four by Giradoux,* trans. and adapted by Maurice Valency. New York: Hill and Wang, 1958)

We continued to be in a state of grace during the actual performances. To play the Countess Aurelia was for me a religious experience. I have never felt either before or after so complete and so completely human, with all the splendor and the folly that it involves, or so totally archetypal and mythic. Although I had done a good deal of theater before and would do a great deal more later, it was as if my entire career in the theater was condensed into that one role. After performing it, I seemed to have accomplished everything that I had ever wanted to do in dramatic arts.

News of the excellence of the production got about, and a number of critics for New York papers and theater magazines came to see it. One day I went to the student mailbox and discovered that I had been given the award as Best New Actress Off-Broadway. I have received any number of awards since then, but none has so stunned and astonished me or filled me with such ecstatic pleasure. The luminous Geraldine Page gave me the award in an event in which I performed a scene from *Madwoman* in front of many theater notables.

After that I majored in religion and theater or, should I say, religion and carpentry (an estimable lineage), since we spent so much time building sets. Our drama teachers were among the finest that the New York stage in those days had to offer—Mildred Dunnock for acting; Norris Houghton, head of the Phoenix Theater for production and theater history; Harold Clurman for playwriting; Patton Campbell for costume and set design, and director Dolph Sweet, with his remarkable penchant for Chekhov, for all-around theater skills. As the drama instructors always brought in their friends and theater cronies, we were awash in the best in the business. News of our special world spread downtown, and many professional actors tried out for our plays. By the end of my freshman year, I was elected head of the college drama society, Wigs and Cues, and got to help in the auditions of these actors.

One day Dolph Sweet and I were holding auditions for the part of Florio, the repulsive but fascinating Machiavellian villain in Thomas Middleton's sixteenth-century tragedy, *The Changeling*. For hours I had been reading opposite a steady troop of actors, but not one fit the bill. Finally, we were about to leave, when a crumpled-up little fellow, who looked like he'd been sleeping in gutters, rolled in and asked to audition. His face looked battered, his breath was alcoholic, and something was definitely wrong with one eye. Yet he had something, and over Dolph's objections and suspicions ("We can't expose our girls to somebody who looks like that!"), I insisted that he be permitted to read for the role. The reading was extraordinary—rich, subtle, malicious, pure evil reeking out of the actor's voice. I got chills playing opposite him. This was our Florio. The actor seemed to know all about the human shadow; he had seen life unvarnished and undisguised. Clearly he had taken the road of trials. We hired him, and, contrary to his appearance, he turned out to be a fine fellow both on and off the stage. Of course, some of his stories of his experiences were hair-raising, but he always told them with a kind of salty compassion that gave the Barnard girls a sense of the larger life beyond the college grounds. His performance was a triumph; Norris Houghton promptly hired him for a part in *Saint Joan* with the great Irish actress Siobahn McKenna, and it was clear sailing after that for the young actor. But I've always thought that playing Florio for Wigs and Cues was what launched the career of Peter Falk.

I continued to perform many roles at the Barnard theater and was invited to act and later direct in professional companies off-Broadway. I tried to keep my off-Broadway career for the summer months, but sometimes it overlapped into the fall, and for a time I would lead a madcap existence, racing between worlds of college and professional theater, skipping sleep, food, friends, and even identity. The subway became the channel that linked my various lives. Like Clark Kent with his phone booth, I would enter the subway wearing one persona at 8th Street and leave it at 116th wearing quite another. Scripts would give way to textbooks, theatrical élan to collegiate sparkle. A doubled and tripled life became my mode, and like my friend Margaret Mead thirty-five years earlier at Barnard, I tried to see how many different lives and activities I could squeeze into mine. This early fractal of racing space and stuffing time has rarely left me, and I fully expect that at my deathbed, many people will surround me, insisting that I hold on a few minutes more so that I can write prefaces for their books, give them a bibliography off the top of my head, and offer the name and telephone number of a suitable mate.

Throughout college I enjoyed the finest possible male companionship. Early in my freshman year at Barnard I met Charles de Geoffroy, a blue-blooded French-man who lived off his investments in a noble old house in Greenwich, Connecti-cut. Charles was elegant, intellectual, athletic, and splendid looking. He was also a good deal older than I (how much older he would never tell me), but that made him seem even more charming. I was the envy of my college friends, who would come to our cast parties with their vacuous pimply-faced boyfriends, while I would arrive squired by Cary Grant with brains. Charles had a mind out of the eighteenth-century French Enlightenment and was always looking for the rational explanation behind phenomena. An avowed atheist, he was nonetheless fascinated by religion and was forever trying to disprove its premises by logical arguments. He would prepare for our engagements by gathering supportive articles as well as notes he had written, and our dates were generally intense exchanges of varying viewpoints on politics, art, and religion, interrupted only by handing each other picnic items or by running through the woods. We honed each other's minds and spirits, for despite the difference in our ages, he treated me as true peer and never used his far greater experience of life to disparage mine. Our relationship, which continued nearly until I married Bob, was both enthusiastic and chaste. Though he continued to have many romantic adventures, Charles did not want to spoil our friendship with an erotic entanglement. I was similarly inclined, and I had my own beliefs supporting chastity before marriage. In this vein, we saw each other frequently for the better part of nine years. We traveled together in the summers and went to theaters and movies. We attended discussion groups on spiritual sub-jects at which I held forth long-windedly, always upsetting the presiding clergy. We discovered and swam in little-known coves on the New England coast, visited a growing group of mutual friends, and enjoyed a kind of rare companionship and transformational friendship that few men and woman ever achieve. I tried going out with other men, but after Charles, there was simply no comparison.

My rising tide of pride brought its own prejudice, a sense of my own invincibility and capacity to conquer any field of endeavor, whether in theater or scholarship. One of my chief activities was to hole up in the college library with the many vol-umes of Arnold Toynbee's *Study of History*. The philosophy of history has always been my passion, looking for patterns of recurrence through many cultures and civilizations. For all practical purposes, I cut my intellectual eyeteeth on Toynbee. As a project for a course, I took on the task of writing a book comparing Toynbee's *Study of History* with Augustine's *City of God*.

When I told my dad about my project, he said, "You've got about as much chance of accomplishing that as you have of getting a milk cow to dance and then squirt butter!"

Dancing cow or not, I arrogantly insisted that my intellectual equipment was equal to the task. My father's doubts just fired me to greater efforts, and I worked away at the project for well over a year, continuing to get extensions from my professor, as the book got longer and longer. I made only one copy because it was getting too tiresome to make so many corrections on the carbon copy. Just before I was to turn it in, a friend who worked at Houghton Mifflin asked to see it, saying that if it was any good, he would recommend it for publication. Hubris hooked me, and I cheerfully handed over my smudged and eraser-streaked manuscript, envisioning a front-page discussion in the *New York Times Book Review.* A month passed, and my friend didn't get back to me. When I finally tracked him down, he ruefully admitted that my manuscript had been handed around and somehow gotten lost in the editorial morass of Houghton Mifflin. It never turned up, although someone reported to me that she thought she saw a typed page containing the words *Toynbee* and *City of God* lining the birdcage in a friend's apartment. My professor was ill disposed to my explanations and gave me a C-minus for the course. He even expressed doubts as to whether I had written the manuscript. This was only the foreshadowing of much more humiliation to come. (I now suspect that the bottom of a birdcage was probably the best possible use for that first manuscript.)

Until my junior year, I was the Barnard golden girl. In addition to my theater activities, I sat on the student senate, directed the junior class play, continued as president of Wigs and Cues, and was that girl in class that everyone hated, the one whose arm was raised so continuously that a bird could have built its nest in her hand. I had mastered the art of the wowing comment and, in my dramatically trained voice, would answer the professor's questions with velvet-toned non sequiturs displaying, I thought, a remarkable range of knowledge. I was also given to word dropping. Consider, for example, the following typical exchange:

PROFESSOR ROBERTSON: What does Hamlet mean when he says, "To be or not to be, that is the question"? Yes, Miss Houston? Your hand went up first.

ME: I believe that it is a statement of existential ennui. Hamlet is positively Chekhovian, filled with ontological guilt over the human condition. He supports Toynbee's theory that the death of a civilization occurs when its citizens lose the structural givens that served as previous endowment of both matrix and metier. I would compare Hamlet's question to the nausea of Jean-Paul Sartre when he confronts the chestnut tree. It's an issue of *en soi* rather than *pour soi.*

PROFESSOR ROBERTSON: Yes, uh, thank you, Miss Houston.

Behind me, latter-day Lillians and Roxannes would mutter in fractal whispers, "Show-off bitch." I was the envy of all my friends and was perpetually in a state of galloping chutzpah. I was also an excellent candidate for nemesis, having fulfilled all the classical conditions for hubris, overweening pride.

My universe crashed with great suddenness. My father had moved to California, and I did not see him again for six years. I had received a letter from him telling me that the only work he could get was delivering phone books. My beloved Uncle Paul, who had lost his legs in World War II and had been an important teacher to me, shot and killed himself shortly after learning that his wife had fallen in love with the Catholic priest who had given them religious instruction. Several weeks later, my Sicilian grandmother died in my arms. Almost immediately after that, a young man whom I loved very much died of a burst appendix while in the woods on a camping trip. Then the scenery of an off-Broadway production I was starring in fell on my head, and I suffered a serious concussion, which left me mostly blind for the next four months. Between the concussion, the blindness, and the mounting personal tragedies, I found that I could no longer think clearly or see the connections between things. Nor could I speak; my former eloquence had become, under the weight of all this grief, a hesitant stammer. My grades as a result went from being fairly decent to a D-plus, and I was put on probation and stripped of all my school offices, including directing the junior class play. Public elections were held to fill my college offices. I was not allowed to take any roles in the school theater. My friends departed from me out of embarrassment, and I isolated myself because I thought I was no longer worthy of them. In the end, I was called into the adviser's office and told that I would not be permitted to return to Barnard the following term because I did not have "the necessary intelligence to do academic work." When I protested that I had shown sufficient intelligence in previous years, the adviser offered a sympathetic smile and the dictum that "the rapid decline of the intellect" frequently occurred among young women when "they became interested in other things. It's a matter of hormones, my dear." Today, the young women of Barnard would thunder "sexism" and punch her in the snoot, but in the fifties, we still swallowed our objections and nodded submissively.

Still suffering from near-blindness following the concussion, I had taken to walking through campus with the help of an umbrella; I had given up my cane when fellow students began deliberately tripping me in the hall. When I protested, one of the Lillians told me, "Everybody knows you are just making all of this tragedy up. You're just playing the big romantic. Shades of the Brontës, my dear." This view, I discovered, stemmed from one of my teachers in whom I had foolishly confided my misfortunes. She then took it upon herself to write to all my professors, telling them not to believe anything I said and that I was making a fantasy out of imagined tragedy in order to get attention. I found this out when I received what I thought was a deliberately lower grade than I deserved on an exam. The professor told me that he had given me the grade because of Mrs. N's letter, which also warned that I should not be given any benefit of the doubt. This blow destroyed any remaining confidence I had in myself, and, since my stock now was so low in classes, I took to huddling in the back row in my oversized camel-hair coat, generally unable to understand much of what was being said. I remember a class in Milton, taught by the excellent Rosalie Colie. *Paradise Lost* seemed well named, for my mind had been vaporized in hell, and, making no sense of Milton's majestic poem, I duly flunked the course.

So there I was, blind, bereft, brainless, and disbelieved. Every day seemed to bring further losses and defeats—or at least, that's how I saw it. When you've lived a relatively blessed existence, your fall seems more acutely painful and scarring to the psyche than if you had lived a more normal life with a regular rhythm of ups and downs. I began to think about my condition theologically and to wonder what in the cosmic plan ordained that bad times should pile up unceasingly. I took to eating my lunch alone in the Green Room of the college theater where I had spent so many happy hours rehearsing and blithely playing tragic heroines. I would lock the door, bite into my peanut butter and jelly sandwich, and yell at God. I wailed like Job, "Where are the boils? Because that's all I'm missing. You've sent every other kind of affliction. Come on, dammit. Do your worst. Bring on the boils."

These fulminations led me to take a course in Old Testament studies. I wanted to understand the debacle of my life and thought that scripture, especially the book of Job, might hold the answer. Jacob Taubes, the young European professor who taught the course, announced at the opening session that he did not intend to follow the course description but would be teaching something along the lines of the implicit dialectic between the apostle Paul and the German philosopher Friedrich Nietzsche.

Taubes brought to the American classroom the mind and style of the most exciting intellectual traditions of postwar Europe. His rendering of Hegelian philosophy, gnosticism, structuralism, existentialism, phenomenology, and the savants of the Sorbonne built a bridge across the abyss of my personal void, and I began occasionally to ask a hesitant question from my hiding place deep in my coat at the back of the room. Taubes would stand on his toes in order to find me and then direct a stream of brilliant reflections my way, past my coat and into my mind. Before long, I was asking more questions, for I was finding his teaching and ideas more involving than my own particular suffering.

One day, locked in the Green Room, still railing at God and feeling I had lost my chances for a life of any significance, I sensed myself being visited by a thirty-eight-year-old version of myself. I didn't actually see or hear her, but I felt that she was there just the same, coaxing me out of my despondency. "Don't worry, kid," she said. "It's going to be a far richer life than you can imagine. This is temporary. You are going to do things of significance, invent new fields, travel all over, and have a remarkable time."

"Who are you?" I asked.

"I'm yourself, twenty years down the road."

"How did you get here?"

"I willed myself here. Look, I've got to run. But do something for me, will you? Take a walk across the Columbia campus. Get yourself some air. See you!"

And then, just as suddenly as she had arrived, she was gone. Bemused, I got up and with the help of my umbrella began to walk across campus. About the middle of the campus, a voice with a Germanic accent called my name. It was Jacob Taubes. "Miss Houston, let me walk with you. You know, you have a most interesting mind."

"Me? I have a mind?"

"Yes, your questions are luminous. Now please tell me, Miss Houston, what do you think is the nature of the transvaluation of values in the apostle Paul and Nietzsche?"

What was left of my mind dwindled and blanked, and I stammered, "I d-don't know."

Still Taubes persisted. "Of course you do! You could not ask the kinds of questions you do without having an unusual grasp of these issues. Now please, once again, Miss Houston, what do you think of the transvaluation of values in Paul and Nietzsche?"

And then he added the statement before which there was no turning back: "It is important for my reflections that I have your reflections."

At that moment I felt called, seen, evoked. The ice of my self-negation dissolved under the sun of his regard. My essential self, the core of my being that could never be hurt by trial or circumstance, threw off its sad and sodden wrappers and practically shouted, "I'm back!" Words tumbled out of my mouth answering his question, words that linked the yearning of souls in the first-century Roman Empire to nineteenth-century Germanic angst, words that bespoke the rhythmic wave that recurs whenever the world is about to turn a corner, words that spoke of history's fractals before that word was ever coined. As I continued to speculate aloud, I noticed that at the corner of my eye a few things were popping into droplets of clarity. The cloudy soup that had been my vision was interrupted by distinct and differentiated items—passing students, the steps of Butler Hall, the statue of Alma Mater.

In the days and weeks that followed, my vision gradually returned, as did my mind, though in a more serious and reflective vein. Knowings were added that had not been there before, a sense of tragedy, of the tears that are in things, and an almost excruciating empathy for those fellow souls who were in states of despair, breakdown, or disregard. Never, I promised, would I let people I saw in such a state go unnoticed. I would seek them out if I could and try to speak to their Essence, knowing them as God-in-hiding. I would come to them humbly, asking them for their thoughts and advice, as Taubes did me, for people who are deeply wounded often have a perspective and a depth that is lacking in those with a happy, satisfied point of view. Subsequently, I have received some of my greatest teachings from the greatly wounded and, perhaps, by acknowledging and empowering them, have opened the door to their recovery.

Wounding often involves a painful excursion into pathos; we experience massive anguish, and the suffering cracks the boundaries of what we thought we could stand. And yet, time and again, I discover that the wounding pathos of our own local stories contains the seeds of healing and even of transformation. This truth is woven into all classic tales of the human condition. Witness the Greek tragedies in which the gods force themselves symptomatically into consciousness at the time of wounding. All myth, in fact, has wounding at its core. I continually joke that Christ must have his crucifixion; otherwise, there's no upsy-daisy. Artemis must kill Acteon when he comes too close. Job must have his boils. Dionysus must be childish and attract Titanic enemies who rip him apart. We are drawn to these stories over and over. We do not flinch before their terrors, although they may mirror our own. Is this because they carry us into the mystery, the marvel, the knowing that with wounding, the sacred enters into time? From the point of the wounding, the journey of gods and humans proceeds toward new birth, and in that new birth is the unfolding of a sensuous acuity to the needs of others, a sensitivity not previously possible. Being more vulnerable, we reach out, we extend our hands and our hearts to others who are wounded. It is only at such a pass that we grow into a larger sense of what life is about and act, therefore, out of a deeper and nobler nature.

It is difficult, challenging, and yet extremely necessary at the time of wounding to revision our situation so that its larger story is revealed. This means, first of all, that we stop repeating to ourselves the data of the local events or personalities that have caused us pain. This is not to deny the facts but to move out of the easy seductions of tunnel vision into the broader landscape that reveals potent opportunities for growth. We then ask ourselves, are we in a cauldron of pain or a chalice of opportunity? Shall we fret and whine, or can we see our suffering as the hand coming from the gods to pull us into a new story? By viewing our humiliations, illness, accidents, and acts of violation in this way, we take our story from the This Is Me level to the We Are level, allowing the I Am to guide the process. I always ask my students to put to themselves the great and terrible questions: Where and by whom were you wounded? What or who is trying to be born in you from that wound? Then I ask them to tell the story again—not as a repetition of historical detail, but as a myth in which the wounding is only the middle of the story, the ending of which is the birth of a new grace.

Moreover, wounding is the traditional training ground for the healer and teacher. By allowing my own wounds to remain open, I can be more helpful to others who are seeking to re-vision their own sufferings in a more profound and useful way. Of course, such sensitivity can be both a boon and a trial. In the course of my teaching and seminar work, many of my students have been brought to the brink of the spiritual chasm, the crossing of which requires a change in being. When they go through the dark night of the soul that precedes such transformation, I find myself experiencing it with them, sharing their pain and grief as if it were my own. My hypersensitive availability to others' wounding makes for a constancy of inner pain that belies the outer merry face that I present to the world.

As I travel around the world, for example, especially in countries where people have little hope, I am haunted by the eyes of children. In a tenement in Bangladesh I will look into the eyes of a child so bright with intelligence that I know that given other circumstances she could be just about anything she chose to be. Here, however, her future will consist of being married very early, constant childbearing, a strong possibility of being abused by her husband, disease, and early death. In a desiccated field in West Africa I have nearly drowned in the pools that were the eyes of a farmer's boy, for in them I found a person who could build bridges between spirit and matter, a scientist of the first order, a Renaissance man. But I knew that he would spend his time on Earth as millions of his forebears have, straining his life away behind a plow. They are everywhere, these children of so much promise with their hungry spirits that will not be fed. I do what I can wherever I go, setting up scholarships, arranging for further education or spiritual adoption by those who are able to recognize these children and train their gifts. But I would love to do more, and I urge the readers of this book to push to your edges and discover what you can do to rescue the little gods who are caught in lives that will render them impotent to their own enormous gifts. Most especially, in our own families, let us become aware of how we may be wounding our children through harsh or unfeeling words, thoughtless actions, or mindless dismissals of their enormous awareness and sensitivity. To ask forgiveness of one's children is a courageous act, one that can change the entire quality of your relationship and even move parenting into partnering. I know this is so, and it happened for me and my dad.

I am on the plane heading toward Los Angeles and my dying father. A movie is playing on the screen—a dog picture. I am too anxious and grief stricken to rent the headphones, and only occasionally do I glance at the screen. Suddenly memory erupts on the screen behind my closed eyes, and I am back with Chickie, my childhood dog. Chickie was a has-been movie star. She had played one of Blondie and Dagwood's puppies until she got too big for the part. She was half bearded collie and half Welsh corgi with long black silky hair, white feet, a white star on her chest, and a magnificent fan of a tail. Always laughing, she was my father's most appreciative audience when he was reading us his comedy scripts. Chickie could do anything and did. She had been trained by my father to respond to many hand signals like a circus dog, but that was the least of her accomplishments. More important, she took care of us, babysat, tried to get us to the train on time, shepherded the rest of the animals, and taught me my best lessons in ethics and responsibility. I thought of her as my sister, and with all of our travels, she was my constant and closest friend. Thus it was a shock when one day one of the actors at my dad's studio came home with him, saw Chickie, and immediately wanted to buy her.

"Jack," said the actor, "that is the greatest dog I ever saw in my life. I'll give you fifty bucks for that dog."

"Can't do it, pal," said my father. "It's the kid's dog."

The actor persisted. "I'll give you a hundred bucks for the dog. I know you need the money." Indeed, we did, and, driven by the panic of incipient poverty, the one thing he dreaded more than anything else, my father acted in an uncharacteristic manner.

Excusing himself, he went into the kitchen to discuss this with my mother.

"Certainly not!" said my mother. "It's Jeanie's dog."

"You're right, Mary," my father sheepishly agreed. "It's just that I think I'm going to lose my job at the studio and am damned scared of not being able to bring home the bacon."

"Well, you certainly cannot bring home the bacon by selling the child's dog," my mother fumed. "Anyway, if we go broke again, I'll just do what I always do, start an acting school for children."

A few days later the actor came back saying, "Jack, I've got to have that dog on my ranch. I want that dog. I'll give you two hundred fifty bucks for the dog."

During this ordeal, Chickie and I were sitting on the floor behind the couch, listening in horror. I couldn't believe that my father would do such a terrible thing to me. The very foundations of my life were falling away.

"Well, I sure do need the money," said my father. "Just a minute; I've got to talk to my wife."

"Mary, he's offering two hundred fifty bucks for the dog! We can always get Jeanie a new dog at the pound!"

"No way!" said my mother.

The next day the actor returned. He had rarely known failure and was not about to start now. "Jack, I'll give you two hundred fifty bucks and my secondhand car. I know you need a car to get around."

"Wait a minute," said my father. "I'm sure this time I can convince my wife."

Upon hearing the latest offer, my mother, bless her heart, stormed out of the kitchen, stalked up to the actor, and chewed him out. "Ronald Reagan," she railed, "how dare you try to take away my child's dog!"

At least he knew a good dog when he saw one.

For the next few days I refused to talk to or look at my father, I felt so totally betrayed. I also wouldn't let Chickie out of my sight and insisted that she sleep next to me under my covers and even take my baths with me. Finally, desperate to gain my forgiveness, Dad offered to take me to the MGM studios where he was working on a picture. And that's where I got to see the fractal waves of my life and discover my own metaphor for a mythic life. So out of this wounding came the healing knowledge of the Dreamtime and its many sets and faces.

As I remember these things, I am suddenly aware of my dad's presence up there at thirty-five thousand feet. I seem to hear the sharp whistle between his teeth that he always used to get my attention. I think I hear his voice saying, "Hey, Jeanie-pot. I gotta go!" I get up and make my way to the telephone at the back of the plane, where I call my husband. Through the static on the other end I learn from him that my dad has just died.

If we become conscious of and stop the projections we make on each other, we can go a long way toward preventing the careless wounding we inflict on others as well as on ourselves. The wall of projection through which people and nations often see each other undermines confidence and makes others less able to respond from the fullness of who or what they are. So much suffering in the twentieth century and in all of history stems from the deep resentments generated by lack of recognition between those who use each other as a screen upon which to project their own shadows.

Now, as we approach the end of the millennium, it seems as if every shadow that ever was has been brought out to dance in the Walpurgis Night of the closing century. I learned this to my sorrow in one of the most formidable roads of trials of my career. I had been asked to chair a gigantic week-long conference of the world's religious leaders. This conference, held in 1975 to celebrate the thirtieth anniversary of the U.N., was a joint effort of the United Nations and the Temple of Understanding, a well-known ecumenical organization that fostered dialogue among religions. The founder of the Temple of Understanding, Juliette Hollister, was the Auntie Mame of the religious world, a great original, fearless and formidable, and a clown for God. She would do anything to take her message of ecumenical understanding to the leaders of the world. On one occasion, she went to Delhi and, in order to get the attention of Prime Minister Nehru of India, paraded back and forth in front of his house all day and all night. She was dressed up to look like Nehru's daughter, Mrs. Gandhi, while her eleven-year-old red-haired son was dressed in an exact replica of the prime minister's clothes, complete with Nehru jacket and cap. Needless to say, Nehru was intrigued; he brought Juliette inside and ultimately gave her all the help that she wanted. On a less successful occasion, she dressed as a chambermaid in Cairo and got into Nasser's private rooms by going down the dirty clothes chute and arriving in his laundry bin. This stunt got her arrested. Ecstatic and eccentric as she is, a master of comical spontaneous performance art, she staunchly opposes anyone who tries to maintain the status quo on anything that she thinks needs to change. I've even known her to attend a private audience with the pope dressed and painted as a clown and behaving accordingly. The problem is that one never knows what she is going to do, so that all plans and decisions made by committee are like the works of Thomas Aquinas— mere chaff in the wind in the wake of the roaring, mischievous, spiritual cyclone that is Juliette Hollister. All in all, she was a most interesting partner for the delicate enterprise of bringing together the world's religious leaders to meet with the officials of the United Nations.

Our committee meetings went on for a year, and during that time my house was regularly full of theologians, bishops, emissaries from the Vatican, monks and nuns of every possible denomination, including some nobody's ever heard of, rabbis, Native American spiritual leaders, Sufis, New Age gurus, and Margaret Mead, who shouted everybody down. Well, not quite everybody. My quirky Airedale, Oliver, had a nose for shadows, and whenever he sensed darkness moving among us, he set up a piercing barking from behind the door and wouldn't stop until the religious folk had left.

The idea of the conference was to bring together for the first time, under the auspices of the United Nations, those who held the brief for the human spirit with those who held the file on the human race. Thus, it was hoped, religious leaders and U.N. officials would speak long and deeply to each other, sharing ideas, information, and perspectives. It was expected that the religious leaders would offer ethical and moral advice, while the politicians would fill them in on what was really going on behind the world scene. In the end, we anticipated, a mutual statement of resolution would come out of the proceedings. We on the organizing committee were very proud of a special coup we had achieved. The Dalai Lama had agreed to come to the United States for the first time in order to speak at our event. The newspapers were full of stories about the upcoming events.

Personally, I was exceedingly happy about being asked to chair this conference, a position that seemed right on track. For the previous two years, Margaret Mead had been grooming me toward filling some of the roles in international affairs that she had pioneered.

When serious planning got under way, Juliette and I decided that since this was to be so momentous an occasion, there must be ritual, and not just any ritual, but a Sufi Cosmic Mass involving some six hundred players in elaborate costumes and all their friends. There should be special music written for the occasion—a major symphony with the full U.N. orchestra and a hundred voices. (To create this work, I put a composer friend into trance and gave her the suggestion that she was to travel to the realm of music and come up with a full symphony in five minutes of subjective time. She did so, but the piece was so elaborate that it took her many months to transcribe onto paper the music she had heard in her head.) Also, we decided, there should be art, and so artists from all over the world began sending us paintings, drawings, monumental sculptures, visionary fantasies in clay and alligator skin, and sacred art from the jettisons of the day's garbage. There should be drama, and full-length plays arrived on the lives of Christ, Krishna, Buddha, and Mechthild of Magdeburg. There should be dances, and the world arrived in dancing shoes—nuns who had studied with Martha Graham, Sufi whirling dervishes, Japanese artists performing thousand-year-old dances from the imperial court. We decided to rent the entire Cathedral of Saint John the Divine for this occasion.

the scope and complexity of the task, we were in sore need of production nts. To make a minimalist statement, I did not hire the best possible person for the job. But to be fair to this person, it was a job for David O. Selznick, after he had been seasoned by the experience of directing *Gone With the Wind*, including arranging for the burning of Atlanta *and* finding the right actress to play Scarlett O'Hara.

From the moment the event opened, everything that could go wrong did. Thousands of people streamed in to be part of this historic happening. For some reason, they all brought their own lunches, so each day we had to pay off the expensive caterers Juliette had persuaded to sell elegant meals to these multitudes. However, these free gourmet meals did not go wasting. Although we had invited seven spiritual leaders of Native American tribes to be part of the formal conference, two hundred Native Americans showed up with no money, no food, and no place to stay. The 105-year-old keeper of the Hopi prophecy, Thomas Binaca, had had a vision that they should go to the tall glass house on the river where they would be recognized for the first time by all the nations. This proved to be true. As soon as they arrived in the backs of pickup trucks from all over the Indian nations, Dutch Marxists (known as *provos*) started putting up signs reading "Unfair to Indians!" We hadn't even had time to be unfair to Indians. I called a meeting with some of the Native elders and asked them what they had to offer that the representatives of the other religions did not. Mad Bear Anderson, a leader of the Iroquois people from upstate New York, put it wonderfully well: "The Eastern religions represent spirituality that looks inward. The Western religions represent spirituality that tends to look outward. We are the people whose spirituality is of the middle. We stand for the spirituality of nature, for the sacred ways of the Earth. Therefore, we can be the mediators between East and West and remind the great leaders that nature is holy and full of the Great Spirit."

"But, Mad Bear," I asked, "what shall I do with all of you? There are so many of you, that there will not be enough room for the representatives of the other religions, let alone the U.N. officials, if we fill each meeting room with your people."

"We will go into council now and elect representatives, for that is our way."

And that is what they did. As a result, in each of the meeting rooms to which we had assigned a balanced group of religious leaders, it was these Native Americans who listened most deeply to the issues of politics and spirit and then provided the most penetrating reflections on the serious choices we all had to make together if the Earth and its peoples were to continue. After each meeting the Native representative would discuss the content of the session with the rest of their people, so that all felt they had taken part. As for food and housing, they relished the free gourmet meals—"as good as bear claws," one Onandago elder said to me after chewing lustily on beef Wellington—and as for lodging, Reverend Miyake, a wealthy Shinto priest, put all the Native Americans up in the luxurious Waldorf-Astoria. He also passed out many thousands of dollars in hundred-dollar bills so that the Indians would have adequate funds. It was wonderful seeing the Native leaders holding their powwow each morning in the lavish lobby, squatting on the Persian carpets under the great crystal chandeliers. So richly appreciated was the Native American contribution that they were invited to enter NGO (non-government-organization) status, which they did, setting up an office near the U.N. as well as becoming members of other international organizations.

That was the best thing that came out of this conference, and whenever I remember all the awful things that went on, I also must remind myself that something beautiful occurred. We tend to remember best the painful things, the sore places in our lives, and we do a great injustice thereby to the truly creditable happenings. This said, I can now recount a few of the disasters.

Take, for example, the wooden stage built for the Cosmic Mass and other events. An ongoing brouhaha between the Sufis and the production team resulted in the construction of a dangerously substandard stage. With a cast of six hundred cavorting all over this flimsy structure, I was in a constant state of terror. Then, when Pir Vilayat Khan invited the whole audience to join the cast on the stage, I did the only thing I could think of. I grabbed hammer and nails and crawled under the stage to try to install a few more support struts. As soon as I emerged, I noticed that the equally substandard iron circle to which the special lighting was attached was swaying ominously. Masses of people seemed about to die from either crashing down with the collapsing stage or being smashed by bolts of lightening with electrical wires attached. It all seemed grimly theological to me. Mad Bear, seeing my dismay, held my hand and gave me his beartooth talisman to wear. "We must pray to the Great Spirit," he said.

Then there was the rancor between the religions. Granted, one could not expect the altercations of thousands of years to be cleared up by one conference, but why was the air so heavy with theological napalm? Why were so many brushfires within and between religious groups constantly breaking out? I ran from group to group in this creedal war zone, trying to conciliate and dedogmatize. Then there was the shock of the personalities of a number of the most esteemed of the spiritual leaders. Never before had I seen sanctity of spirit joined to such elephantiasis of ego. Each wanted the lion's share of publicity, and since that was not possible, someone had to be blamed for it. One maverick Native American healer got up on a platform in the middle of the cathedral and railed against white people. That might have been expected, but not what happened next. He was packing two guns on each hip and was accompanied by a squad of toughs. He told his meekly receptive audience that if anyone tried to take his picture, he would shoot that person through the head, and he whirled his loaded pistols to prove his point. While the crowd was thus distracted, someone stole the large gold cross that was one of the sacred treasures of the cathedral. "This man has nothing to do with us," Mad Bear assured me, but someone had to be blamed for it. As events continued to unfold in this vein, money poured out like water to shore up disasters and to prevent further mayhem, and somehow it was not arriving where it should. It soon became clear that financial perfidy was loose upon the land, and someone had to be blamed for it.

Chaos compounded with calamity—artists having breakdowns before their performances, the Chinese and Russian delegations to the U.N. refusing at the last minute to allow the Dalai Lama to come into the United States to attend, Secretary-General Waldheim threatening to cancel the event scheduled for the United Nations even though it had been planned for over a year and thousands had come to New York for the occasion. Through all of this, Juliette swooped in and out like a great eccentric bird, overriding plans, maximizing costs, full of light and good cheer.

To be perfectly truthful, the story of the conference is much, much worse than I am telling here; suffice it to say, during much of this time, I would have relished a vacation in hell. I remember making an appointment to ask the advice of a distinguished spiritual leader whose books I had found wise and enlightening and who was said by his disciples to have a heart of unparalleled compassion. The great man, dressed in splendid sacerdotal regalia, heard my tales of woe and my earnest questions about the rise of so much apparent evil and chaos in the midst of what should have been spiritual grace and harmony. He turned a cold eye to me and said, "All of this is probably your fault. I have nothing to say to you, except, what are you going to do about our . . . ?"

Everywhere I turned I was catching the blame for everything that was going wrong. I felt like the character in Kafka's *The Trial*, confronted with accusations that had no basis in reality and no possible way of being defended against. Still I persisted. I wrote most of the mutual statement of the U.N. officials and religious leaders, which was widely acclaimed, and did not care when others took the credit. With Margaret Mead by my side, I ventured into the hallowed offices of Secretary-General Waldheim and persuaded him to let the conference continue at the United Nations. The fact that Margaret shook her stick at him didn't hurt, either. What did hurt was the booing I received when I stood up at the final banquet in the Waldorf to give the concluding speech.

Only Mad Bear offered some kind of solace. "When so many new good things are trying to happen, all the bad things try to stop them. The world religions are trying to come together, the Native Americans are finally being recognized. How could the dark not rise?"

"But why is the blame for the dark all falling on me, Mad Bear?" I asked.

"Because someone has to be the lightening rod, to catch the fire. Otherwise all would burn up. The Great Spirit has decided that you are the one who is brave enough and strong enough to receive it. It is a very great honor."

At the time, however, the honor was cold comfort. What the world saw of the conference and its many events was deemed a critical success. (Among other things, the conference brought Mother Teresa into wider public consciousness.) But my own reputation was in shreds, and my career as an international agent of change had to go underground for many years. I went into intensive seminar work, studying even more deeply the nature and application of human potentials and trying to understand the shadow's place in all of this. My teaching took on added dimension, for I had learned the hard way that we cannot hope to change societies until we change ourselves.

However, the anguish and humiliation I felt also took their toll on my body. Several months after the conference, I had a lump the size of an orange growing on my right breast. My physician, Marvin Thalenberg, a man of great gifts and deep humanity, sent me flying to a surgeon, who said that judging by its size and rate of growth, the tumor was very likely malignant. Both doctors agreed that an operation was called for immediately. I asked Thalenberg to give me four days to see what I could do using my own methods. He looked at me sadly, suspecting the hopelessness of it, but, knowing that I had to be true to my own philosophy, he agreed.

At once Bob and I went to work. I refused to accept the reality of the tumor. I felt it to be a by-product of angst and not of my essential self. So the first thing I had to do was dive deep within my own being and recover the self that had been lost during the long months of trial. Although I am not usually given to deep trances, guided by Bob's hypnotic suggestions, I went deeply down and stayed in trance for from five to seven hours at a time. While I was in an altered state, in which I could readily identify with my essential and perfectly healthy self, Bob fed me images of the tumor shrinking. Then, while he sent energy to dissolve the tumor, he also continuously reinforced the idea that my unconscious mind had the power to modify my body in many ways, including eliminating the tumor. Using powerful imagery, he appealed directly to my brain and nervous system, telling my brain that it could dissolve the tumor and would now do so.

What he was doing with me then was providing an experience sufficiently intense so that my belief system accepted it. His suggestions were reinforced by the fact that I was in a state of consciousness far removed from my ordinary one and thus receptive to ideas and images that my everyday consciousness might be skeptical about or reject altogether. Then he gave me specific images of the tumor shrinking and dissolving so that my brain knew what it was to do. All of this was based on a basic principle of our work: that whatever the brain can organize, the body will execute.

When I was not in trance, I drove daily to New York City to work with the wonderfully resourceful Chilean healer Carmen di Barrazza. She did her remarkable energy healing on me, and undoubtedly that also had a positive effect. Certainly I was in a state in which I had determined to suspend all disbelief, and so my body and mind cooperated to the highest extent. After four days of intense work with Bob and Carmen, I went back to Marvin Thalenberg's office, where he sat me down to look at pictures of what my operation would entail. "Marvin, don't you think you should examine me first?" I asked.

"All right, Jean," he said, clearly wanting to humor me in my crisis.

As I lay on the table, I suddenly felt hot tears falling on my chest. They came from Marvin. "I don't understand," he said in considerable shock. "Where could the tumor have gone? I can understand a remission, but it should need at least a month for all the tissue that was there to dissolve." Would that the wounds to my career and reputation could have been healed so easily.

These experiences, felt as woundings, led me to reflect long and hard on the place and purpose of suffering in our lives. My own experiences of wounding—physical, psychological, emotional, loss of status, prospects, friends, and what had been my place in the world—led me to understand that in times of suffering, when you feel abandoned, perhaps even annihilated, new life is entering into time at levels deeper than your pain, in realities at once more subtle and more evolved. Thus I offer the conundrum that as baby-making occurs through the wounding of the ovum by the sperm and the sperm's explosion and dying into the ovum, so soul making occurs through the wounding of the psyche—quite possibly by the gods. And by *gods* I mean not old atavisms, but those psychospiritual potencies yearning at the threshold of existence to enter into time and, through our lives, to "redeem the unread vision of the higher dream." Maybe the gods also suffer and even die, as we do, out of their old archaic selves, to be rebirthed as emergent culture, art, story, and spirit.

All this may seem cold comfort to those going through a time of suffering. Living as we do in a fix-it society, people tend to view their woundings as pathologies that can be redressed with the right kind of tool kit. Too often, we seek not to understand our pain, but to mend it or find relief from it as quickly and comfortably as we can. Or we resort to blame and seek to avenge the wrongs we feel have been done to us. In reacting so, we turn our backs on the growth that is knocking at the doors of our souls: "What is the knocking? / What is the knocking in the door of the night? / It is someone who wants to do us harm. / No, no. It is the three strange angels. / Admit them. Admit them" (D. H. Lawrence, "Song of a Man Who Has Come Through"). Looked at through the lens of a psychology that embraces the sacred, our woundings can deepen our growth. For woundings make us stop, shift, move in new directions, face what had been hidden. They prune us of our primal growth so that we can bear fruit.

It may be, and indeed it probably is true, that we are never completely healed. I still suffer from the devaluation of my own worth that occurred with my dad's letter. After that incident, I never truly took my own life very seriously again. But somehow, that wound also has made me more available to others experiencing a period of self-diminishment. I find that I can embrace and therefore help redress the pain of others, and, because of my own diminished ego, be able to appreciate not only the pain they are feeling, but also the deep inner truth, the absolute worth of their lives. And I tell them about it.

When we are wounded, the body goes into an electrical trauma. The memory of the electrical discharge that takes place in psychological woundings remains stored in our cells. Certain kinds of venting therapy, such as varieties of Reichian bioenergetics and the acting-out varieties of psychodrama, have had some success in discharging this energy. However, these techniques often do not look far enough beyond the therapy itself, and thus the healing is not as complete as it could be.

Now suppose that instead of releasing the charge, we find ways of using it. Too many people, terrified of the pain of looking deeply at their own woundings, recoil from facing that pain and channeling the charge into new and expanding functions. Then the stored charge debilitates them, and they organize themselves around lesser or safer lives. But we can reactivate the memory of failure or of wounding and then take that charge and select for an entirely different set of variables—say, a movement toward creativity and compassion rather than toward collapse or safety. We can do this in a number of ways, according to our beliefs and what we are willing to invest in the process. For some, this might involve asking, through prayer, for the miracle of grace to relieve the pain of the wounding: "Dear God, please give me the grace of release. Let me be born again."

What do I mean by being born again? If we think about birth in its most literal sense, we plumb a potent truth. The wound can serve as a gate of life—a stretched and bleeding birth canal through which the fetus of our higher self, now come to term, can enter into world and time. In this process, energies tied up in the wounding are released back into life. I suspect that fundamentalists, despite their limitations, have been so successful because they give people a radical reassurance of reconstruction after deconstruction. One feels "saved" from the continuing trauma of disintegration and ongoing despair, and life again become possible. The same is true of those people "born again" through Eastern spiritual disciplines, politics, or psychotherapy. Of course, the problem is that when one is "converted," one is always in danger of becoming the happy missionary and then, through innocent though mindless zeal, wounding other people.

So the challenge is to take one's woundings and open them to the treasures they contain without becoming fixated in the sense of one's salvation. We have to find a way to extend our bliss tolerance so that growth from our wounds can be continuous and powerful, without allowing our minds to be caught in a particular theological or political prism. If we do so, we can experience the inpouring of light or grace, a sense sublime of living in a felicitous universe whose ground is love and whose gift is utter forgiveness for what we have or have not done. We open then to a reality larger than any particular path—open to the dazzling glory and wonder of it all, a wonder that exceeds all known boundaries of time and space.

Our woundings, then, seen in their fullness, can be doorways leading us into a richer and more complex universe, one in which our usual bounded perceptions of space and time are stretched. Time has many quirky turns, and to paraphrase T. S. Eliot in his eloquent description of the fractal patterns of the temporal domain, time future may be gathered in time past and time past in time future and all of these fractally rolled together in time present. Thus, a future self may already exist and be as real and as full of qualities as a present or even a past self. My research indicates that the different times zones of our lives seem to persist as separate entities, with our five- and ten- and eighteen-year-old selves, as well as our twenty-five-, thirty-eight-, and fifty-year-old selves, continuing to exist in some portion of our brain-mind system with little if any knowledge of the selves to come. Through altered states and experiments in age regression, it is possible to demonstrate that complete personalities and their memories belonging to these earlier stages can emerge.

The work of brain scientist Wilder Penfield suggests the neurological basis for this phenomenon. During surgery he would stimulate a tiny, discrete area of the cortex, and the patient would report himself back in some previous time of his life, living out the sights and sounds and feelings he once had as if they were happening now. Stimulation of another discrete area would evoke other distant memories, experienced as living realities. I find it useful to create exercises that allow people to get in touch with these earlier selves so as to offer encouragement and psychological nourishment to the persons they once were and who still persist in the nether world of their minds. I send my students walking backward through the decades to meet these earlier selves in maturity, in adolescence, and in childhood at times when help was needed, using appropriate music and suggestions to deepen the process. They even meet their infant selves and hold themselves in their arms, offering gifts that are the equivalent of gold, frankincense, and myrrh to the holy children that they were. Then I take them back to years before they were born, where they enter the chamber of the great pattern keepers in the time beyond time when the possibilities for their lives were laid down. I invite them to offer suggestions for new patterns or turns in the design of their lives from their present ages on, and they thus become management consultants in life design. Then, going forward in time, they bring new blessings and empowered life to themselves from infancy up to the present. I ask them to become aware in the distant future of the presence of a very wise elder. The elder approaches, and they see that it is their future self, who then embraces them and gives them fortitude and grace from the future. In a final celebration, all deepened versions of each time traveler's different ages come together in a testament to the redeeming capacities of time.

Many changes emerge from this process. I do not believe that the past is altered; rather, the track of the past as it continues in the brain is modified by empowerment from the present self. Thus, after having met oneself at various ages, one often feels considerable change in oneself, because the past now bears the frequency of empowerment. You were there, as great friend and ally of your needy earlier self, and this seems to play upon the fractal scale of time in body and memory, releasing bad habits, freeing new mind, bringing soul back to times in which soul may have been dirtied or lost.

I discovered this miracle for myself in a most remarkable way. One day when I was about thirty-eight years old, I was giving a seminar and walking students backward through the decades of their lives. I sent them, accompanied by their newly evoked younger selves, out into the bright summer day to walk through the gardens, play by the pond, and generally befriend and empower the children they once were. As my students left to perform the process, I decided to join them. As my young childhood had been an exceptionally happy one, I determined to find a time in adolescence when I could have used a wiser and older friend. I then thought of that poor girl eating her lunch behind locked doors in the Barnard College theater's Green Room, suffering so much misery. I sent my mind back in time and found myself standing before her. She was in an agony of hopelessness, thinking her life was over. I said to her, "Don't worry, kid. It's going to be a far richer life than you can imagine. . . ."

It was only recently that I remembered that I, at thirty-eight, had in fact shown up to myself at eighteen. The reader will undoubtedly say that my unconscious made me visit my younger self in order to fulfill the terms of the imaginative occurrence of years before. But I'm not sure it's all that simple.

It is ten days after my dad's death. I am in the middle of a seminar, conducting an exercise in which I ask the students to imagine a series of doors that they pass through, gradually taking them to deeper states of consciousness. I decide to join them in the process. I shut my eyes and eventually find myself in front of a very unusual door. The bottom half is paisley, while the upper part is glass. Suddenly, through the glass I see my father grinning at me. I am shocked because my capacity for internal visual imagery is very weak, and yet my father appears as clearly as if he were right in front of me with my eyes open. For some reason I say, "Dad! What shall I call you?"

"Call me Popsicle!" he replies and, waving, turns and walks away.

Later that day, I call Polly, his wife, to tell her the incident. She breaks into laughter and says that she had received a call from Forest Lawn, the funeral home that attended to my father's remains. Due to a backup of bodies for the crematorium, they tell her, my father had to stay "on ice" much longer than usual. Thus the reference to Popsicle.

Several months later I find myself asleep but in a lucid dream. My father shows up, and again I am shocked.

"Dad, how come you're here? I know I'm dreaming, but you're supposed to be in the next place."

"Yeah," he says, "but they gave me time off for good behavior, and you're asleep so I can reach you. Now, Jeanie-pot, I've been going to comedy clubs all over the world. I've been getting in free 'cause they can't see me. Now there's a great chicken act at the

Dirty Rascals club in Manchester, England, that you've just got to see. And then at the Comedy House in San Diego they've got a Martian stunt that's got them rolling in the aisles. Now a couple of guys at the Kangaroo Club in Sydney, Australia, do a riff on politics that will, you'll excuse the expression, make you die laughing."

My father continued to name a number of other comedy skits he'd been seeing in his time off. Finally he said, "Now, kid, this is what I want you to do. When you wake up, try and remember these clubs I'm telling you about, and go around to them and write down as many of the jokes and routines as you can. Do a little rewriting, punch them up with your own material, and you'll have a great comedy act. Then you can quit this scam that you're into!"

One thing you have to say about my dad—he never gives up!

11

THE FEAST OF MATURITY

It is early evening, around five o'clock. You are here with me now in my kitchen, about to embark on a feast that will take us at least until midnight, what with all the courses and discourses. I have planned this dinner for a long time, in fact, all my adult years, for it is to be a feast of maturity, each dish representing a commemoration of life when it has ripened enough to celebrate.

I should tell you that I am a cook. I have always been a cook. In fact, cooking is really the only craft I do well. I've even thought of writing a book called Philosopher in the Kitchen, *with chapter headings like "The Metaphysics of Crunch" or "The Ontology of Taste." But I gave it up, for, truth to tell, all philosophy is already inherent in the splendors of cuisine.*

In ancient times people would burn the most succulent foods on the altars of the gods or, as in Bali, prepare an elaborate offering of beautiful food so that the divine beings might savor the tastes and aromas of these riches and declare us worthy of their favor. Relishing the many tastes and textures of our mature lives, we too can be the offering, a feast for the gods, sustaining and nourishing the divine within us. This is perhaps one of the richest mysteries there is.

A Sufi spiritual exercise offers a meditation on becoming divine food. To begin, you concentrate on your eyes, and as you do so you also become aware that God is looking at you and you know yourself as good seeing. Then you focus on your ears and know yourself to be good hearing. Then you meditate on touch and then on smell and finally on taste and know that God finds you to be good touching, good smelling, and good tasting. Finally, you are consumed by God and become part of God's body.

To nourish is to be deeply nourished; to savor is to be deeply savored. We come to understand and call forth the beauty of the world wherever we may find it. The world has suffered much in the last few centuries from those who directed their appreciation only to goals and not to the enjoyment of what they met on the way. In maturity we finally have enough ingredients to celebrate the path and where it leads us.

This evening I invite you to a feast that embraces the full flavor of our lives, relishing the tastes—both simple and complex—that feed us. Such a banquet is also an initiation, a preparation for a life of true service—to the Earth, to all sentient beings, and, yes, even to the gods. So bon appetit, and let us begin!

A special guest is present in the background, Herr Wolfgang Amadeus Mozart, himself a devoted gourmet, whose music now will feed our souls as we feast our bodies. First let me give you something to drink, something bubbly to launch the appetizers, little epiphanies of taste. Do you like champagne? Then let me pour you a glass of Veuve Cliquot, a dry, witty, cleansing quaff. And for you non-drinkers, Pellegrino water from Italy with its bright effervescence that surprises the palate without attacking it.

And now for my first course, *L'horloge gastronomique,* the gastronomic clock. Here, for each of you, is a large plate with the numbers of the clock inscribed in roman numerals around the edge. At each number I've placed what the French call an *amuse gueule,* a small but provocative portion of pure delight. Mine are meant to take you on a journey, an opening processional of the feast of maturity.

At one o'clock I invite you to eat a baby artichoke heart, flattened to look like a sunflower and sauteed till golden brown in olive oil and garlic. It is a sunny morsel, a wake-up call for the taste buds, an invitation to a heightened state of awareness. This little burst of "Yes!" is newness incarnate, and in it we recall our own beginnings.

From the time I was three years old, the only thing I ever wanted for Christmas was a stove. I would climb up on the department store Santa's knee, and just as he began his mantram, "And what do you want for Ch—" I would interrupt with "a stove, Santa," and then hop down and bounce away. When Santa complied on Christmas morning, I was in ecstasy. Here was destiny realized. Little Mozart had his piano, little Picasso his brushes and paints, and I had my stove.

Destiny had to be deferred, however, as my father had found a bargain in children's stoves, one with DC current. I carefully prepared the batter for sugar cookies, plugged the cord of my stove into the AC socket, and before you could say "Julia Child," watched my dream destroyed in a sorry spectacle of smoke and seared wires. The following year, a similar scene repeated itself and with the same curling smoke and acrid smell I had come to dread. This time my mother came to the rescue. "Never mind, Jeanie. We'll make the cookies on the regular stove." And from that moment on, the kitchen became the center of my household activities.

As I grew taller, my head slowly rising above the level of the burners, I took on more and more of the preparation of the family's meals. Comic books were supplanted by cookbooks, and soon I began my ritual, continued to this day, of reading recipes while eating my morning Wheaties. I must explain that as an infant I went from mother's milk to Wheaties, largely skipping the pablum stage. Thus I am constituted by Wheaties, and I eschew all attempts at granola or bacon and eggs. Because I am a gustatory thinker, I can read almost any recipe and taste its flavors within the prima materia of the Wheaties. Thus my breakfasts are extravagant feasts, the Wheaties transformed into ballottine of duck stuffed with pistachios and truffles. An Indian lamb curry of Rajasthan, spiced with fenugreek, cardamom, black mustard seeds, and pickled lemons fills the bowl, where anyone else would see only the familiar brown flakes floating in milk. I arise from table sated with the cuisines of many lands and planning my evening meal from the recipes that I have so richly savored. (A sad, late note: Wheaties has just been "improved" and toasted into paper. It has lost the qualities of resonance that made it so absorbing of imaginal feasts. Thus I am experimenting with Cheerios.)

Have a sip of whatever you are drinking, and try my offering at two o'clock. It is an unctuous morsel of gravlax cured in pepper-flavored vodka with lemon juice added, sitting in a sweet mustard seed–dill sauce. Gravlax is salmon, cured, not cooked; its essence is not changed, merely deepened by spirits. It is met by the spice of adventure, for mustard seeds have long been carried in travelers' pockets as a protective talisman. And, of course, as that great compendium of recipes, the Bible, tells us, if you but have the faith of a grain of mustard seed, you can do most anything.

Salmon is a holy fish, a storied fish; to Celtic folk it is always associated with wisdom. And why not, for a salmon will always find its way. Spawned in fresh inland waters, it follows streams and rivers into the salty ocean, there to live out its adult life until, finally, pulled by a call it must heed, it swims immense distances, leaping falls and cascades, to come home to the place it began. Maturity knows the eternal return—its risks and waterfalls, its sureties and comforts. Life fractally repeats itself, and this cyclical awareness more than anything else gives wisdom and remembrance.

Taste now what is there for you at three o'clock—macadamia nuts. A macadamia nut is everything that a nut would be if it could grow up to perfection. It is the hardest nut to crack in the world, and the fact that it is accessible to us at all symbolizes that nothing is impossible. Bite into it now and notice how this salty, gnarled, but golden stalwart of Hawaii is so totally itself, so possessed of its own macadamiality. When crushed between our teeth, it is not vanquished but gives of its essence, of its utter suchness, awakening the temples of our mind. In its generous, abundant, compassionate richness, it reminds us of the treasures of our own life, our talents and skills.

What does it take to crack us open and discover that our inner treasure is already fully formed? Within a protective coating of ego is a kernel of glory. Do but the work of stripping away, and it is there to be found. We are all already enlightened, say certain schools of Buddhist thought. Only peel away the shell of delusions, crack the bark of defenses, and discover yourself to be a full being, rich, compassionate, complete. And now in this feast of maturity, you are worthy of being macadamia, ready to give utterly of yourself and to make perfection in large and small ways wherever you go.

Now let us consider what we find at four o'clock. At this hour we move from the solitary splendor of the individual to a more social reality that speaks to the meeting of cultures. For here we have chicken sun-dried tomato spring rolls. Soak two ounces of bean thread noodles in warm water and squeeze out the moisture. Then combine cooked chicken strips with salt, pepper, olive oil, marjoram, chives, and sun-dried tomatoes—a classical Italian mixture. Sun-dried tomatoes: memory and desire, Earth-bound, sun-kissed, crossed into something ethereal. Add the noodles and let the mixture meld for an hour.

Then dip a Vietnamese rice paper round in water to soften. Place the chicken and sun-dried tomato and olive oil mixture on the rice paper and roll it up. Heat peanut oil and fry. Spring rolls extraordinaire. Bean threads, rice paper, the ancient seeds of Eastern life, encased in and encasing what is essentially an Italian reality. When you bite into it, can you imagine what it does to your brain-mind system? Does it throw it out of kilter? Does it blow open the old categories? Does it spin the mind out of its usual culinary track? Born of a marriage between Vietnam and Italy, this is the movement toward planetary culture in two bites. Politicians may fret, fundamentalists may fume, but it is too late; multiculturalism has found its way into the mouth, and there is no turning back. The food of fusion changes the very way our minds and brains function, lends them a planetary wisdom born from different soils, different realities. Swallow this dish and you are no longer culturally innocent. You have tasted a mature society that embraces the harvest of many cultures, many lands. In cuisine is the key to a metademocracy, the lineaments of which we do not yet know but the taste of which we begin to fathom.

I learned culinary politics firsthand by my ninth year, doing most of the cooking for my hybrid family. This required at least four burners going full blast. In one pot the flavors of Italian tomatoes, meat, and garlic melded into sauce to serve on pasta for my mother and her relatives, while in two others, chicken-fried steak and hush puppies sizzled for my dad, who couldn't abide the taste of garlic. But always there was the burner that I thought of as my very own, the one on which I would cook my own particular food, sometimes a mixture of the two cuisines, ending up with something like hush puppy polenta balls steamed in chicken-fried-steak tomato sauce. Gradually my concoctions assumed their own distinctiveness, a youthful fractal of the latest in the cross-cultural dishes offered by today's cutting edge chefs. I was generally the only taker for the fourth dish, my early attempt at fusion food. Thus began my complex and, some would say, surreal relation to cooking.

At five o'clock we return to basics. Here we scoop up with a bit of lavash—the crisp flat bread of the Middle East—a potent amalgam known as peasant caviar. It is eggplant, charred over a fire until soft, its blackened skins peeled away, and the creamy flesh chopped up with onions, garlic, olive oil, lemon juice, and a bit of dill. One taste and one remembers things one never knew, caravans in the night and the footfall of camels, men drumming and singing in the firelight a verse of Rumi about his finding of the beloved:

The result is not more than these three words:
I got burnt and burnt and burnt.

(Quoted in Annemarie Schimmel, *The Triumphal Sun: A Study of the Works of Jaloloddin Rumi,* London and the Hague: East-West Publications, 1980, 24)

The eggplant's bitterness is taken by the burning, and in its place is a smoky afterglow. This process is germane to the human condition, for we have all been burned and, if not destroyed, then like the eggplant we are rendered vulnerable, available to a new appreciation of the simple givens of life—onion, garlic, olive oil, the hand of a child, the smile of a friend, the wonder at the dawn.

At six o'clock, we reach the halfway point on the gastronomic clock, and we renew ourselves with a tiny hillock of mango sorbet held in an icy silver cup. It is the taste of refreshment—pure but with many latitudes. In 600 B.C.E. a special mango grove was presented to the Buddha as a quiet place for his meditation. A place of reflection, mango sorbet is a precious moment in time, reminding us of our need for solitude, an interval each day, sacred and inviolable, when we may reflect and clarify. Icy yet sensual at the same moment, mango sorbet is a paradox that resolves our own. Go too long in the steamy succulence of life without an interval of purification, and one becomes cynical and sated. Receive it now, and, as it melts, a tiny chime in consciousness sounds a pure call to wake up.

Seven o'clock is luxurious, an evening fete of diamonds and sybaritic pleasures, dining at the court of the czars in the grand old days before the revolution. A purse of caviar—not just any caviar, but gray, translucent pearls of Beluga, eggs fitted together like molecules, the DNA of the sea. They sit on a small dollop of sour cream and chives and are wrapped in a tender, almost translucent crepe like a membrane of consciousness. One bite and the shadow of your knowing awakens as memories of ancient waters or Earth in space. You do not chew but press it on the roof of your mouth like a holy word, where it explodes like the outsparkings of a trodden star.

At eight o'clock you get down and dirty, stomping in the red Earth of the Southwest. A little corn cake, about the size of a silver dollar, with a green smear of guacamole and a touch of chipotle salsa, and don't miss the garnish of cilantro. This is goddess food, Corn Mother food, the mothering gift of this continent. For Navajo, Hopi, Zuni, corn is queen and the eating of it is a conscious, celebratory, devotional act. Taste corn and be enlivened. Dip it in salsa, and your crown chakra blows open. You are illumined in more ways than one. The brain says, "There's a fire down there!" and sends in endorphins, a cascade of pleasure streamings. You get high on it, this dark food that brings you to light; it is shaman food, nearly psychedelic. This maize and its dark and peppery companion becomes a maze food. Something is chasing you through the labyrinth, the fabled Minotaur, perhaps, but when you turn around, you find it is yourself. Freed now from insubstantial fears, the inner teacher comes forward, a dancing kachina, eagle headed, conferring Earth power and sky sentience.

A simple and needed perfection resides at nine o'clock: seedless red grapes. Little circular spheres that look like Mars, they are serendipity, happy chance. Englobed and nubile, ready to burst, grapes pop in your mouth, a sparkling wonder, the inner life of rubies. These are thirst quenching and perfect, like a sunset on a mountain. Grapes have hidden colors, pure joy with a hint of sour—life as it is supposed to be. A joie de vivre about them, but mutability, too, turning into wine or vinegar as you choose. A dancing kind of food, Januslike, grapes face both the sour and the sublime.

At ten o'clock, a curl of prosciutto of Parma shaped into a rose. This is poetry in flesh, a buttery, blushing meat. There is an innocence about it, perhaps because until this moment, it is untouched and air cured. That so feminine, sensuous, and silky a taste comes from the pig is no surprise. From Borneo to Ireland, pigs are holy creatures, always knowing where to find Earth's hidden treasures, and having knowledge of the underworld, too. In the choosing of totems, goddesses stand in line, hoping to be selected by the Great Sow.

But now, enjoy it, this succulence softened beyond its own excellence. How did it happen? Like coal transmutes to diamond from the pressure of the Earth, prosciutto is pressed until it becomes a dense jewel of flesh. This is familiar, yes? Our lives at maturity are compacted of everything we have ever experienced, everyone we have ever known. We are wisdom compressed into a core of excellence that, like prosciutto, is smooth, supple, protean, able to take on any shape.

Eleven o'clock presents us with a variety of olives, roasted in thyme, sage, olive oil. Olives are the gift of Athena. I wish I could take you to her groves, the ones extending twelve miles to the sea from the Tholos, her circular temple at Delphi. Olives are the ambassadors of peace and possibility; their leaves crown those who have surpassed themselves. As you eat an olive, note how you are encompassed by the experience. It is so assertive that you cannot ignore it, for it has been cured but still retains its integrity of flavor.

Olive trees live forever—well, a thousand years or so. Their fruit—Niçoise, Kalamata, Gaeta, wrinkled old Sicilian, from green to brown to purple to black, salt-packed, oil-logged, or steeped in a briny, acerbic bath—tastes like all the tears you have ever shed, tears that have tenderized you. Olives remind us of the healing that takes place between generations. One thinks of the end of Shakespeare's play of overripe maturity, when King Lear and his daughter, Cordelia, come together and he reaches out to touch her cheek and asks, "Be your tears wet?" After being so maddened and so humbled, he cannot believe that somebody will weep for him. Is he dead, he wonders, and in heaven, and this lovely girl an angel? When he realizes that she is his beloved daughter Cordelia, from whom he has been desperately estranged, he reaches out and tastes her salty tears. The olive is the Lear of trees. Gnarled by the elements, tortured and wind tossed, withstanding time and change, its fruit is at first bitter and then forgiving. . . . "When thou dost ask me blessing, I'll kneel down, / And ask of thee forgiveness; So we'll live, / And pray, and sing, and tell old tales, and laugh / At gilded butterflies, . . / And take upon's the mystery of things / As if we were God's spies."

We have come to the final hour of *L'horloge gastronomique,* and for it I have chosen a marriage of many flavors in one. Thus, at twelve o'clock, I offer you a tiny box of phyllo dough containing curried coconut shrimp with a touch of coriander. Here at the place of the end, we have also returned to the beginning, for spices act as a melding of ancient wisdom and new beginnings. Curry is an evolved mélange of spice, containing all previous evolutionary levels, and shrimp, a density of protein, is a paradox of the tender and the firm. These two, shell-encased—shrimp walking on the bottom of the sea and coconut heady at the top of a tree—come together, both eminently crackable. So like a human head coconut is, with eyes to boot, and therapeutic, too. Hawaiian kahunas tell us that wearing half a coconut on your head, wrapped around with a white cloth, relieves head pain. At the same time, coconut draws out the pain of life, evoking spirituality, psychic awareness, purification. Together with shrimp and spice, coconut restores our wonder, for often at maturity our enthusiasm begs to be renewed. Thus this delicate piece of "Oh, wow!" enclosed in phyllo, a dough stretched tissue-thin and folded with butter; it is a luscious crackle, an archaeology to the tooth.

Perhaps after all this you need a respite, an interval, a breath of fresh air or a stroll around the garden. Do so, but come back, so I can tell you a story, a new myth, born of my love of food, one that has haunted me for many years. I call it "The Myth of the Bests in the World."

A family called Bests have a restaurant on East 49th Street called "The Bests in the World." Everybody thinks the Bests are a wonderful family, but they're not quite what they seem. They are here to stimulate through exquisite tastes a new possibility for humanity. To eat their cuisine is to be inspired to be better than one ever was. One's ethics are deepened, one's sensibilities are expanded, one's heart is opened, and one is moved to become a social artist. As a result of eating the Bests' cuisine, you change, and gradually the world changes, too.

You see, the Bests in the World are not exactly human beings. They are Elohim. Who are the Elohim? They are members of Type Three High-Level Civilization. Right now we're at Type One, in which human beings have become responsible for the biological and evolutionary governance of the planet. In Type Two High-Level Civilization, a few hundred years into the future, we will have evolved to assume appropriate stewardship of the solar system. Type Three is further away still, but then we join the galactic milieu and help to create worlds, entering into these worlds to stimulate spiritual growth, create novelty, and help societies evolve.

The Elohim have a number of bodies, both corporeal and subtle. Sometimes they spore themselves and meld with human DNA, showing up as moral or spiritual evocateurs like Buddha or Krishna or the Marys. I imagine that the Elohim feel some consternation about present crises in this world and gather to discuss what will work to save the planet and its species. They say, "Well, what about going in as another avatar incarnation? In a time of whole-system transition, maybe that's what humans need, another Christ, another Buddha. They're always claiming that Christ or Buddha is coming again. Why not rise to the challenge and send one in?"

But then the others say, "No, that creates more problems than it solves; it makes people dependent rather than independent."

"What about inspiration?"

"Well, inspiration serves, but it doesn't sustain."

So the Elohim then ask each other, what is it that all of humankind love to do? What is the most social of their activities? It isn't sex because that's too private. It isn't art because large numbers do not participate at all or only dabble or watch. Sports, too, reach only a segment of the population, with the rest as spectators. Also sports can be divisive, especially of husbands and wives. There is only one activity that truly touches and joins all humans, and that is eating.

And so the Elohim agree to come down to Earth as cooks. They come in as a husband and wife and seven grown children whose last name is given as Best. They begin with a trial run, a consumer test restaurant. The woman and two sons and a daughter prepare the food, while the others help. The father and one son get the best produce, the other two daughters serve the food, and one son manages the cash register. However, there is no price list. You pay what you want to. That's part of the test.

Now the Bests can, with very special quantum catch-it equipment, tune in around the world to what is the best and tastiest food being cooked that day. Is it the corn and crab soup served in Hong Kong at the Peninsula Hotel? Is it the barbecued ribs at the Rendezvous in Memphis? Is it the salmon with sorrel sauce at the Connaught Grill in London? Is it the tofu stuffed with wild mushrooms served at the Oriental Hotel in Bangkok? Is it anything that master food designer Paula Perlis is cooking up this evening? Whatever it is, they can beam it in and replicate it before returning it to the counter or stove from which it has so mysteriously disappeared. They taste it and then enhance it, filling it with manna, the ultimate soul food. Remember in the Old Testament, manna sustained the people of Israel on their forty-year journey through the desert? Earlier yet, if Eve hadn't eaten the tempter's augmented fruit, we would still be featherless bipeds living on welfare in the garden instead of going out there and finding division and delectation, trauma and transcendence—the matters that underscore all growing civilization and stop the gods from being bored.

More often, however, the Bests use their own recipes and genetically evolved produce; they are also genius agronomists and have a magical truck farm and hothouse across the river in New Jersey.

Their cooking has themes: primavera dinners for the first day of spring, the comfort foods of childhood, medieval feasts, food of the steppes. Sometimes they even surprise guests with a junk food theme, but they serve the ultimate hamburger, the ultimate french fry, the ultimate milkshake. Other times, the main course is something exquisite, laden with truffles (which they've beamed back from the mouth of a very surprised Lulu, the champion sow truffle finder of Perigord), that makes nouvelle California cuisine look like child's play. They add some special magic that brings any food they prepare to perfection, not just of taste, but of Essence, because all who eat it enter a state of complete happiness and pleasure. The Bests' food enhances their diners' entire being, calls forth their entelechy, amplifies their highest qualities. People are retuned by the eating.

Somebody with a cold is invariably given chicken soup, served in a big glass bowl. But in the chicken soup at different levels float various delectable wonders. At the top, a paper-thin crepe wrapped around a gossamer pâté of foie gras. Beneath that, a greening spray of snow peas. Lower still, a quenelle of chicken breast. And so it goes, through noodles and nuggets of sensation, layers of floating little worlds, until finally, when you get to the bottom, the soup's ground of being, you reach the *Ursprung*, a wild mushroom with a slight magic to it. Thus one eats one's way from the most ephemeral reality to the deepest and, on arriving, finds it to be an epiphany.

The Bests' food acts upon the entire body and mind as an evolutionary accelerator. Patrons are in such a state of bliss that they agree to evolve out of pleasure instead of out of pain, for that is the way of the Elohim. The food enhances one's maturity, one's gift for social artistry. Say a very ordinary doctor sits down to dinner. After the meal he thinks not only of what he can do to provide better medical care for the homeless on the streets of New York, but also how he can create environments of hope by teaching the homeless to be paraprofessionals in medicine. He becomes not unlike the great Jewish Zen roshi of Yonkers, Bernie Glassman, who teaches the homeless to rebuild crumbling buildings and also create cake and cookie factories that turn out extraordinary pastries for the best restaurants. That's what I mean by the social artistry. In my experience, great social artists are also great savorers. Margaret Mead went through life saying, "Yum, yum, yum, yum, yum!" That's why she was such an evocateur of people and cultures.

Perhaps you have visited the restaurant without even knowing it, because the Bests can show up in dreams as well, and their restaurant resides also in the archetypal domain on some evanescent 49th Street where anyone can enter. Have you noticed that your bliss tolerance has been extended? If so, perhaps you've been there. If not, make reservations for tomorrow, for tonight you are dining with me.

And now for the soup. But first another wine, a sauvignon blanc—the 1990 Pavillon Blanc du Château Margaux from Bordeaux, a wine of exquisite elegance and complexity. With it I serve you now a wild mushroom soup covered by a golden dome of puff pastry. As you shatter the dome, the aromatic steam rises up to meet you, and you spoon up a thick brew of forest mushrooms, picked by moonlight—shiitake, porcino, morel, chanterelle.

This stew of Earth essence is accompanied in its rich chicken broth with morsels of carrot, leek, onion, and barley, a touch of madeira, an enrichment of cream, subtle herbs. This is moonlight food, well met by rich pastry, prophecy in the mouth, an oracular taste born of the friendship of Demeter and Hecate. Leeks you wear in your bonnet, if you are an old Welshman, for they strengthen you and help you win your endless wars against the Anglo-Saxon hordes. Barley, Demeter's own, is the oldest of grains, the nourishment of pyramid builders and cuneiform scribes. Cream is from sun and cow—the green of grasses translated to thick, white richness; it raises the soup to another level. Thus sun and moon marry beneath a topping layer of buttered wheat, pastry that expands into a strong and supple shell. Wheat is the kiss of the sun gone right; in fine baked pastry it is born again to its golden self. How like a life this is—a sunny surface perhaps, a smiling face shown to the world, but, once cracked, it reveals a mystery both chthonic and cosmic, a remembrance of our hidden origin as spores of God.

Some think that mushrooms are the spores of the galaxy, the life bringers, so coded with secrets that they must remain hidden, sequestered with the magic of their knowing. Thus their association with moonlight, the heartbeat of the woods, and fairies; a grounded ethereality is theirs. The Greeks always included in their feasts for the gods not just roasted flesh but also ambrosia. What was ambrosia? It was described by the second-century Greek scholiasts in Alexandria who wrote about such things as compounded of *mele,* which is honey; *udor,* water; *karpos,* fruit; *elias,* olive oil; and *muke.* Therein lies a mystery, for *muke* means sacred psilocybe mushroom. It was a secret that the food of the gods was a psychedelic substance so that the gods could get stoned, which is what gods do, you see. We are told that at Eleusis, initiates were served ambrosia, after which they had dreams and waking visions. A little side trip through the fields of theobotany may lead us to the origins of the expression *holy cow*. For way back when, say some fifty or sixty thousand years ago, if you were a hunter-gatherer, you dutifully followed a trail of ungulates' droppings to find your dinner. And what grows out of these droppings but the psilocybe mushroom! We might picture these not-too-bright people following the trail and eating magic mushrooms, which, as we now know, activate the speech centers. The verbal mind—what I call the logos laser—was primed, perhaps, by cow patties. Such is the ecology of things in this divine world!

We are approaching now the alchemical courses, which transmute while they raise the vibration. For what is maturity but the turning of basic substances into rare and precious ones with the skillful addition of just the right thing at just the right moment? In the ancient traditions, preparing food for the gods required just such alchemical practice and knowledge. Indeed, medieval alchemy grew directly out of these ancient practices of Greece and Rome, Babylonia and Egypt. The preparation of an offering was not merely finding something expensive like a haunch of ox and burning it on an altar. The haunch was merely a template, upon which honey, oil, wine, and herbs were placed in meaningful proportion.

The later alchemists regarded their own preparations as a meditation, grinding salt and saltpeter, mercury and metal into powder and, at the same time, grinding down their own inner obstacles and impurities. A similar kind of alchemy is practiced in the Eastern traditions. A practitioner of deity yoga in Tibetan Buddhism transforms through mantra each morsel of food before eating. *Om* purifies it of all faults of color, smell, and potentiality. *Ah* multiplies and increases it. *Hum* transforms it into an ocean of nectar, ambrosia, food fit for the gods and for the deity that is the self's highest essence.

The ancients believed that humans could speed this evolutionary process, this alchemical transformation, and participate in it as well, thus achieving health, immortality, and conscious growth of the soul while helping to perfect God's creation. Now we reenact cosmic processes within ourselves for the purpose of becoming Godseeds, cocreators. It is thought that if we can alchemize food within ourselves it will be transmuted into something extraordinary. Rumi wrote a wonderful passage in which a housewife throws chickpeas into the boiling water, and they yell bloody murder, "Get us out of here! Get us out of here!" She starts to beat them in the boiling water, and they say, "Stop that! Stop that! First you boil us, then you beat us. What kind of good Islamic woman are you?" And she says, "Don't you realize the great gift I'm giving you? Being cooked and eaten is the only way for chickpeas to reach a higher level of development." After realizing the transformation they are undergoing, the chickpeas say, "Since this is the case, O woman, let me boil happily—aid me well! In this boiling you are like my architect. Strike me with the spoon, for you strike delightfully . . . so that I will give myself to the boiling and be delivered into the embrace of the Beloved." Remember that the next time you eat hummus!

In personal alchemy, food that is eaten mindfully, sacredly, activates spiritual taste buds that then actuate a higher, more conscious mode of life. In some esoteric traditions, especially among Taoists, food can be transmuted to create a subtle body more perfect than our ordinary one. This subtle body then plays back upon our physical one, rejuvenating while eliciting new capacities. And yet there is more. I can imagine eating with such an exquisite *saveur* that one is also feeding the gods, the higher spiritual principles, one's archetypal support system. Why, after all, should we be the only ones having fun? As David White explains, "The alchemist's craft is conceived of as a spiritual exercise, a ritual, a sacrifice, an act of devotion, and a participation in the divine play of an expanding or contracting universe." This is how I see food—as the primal matter, the alchemical conundrum, the sympathetic energies we add to our matter—and our adulthood is the Philosopher's Stone.

For our next course, I offer the very essence of maturity, a stuffed artichoke, prepared in the way I was taught by Nana, my Sicilian grandmother. The artichoke is the great bulb of life. It is prickly on the outside, a fortress of walls within walls, yet within it contains both a culture and a psychology. In this it is the mirror of yourself. You may be surrounded by walls of egotism, arrogance, and fear, a well-defended citadel of mistrust and misunderstanding, pocked by too many assailants. But inside, as with the artichoke, is a very soft heart. Because one's heart has been wounded so many times, it is shielded by tough, pointy leaves and must be opened very carefully.

Like a life, the artichoke gains richness and savor from being combined with many flavors. I slice off just the top third. Then I crush the bulb a little bit so that the leaves open up, as we've all been crushed and our layers exposed—wearing our hearts on our sleeves. Then I make a stuffing of bread crumbs, the sacred grain, the staff of life, to which I add basil for greening, oregano for piquancy, and garlic—much garlic—for pungency. I also add the bite of freshly grated aged cheese, romano or peccorino or parmesan, the kindness of olive oil, and the grounding of salt. And for spiciness, I will often put in a bit of cardamom, which I'll grind, or coriander as a strange Sicilian undercurrent. Sometimes I even throw in a little bit of pickled oregano bud in the form of chopped caper. Then I mix that up and carefully stuff each leaf, spiraling inward to the center choke.

When it has been slowly braised to just the right moment of tenderness, the stuffed artichoke becomes a hologram, each part containing the whole. It symbolizes how each aspect of a life has the potential for a full relation to the totality. The sweet does not remain simply sweet. It is set off by the sour and the bitter and the pungent. The same is true of the salty parts: even tears contain a bit of greening. Life as usual imitates cuisine, and the art of cooking is a metaphor for composing a life.

For the fish course I am placing before you a grilled paillard of salmon in a sorrel sauce. Here, a salmon steak is pounded into a single flat broad leaf, and this fish of wisdom settles into the sauce of bittersweet remembrance. Sweet things may have left your life but are recalled with poignancy, a *tristesse* that still is happiness, but such as only maturity knows; a loss that is a foundness—children growing up, the completion of a creative act, a knowledge of transitions and rites of passage, and, finally, the rueful honoring of time's takings in the celebration of lives that have ended. This is no limpid dish but one with crunch, leavened with a little cream to give it a savory character. Still, with sorrel, it is poignant but not bitter, a flute note, not a whine. You now have hindsight and more than a little foresight. You have moved through, aware of your transitions and hopeful of what is yet to come.

Enter now the entrée, bright with glistening colors, settled on its plate like a medieval pageant. I have made for you a marguet of duck breast surrounded by ancient forbidden fruits found in the garden of paradise: persimmon and pomegranate and slices of blood orange and figs caramelized with a touch of honey. I cannot believe it was a McIntosh that tempted Eve in Eden! The plush dense duck meat, medium rare and so deeply comforting, is sliced and fanned out under its rich but tart wine-citrus sauce. Sprinkled about are six pomegranate seeds to make the whole shimmer and also to remind us of what Persephone ate, so that we may recall our regular sojourn in the underworld or our continuing life in the unconscious. And on top of it all, angel wings—a white spray of filaments of onion cooked in a coating of lacy tempura batter. This dish seems to say, "This is the main course of your life, oh, good and faithful servant, a gathering of all the fruits of your work, your true reward, substantial and yet so sweet."

Accompanying this is a deserving wine, a majestic cabernet sauvignon. My choice for you this evening is a rare vintage, to me, the finest ever produced in America. It is the 1979 Valley View Cabernet from southern Oregon, and I have never enjoyed better. Fortunately, I bought a few cases when the price was still feasible, but now there is not much left, and should we run out, I will offer you a fine consolation in a Beringer Reserve, 1992, heady and aromatic, a wine of many overtones, fruit, spice, oak—summer and smoke.

A saintly handmaiden is in attendance in the form of endive braised in lemon and butter, then, at the last moment, broiled to give it a necessary earthy touch. Endive looks like prayers, pale leaves like hands steepled in devotion. As it unfolds, leaf upon leaf, it has nothing inside but itself. Endive speaks of commitment to one's own integrity. Lemon adds a subtle awakening; butter gives it sunlight so that it comes out of the dark cloister. Butter can temper solitary devotions, for butter is merry and in some places is used to surprise the gods with joy. I remember the great Menakshe temple in Madurai, India, where devotees hurl pats of butter at the statues of Shiva and Parvati. They stick, which evidently tickles the gods, and they respond with benign irony, as is their fashion. Contemplative endive prepared in this manner gives us pause lest we get too caught in our own interior states. A good balance to duck in paradise, wouldn't you say?

Why do people like feasts? Because at feasts we agree to be happy, to let go of our cares, to be convivial, not to be self-conscious. In short, we agree to a kind of collective renewal. But suppose every meal were a feast, what would happen to our bodies and minds? In the Renaissance, feasting typified the Promethean gusto of men exalting in their growing sense of power over nature. In 1581, a feast was given in Mantua, Italy, to celebrate the marriage of the duke's daughter. Imagine, if you will, a table covered with an embroidered cloth and decked with napkins folded in intricate shapes of arches and columns. To this blazing napery were attached streamers of colored cloth gilded with the coats of arms of the noble families in attendance. The first course, to quote from a contemporary description of the event, was "salads decked out with various fantasies such as animals made of citron, castles of turnips, high walls of lemons; and variegated with slices of ham, mullet roes, herrings, tunny, anchovies, capers, olives, caviar, together with candied flowers and other preserves." The entrée, according to the accounts, included "venison patties in the shape of lions, pies in the form of upright black eagles, pasties of pheasant, which seemed alive," and other wonders. Dessert, for those who were still upright, was "three large statues of marzipan, each four hands high," representing famous mythological personages and events. I cannot help but wonder if the gods make statues of us for their dessert? I'm partial to seeing myself done up in halvah.

Feasting was a kingly activity. One of his biographers reported that England's Henry VIII "ate enormously, stuffing the meat into his little mouth with his knife. As he munched, the meat and vegetables popping from cheek to cheek, his eyes shone with happiness. He jabbed his knife, greasy as it was, into the salt cellar, blew his nose into his napkin, spat into the washing bowl—he was the king." Henry's repast too was royal: "meat soaked with sauces of parsley, garlic, quince, pear, wine," "pasties glittering with sugar or hiding haunches of venison," "veal boiled with sage and smeared with cinnamon, cloves, and saffron, stiffened with eggs, all buried under pastry dotted with dates." Would that we all could savor the feast of our lives with Henry's royal gusto and still have time to write lyrics, compose airs for the lute, dance elegantly, and be a patron of the arts as Henry was. Still one wonders if it was the sight of his dinner popping from cheek to cheek that so charmed the ladies . . . "Ohhhhhh, Henry!"

And now for my favorite course, wildly expensive, a consummation devoutly to be wished—risotto with truffles. For me, making risotto is a moving meditation, a dervish dance of stirring, a masterpiece of timing and motion and time in motion. First, the Arborio rice, itself a concentration of riceness, round kernels bursting with the most amazing starch content. Blessed be the starch that binds. Sauté these kernels along with a little chopped onion in butter until translucent: windows on eternity. Then add stock, let it absorb; then champagne, let it absorb; then more stock, let it absorb; and yet more champagne. Finally, though little room remains in the engorged kernels, let them imbibe a last drink of liquid butter, like Brendan Behan closing down the bar on a night out in Dublin. Sated, the rice turns into a creamy, totally completed miracle, a muchness that exceeds each of its parts. Here is a parable, the rich marriage of butter and wine and starch layered in at just the right time, signifying the verities that bind us together through the motions of our lives. And with a final shaving of white truffle, risotto becomes food worthy to grace the inside of the Holy Grail.

A little dissertation on truffles, my friends. They are found by pigs and dogs, those stalwart keepers of underworld mysteries. They are rarely less and hardly ever more than three to twelve inches underground, generally near the roots of oak trees, though also known to take up domicile near chestnut and hazel and beech. Never do they journey beyond the range of the branches, for they seem to require the presence of strong roots and a canopy of leaves overhead. Lady pigs have the keenest nose for truffles, for they smell to them like lusting boars, and the sows always demand a small piece of their find in lieu of love. Dogs, though less prescient about truffles' whereabouts, do not gobble them up but are content with chunks of liver. Truffles are so primal that only original noses can find them. When put to human use, such as crowning risotto, truffles return the mind as well as the mouth to their Maker. Taste them now and see. This is no mere ecstasy; it is love that exceeds all human understanding, the recovery of everything you held dear that had been lost and now is found—grandma wisdom, the roots of things, an amazing and unexpected grace.

Wake up! The best is yet to come, a refreshment for tired palates, with greening power. Our salad arrives with accompaniments, a stellar cheese and stunning breads. Just when you think you could take no more, nature shakes her cornucopia and more gifts of Earth pour out. The salad is composed of fairy food, little deva leaves of mesclun, mache, tiny oak lettuces, a whisper of garlic, and a few nasturtium leaves and flowers for bite, all tossed together with extra virgin olive oil, aged balsamic vinegar from Modena, and a drop of roasted sesame oil for a back note of smokiness. This salad takes you back to the future. It gives you everything you need for awakening to another level: lettuces so innocent and open, translucent greens mixed with dark opaque emerald—the glory of *viriditas* hymned by Hildegard of Bingen as the vigor of love that "hugs the world: warming, moistening, firming, greening it." Nasturtiums gather solar power and teach you to speak your truth, say savvy, gutsy things, risk expressing what you believe. And it's about time, too.

And now for a showstopper, blue castello cheese. Cheese, as author and wit Clifton Fadiman once noted, is milk's leap toward immortality. I would add that it is also immortality's yearning for us. Blue castello is a triple cream cheese, a theological cheese, a Trinity in cheese. Its sumptuous melting flesh is streaked with the life force of blue veins. Bred in caves, a marriage of milk and mold, it ages into inwardness. Its first appearance is deceptive, a white downy casing, soft to the touch, like baby skin. But inside, mad gestation and Dionysian revels go on between milk and yeast and mold. The inner life of this cheese would make for a best-selling and slightly salacious novel. Soft and runny in your mouth, it hits the back of your throat, stunning you with its fullness. Then it becomes intellectual, philosophical, a commentary on life and on aging beautifully. For with aging comes the real flavoring and richness of life. In the interior cave of the psyche we ripen to become pliable and wise. What had been hard in us turns out to be coded with perfection, like this cheese, an edible marble, its forms emerging with no sharp definitions, like a last work by Michelangelo.

In full maturity, distinctions between the inner and outer worlds dissolve. The encasement of personality turns out to be an illusion, a permeable membrane, which allowed for an exchange of nutrients between here and there, I and thou, body and spirit. You have the sense of touch that comes only with experience and the instinctive knowing of the right time to cut through the illusion of boundary and share your riches with those about you. If cut into too soon, you may initially taste fine, but at the center will be a hard core of intransigence and immaturity. If too late, then what remains is runny sentiment, like some very old women I know who exude laughter and tears at the slightest provocation. They want to kiss you all the time, too!

Bread comes to your rescue, surprise locked into the staple of your life. A guardian of the threshold, bread will be a welcoming host only to cheese of the proper consistency. If its proposed companion is found lacking, bread will look the other way and resolve to save the day with its own firm flavors. With the perfection of blue castello, I offer you a fine crusty yeast bread studded with walnuts and, with it, a loaf of sourdough. Both breads are elevated by airborne yeasts; with sourdough, the starter can be some hundreds of years old, passed down through generations. This makes it poignant to chew, its taste coming down to you direct from the fourteenth century. Your great-great-grandparents many times over sit down at table with you, dissolving time barriers in the mystery of breaking bread together.

We have arrived at last at the desserts and, with them, dessert wines. Billionaire Doris Duke once gave me a 1921 Château d'Yquem, and I've been saving it for this occasion. Its sweetness has been brewing in cellars for generations. Now we open it, and . . . you tell me how it tastes. Because there is so little of it, I have arranged to pour you as well my own particular favorite, a Greek muscat wine from the island of Samos. Byron sang of it, as well he might, for it is at once sinister, sugary, and sublime: a beneficial mold, the noble rot of the grape, is the basis for dessert wines.

Our first dessert is that elegant old standby, floating island, also known as *oeufs à la neige*. Deep, rich vanilla custard, a blending of egg yolks and cream, becomes the sea upon which float evanescent islands made of sweetened egg whites whipped and poached in milk. Over this I place Olympian golden crowns of spun sugar, a sign that the old Greek gods are with us and watching. We are eating slower now, reflections are longer, even mildly hallucinatory.

We sit back and tell tales. The floating islands before me bring to mind the grand Homeric adventurer and the finest trip I have ever taken. In May 1988 I retraced with my students on sailing yachts the adventures of Odysseus. The voyage, one of clear skies and fair seas, began with the miraculous appearance of great schools of dolphins, who ran before our ships for more than an hour. The captains were tremendously excited and ran to the prow and took many pictures, for seldom had they seen so many dolphins stay around the ships for so long. "It is a voyage blessed by the gods," they said, tucking their Greek crosses under their shirts and giving themselves over to the ancient spirits, which followed us with sunshine and serendipity for the rest of the voyage. On many of the islands that scholars feel are the actual sites of the great adventures, we stopped to relive the episode through drama and experiential process, aligning our own reality to the one known by the wily Odysseus. We began in Troy, where we remembered the horrors of war and siege, and on the sixth level of Troy—thought to be the time of the Trojan war—Peggy Rubin performed the great scene from Euripides' *The Trojan Women* in which Hecuba says good-bye to her last grandchild before he is killed and she sent off to servitude. In partnership with the mythic hero Odysseus and his great friend, the goddess Athena, we wandered into an island cave, where we put out the eye of our own Cyclopean limited vision and automatic behavior. Later, we basked on another shore among sweet fruits and sweeter airs, where we found some of the mindless bliss that may have been known by the Lotus Eaters. On Circe's Isle, at the place where Odysseus saw his men changed into wolves and pigs, we adventured in evolution, recapitulating the movements and sensations of the earliest to the present stage, emerging out of the Ionian Sea. Greek sailors and waiters joined us with gusto and great fun. Perhaps my favorite process was the one we performed at the estuary of the Acheron River, where, it was said, the souls of the dead would board the ferry to Hades. Some think that this was the entrance to the Underworld, which Odysseus traversed on his way to meet the souls of the noble dead as well as the shade of Tiresius. Diving into the place where the Acheron met the sea, we swam backward into the dark and brackish current to meet our own ancestors and commune with them. Ancient mothers and fathers seemed to rise up in the chilly waves behind us as we chanted the words of the Eleusinian mysteries, *Oide men bio teleutan oiden de di-os-doton archan* (Blessed are you who have known these things. You have known the end of life and you have known the god-given beginnings). Then I had my fellow travelers swim forward through the years until they reached the present time and then swim further forward to meet some descendants of their minds or bodies in the future.

On Corfu, the site of Odysseus' probably meeting with the noble Phaecians who offered him hospitality and to whom he told his adventures, we each recalled our lives in song and poetry and made a festival of games and celebration. At last we reached Ithaca, perhaps the most beautiful island in Greece, and felt that we had come home to our beginnings as well as our endings. In the Cave of the Nymphs where Odysseus, with the help of the goddess Athena, stored his treasures, we chanted our own treasury of sacred words and convictions. We made plans for "cleaning up" our own houses of mind and body and invoked and met our own inner archetypal guide and partner of the inner world, as Odysseus had been reunited with his beloved Athena. Finally, after dancing in the tavernas and singing ancient songs and lays, we ended by ritually bathing in Penelope's bath and then climbed up to the rocky ledge that is known as the School of Homer. There, it is reputed that Homer wrote the *Odyssey* and trained other poets and bards to follow in his path. Standing on this magical outcropping of holy stone, each participant became bardic and sang or spoke words mysteriously invested with the metaphors and fire of ancient lays. And, once again, Homer sang.

Such is the inspiration of floating island.

In this meal of transformation, I have invited reflection on a higher truth and meaning of the most commonplace of human activities. Food that has been raised to its Essence, transmuted into an offering and a sacrament, as have the dishes of the imaginal meal we've been sharing, can inspire us to raise our lives also to another level of service. We can live life as social artists. By *social artist* I mean anyone who works creatively with students, with patients or clients, with business, with families—in other words, just about everyone. I practice my own version of social artistry by giving seminars and workshops around the world, through which I try to embody and transmit the principles for transforming life individually and culturally into a many-flavored repast. To explain how I do this, let me use as my text my favorite dessert, with which we will close our fabled dinner. It is minted deep chocolate mousse mounded on angel food cake with whipped cream. Please dig in and enjoy it while I tell you its secrets.

My recipe calls for 12 ounces of bittersweet chocolate morsels, 8 eggs separated, 3 tablespoons of peppermint brandy or liqueur, half a teaspoon of cinnamon, 1 teaspoon of instant coffee, and 10 tablespoons of boiling water—lovely things that turn into an epiphany. Coded into this recipe are the principles of working as a social artist—principles I have learned on the job, as it were, in widely different cultures and conditions and all over the globe.

The first principle of social artistry is to use a good mix of ingredients. Peggy Rubin and I always make sure that those attending our workshops represent a mixture of both the freshest and the most aged ingredients in the society. We will not work with all coffee or all brandy or all new eggs—all management consultants or new trainees or secretaries or teachers. A homogeneous group is not the best vehicle to effect change. You need a stimulating medley of the low, the high, the old, the new, the middle—many professions, many points of view. Social artists are lifelong learners, getting their inspiration not just from books, but from being immersed in all aspects of the culture they are working in. In a corporate culture, the social artist knows everyone from the mail room clerk to the president; in India, everyone from the leper begging on the street to the maharaja on the polo ground. Any really effective social artistry appreciates the differences, respects the perspectives. If you find yourself having to work with just corporate V.P.s or teachers, your first task is to mix it up a bit. Add a few of your more congenial friends; bring in some artists. Do not allow the group to be only one thing or another; put in some leavening.

Next, the ingredients needed to compose the dish of social artistry have to be at room temperature. This requires a warming of all present through dance and jokes and songs. That is why no matter how serious the occasion, I generally try to begin with a dance, because that way everybody gets to at least see everybody else. Generally, I use one of the most ancient of dances, such as the Ur dance of deep seeing and deep greeting known as the Labyrinthos. It is performed to the haunting strains of the old Greek song with words by Sophocles, the "Enas Mythos," sung by the evocative Nana Mouskouri. In teaching the dance, I tell the group that as they move in the double circle from person to person, they will look deeply into each other's eyes and recognize each other from time out of mind. This takes people out of their ordinary time and consciousness. I also kid around. "I know you," I might say to someone in the dance circle. "I remember the time that you were the Pharaoh and I was a slave. You used to whup me. Do you remember that?" And they often reply, "I sure do!" Once I said, "I remember when we dragged our great long tails as dinosaurs across the swampy marshes. Surely you remember that?" "It was just like yesterday," one fellow replied. Social artists look at everyone with great respect and familiarity—as if to say, "I have known thee of old." This is very important, for a true social artist must really re-member people in terms of their total potential. Regardless of how unskilled their apparent behavior may be, social artists must see the essential being, the God-in-hiding. And quite frankly, after we get to a certain age, everybody seems very familiar—cut from a psychic swath that we recognize. Thus, for raising the temperatures of the ingredients, always the dance and a few jokes and more than a little kindness in seeing. By the way, if you don't know any jokes, learn some, preferably the favorite jokes of the culture. I've learned jokes in Bangladesh that I still don't understand, but when I told them there, everybody dissolved in hysteria.

Another way of warming the room and bringing the eggs to room temperature is by telling the group something of your own life from both a horizontal and then a vertical viewpoint. First, you tell your life horizontally—this thing happened, that thing happened, one thing after another. Then you tell a vertical story; I often speak about my walking the dog with Mr. Tayer or about my religious experience at six. This tells a more essential truth about who I am and how I came to be that way. Barriers come down, the group warms. Then you invite everyone present to do the same with one or two other people. Thus everybody gets to tell their life stories as they usually relate them in meetings and then to tell the vertical experience that really blew them open. These warmers are not just games; they take people to the depths very quickly. By the time these preliminaries are over, people have lost their edges and are ready to be fluid with each other.

Next you break the eggs and separate the yolks from the whites. This means that you do not permit those who think of themselves as inseparably linked—secretaries, teachers, government bureaucrats, health professionals—to stay yoked together. People will always tend to gather in what they think of as safe clusters, staying together by age, gender, or profession. The social artist has got to break these eggs. Separating people provokes them to discover more of their unique Essence, either on their own or in relationship to those whom they would not ordinarily meet. To do this, I might have people dance through the room with their eyes closed until they bump into someone, probably a stranger, who becomes their partner for the next exercise. Or I group people by birth month, so that all the Decembers have to work together.

Next, you put the bittersweet chocolate into a blender and immediately add dark things—a teaspoon of coffee crystals, a half-teaspoon of cinnamon. In this simple act lies an entire philosophy of social artistry! The bittersweet chocolate represents the sweet sad shadows, and the spicy additions are those things that give them piquancy or depth. The social artist does not balk before these shadows or try to reconcile them or offer cheery words. Rather, you address the fact that there are problems in the society—racism, religious conflict, poverty, pollution. You see and acknowledge the dark, recognizing that it contains the seeds, the crystals, the stuff, the spice, the elements of transformation. It is because of the dark that we are ripe for change. Having acknowledged it and seen its power, you add to it hot boiling water. This is to say, you add a stun ray of ideas and a huge emotional sweep of feeling. You speak from your heart about issues and problems, invite others to do the same, and together form ideas about what to do about them. A social artist can't simply perform or give her practiced aria. To call forth the mind and heart of others, one's own work has to be from the mind and heart. You must be willing to ask real questions: What are the issues? What are the possibilities? What do you feel? What local stories do you have to tell? The hot boiling water of passionate ideas and heartfelt thought allows the dark flavors to melt into each other in an agon of feeling, so that many present dissolve some of their boundaries.

The melting also requires a physical loosening, so at this point I often add processes of a physical nature. Surprisingly, throughout the world, people will generally agree to participate; they feel safe with physical movement. These exercises show the participants that just as they can extend their bodies, they can also extend their minds and open their hearts. Physical movement is like blending ingredients at high speed into something that is neither one thing nor another, a sweet thick soup, a dark porridge of possibilities that has yet to find its identity but stands warm and waiting.

Then I tell a story. I generally find a core story of the culture, like the *Ramayana* or the life of Gandhi in India, or the search for the Grail in northern Europe. Or I bring in a potent legend or myth from a parallel culture. The Iroquois legend of the peacemaker Deganawidah, which I have written about in *Manual for the Peacemaker,* has worked beautifully among Australian Aborigines and other native cultures. Through such stories, social artists help members of a culture or organization preserve and honor their unique genius as well as discover and move toward a new story. When traditional cultures are upset by waves of immigration or, as in the corporate culture, through mergers and acquisitions, the social artist helps model a new story that celebrates and appreciates the diversity and complexity of the new brew. Just as the Maori and the Anglos of New Zealand are coming to appreciate each other's stories, so too the Samoans and the Vietnamese and the Koreans and the Hispanics and the whites and blacks in a typical urban school are beginning to tell a multileveled story. The new myth of our time has to do with disparate cultures coming together to meld into a new form while still keeping and celebrating their individual identities. As cultures tell their own stories and attend to the stories of others, they reach a higher communion that is the emerging myth of the time.

Just as you need to work quickly in cooking so that ingredients stay at their peak, social artistry needs to proceed at a fine pace. Most of my seminars last just three days. The very speed of the work dissolves most resistances. With the barrage of jokes, ideas, dances, processes, and myths, presented with such rapidity, there is simply no time for barriers, no way to impede the process of transformation.

As the facilitators of this process, social artists must have an exquisite sense of timing and be able to seize the *kairos,* the loaded time for change, and then act with power and decisiveness. They understand that sometimes what seems like depression is, in fact, a time of ingression, when a society or an individual needs to go inward to let the sap rise. Social artists know that you don't necessarily have to act; they understand as well when *not* to be social artists. It isn't always appropriate to say, "All right, boys and girls, upward and onward!" There may be times when stillness is the only path—a time of reflection and inaction. Thus social artists have to understand negative capability, the capacity to dwell in uncertainty and doubt and mystery, and they laud this state of unknowing as the source from which some of our deepest, darkest, and richest possibilities rise. This is Plutonic knowing, the wisdom of when to approach the treasures of the depth world.

In our recipe it is now the moment to bring in the sun. Into the blender containing the dark chocolate soup are poured the egg yolks—bright yellow, full of promise of the new day. This means that the future of the society is suggested. New paradigms are presented, a fresh way of looking at old ingredients. Light and dark meet, and before they can establish lines of defense, they are again blended at high speed into something rich and strange, an amalgam of the old and settled forces with the more innocent yolks of the society. The result is heavy with promise, succulent and overpowering. Suddenly everything is blended together— suggestions for the future, ways of creating ongoing patterns, an open vision of what the society can be.

But almost immediately, when everything has been stirred in, the ingredients want to separate. Almost immediately, questions and doubts arise. "Wait a minute," the mixture seems to say. "This is too much. You seduced us! You carried us too far! You blended us in a way we're not sure we want to go." The new brew, however, is patently fascinated with itself but is weighted down by its own special- ness. How will the others "out there," the ones not in attendance in this Mousse of Transformation, ever accept so heady a concoction? "We can, of course, 'cause we are further along on the path, but 'they' can't. What shall I do at nine o'clock on Monday at the office?" Those questions come up every time. Depression threat- ens. It will never work. We know we're going to return again, separated and banded into the same tired old tribes and tribulations. Nothing, after all, ever changes. *Plus ça change, plus c'est la même chose.* "This is wonderful, Dr. Houston and Mrs. Rubin, but it is not the real world."

Social artists skillfully show people that their inevitable resistance is not patho- logical but rather a necessary stage of homeostasis. This being understood, social artists can show a group or individual how to move from homeostasis, where things remain the same, into healthy movement. In a state of homeostasis, an or- ganization, society, or person is stable and effective within a limited range. But after a certain period of time, this stability naturally begins to decay. The in- evitable process can proceed in two ways: either members can observe the signs of decay and make needed changes, thus bringing about a state we could call home- okinesis, which is characterized by a natural and gradual flow of new ideas. Japan- ese business practices are thought a good example of this process of homeokinetic growth. Workers are encouraged to make suggestions for change, and the cor- poration acts on many of these suggestions. As new ideas and projects become accepted, a stabilized flow of new ideas becomes a healthy and sustained develop- mental growth. But suppose, on the other hand, that as the state of homeostasis or balance stops working because of unsuspected events or global conditions, its members become afraid or unable to make needed change. Then society becomes mired in hyperstasis, heavy-duty stuckness. Functions become mechanical, work is done only for the paycheck, and, faced with demands for change, members are either unresponsive or radical. The demands for change as well as the radical ele- ments become stronger. In-fighting, accelerating tensions, and ineffectiveness in- crease. When new ideas and projects begin to sprout and leaders do not listen or hearken only to their own counsel, everything gets frantic and moves into hyper- kinesis, revolution. A lot of people get killed, or the organization itself blows up or becomes vulnerable to takeover, often from the worst but loudest constituents. Faced with this threat, the organization can either adapt to change or regress or even die.

Social artists understand this dynamic; they teach people both that their resistance to change is natural and that change can be handled creatively. When the inevitable resistance arises, the social artist brings in the forces of strong persuasion. I generally just stop the seminar and begin to entertain. This is akin to adding a bit of strong spirits to the mousse, such as some brandy and mint extract. Peggy will recite a poem or perform a speech from a great play, or another associate will offer a musical interlude. Invariably we discover that some attendees themselves are artists of merit. In Bangladesh we had the country's finest singer suddenly rise from the audience and thrill everyone with her songs. In Brisbane we had performances by Aboriginal dancers and an Australian comedian.

Finally, a fresh ingredient is added, one that adds spirit to the whole. The egg whites are blended into the brew, and it gets lighter and rises and gets airier. This is the moment of the larger vision, the new frame of meaning. It is often a spiritual or highly creative experience. In my seminars, participants create and perform a comical play or everyone takes part in a ritual of transition, which ends with hilarity and general whoop-de-do. This addition makes the whole experience foam and froth and become a vehicle of grace. All previous heaviness is gone. There is an angelic cast to the whole. Hope is renewed and, with it, heart. A whole-system transition occurs. One is full of light and love. One wishes one could never leave this space, these people, these ingredients.

And yet the result is still too light for complete enjoyment. The mousse must be set and chilled for a few hours. This means that objectives and plans that bring these new understandings must be given time to form. Networks can be established and plans for further meetings made; creative structures can be put in place in such a way as to offer something that the world can understand and benefit from. At this stage, the social artist in the field helps to build collaborative teaching-learning communities at every level of social groupings and to persuade others that this is the challenge and the way of the future.

In Peter Vaille's wonderful book, *Managing as a Performing Art*, we learn that business and, by extension, society as a whole requires us to navigate now in permanent white water. In the 1960s and 1970s, we navigated between quiet ponds and relatively short stretches of white water. Now it's white water all the way! The social artist presents a model for a constantly learning society, offering a compass for a white-water culture in which we can no longer manage by objectives. To continue the analogy, social artists aim to give people a paddle, a crash helmet, a sense of exhilaration, and the ability to enjoy the scenery as it flashes by as well as wave at others who have chosen to remain on shore. Ideally, the social artist also imparts the ability to give a helping push to those caught in the eddies and the backwaters.

Social artists help organizations see that changing times also require a revolution in management styles. The hierarchical management style of the past eighty years led upward through levels or workers and managers to the CEO at the top of the pyramid. This model was stable, but all decision making had to ascend through a series of cross-functioning executives at higher and higher levels; it took forever to get a real decision. In a white-water culture, what is needed are multifunctional groups pulled out from all levels of the pyramid and formed into clusters, task forces, or problem-solving teams.

This so-called new management model is really an old method, one that has been practiced with success in native and Aboriginal cultures around the world. The beauty of a multiwindowed task force is that it gives each member multiple frames of understanding. It is not unlike the way that African tribes I have visited solve problems. First they sing about the problem; then they dance about it, vision it, draw it, talk about it, dream it, and then mutually arrive at the solution. What works for human beings who learn to cook on many burners will also work for a society. Multiple frames, many participants, mutuality and connection—an ad hocracy rather than a bureaucracy—lead to solutions that are of the moment and that work for the times.

Now the process is complete, and the mousse is lathered over angel food cake. Let me top your portion with a mound of whipped cream to remind you that solutions must be presented to the world with a light touch. Take a bite and experience initial success; the sweetness is exquisite. One is made new. One loses one's disbelief. Everything is possible. In the great words of the Madwoman of Chaillot, "We can begin again."

Would you like some coffee? I have a dark Kona roast ready, steaming hot, or for those of you, like me, who do not drink coffee, a cup of Twinings Earl Grey tea. Steaming, comforting, aromatic brews bring us to natural conclusions, confirm the warmth we all feel for each other, and prepare us for the road home. My husband Bob prompts me to offer you a liqueur or brandy and brings out his favorites, Calvados and old Armagnac. (He also grumbles, "Where was the beef?") But, please, stay awake on your return and never forget that your life is a feast. And as actress Loretta Young used to say, in a swirling skirt and a blazing smile (for those of you mature enough to remember), "Good night. And shall we see you next week?"

12

ATHENA

It is February 1990 in Rishikesh, India. I am steeped in Hindu mythology and culture, having just used the great Indian epic poem, the Ramayana, *as the basis for a ten-day seminar for leaders of India's educational, business, health, and governmental communities. The seminar was the culmination of six weeks of deep exploration into India's human and cultural potential, and I lectured, advised, and lived and worked with various groups and castes throughout India. I have stayed with the richest maharajas as well as with the poorest untouchables, convened with lepers, and consulted with Mother Teresa. I had been through every temple I could convince my companions to stop and see, and my dreams are phantasmagorias of many-armed deities, elephant-headed gods, dancing Shivas, and the terrible eyes of Kali.*

In this god-intoxicated country, I myself have been taken for more than I am. One day I was wearing a white caftan that flowed to my feet, my long hair was down, and my eyes were covered in dark glasses to keep out the astonishing brightness of the

Indian sun. In the morning we visited the temple of a mother goddess. Some teenage boys happened to look my way and began to make fun of my height and unusual appearance. Suddenly I swept off my dark glasses and gave them my most sinister stare. "Kali! Kali!" they shrieked and went running off. Later that day we were visiting the temple devoted to the goddess Lakshmi, who gives prosperity and all good things. As I emerged from the dark temple into the sunlight, an old beggar woman who was waiting outside fell back and then timidly came over to me. Our guide translated what she was saying. "When I first saw you, I thought you were Lakshmi herself come into this place." Needless to say, I gave her considerable baksheesh. But the crowning event occurred toward sunset. We were visiting the cathedral of Saint Thomas, which was so full for the Sunday service that we couldn't get in. (Thomas was said to have traveled from the Holy Land and set up a Christian mission in southern India in the first century. The church even housed the bone of doubting Thomas's finger, the one that Jesus had invited to touch his wounds. One is encouraged to touch the bone through the wad of scotch tape that is its only covering.) As we were wandering around the precincts of the church, the mass suddenly ended, and a group of young children, dressed in white Western clothes, came running near us. Suddenly they stopped, pointed at me, and screamed, "Jesus Christ! Jesus Christ is here!" I made tracks and headed back to the car, followed by many, many Christian Indians. Only in India could one be mistaken for a god three times in one day. My companions, Hindu, Muslim, and Christian, found this wildly funny, and I was teased unmercifully throughout the remainder of the trip.

Still, I am drawn to one figure, the goddess Saraswati, who guides the arts and literature as the goddess of education and culture. Riding on a swan, she holds a book in one hand and a stringed musical instrument called the vina in the other. She is an entirely beneficent goddess, thought by many to be the Hindu equivalent of Athena. On the day that honors Saraswati, many scholars, poets, teachers, and students come to one of India's great rivers to bathe and ask her blessings for their endeavors. Especially important in her rite is bathing in the Ganges near Rishikesh, and so on Saraswati day, there are often thousands of scholarly pilgrims doing just that.

I find myself, then, on Saraswati day sitting on the bank of the Ganges looking into the vista that has helped so many yogis and holy folk meditate on spiritual matters. I, however, am intent on getting a glimpse of Saraswati herself. I could certainly use her help with the pile of manuscripts I have committed myself to writing. I close my eyes and call upon her. No Saraswati. I open my eyes and hope she will appear. No Saraswati. I recall my similar attempts years before with the Virgin Mary and remember that although she did not show up so that I could see her, something much more did appear. I renew my efforts to invoke the epiphany of Saraswati. Nothing. Nada. The only voice I hear is that of my friend and associate Peggy Rubin, who calls, "Jean! Jean! It's time to get back on the bus!"

Seconds later, the most beautiful voice I have ever heard begins to call my name, a voice with a lilting Hindu accent and full of the music of birds and the vina. "Jean,

Jean," the melodious voice continues to call me. I scramble up the bank and find a tiny woman crouched in a fetal position lying on the sand. She is wearing a pink sari and seems very old and sick. Her eyes are bright with fever and yet with something else, some unquenchable fire of life.

I sit down next to her, and she tells me her story. She had come down the day before on the train from Delhi to bathe in the waters of the Ganges in hopes that Saraswati would relieve her fever and her illness. She had been an educator all her life and had taught all grades from kindergarten through graduate school. Her specialty was English literature. We continue talking for the better part of an hour about education in India and in the United States—education as the major hope for the world's peoples. We share our schemes for improving education and agree that every child is different and that there is no such thing as a stupid child, only incredibly stupid systems of education that diminish the mind's powers and demean the soul. We talk about restoring art to the curriculum and about inviting children to learn through all their senses. My friends try to get me to board the bus we have rented. I wave them away and continue talking to this luminous woman. She tells me that she had missed the train because of her fever and now is waiting for the fever to pass so that she can get up enough energy to find another train. I give her aspirin to take her fever down and even try out a little energy healing through my hands, which seems to help her feel better. I ask her if she is now teaching, and she replies that she is not, owing to the fact that she is too old and too sick. "How old are you?" I ask, thinking by the looks of her that she must be in her seventies.

"I am forty-eight," she answers, and I become very quiet.

I offer to take her with us on our trip north, but she refuses, saying that she will eventually be fine. I discover, however, that she has little money on her, so I insist that she take some of mine. She refuses, I insist, and finally she takes it. Although it does not seem to be much, she tells me that it is enough for her to live on for six months. I offer to arrange for her to have a support community of fellow educators belonging to the Institute of Cultural Affairs, if she wishes. She thanks me and struggles to sit up.

She takes my hands, looks in my eyes, and says to me, "I came here to the Ganges to find Saraswati. I have found Saraswati. You are Saraswati."

I hold her hands in mine and say, "No, you are Saraswati." And we both laugh and bow to each other, hands pressed in the namaste position, and I turn and leave.

Sitting by the window in the bus watching the Ganges go by, pilgrims bathing, cattle and children and clothes being washed in its holy waters, I knew that I had met Saraswati, the principle of education in her current form. Sick, feverish, unsupported, perhaps even dying, she was possessed, nevertheless, with a spirit so bright and a hope and vision so earnest that there was no doubt that she would soon rise out of the sands of her diminishment. I had gone looking for Saraswati in her ancient form, and, as with my quest for the Virgin Mary, had found her in her current guise, a Lady of sorrows and sickness, yes, but also a Lady who knew and honored the genius in all of us and who was resolved to bring it into light.

"What is the most beautiful island in Greece?" we asked the elegant Greek gentle-man on the plane to Athens. My college friends Jenny Ballard, Mary Lou Jacobs, and I were beginning our postgraduation adventure. We hung over our seats on the plane, straining to hear the gentleman's travel advice.

"Why do you want to know such a thing?" he asked.

"Because my friends and I want to sit on the shore and read Plato there," I replied.

"Ah, well then, you want to go to . . ." The plane suddenly dropped a few hun-dred feet, and the man's words were lost in the downdraft and his thick Greek ac-cent.

As we left the airport in Athens, we debated the name of the island. "He said it was Siros," Jenny assured us. "No, he definitely called it Skyros," Mary Lou de-murred. "I sat closest to him, and I'm sure he said it was Siphenos," I insisted. "Or maybe it was Spyros, like the name of the movie producer."

We were still arguing later that evening while we climbed up to the Acropolis to see it by moonlight. On the night of the full moon, they were keeping it open for visitors.

At the first sight of the Parthenon, I crossed the threshold into forever. Time stopped or was flooded by eternity. All temporal tenses were strained. I was here. I had been here. I would be here thousands of years before and yet to come. A shaft of lunar light appeared under my feet, a pathway sent from moon and marble col-umn, and it beckoned me into the Parthenon. I climbed the steps into the temple and found myself standing in the center, looking up toward where the forty-two-foot statue of the goddess Athena would have been, but I saw only the full moon.

It was then that the chanting began, an archaic hymnody, intoned in a minor key by many marrow-chilling voices. It swept around the columns and moved to the other temples, a ghost sound from thousands of years past traveling through the Acropolis. We tried to follow it, first into the little temple of Athena, then into the Erechtheion, then back again into the Parthenon. The chanting circled us like smoke, raising the hair on the napes of our necks, making our flesh crawl, our breath quicken.

After about fifteen minutes of the most exquisite terror I have ever known, we finally discovered the source. Not a hundred yards below us was the ancient the-ater of Herodes Atticus, where a rehearsal of Sophocles' *Oedipus at Colonus* was going on. The acoustics were such that the sound echoed from temple to temple, a mystic liturgy that was to me an initiation, a sacrament of light and sound, a re-membrance of things past and a new ordering of my future.

The next morning I returned to the Acropolis and, to the consternation of my friends who wanted to go sightseeing, refused to leave. "I've found my place," I told them, settling on the steps of the small Temple of Athena Nike across from the Parthenon. "You go on without me."

Throughout the morning and afternoon I sat there, almost unmoving, having come home. I had no thoughts, no memories, no desires. Everything in my life, it seemed, had led to this point, this perfect point, poised between the sun-washed white and blue of temple and sky. Then, late in the afternoon, my friends returned.

"Here, read these," Jenny said as she thrust into my hand three telegrams that she had picked up at the American Express office. "Have you been sitting in the Temple of Athena all this time?"

Reluctantly, I opened the telegrams and found myself at a crossroads. Over the past several years I had received a number of off-Broadway awards for acting and directing. On the basis of these, I had been invited, in the weeks before graduating from college, to audition for several acting companies. Now they were notifying me of their decisions. One telegram was from a major Hollywood studio offering me a seven-year contract. I crumpled it with an air of disdain. Having grown up in show business, I thought I knew all about those contracts. The second telegram was more interesting. It was from the estimable director Margaret Webster, offering me a chance to participate in the finals for the role of Jane Eyre opposite Errol Flynn. I knew that casting wouldn't work. I had no real ingenue-ity, and besides, Errol was three inches shorter than me. But the third telegram held it all. It was from the remarkable producer and director Joseph Papp, inviting me to play Viola in *Twelfth Night* at his annual Shakespeare festival in New York's Central Park. Papp had played Olivia to my Viola during the auditions, and each of us had been moved by the other's performance. The telegram said I would have to return immediately to begin rehearsals. I was thrilled by the prospect and could feel the adrenaline rising to catapult me down the Acropolis and onto the next plane home.

"Yes! Yes! Yes!" all my years of training in the theater shouted. "This is it. This is what you were meant for!"

"No," a still, quiet voice whispered. I shivered as the presence within the voice became stronger.

"What do you mean, no?" I retorted to the great No Body who now filled the space.

"No," it replied. "If you say yes to this, it will mean a life in theater and films."

"That's right!" I exclaimed with enthusiasm. "Let's go!"

"No," it or she countered. The presence seemed to be feminine and strong— very strong. "Your life can have another meaning, take a different direction. You can be part of a larger story."

"Larger than the theater?" The notion seemed shocking, almost amoral. Who was this, anyway, and why was she bothering me? Was the voice behind me or within me?

"Yes, larger than the theater."

"Okay." At that moment *someone,* whom I later felt to be Athena, the lady my mother had met in dreams in the temple while she was pregnant with me, moved into my life and *something,* a life in the theater, definitely moved out.

The next morning my friends and I traveled to Cape Sounion to see the beautiful temple of Poseidon. As we drove down the coast, I regaled them with tales of

the bitter feuds between Athena and Poseidon; how Athena had become the goddess of Athens when the city's mothers and fathers thought her gift of the olive
tree much more useful than Poseidon's gift of the horse; how she had rescued
Odysseus from the wrath of the sea god Poseidon by pleading his case before her
father Zeus and the Olympian gods while Poseidon was off to an Ethiopian party
in his honor. As we reached the temple site, I remarked, "You know, there are some
archaeologists who believe that this temple was really dedicated to Athena and not
to Poseidon." I probably shouldn't have said that.

As we wandered around the magnificent ruins, I discovered the place where
Lord Byron had carved his name into a pillar. I listened as a group of English
tourists were told by their guide that Byron had dived into the sea from the rocks
below the temple. Within minutes I was in my bathing suit and swooping into the
wine-dark sea, emulating the romantic poet. As my hands hit the water, I saw too
late that I was about to plunge through a huge Portuguese man-of-war jellyfish. I
managed to flip my legs away from the jellyfish, but my hands and arms up to my
elbows sank into the stinging blob. The wrath of Poseidon was no mere metaphor.

As we drove back to Athens, my hands and arms began to raise welts and itch
furiously. "Let's get to the island of whatchamacallit, and I'll recuperate there," I
told my worried friends. At the ticket office near the boat docks, we tried out the
names of the island to a growing crowd of interested Greek men. After much de-
bate among themselves, they put us on a boat that was just leaving for "island very
beautiful, very quiet, very few people, no problem." We sat on the deck among
chickens and goats and old women dressed in black. I felt like Odysseus ready for
an island adventure. To keep from scratching my now bubbling hands I pulled out
my tattered copy of the *Odyssey* and read of the Cyclops and the winds of Aeolus
and Circe of the braided tresses. A little piglet nudged me, looking for food.

When we finally landed, we discovered that the island was indeed beautiful and
quiet and rarely had tourists. There was a small hotel on the other side, where we
promptly repaired to settle in and read Plato. News of my hands, however, had
spread, and we were soon visited by many of the island's residents, who came to
view my stupendous appendages, which now looked like two big pots full of
burned tapioca pudding. No one spoke English, but each after viewing, locals
would make a sound like "po po po po po" and offer archaic forms of help. An ancient crone came riding up on a donkey and covered my hands with garlic, lemon
juice, and olive oil. That seemed to help. A man lathered them in baby powder and
tied on tight gauze bandages. That didn't. The richest man on the island, the one
with the 1939 automobile, poured on hot retsina wine and fish roe as others
watched respectfully.

With each of the visitors, Jenny tried out words for *telephone, telegraph, doctor,
hospital,* and *boat back to Athens.* She received in response shrugs and negatives,
except for the boat part. The boat, they indicated, wouldn't be back for a week.
Meanwhile, the pain and swelling worsened. My hands were turning interesting

colors—blue, green, iridescent. Each morning I would go down to the shore and try to read Plato on virtue, love, education, and the perfect state. Mostly, however, I found myself praying to Plato for some miracle. I no longer could sleep for the pain and itching. I couldn't even get my dress off over my hands, they were now so huge.

One morning at dawn I was running along the beach to escape the pain, when I heard a motorboat. It headed toward the dock of the only other house on this part of the island. I ran toward the dock waving my monstrous hands, hoping to flag down the boat. But I was too late, for it deposited a number of passengers and immediately sped away. I ran wild-eyed toward the four passengers, a couple and their two children.

The husband looked at me and said calmly in excellent English, "I had better have a look at those." He picked up a black bag and immediately began to tend my hands by lancing them and applying the latest in cortisone treatments, which he "just happened" to have with him. As he worked, he and his wife introduced themselves. He was a physician, head of the Veterans Administration hospital in Athens. He had earned his medical degree abroad in New York at Bellevue Hospital. There he had met his wife, who had attended Barnard College about twelve years before I had.

I was on the verge of developing gangrene, he informed me, and it was a miracle that he showed up when he did; otherwise I would have surely lost my hands or worse.

"But how did you happen to come here?" I asked. "Nobody ever comes here."

"It's true, " the doctor responded. "Normally on our vacation we go to one of the better-known islands like Corfu or Kos, but this time something different happened. Tell her about it, Virginia." His wife filled me in on the miracle part of the story.

"As a child," she said, "I grew up on the stories of Dr. Doolittle. I especially liked the parts where he would put a blindfold on one of the animals while he spun a globe and had the animal point to a place on it. Then Doolittle and the animals would travel there. When I read these stories to my own children, they begged that we let them do the same. We said we'd do it, but only on the map of the Greek islands and only if they got good grades. So a few days ago we blindfolded little Penelope, spun her around, and pushed her to the map to stick her pin in. This is the island that she stuck it on. We were able through friends in Athens to find a house for rent here and charter a boat from another island, and here we are."

"But clearly we are here for you," the doctor added. "The gods must love you."

Perhaps they did, but as with Odysseus, they had strange ways of proving it, for a month later I found myself caught up in another harrowing adventure on yet another Greek island. I had blithely eaten and drunk everything offered me, until I came down with typhoid fever in Crete. In the throne room of the reconstructed palace of Minos in Knossos, I slid to the ground as the fever overtook me. Jenny dragged me onto the bus that was heading for the mountains, thinking that I only had the usual case of *turista*. The bus driver was drunk, singing loudly as he lurched the bus around hairpin curves that overlooked thousand-foot drops.

Several old women came over to look at me as I lay dying, it seemed, on the floor of the bus and then, with the characteristic "po po po po po" that I had learned to dread, went to argue with the bus driver.

He loudly refused their request. "Oheeee" (no), he shouted over and over again but finally capitulated to their threats and berating and drove his bus into the interior. There the old women led me out and into the ancient fifth-century church of Aghios Yorgias (Saint George), the patron saint of healing on the island. The church had itself been built over a healing shrine to Asclepios, the healing god of ancient Greece.

Inside I was introduced to a very tall and beautiful old priest whose long white hair and beard had yellowed with age. He gently led me to the altar, and I saw that the church was covered with small votive images in silver and gold of parts of the body—legs, arms, stomach, liver—representing body parts healed by the good Saint George. The priest prayed over me, and the women brought me back to the bus. We got off in a remote village where we were asked if we wanted a first-class or a second-class hotel. "Second class," we exclaimed and were led to a fifth-class pensione. "Class Epsilon," it said on the wall, and we were given straw mats to sleep on and hot egg and lemon soup to drink.

"Never have I seen anyone so sick with so much," a strange little doctor giggled as he examined me. He left a few aspirin tablets and departed, afraid for some reason to treat an American girl. As my temperature mounted, I began to have hallucinations. I had been reading Robert Graves's *The White Goddess* as well as viewing the murals on the walls of Knossos, and it seemed to me that the goddess of ancient Crete, complete with flounced skirt, major hairdo, naked breasts, and snakes crawling up her arms, walked back and forth across my room all night, chanting ancient Cretan hymns. I remember regretting that I didn't have a tape recorder handy. Jenny stuck a thermometer in my mouth and gasped when it read 105.5 degrees Fahrenheit. "But you're supposed to be dead!"

"Well, I'm getting there," I muttered. And in fact it seemed that I was fast approaching some kind of end. I felt electricity leaving my body. I found myself at a kind of open doorway, and as I put one foot over the doorstep, it seemed that the light in the room where I was lying dimmed, while the light in the room I was about to enter grew brighter. It seemed very pleasant and quite normal in that room I was about to enter.

"Wait a minute," I suddenly said to my departing soul. "I'm only nineteen years old. I'm not ready to go into that room yet. No!" And with an enormous effort of will, I pushed myself back across the threshold and returned to my sickroom, whereupon the light in it grew brighter again. Shortly after that my fever broke, and I slowly returned to full health.

Several months later, in lieu of my theater career, I entered graduate school, where I plunged into a study of the philosophy of religion including its myths, archetypes, and symbols. I was blessed with great teachers—Jacob Taubes, Paul Tillich, Reinhold Niebuhr, Paul Ricoeur, Tom Driver. I also studied ancient Greek, and while I had never been a good student in modern languages, learning Greek seemed more like remembering, so that within the period of an intensive six-week summer course, I had a fairly good grasp of it. The only problem was that the course, taught at Union Theological Seminary, was in New Testament Greek. The textbook had been written by a minister of the previous century, so we found ourselves declining verbs with a calculated slant: *I sin; you sin; he, she, it sins. We atone; you atone; they are guilty.* Wanting to read Homer in the original, I continued my studies myself, discovering quite a different vocabulary than the one offered in the course.

For all the joys of the life of the mind in that first year in graduate school, my face betrayed a different experience, at once both curious and macabre. The poisons that had entered my system in the dive through the jellyfish began to emerge again under the slightest provocation. The dog would graze my face with his paw. Almost immediately the scratch would become virulent, the skin of the entire face and neck and shoulders heaving with running sores. I would get angry at someone. Instead of merely turning mildly pink, I would soon have the face of Job, which I had once dared God to bestow on me. In a class on Hebrew Scriptures, I looked so much like a bad day in the Old Testament that students nervously moved away from me lest they catch the plague. The only way they could stand me was if I showed up swathed in bandages like the mummy of Hatshepsut. Did I have a penchant for ancient diseases as well as ancient languages? It seemed that from that moment in late spring when the voice in the Temple of Athena caused me to turn down a career in the theater, I was haunted for a year or more by life-threatening situations, crushing losses, inexplicable events. It was as if, having denied a natural calling for which I had been highly prepared, my mettle was being tested to see if I could withstand the blasts of an angry fate before I would be allowed to continue on my new path.

What that path was to be I still was not certain, even though I soon began to lecture in the department of religion at Columbia, enduring a pedagogical baptism by fire as I taught hundreds of male students who were generally older than I. By the age of twenty, in addition to my graduate studies, I was teaching six courses, marking almost a thousand papers, and being paid the princely sum of five hundred dollars a year as salary. Shortly thereafter, the LSD research began and, with it, my career in human potentials research.

Thus those early adventures in Greece not only set me on the journey toward my life's work but also began what has been my most significant spiritual relationship. Whatever it was that came so forcefully into my life and consciousness—construct of my unconscious, goddess, archetype, numinous borderline person, beloved partner of the soul—soon became for me both path and goal, a pattern for my self's unfolding, an adviser on matters both practical and spiritual, a companion on the journey, and my deepest and most original friend.

For many years after those events, however, I was not particularly conscious of this relationship. My situation was not unlike the scene in the *Odyssey* in which the hero, disguised as a beggar, is talking with his wife Penelope, who does not know that the man before her is actually her long-absent husband. Finally, Eurycleia, Odysseus' old nurse, bathes his feet and recognizes him by a scar on his leg. Her excitement should betray the beggar's identity to Penelope, but for reasons of plot and circumstance, Odysseus must not yet be revealed, and therefore Penelope does not notice the hysterical joy of the nurse. As Homer tells us, speaking of Penelope, Athena "had turned her thoughts aside."

My thoughts were also turned elsewhere, and I probably would have continued in this state of only mild interest in Athena but for the fact that around 1969 my mother gave me a medallion based on an ancient coin that showed the face of Athena. At the time, I put it away, being something of snob about wearing a modern reproduction when I was surrounded by so many genuine antiquities. Then in 1972, I found the medallion while cleaning out a drawer. Evidently the time was right, for I began to wear it. As I did, I became aware that Athena had always been a part of my life. The *Odyssey,* in which Athena is the leading archetypal character, has always been my favorite book, and I had read it yearly. My favorite high school teacher, Mrs. Finnegan, was in appearance and manner an Athena look-alike. I had designed my own wedding dress to look like the garments worn by an ancient statue of Athena in the Louvre. Under LSD and in trance, research subjects frequently and spontaneously identified me with Athena. This is not surprising, for since I am tall and sturdy and have a face described as classical, a person in an altered state of consciousness could easily project this archetype onto me. I could never be taken for Aphrodite, and Isis belongs to another ilk as well. However, as I began to use the medallion as a focus for some of my meditations, it became clear that the fractal waves of recurring Athena imagery were not just an outer phenomenon in my life but resided in the inner reaches of my mind.

As my meditations continued, the relationship became stronger, and I began to feel myself accompanied by the archetype. Over the years of living this relationship, I have asked several times for proof that this being, who seems so near, is more than merely a figment of my classically attuned imagination. It seems, as I look back, that every three years or so I enter into a state in which I decide that I know nothing and it's time to start all over again. At those points I sometimes challenge the gods. I have a long fractal history of doing so: witness my pleading with the Virgin Mary to show up in the closet, the challenge that my ten-year-old self made to the supernatural allies to come forth, and my yelling at God when I was a devastated eighteen. But there have been many other occasions as well, which leads me to wonder if strong emotion allied with some form of *kenosis*—a

giving up or giving over—perhaps sparks a response from a higher frequency domain. This has always been the case with the archetypal presence that I have come
to think of as Athena.

In March 1979 I was in one of those three-year cycles of roaring self-doubt.
Margaret Mead had died a few months earlier, and I was about to lead a major
conference of government leaders, for which I felt I was profoundly unsuited. So I
ran away for a week to Greece, which I continued to think of as my soul's home.
Bob and I decided to go to Crete, as I had not been there since my near-death experience with typhoid fever. When I arrived, my inner darkness increased, and
being on Crete definitely had something to do with it. "If I believed in reincarnation," my husband said, observing my dolorous mood, "I'd swear you went
through some very bad times here a couple of thousand years ago or so. Why
don't we walk the Samarian Gorge and see if that won't snap you out of it." The
Samarian Gorge is a chasm of Dantesque proportions well known to hikers. One
climbs and descends and scrambles over boulders and fords streams through
about eleven miles of spectacular if daunting landscape. Wiser travelers ride don-
keys. As we hiked the gorge, every belief I held dear fell away, every sense of purpose or meaning was discarded, and when we collapsed many hours later at the
sea, I was nothing but a great quivering blob of doubt and despair.

"Let's get to Delphi," I said, hoping that in that high and holy place I might find
my soul again. A day later we were in Delphi, and out of my moroseness I decided
to challenge the gods, specifically Athena. I fingered the modern Athena medallion
around my neck and said, "Athena, if you really exist, I want you to show up as a real
coin from the ancient world." I knew how well-nigh impossible this was, since such
coins were rare and even more rarely sold in Greece, which had strict rules about
selling any antiquities. Less than a minute after offering this challenge, I found myself looking at modern reproductions of Athena coins in the Vafiades shop. As I
sadly contemplated the beautiful reproductions, Mrs. Vafiades, an English woman,
came over and said, "Would you by any chance be looking for a real one?"

"You have ancient coins with the head of Athena?" I asked in some surprise.

"We have two," she replied and brought them out. One was an archaic Athena
from the early fifth century B.C.E. It was in poor condition, however, and the features were blurred. But the second coin, a large Tetra Drachma from around 87
B.C.E. bearing a Hellenistic head was in perfect condition. "Get that one, Jean,"
Bob said. "It looks just like you."

Still I needed proof, and Mr. Vafiades came over and introduced himself. I realized from my reading that he was considered one of the leading numismatic experts in Greece. He gave me letters of proof of the antiquity of my coin, and I paid
the asking price. You do not quibble with the gods when they come through, and
I've been wearing the coin, set in a medallion, ever since.

Three years later, I found myself back once again in my usual state of discovering that I knew nothing. In a slough of despond and needing some proof from the

universe that meaning and purpose could be found in it and in my life as well, I said, "Athena, if you exist, please show up as a statue or portrait bust from the ancient world." Now I knew that this was impossible, since most of these statues were in museums and those few in circulation were prohibitively expensive. Two days later, unsought and unexpected, a xeroxed page showing Greek and Roman antiquities arrived in the mail. On the page was a blurred picture of a bust of Athena for sale. It didn't look like much, and it seemed small, and the price, twenty-five thousand dollars, was far more than I could afford. Nevertheless, since apparently my challenge was being taken seriously, I decided to go along with it. I asked my mother in her role as an interior designer to contact Dr. Jerry Eisenberg, owner of the Royal Athena Gallery who was offering the bust, to see about buying the statue for me. After examining my financial resources, I offered the most that I could, twelve thousand dollars. My mother phoned me back within the hour telling me that my offer had been accepted and that the Athena head would be shipped immediately from the gallery in La Jolla, California. A week later a large and heavy shipping crate arrived. Why was the crate so big, I wondered? The head had seemed very small from the picture. We pried it open to reveal—a masterpiece! Here was a larger-than-life marble head of the goddess made by a Greek master sculptor in the first century. The next day Eisenberg called me in a state of shock. "Do you realize what I have just sold you and at a fraction of its value?"

"Yes, Jerry. Why did you do it? And why did you offer it in the catalog at such a low price?"

"That I can explain," he answered. "I had had a fire in my gallery, which destroyed a number of antiquities I was showing on commission. In order to pay back the owners, I needed to sell things from my own collection quickly. That's why I priced them below their normal value and sent out xeroxed pictures of my collections to everyone who had ever bought anything from me. When your low offer came in, I don't know what happened to me, but I accepted it."

"And now you want the statue returned?"

"No, I sold it to you fair and square. It's yours. I just wanted to be sure that you know you have a masterpiece."

Indeed I do know that. The beautiful head of Athena now occupies a prominent place in my home and is central to my meditations.

My most recent challenge to the goddess took place a few years ago in yet another period of unknowing. This time I said to her, "Athena, if you exist, I'd like you to show up as a surprise." Several days later, Elizabeth Shuey and Annie Roberts, mystics and nature conservationists whom I knew at the time only slightly, called to tell me that they had received in meditation the awareness that they were to build me a meditation cottage on their beautiful land in southern Oregon, since I needed a quiet and serene place in the middle of a forest to recollect myself and be nurtured for my work in the world. I was to help in the costs of construction, which would not be very much since they were using their own lumber and doing most of the work themselves. I had never had such a gift and protested their generosity, but they insisted that they had their orders and this is what they had to do.

As the year progressed, the cottage grew larger than they intended, with high ceilings, a wrap-around porch, and large floor-to-ceiling windows showing spectacular views of the mountains, waterfalls, and even an eagle's nest. When I arrived to see the completed house, I was stunned to read the name carved in blue letters on a sign by the door—"ATHENA." My friends knew nothing of my history with Athena. They said that while they were working on the house, one of them sensed the presence of an ancient goddess who came down the hill and announced that this was her place and that they should name it after her. The house seemed to design itself and took on the lineaments of the archaic Greek style of temple before pillared marble became fashionable. All my friends who stay in the house sense something going on there: "an opening between the worlds," says one; "a sacred and magical place," say others. "I heard the most beautiful music all through the night. It's as if the house were singing," says one, while a young child insists that "a beautiful lady came by before I went to sleep, and we talked and then she sang to me." I must confess that I do not hear or see anything unusual while staying there except the extraordinary beauty and peace of the house and its environs, but there is no question that the place is loaded with presence. "Athena, if you exist," I often think, "why not show up so that even I can see you with my rational, overly educated eyes?" Perhaps someday she will.

Some years ago I decided to try to dialogue with Athena using my computer. As I have been greatly enamored of computers since the 1970s and have a near-religious belief in their efficacy and magic, I figured that a conversation with an archetype could only be enhanced through using this, to me, holy medium. Whether the conversations that ensued are the product of my own creative unconscious process or something greater and apart from myself, I will probably never know, but the goddess or that part of myself that I have come to identify with that archetype has, over the years, provided me with some deep and wonderful insights. Here is a typical interchange:

JEAN: Athena, Goddess, how then shall we begin?
ATHENA: We should begin with my quandary. I am more than real and less than fact. I live in myth and am felt in time. My image is everywhere, and my body is nowhere. Great cities were laid in my name as well as thousands of institutions, then as well as now, and yet I am homeless. There has not been a moment in the past five thousand years, not one second, when I was not evoked by someone somewhere, and yet practically no one believes that I exist.
JEAN: And do you exist?
ATHENA: I do.

JEAN: You are not a figment of my classically attuned imagination?

ATHENA: No more than you are a figment of my modernistically inclined one.

JEAN: Goddess, have some parts of you been sleeping through the last several hundred years?

ATHENA: Not sleeping, no, but not well used, either.

JEAN: What would be good use of a goddess in our time?

ATHENA: The task is much larger now than it was then. That is why I have to be called on anew.

JEAN: Goddess, what are some of the new things that you do?

ATHENA: Many of them are old things in new form. Remember that I am essentially a weaver, but now I no longer work with wool but with mind and culture, body and spirit. Weaving is always the metaphor for my wisdom and power over human possibilities. I am supremely the goddess or archetype of those who would reweave, who would reorchestrate, who would take the threads of what is given and reweave them for new possibilities.

I am reweaving the planet into new forms, new connections. With humankind, I am helping to reweave their minds, their nervous systems. But this is where humans and gods must partner each other. I wish we were speaking now in old Greek, for the English does not contain the subtlety to hold the thought of gods. But we will give it a try.

In the realm of gods and humans, an alliance is made between those who have much of the same kind of qualities. That's why I say it's very important for each person to find that ally, that archetype, that is deeply appropriate to that person, just as I was the innate and natural archetype of Odysseus. Because the qualities between us were the same, in the larger reality where everything is interrelated, we were and are part of the same family.

JEAN: Athena, where do you and the other archetypes exist?

ATHENA: Our existence pervades yours as well as opening to another continent of spirit. I do not have the same kind of living in space and time as you do. What you sometimes think of as space-time gives some idea of the quality of where and how I live.

JEAN: Are you mainly a psychological or mythic construct?

ATHENA: I am more in the order of an in-struct. I am both coding and pattern, as in many ways you are.

JEAN: Why are goddess archetypes rising in the cultures of the Earth today?

ATHENA: Because you are all in a culture that requires the specificity of the goddess archetype in order to survive and grow its next phase. The earlier forms of more masculine concepts of God, the male metapatterns, although persisting, need the concept of the Earth herself and the goddess archetype to heal and make whole their development. Similarly, the goddess archetype has to be extended, joined with humans, and allowed her next phase of growth.

JEAN: All right, Goddess. How do we begin to establish closer connections with our archetypes?

ATHENA: You might begin by reviewing the parallels between the life and times of your archetype and your own life. Look for the similarities and the correspondences. Often you will find that your strengths and your sorrows, the very progress of your journey, will prove remarkably similar to the mythic life of the archetype. Aspects of the archetypal story are your own story writ large.

JEAN: Having done that, Goddess, I ask now for all of us how we can nurture this knowing.

ATHENA: The nurturance comes about by your being able to hold us in your heart as well. Now that you see the parallels in our stories, we can be emotionally known at a closer, more intimate vantage. Each must try to see his or her archetype in many ways—visually, kinesthetically, as felt or heard presence. You must dance with us if you wish to know us.

Our growing task is one in which we operate as a single beingness, our own identities merged, although sometimes confluent. Then the "we" that is that identity can use more of human and archetypal skills both to understand and to perform the task given us.

JEAN: And that is?

ATHENA: This is to be part of the awakening; to give to many beings—human and archetypal—their impetus to evolve, to serve as planetary catalytic agents of this. The seeding and coding is already within human beings. The impetus often is not, or, if it is, it has gotten fogged by the demands of their lives and the loss of meaning.

There's more. You all must try and devote days to staying with your archetype almost continually, days in which you have a fair amount of freedom to do this. This kind of time builds up the connections between us.

As you grow the relationship to your archetype, the archetype dwells more and more within you. Then we can be bridged into your world, rendered diaphanous to your world, and you to ours. That is the key exchange, not unlike nutrients that pass through the membrane of an organism. It becomes a healing exchange, with the archetype holding the higher "pattern" of "you" that can come through—not just for the healing of you but for the "wholing" of you and the deepening of the world.

Following Athena's advice and my own practice, I advise my students to use their journals to dialogue actively with their archetypes, however they are felt and known, whether as gods and goddesses, the higher self, the lower self, the child self, the self-to-be. Such journal dialogues may take the form of an interview where we ask the questions and the god or other self provides the answers. Or we may decide to engage two or more archetypes at the same time and let them talk with each other, in which case the dialogue may begin to look more like a play. It is also possible to dialogue with people, events, works, the body, the world, the emotions, symbols, and other topics. The dialogue may seem unnatural at first, but the main thing is not to censor what comes out of the pen or the keyboard. Where silence enters in, the silence should be allowed. When the dialogue is complete, I always tell my students to exit gracefully, thanking the other for its time and words.

Although dialoguing with Athena on the computer came easily to me and was a deeply satisfying activity, in general, I do not like to write, in spite of my many published books and articles. I find writing constraining, confounding, and almost always confusing to the point of what I really have to say. I am essentially a teacher, and it is in communing with students and audiences that I find my true voice and the dimensions of my mind. This aversion to writing began when I was about nine years old and found myself in a school that emphasized children writing daily themes as part of their homework. I had already been typing for a year, which the teacher greatly appreciated, since my handwriting in those days looked like a drunken chicken scrawling Sanskrit. One day I took my theme out of my bookbag to give it to the teacher, when I noticed that it didn't look at all like my typing. In fact, it didn't look like my writing, although the assigned topic was the same. What's more, it had an attached note that read, "Hey, Jeanie-pot, Your stuff stinks. Here, I wrote you another one that will get you an A. Love, Dad."

As the teacher came down the aisle to collect our papers, I tried to hide mine in the desk, but she reached for it anyway. "Please, Miss Johnson," I begged, "let me have it back. I don't feel good about it and would like to do a little rewriting."

"Nonsense," said Miss Johnson and snatched my father's work out of my hands.

The following day, Miss Johnson announced to the class, "Jean Houston has written the most wonderful theme. Would you read it, dear?"

I gulped but got up and reluctantly moved to the front of the classroom and, following the family motto that, regardless of all circumstances, including war, catastrophe, and uncertain morality, the show must go on, I read my father's piece with great expression. At least, I figured, I could put something into it that was mine. To the sound of much laughter and applause, I grumped back to my seat.

That afternoon my father asked me, "How'd we do?"

"You got an A. And Dad, don't you ever do that again. It's not right."

"Hot damn," my father chortled. "I got an A in the fifth grade."

That night I took special care with my homework theme, trying to give it a more humorous flavor so that the teacher would not catch on. The next morning in class, as I reached for my theme, I noticed that once again the typing was not mine. The note read, "Hey, kid, This will get you an A-plus. Dad."

"Oh, no," I moaned, hiding the note as Miss Johnson took the theme out of my hand.

My father seemed to regard this as a great joke, in spite of my complaints, and time and again he would try to slip his rewrites into my bookbag. I took to making carbon copies and always having a spare of my own work to hand in, painfully trying to joke it up in my own feeble fashion so as to resemble my father's brilliant and comic replacement. However, whenever I was able to hand in one of my very own themes, Miss Johnson would call me aside and say, "Jean, dear, this is so much less than you are capable of. Is there something wrong?"

As a result, I grew to hate and dread writing, and it was a long time before I could write a decent composition. Some would say that all my books and papers are merely compensation for the long years of trauma regarding writing. Others, however, who believe what I have surmised about symptoms as prefigural fractals of a higher achievement, would say that I was basically a writer but needed the dad-given trauma to shore up the talent until I had something important to say. New Age folk, commenting on my prolific output, often tell me, "We are sure that you channel your writing."

"Like hell I do," I respond in some heat. "I fight for every word!"

Only once in my life have I really enjoyed writing, and that was my book about Odysseus and Athena, *The Hero and the Goddess: The Odyssey as Mystery and Initiation.* Maybe it was because I felt as if I were writing it for Athena, sometimes even with Athena, that I transcended my usual reluctant eking out of words and became instead transparent to images and ideas that arrived in my mind. The images found their way to the computer keyboard as gifts from Olympus—a joyous cocreative telling and interpretation of a tale remembered as if it were my own and, as a happy dividend, a transcendence of trauma.

The Greek playwright Euripides once wrote that myths are the arena for the activities of the daimons, and it is the daimons that give shape to our characters as well as to the unfolding of the events of our lives. In the course of my work in sacred psychology I have sought to help individuals, groups, institutions, and even cultures discover the guiding myth that would make them understand the map and meaning of their lives and the unexplored countries that lie within the province of the myth they are living out.

My life has followed certain patterns of the Athena life, as expressed in ancient Greek mythology. In the old tales, Zeus swallowed Athena's mother, Metis, the goddess of wisdom, while she was pregnant with Athena because of a prophecy that the child would be more powerful that Zeus himself. Athena, clearly a father's daughter, was born from Zeus's head. My birth was also doubtful and ambiguous. My father wanted me aborted since he feared that he would not be ready to support me, and I emerged almost two months too soon. I also sprang from my father's head, while my mother was a source of deep inner wisdom. To my child's eyes, my father, because of his huge personality, absorbed my mother, although she always was there, giving me the benefits of her fey wisdom and deep caring. And as the tale of my father rewriting my themes hints, my relationship with my father might be described as occasionally competitive and always feisty. As with Zeus and Athena, I held his thunderbolts; he regarded me as one of his better productions.

Like Athena, who emerged fully grown and armed, according to my relatives I was also quite a full person by the time I was five. I grew strong and tall, with a face out of the classical Mediterranean. I early showed skill with armaments—in my case, the fencing foil. Like Athena, I was musical and was taken up by wise old men and given an extraordinary education, as Athena was trained by Hephaestus and Prometheus. Below my generally benevolent nature lies a more archaic warrior, fiercely protective of people and projects, ready to launch a mission when I think wrongs are being committed, and capable of rare but considerable wrath when it is justified. As Athena is the goddess of persuasive speech, I am known as a fine speaker, able to convince individuals and groups to enter into a larger life and to take on new ways of being. Like Athena, I seek to reweave the world, bringing technology, culture, knowledge, and spirit into a more beautiful pattern and a more possible society. I am always rescuing people who have been cast aside—the deviants, the mavericks, the wounded, and the unseen—as Athena rescued the baby Hercules. Like Athena, whose favorite epithet is "the ever near," I try to be available to all who seek me out though letter, phone, fax, or visit. I consider it my task in life to be of use to whomever comes my way and in whatever way I can be.

The Athena energy is robust and hearty, and I share that earthy quality in my love of great food, music, friends, celebrations, theater. Athena is both chaste and passionate, and this I share with an essential purity that is almost inviolable. While Athena is very intelligent, she is also crafty, wily, and clever, as I am reputed to be. She is a shape-shifter, showing up as birds, winds, old men, and, in dreams, as other people's relatives. I am known for mimicry. My many accents and the changes in my face and personality allow me to assume a dozen different personas in as many minutes. Also, I seem to show up in many people's dreams. Athena likes and works well with men and has fun with heroes, and I have always had strong and deep friendships and working relationships with men and generally am training a young hero—a Hercules, Bellepheron, or Perseus. But Athena also appreciates and honors women, and like Athena with her mother Metis, I continue to find the greatest wisdom in the minds and souls of my women friends and associates. As Athena was the foster mother of Asclepios, I feel kin to this man-god of healing and have done much to bring back his legend as well as the practices of the ancient Aesclepian. Athena wears the snake-haired head of Medusa on her chest, the signature of the Kali and dark chthonic energy that Athena carries. I hold this energy as an ability to guide people into their own underworlds to face their shadows and their dark crannies but then help them to emerge to live again in the light. For me Medusa is also an emblem of my belief

that in our most fearsome and loathsome quality lies the basis of our most creative and luminous expression.

Athena is preeminently a goddess of timing; she is the one who knows the right
moment to enter a situation and make a difference, as when she is able, for example, to argue the case of Odysseus before the Olympian gods and convince them to
release him from Calypso's isle so that he can return home to Ithaca. In other
myths she is always there to instigate, inspire, and weave new plans when the time
or person is ripe for renovation. Such is my way, and a sense of timing is, perhaps,
my most fortunate quality.

What I have been describing is my own particular sense of correspondence with
an archetype, but this phenomenon is hardly unique to me. Probably, in fact, it
would be recognized as universal, should individuals take the time and trouble to
notice the patterns of similarity between their own natures and histories and
those of archetypal figures. Realizing this connection can result in the individuation and powerful enhancement of both the human person and the personality of
the archetype. As we grow the "gods," the "gods" grow us.

How do we grow these so-called gods? Perhaps it is by pursuing a conscious
partnership with an archetype or psychospiritual power that has the same kinds
of qualities as ourselves. In living and working with these mutual qualities as
gracefully as we can, humans help to individuate and extend the essence of the archetype in the world. It is a high craft, this growing of the archetype, and it would
seem to require what the ancient Greeks called an *enantiadromia,* a big turn-
around in our perception of our place in the order of things. We have traditionally
regarded the "god" as the one who maintains our dependency, and by this we keep
the god ungrown and immature, often fixated in archaic attitudes. But the archetypes do not need to be met as old dependencies. They need to be met as partners,
not as peers, and certainly not as pathetic little hangers-on.

In our time we have suddenly become directors of a world that up to now has
mostly directed us. This exponential growth in responsibility requires a corresponding enhancement in consciousness and psyche as formidable as it is necessary. For in our world, powers once mythically accorded the gods are now lodged
in extremely limited human consciousness. As we try to play catch-up, we find
ourselves seeking the enrichment of an archetypical base that can provide missing
components of intelligence, wisdom, and compassion. But first we have to get past
the conundrum that these archetypal partners still bear the baggage of ancient attitudes, fine for one era, devastating for an other.

Thus, the process that I am calling the growing of the gods may, in turn, be
part of the necessary evolution of the *anima mundi,* the soul of the world. This
evolution can be seen as a historical movement from an undifferentiated noumen
toward the multiple faces and stories of gods and archetypes. Each particular god
bears the holonomic resonance of the original unity, refracted through the lens of

time and culture, a parochial rendering of the sacred. Back in Paleolithic and early Neolithic times, the *Ur*-mother, the Great Goddess, was felt and known in her utter and absolute suchness. She was the One without a second. As the culture of agriculture expanded, communities and roles becoming ever more complex and differentiated, she divided and became many, her powers particularized, her agenda shared. She took on the faces of the seasons—the Triple Goddess in her roles as spring maiden, fruitful summer mother, and wizened winter crone. The Triple Goddess individuated further, becoming the vehicle of stories that reflected not just the agricultural cycle but also the psychological dramas and rituals of everyday life—birth, growth, learning, sex, fertility, family relationships, wounding, death. Thus the Great Mother birthed herself in multiple story lines, multiple matrices.

As humans tell and retell, live and relive these stories, their psyches, too, expand. Throughout time, mystics, creators, crazies, shamans, fey folk, and lovers have so identified their local lives with the larger life of the archetype that they were able to dwell in the realm of myth and goddedness but at the same time enjoy the delights of flesh and firmament. They have felt themselves to be embodiments of the archetype in time with accompanying skills and powers that seemed to belong more to the archetype than to their culture and habit-bound selves. Today, however, what was reserved for the few may be becoming the province of the many. The individuation of the numinous finds a new turn as people everywhere are learning to live their larger stories and tap into the necessary spiritual DNA to become archetypal. A Buddhist statement expresses wonderfully well what it means to live archetypally. In this state, "one sees all beings as Buddha, hears all sounds as mantra, and knows all places as nirvana." To me this means every moment has its magic, every action however small is stellar in its consequences ("stir a flower and bestir a star"), and each word that one speaks is creation.

But there is still a great divide between gods and humans. The gods are not schizophrenic as humans are. The polarities and seeming splits in their nature are more on the order of a healthy polyphrenia. Their multiple selves serve them according to the needs of any situation. They can also elevate us into the One and know that Oneness as their true condition. Knowing the One, they can step down into the many—thus their polyphrenia, their wide play of attributes, their many selves. This protean skill is one that humanity awaits and, perhaps, in our time is moving toward. What myths tell us about the polyphrenia of the gods may be our evolutionary portion as we humans move into the next stage of our becoming.

People may thus, as I have suggested earlier, develop a very different kind of psychological structure. Instead of having a dominant self or ego, they will learn to keep a large cast of characters active, calling them to stage front to fit the occasion. The orchestrator of these selves may not be the ego as we have known it but instead a high self, one that is less culture-bound than present humans and more like a panhistorical archetypal persona. What I am calling Athena may be the emerging archetypal orchestrator of my own inner crew of selves. Thus I do not become the archetype; rather, I allow her a more central role in my psychic development. As I experience it, this is neither inflation nor possession; it is a partnership that instructs, guides, inspires, and sheds light on the meaning and message of hard times—though without making those hard times go away.

What does the living presence of an archetype look like? In my case, it was captured on film. In January 1985 I took all 144 members of the Mystery School to Egypt, stopping en route to visit archaeological sites in Athens and Delphi. Upon arriving early in the morning in Athens after the night flight from New York, I bundled them all, bleary eyed and complaining, into buses, and took them up to the Acropolis. I thought that the first sight of the Parthenon, blazing white against the shining air and blue sky of Greece, would give them the thrill that I had known upon first seeing it, and so it did.

Then I took them into the Acropolis museum, where they wandered around, and I visited my favorite resident—the monumental archaic statue of Athena. Her arms are lifted to do battle against the giants. Striding forward, she bears a cloak that is rimmed with snakes. Snakes also form a circlet around her head. It is a formidable statue, this snake-blazoned Athena, primal in its power and with a living energy that invited me to emulate her stance. Hoping that the guard would not notice, I stood in front of the statue and assumed her posture, while she rose seven feet above my head. I meant my action to be playful, but immediately I felt myself struck through and through with bolts of power that did not seem to be my own. Neither before nor since have I felt such energies, such radiant streams of living fire.

After we returned from Egypt, Ann Breutsch, who had been photographing the expedition and, unknown to me, had taken a shot of my antics before the statue, approached me in some consternation.

"I don't understand," she said. "I am a professional. I took over two thousand photographs on this trip, and they all came out just as I saw them. Here is a picture of the statue of Athena just seconds before you stood in front of it. And here is a picture just after you left, from the same role of film. Normal pictures, see? Now look at this picture of you standing under the statue. It is full of these weird lights that had no way of getting on the film."

I looked at the picture. There I was, surrounded by a luminous corona. Under my outstretched arm and radiating between the statue and me were fiery fingers of yellow and orange light. I was not at all surprised to see this. The alchemy of energies had been so strong that sensitive photographic film would be a natural medium to record it. Whether the picture depicts the actual presence of Athena or my own energies activated by a combination of trans-Atlantic fatigue and stepping into the iconic posture of the goddess at her most energetic, I cannot say. For me it suffices that it happened at all. Such interchanges are not ephemeral; they occasionally break through the barriers of local space and time in frequencies that burn and sear their way into bones and blood as well as into photographic film.

In February of 1992, as part of the celebration of the publication of my book about Odysseus and Athena, I conducted an experiential seminar on the *Odyssey* in Nashville, Tennessee. Why Nashville of all places, home of country music and the Grand Old Opry? Well, the city was not entirely unfamiliar. When I was about two, my father had written jokes for the Grand Old Opry, and Cousin Minnie Pearl had baby-sat me. But this time I was there because of another statue of Athena and another Parthenon. Nashville is the home of a magnificent reconstruction of the ancient Parthenon, and within it had just been placed a stupendous, forty-two-foot statue of Athena. Created by Nashville sculptor Alan Le Quire, it is thought to be a close replica of the ancient statue by Phidias. It is known that when Phidias completed the statue, his studio burned down, and when Alan Le Quire completed his statue of Athena, his studio also burned down. The studio where this goddess is created is clearly incendiary and can allow no further creation. We were able to rent the Parthenon for the last day of our seminar. There we invoked and celebrated the goddess with bardic speech, paeans of joy, and even a little country music. Many claimed to have seen the great lady smile, and I felt that something deep and potent had been reawakened in the world.

In various of my writings and seminars, I speak of "docking with one's angel," becoming the exotype of the archetype. It is then that one assumes, however briefly, something of the qualities of one's archetypal partner. Some shamans, for example, are filled with the god or totem and in this state acquire unusual capacities to heal, to reorder matter, and to envision a probable future for individual or tribe. There are saints, like Francis of Assisi, who enter into such ecstatic states of union with the Christ archetype that they are said to perform miracles and, in the case of Saint Francis and others, to acquire the stigmata, the wounds of Jesus. Many people, known and unknown, in virtually every region of the world, have experienced the suspension of their usual ways of being and the acquiring of metanormal capacities through communion or identification with archetypal energies. Is this because these energies are natural complements of the human condition activated by the belief that one is receiving gifts and powers from the archetypal realm—"not my will, but thine, O Lord"? In my own personal cosmology, I find some truth in this explanation, yet I fear it is too reductionist to be worthy of this grand and glorious universe, which itself is a palimpsest of many layers and domains. I have given myself place, time, and permission to explore this phenomenon in an event that occurs one Saturday night each year in Mystery School: the Night of the Gifting.

Several months before the event, the participants are asked to think about what they really want to receive from the universe and also to be sure that they are willing and able to accept such a gift and its consequences. They are warned of the fact that virtually everybody gets what she or he asks for. What we try to create on the Night of the Gifting is a dramatic context in which one's usual habits and disbeliefs are suspended. Participants turn the huge, high-ceilinged field house where we meet into an imaginative field of dreams, a Renaissance fair of the mind. As they await their turns to be gifted, participants, dressed in celebrational attire, cycle through imaginative stations created by fellow Mystery School students. These stations invite them to experience the essence of the best plays of Shakespeare, for example, or of the twelve astrological signs. To symbolize the balanced polarities of Libra in a recent Night of Gifting, a participant was invited to gaze into a hand mirror while two Librans simultaneously whispered affirmations into her ears, and at the watery Pisces station, she was anointed with scented water to the soothing sound of a rain stick.

My own preparation as the one who gifts is to spend hours before the ceremony in meditation, releasing any concerns or emotional coloration from my daily life. I find myself dropping my local margins, becoming liminal, and crossing a threshold in my mind and spirit in which I am no longer just Jean; I enter into a communion with the Athena archetype, assuming a largesse of being that knows no limitation, sees beyond obstacles, and views each person as a fellow mirror of divine possibilities. By their accounts, others perceive me as strangely intense and otherworldly, and when each person comes up to me and tells me what he or she desires, we meet at another realm, a magic circle of communion, a consensual altered state in which fears are lifted, resolve strengthened, and probabilities seen. I feel myself a weaver, shuttlecock in hand, tying together threads of potential partnerships, if that is what is wished, pulling the lines that connect books to be written, projects to be launched, abundance to be found, and, most often of all, a release from fear so that each can accept the gift her or his entelechy intends.

In the course of the evening, which can last from twelve to fourteen hours, stirring music plays to prime my spirit and keep me on my feet to see the 150 to 180 people who wait their turns to be gifted. The next morning, with swollen legs and feet, I make my way back to my room to rest for a few minutes before the morning session, knowing that it has been a good night and that I have been as much gifted as gifter. I release all remaining archetypal energies, and "just Jean" shows up in the morning session. To date, some 2500 people have gone through this process, and most claim that they have received what they asked for and, in some cases, much more. Perhaps the most delightful example took place several years ago when three women, two in my Denver Mystery School and one in my New York school, made the same request: each wanted to become pregnant. One had been trying for seven years, one for ten, and the third for fourteen years. In each case, the woman and her husband had been unsuccessful even though they had pursued the most sophisticated medical technology available. Within ten to fifteen months after the Night of the Gifting, each delivered a healthy baby.

I doze as the bus moves though the Indian countryside. Suddenly it hits a rut in the road and I wake up. Everyone but the bus driver is asleep, and as I look around I see that their faces have become transfigured, even godlike. I seem to be seeing with the eyes of Saraswati. I see the archetypal natures of each. I look over at wise Peggy Rubin, and she bears now the radiance of the Sophia, the ancient gnostic feminine spirit of wisdom. John, across the aisle, always seeking, always looking for the elusive truth behind things, is Parsifal. I turn and look at kind and compassionate Mary di Souza, a native of India with a face that seems the soul of India and now bears the presence of Mother Mary. I stand up and wander down the aisle and look at my friends. There they are—Merlin, Parvati, Artemis, Saint Francis, Shiva. The bus driver, a plucky funny fellow with a nose worthy of Cyrano de Bergerac, has become Ganesh, the laughing, lucky elephant god. I rub my human eyes, thinking that ordinary vision will return, but the eyes of Saraswati persist, and I continue to see only gods and saints, the true faces of my dreaming friends. In sleep they have let down their local guards and the gods have come through. Perhaps if I look out the window, things will descend to the normal. But when I wave at a pair of little children at the side of the road, Radha and Krishna wave back at me. The bus slows to make a turn, and an old man, the Ancient of Days, lifts his hand to me in salutation. His eyes blaze blessing, and I know that I have passed into another domain where the membrane between the worlds has dissolved. And yet this world is so familiar. I have known it before. Where? When? How? Suddenly I recall that little girl, myself, on the MGM lot so many years ago, wandering through the many sets of movies past and in production, seeing actors dressed up as personages of myth, history, and adventure, fractals of the gods. My funny father—or was he really Loki, Coyote, the Trickster—tells me the truth behind all mystery when I ask, "Why do you call your office Dreamland, Daddy?"

"Because that's where we are, kid, that's where we are."

Dreamland—the Earth, the solar system, the galaxy, the universe, the Mind of God—the place where the great archetypal potencies get to play out their drama, evolve their stories, and where we, as the vehicles of their becoming, get to rewrite the material. We are all fractals of one another and partners to the core, gods no longer in hiding, the players on the many sets of the great lot that is the life of the One in time.

✦

It is now. Right now. You and I are facing each other—you reading these words, I within the page. May I be so bold as to offer you a gift? If I may, read on. I gift you with the courage to be, to know deeply the divine design of your life. I gift you with passion for the possible and the willingness to bring this possibility into time. You are more than you think you are, and something in you knows it. All the hurts and failures, all the wanderings, losings, dyings, and forgettings were but part of the gaining of the rich material of your life. By being wounded, you became vulnerable and available; by being lost, you were able to be found; by dying, you learned the power of new birth; by forgetting, you gained the joy of remembering.

Now I call all parts of you back, a mighty crew, seaworthy and well stocked, to set sail for new continents of spirit, shores of incredible lands where the fractal waves of many people and many times arrive at last, and you know that you have gained your birthright. Welcome home, god and goddess, no longer in hiding.

♦

Acknowledgments

Because *A Mythic Life* is more of a metabiography than an autobiography, I must acknowledge and thank not just everyone I have ever known or will know, but those unseen ones as well. The list would be longer than the book, for a life is nothing if it is not a living planet of ecologies and exchanges.

I have been gifted and blessed by the friendship of many, and many are those who have helped me reflect upon the contents of this book. My mother, Mary Houston, has given me the treasure of her "far-memory" and has recalled in detail the events of a half-century and more. My husband, Robert Masters, with his passion for truth-telling, has kept me honest. My good friends, Peggy Rubin and Elisabeth Rothenberger, have reminded me of the meaning of my life and work whenever I have come close to losing the thread that weaves it into form. John Loudon, my editor at HarperSanFrancisco, wisely sent me back to the drawing board with pungent instructions when a first draft was more comedy than content. Brenda Rosen, my in-house editor, did a splendid job in orchestrating and conducting my myriad instruments and melodies. And Priscilla Stuckey turned in the finest and most skillful copyediting that I have ever seen. I am also grateful to

Mimi Kusch for her fine production editing, as well as for the ready and willing assistance of Karen Levine. The deeply wise Mary Catherine Bateson saw the gold amidst the detritus, while Normandi Ellis surprised me with inventive takes on turning life into art. Strident reality checks to present mythic aspects of my life were provided in a Neopolitan patois by my business manager, Fonda De Cillo Joyce, while Donna Liers, my practical and spiritually gifted assistant, helped in bringing order to my madness as well as in printing and collating reams of manuscript. Paula Perlis, my gastronomic guru, helped me imagine and prepare the delicacies offered in chapter 11. And then there is my agent, that great original, Roslyn Targ, whose heart is as large as her immense personality. Her high spirits and sense of the absurd keep me buoyant, keep me writing.

And thank you for reading *A Mythic Life.*

Index

✦

For further information concerning Jean Houston's seminars, books, and tapes, please write to her at Box 3300, Pomona, New York, 10970.